THE ULTIMATE CRIME
Who betrayed the UN and why

Also by Linda Melvern

Techno Bandits (co-author)
The End of the Street

THE ULTIMATE CRIME

Who betrayed the UN and why

Linda Melvern

First published in Great Britain in 1995 by
Allison & Busby
An imprint of Wilson & Day Ltd
179 King's Cross Road
London WC1X 9BZ

A catalogue record for this book is available from the
British Library

ISBN 0 85031 939 0

Typeset by N-J Design Associates
Romsey, Hampshire

Printed and bound in Great Britain by
WBC Book Manufacturers, Bridgend, Mid Glamorgan

CONTENTS

To Phill Green

1. GENOCIDE

In peacekeeping, the transition period, when warring factions vie for power, is the most dangerous. It is the time used by extremists to make the most of the vacuum, to derail peace.

In the case of Rwanda, by the time the UN peacekeepers arrived, it was already too late. The peacekeepers, identified by their distinctive blue helmets, had no combat training and were ill-equipped. Their job was to provide a neutral buffer between two enemies, in this case identified by race, the Hutus and the Tutsis. They were not meant to use force. This was classic peacekeeping and, to work effectively, the peacekeepers had to have the consent of the parties and a ceasefire agreement in place. Peacekeepers observe, they mediate, but they do not compel the parties to cease hostilities, nor do they try to end human rights abuses. The best equipped and trained were the Belgian para-commandos, 440 of them, from the second battalion of Flawinne, who were responsible for the central Kigali sector.

At 5.20 a.m. on the morning of April 7, 1994, ten of these crack Belgian para-commandos arrived at the home of the Prime Minister, Agathe Uwilingiyimana, a Hutu, to escort her to Radio Rwanda, where she was expected to make an emergency appeal for calm to her people. But the Prime Minister was not ready to leave and she asked the UN soldiers to wait.

The officer in charge, Lieutenant Thierry Lotin, wanted her to hurry. He could see armed men crouched on roof-tops and hear shooting in nearby streets.

Inside the house, the Prime Minister was trying desperately to contact her ministers and to speak to the army commanders. There was nothing

1

but bad news: the President of the Constitutional Court, Joseph Kavaruganda, had been murdered and the Minister of Information, Faustin Rucogoza, was taken away by the Presidential Guard.

Suddenly, there was an explosion outside. One of Lotin's white UN jeeps, parked near the gate of the Prime Minister's house burst into flames from the impact of a tank shell. Within minutes, the Prime Minister herself took flight, clambered over the wall at the back of the house and was gone. Momentarily confused, Lieutenant Lotin radioed UN headquarters and spoke urgently to his Belgian commanding officer. He was told not to follow her, to stay with the jeeps, his only radio contact. There was suddenly the sound of tyres screeching to a halt and Lotin and his men found themselves surrounded by soldiers.

A Rwanda major steps forward. He gives Lotin his word that he will personally escort all ten of the Belgian peacekeepers safely back to UN headquarters. He asks Lotin to disarm. Lotin keeps his head. He radios again from the jeep. "What shall I do?" he asks. They answer that he must make the decision himself. Lotin is 29 years old. He has a pregnant wife back home. He has two years' peacekeeping experience. He reflects, then decides to disarm. He and his men are led to a lorry and it pulls away from the gate.

Across the city, Mary Vianney Benoyeze, a receptionist at the Hotel des Mille Collines, sees peacekeepers as she hurries to the Swiss Embassy where her fiancé works. "It's started," he says and rushes off to collect his family and hers. All night she waits, and the next day. Early on Friday, April 8, he telephones. He tells her that her family is gone. Her mother, father, her four brothers and her grandparents are murdered. She is the only member of her family left. He says he is trying to get back to her, but he is surrounded by the militia. He says goodbye and that he loves her. She will never hear from him again. Soon all the Swiss are gone and Mary is alone. All around she hears shots and explosions, and she climbs into a metal stationery cupboard where she hides for three months, venturing out rarely, and only at night, for the scraps which someone, at risk to his life, leaves her.

One day the doors of the cupboard are flung open and, miraculously, it is a rescue instead of a death squad. Emerging from the darkness of her hiding place, Mary sees her city, Kigali, which was once vibrant and alive. It has been ransacked. There is a foul stench of rotting bodies. The dogs through the night are howling.

The horror of Rwanda was exactly what the UN was created to prevent, the crime of genocide. But the generosity of the UN founders, reeling from the image of the Nazi death camps, faded with time. Governments have practical, political concerns and the UN could never be stronger than the will of the world governments.

On the face of it, the assignment was unambiguous. A three-year civil war ended in peace, with a handshake between government and invading rebels. A more tangible peace was enshrined in the Arusha Accords, signed in Tanzania in August 1993. The accords promised a new Rwanda. There was to be reform of the corrupt government and power-sharing. A timetable was agreed that would lead to multi-party democracy. The UN, the world's last resort, was needed to oversee the transition. But it was not so simple. No sooner were the blue helmets deployed than there was a rapid and dramatic deterioration in security. Armed thugs terrorised the population. The UN soldiers were put on Phase Two alert, a high-risk assessment. It was so tense and dangerous that the troop commander, Major-General Romeo Dallaire, with tactical control on the ground, realised the peace process was unravelling. It was impossible for him to meet his mandate. He had no equipment; he did not even have helicopters. He needed more and better trained troops with the power to disarm.

Peacekeeping requires ceaseless political direction. In every operation throughout the world, the mandate, authorised by the Security Council, provides crucial guidance. It establishes what the peacekeepers will do.

Dallaire, a French Canadian, had trained in an army in which peacekeeping was a tradition, and he was well acquainted with UN mandates. He knew how often they had been inadequate, how often they were written with scant consideration for the realities on the ground. There had been tragic mistakes in the past, when the Security Council sent peacekeepers into situations with orders they could not follow, and which the Security Council would not change. In Cambodia and in former Yugoslavia, soldiers died as a result of inappropriate mandates. In the case of Rwanda, Dallaire realised that the international community, hiding behind the Security Council, was not fully committed.

3

The Security Council discussed the mandate for Rwanda on several occasions. Each time, the permanent five, Britain, France, the US, the Russian Federation and China, refused a change. The Council wished instead for speedy implementation of the Arusha Accords.

Peace never stood a chance. Rwanda was controlled for twenty years by the same ruling clique, fiercely loyal to the President, Juvenal Habyarimana. The 700-strong Presidential Guard was mostly comprised of his relatives. Both before and during the transition period, the Guard was financing a militia. The militia was trained by the Rwanda Army, and the army was already 35,000 strong. Rwanda became a country awash with arms. Weapons were distributed to the police, the local gendarmes. There were rumours that the civil administration was compiling lists of names of Habyarimana opponents. There were massacres and political assassinations and increasingly the peace was postponed.

In February, 1994, the UN's Secretary General, Boutros Boutros-Ghali, telephoned Juvenal Habyarimana to talk about the serious delays which had occurred in the transition programme. He was warned about moves in the Security Council to pull out the peacekeepers. The Council was fed up with postponements. Habyarimana shrugged it off, seemingly unruffled at the prospect that aid donors were beginning to back off too.

But the UN Commander, Major-General Romeo Dallaire never gave up hoping the peace plan would succeed. "Once ministers were round a cabinet table, I thought they would be able to reach compromises", he said. Others thought so too.

On April 5, 1994, Habyarimana was invited to a regional summit in Tanzania where the Secretary General of the Organisation of African Unity, and the Presidents of Tanzania, Uganda and the Vice-President of Kenya reminded him of the efforts which were made to broker peace. There must be no further delay.

That same day Rwanda was discussed in the Security Council, which reached a deadlock. The US argued for a total withdrawal of the UN but there were several objections.

The Security Council has fifteen members. Five of them, Britain, the US, France, China and the Russian Federation, are permanent. The other ten are elected by the General Assembly to a two-year term. That April they were: the Czech Republic, Djibouti, New Zealand, Nigeria, Oman, Pakistan, Spain, Argentina, Brazil. It was not a promising line-up for the US, which would need to command nine votes to win – always provided, of course, that none of the permanent members used its veto.

In opposition to the American view, Nigeria argued that a pull-out would be shameful and eventually the meeting ended in compromise. Habyarimana was given six weeks. Unless he proved his commitment to peace within that time, the UN would leave. The very next day, on Wednesday April 6, 1994, at 8.22 p.m., Habyarimana was dead. As he returned to Rwanda in his Mystère Falcon jet, it is alleged he was blown out of the sky by a missile.

The consitutional head of Rwanda was now the Prime Minister, Agathe Uwilingiyimana, known to everyone as Madame Agathe, and a keen advocate of power-sharing. Dallaire talked to her several times. Madame Agathe had fled to a house where UN volunteers lived. The Presidential Guard had surrounded the compound and she was frightened for her life. Dallaire decided to go to her rescue, but on his way he was ordered out of his Toyota jeep at a road block and Rwandese army officers insisted he ride with them. By the time he reached Madame Agathe, she had been dead for two hours.

For a time, Dallaire remained confident about Lieutenant Lotin who had gone to protect Madame Agathe but who had been taken away with his men in a lorry by the Rwanda Army. Dallaire assumed they were being kept in a Kigali barracks and would shortly be released. In the history of peacekeeping, the hostage-taking of UN troops was not unknown. In Kigali, only hours before, a similar incident occurred when peacekeepers at the airport had laid down their arms and were unharmed.

It was not until dusk that he found them. Lotin and his men were piled high, in a heap, like sacks of potatoes in the courtyard of a Kigali hospital. At first, Dallaire wondered why there were eleven of them. Then came the sickening realisation: mutilation made their number impossible to determine.

Dallaire, stunned as he was, ordered photographs taken. He negotiated with the Rwanda gendarmerie that his men be laid out with more dignity. He wanted the remaining pieces of their torn uniforms kept safe. This he accomplished.

It took two full days to get their bodies back to UN custody. They remained under guard, in a lorry in the Hotel Meridien car park, until a plane carried their remains home.

No one ever saw a country collapse so quickly. When the Security Council convened in New York on Saturday, April 9, 1994, Rwanda was falling apart. The 600-strong battalion of rebel forces, which under the peace accords was to be integrated into the Rwanda army and stationed in the middle of Kigali, found itself fighting Rwanda Army troops. The rebel army in the north had launched a simultaneous offensive across the demilitarised zone. The rebel army also sent a vanguard party to rescue the battalion in the city. Now ten of the peacekeepers were dead.

The UN presence in Rwanda consisted of 2,000 soldiers from Bangladesh and Ghana, most with no combat training, let alone flack-jackets. They were not fighting units and they had bunkered down as soon as the fighting started.

The Belgians had already decided to pull out – with or without Security Council authorisation. Belgian diplomats to the UN began a campaign to persuade everyone else that it was madness to leave a peacekeeping force in a civil war. The Americans agreed. The recent bungled UN operation in Somalia taught the overwhelming military difficulties of trying to enforce peace.

There was dissent. Colin Keating, the New Zealand ambassador to the UN pointed out that it was precisely because of the failure of Somalia that someone in Rwanda had worked out that to get rid of the UN, you had only to kill some of its peacekeepers. Keating wanted a small force to remain in Kigali with a mandate allowing troops to fight. Nigeria's UN Ambassador, Ibrahim Gambari, thought it unthinkable for the UN to leave. Had Rwanda fallen off the map of moral concern?

Keeping ahead of events, the Organisation of African Unity in Dar es Salaam, issued a statement expressing shock at wanton killing of civilians in Rwanda and calling for an end to the "carnage". In New York, the Security Council could think of only one action – it urged a ceasefire.

Rwanda was one of the oldest problems on the international agenda. First brutally colonised by the Germans when it was part of German East Africa, in 1916 it was occupied by Belgian forces, a spoil of the First World War. From 1920 it was administered by Belgium under a League of Nations mandate but this made little impact on Belgian rule which was coldly efficient.

In 1945, the Charter of the UN promised a great deal for the colonised peoples of the world. Apart from its well-known determination to prevent the scourge of war, the Charter guaranteed freedom for all under colonial rule – at the time, one-third of the world's population. The Charter was a sacred trust for these people. Article 73 promised them justice and protection. UN member states set up a special council, called the Trusteeship Council, established to oversee their transition to freedom and to this end anthropologists and other experts were hired to work in UN headquarters but there was little benefit for Rwanda's people; the UN had no great impact on their lives. Rwanda did not reach independence until 1962 and, like other Belgian colonies, it was ill-prepared to govern itself. Rwanda, with sparse natural resources, was not a high priority for the international community. Worse, Rwanda had a deadly fault-line – an ethnic divide.

Historically, long before the arrival of the Germans and Belgians, Tutsi invaders swept down from the Horn of Africa and imposed themselves as the aristocratic ruling class over the more numerous Hutu already there. The country became a highly organised monarchy with a Tutsi aristocracy; the lower, less educated class formed by Hutus. The Belgians used the ethnic division to help them rule. To keep European staff to a minimum, the Belgians froze the power structure and ruled through directives given to the Mwami, or King. In 1933 the Belgians came up with the idea of a census and everyone was given an identification card. Teams of Belgian bureaucrats were sent to count and measure everyone – and notes were taken of their height, the length of their nose, the shape of their eyes. Everyone was classified: the Tutsi were the taller and the Hutu, shorter and broader. Hutu and Tutsi lived in the same valleys and villages, spoke the same language, and had the same traditions. For many Rwandese, it was not possible to determine ethnicity on the basis of physical appearance.

In 1959 the downtrodden peasant majority fought back. There was an abrupt and violent end of Tutsi rule and tens of thousands of Tutsis were massacred by Hutu, both before and after independence. A newly installed Hutu government operated a policy of apartheid; Tutsis were discriminated against in education and in employment and thousands were forced into exile into neighboring countries, including Uganda, where Tutsis were refused citizenship. It was among stateless refugees in Uganda that a rebel army was formed, called the Rwanda Patriotic Front. A number of Hutu politicians disagreeing with the one-party rule back home joined up.

In 1990, claiming to enforce the right of Tutsi refugees to return home, the rebel army invaded from Uganda. The Hutu government believed that the Tutsis were coming home to dominate and the result was a three-year civil war, with the Hutu government clinging on to power, thanks in the main to arms and military training from France. Thousands of people were killed and a million displaced and the civil war was an economic disaster.

In August 1993, a fragile peace was agreed, thanks largely to outside pressure, particularly the Organisation of African Unity. Afterwards, both the Rwanda government and the rebels came in delegations to New York and asked for UN help with the transition to democracy. The Security Council met the request with considerable reluctance. The big powers were not keen. The UN was already over-committed in other troublespots. But the non-permanent members had been for moral obligation. Here was a small, pathetic country struggling for democracy, asking the world for help. The UN could not turn its back.

The result was a UN fudge. On October 5, 1993, the Security Council authorised a small, cheap peacekeeping force. The following day, President Habyarimana expressed his gratitude in a speech to the General Assembly in New York. The UN was his last hope. "My country's recovery", he said, "depends on the generosity of the international community".

When Belgium decided to contribute troops for the UN mission, Habyarimana went personally to Brussels to thank the King.

Within minutes of Habyarimana's death on April 6, 1994, there was gun-fire and explosions. It lasted intermittently throughout the night until, at around four in the morning, it became intense. At six, the Rwanda's Minister of Defence broadcast on Radio Rwanda to announce the death of President Habyarimana. He also announced a indefinite, nationwide curfew.

Curfews had previously been used to imprison people in their homes, making it easier to arrest them. In the past, thousands of

Tutsi men had been thrown into jail by using this method. Thus it had aggressive, threatening overtures. In the streets of Kigali dozens of road blocks were set up. Some domestic telephone lines were cut.

"I started to hear about people being killed. No civilians or cars were on the street. Only military vehicles could be heard and seen . . . the interahamwe (militia) were cruising . . . " a survivor recalled.

Almost from the time of the Presidential plane crash, the militia, instructed in Hutu supremacist ideology and trained to kill, was loose. Its members were told that Tutsis had killed their President and that their country was being invaded by the rebel army. Hatred against Tutsi spewed out of the airwaves to a mostly illiterate population. "We need over 100,000 people to clean the country . . . Look at the size of the person, and how small the nose and then take your machete". This newly created propaganda machine, a Hutu radio station called Radio-Television Libre des Mille Collines, called for the extermination of the "inyenzi", a word made popular by the Habyarimana government, which means cockroach. It was used to describe the Tutsi soldiers of the rebel army.

"Even before the President died, the consciousness of the Hutus in our area had already been awakened . . . they had been given a very clear idea. Hutus in our hill were always being called to secret meetings with the bourgmestre, councilors and other officials . . . I ran as fast as I could," said one of the survivors later.

To the outside world, the murder in Rwanda was an outburst of tribal violence but it was a convenient description only, and it hid a greater truth – three days into the slaughter, by Saturday April 9, Rwanda's opposition to Hutu extremist ideology was wiped out entirely.

Everyone who wanted power-sharing, or who had spoken out against Habyarimana, was dead. Every journalist, every lawyer, every professor, every teacher, every civil servant, every priest, every doctor, every clerk, every student – all were hunted down in a house-to-house operation. It was systematic. The lists of the victims were prepared beforehand, kept on white index cards, neatly stored in wooden boxes on grey metal library shelves. The first targets had been members of the transitional government and, while one part of the government was being killed, the other half was whisked away.

The Presidential Guard took certain ministers to the French Embassy. France was an ally, had given Rwanda arms and military assistance. After a brief period at the French Embassy these ministers were installed in the Hotel Meridien. There, three days later, a Hutu extremist government was formed, where, for a time, it pretended the killings all around were a spontaneous expression of Hutu grief at the death of the President.

The militia grew. A survivor recalled: "Everywhere neighbours were screaming; here she is, here she is. I jumped over fences and they were yelling instructions to the interahamwe, to point them in my direction."

People were coerced to join through rape and murder. Neighbour killed neighbour, and looted the victim's house. The killing seemed random, but all the time the militia was being instructed by government-appointed local officials. The militia was armed by the communal police and, when victims were herded up, the Rwanda army arrived in buses to seal exits, or to stand guard, while the militia used machetes and spears to maim and to kill.

Some Tutsi tried to flee but found road blocks and thus death. The gangs used the identification cards at first, but this took too much time. Soon the gangs resorted to the size of a person, singling out those who were tall, with straight noses and long fingers generally to be slashed with a machete on the spot.

A casualty toll quickly became impossible. Hundreds of bodies piled up outside the morgue. Rows of the injured blocked the entrances to Kigali hospitals. Wounded people seeking medical attention were killed either before they arrived or in the hospitals themselves. Philippe Gaillard, the head of the Red Cross mission in Rwanda, said he managed only a drop of humanity in an ocean of blood. There were thousands and thousands who needed help.

In his UN headquarters, a run-down hotel in the middle of town, Commander Romeo Dallaire could smell death, he could see it and he could hear it. He kept some convoys patrolling, but after finding Thierry Lotin, he pulled back and increased the Belgian contingent at the airport. It was his only lifeline. Dallaire's priority now was the protection of his terrified soldiers and staff and the desperate civilians seeking UN protection. He awaited a decision from the Security Council.

The Security Council consists of a room full of ambassadors, cautious to pronounce on anything and loath to take action. They sit around a horseshoe table in a large room in the grey and dreary UN headquarters. A week goes by and there is no decision for Rwanda.

"It was rudderless," one of them said. "No one was sure what, if anything, needed to be done. Into this absolutely bizarre situation came the big powers . . . who said they could do nothing."

The Czech Republic was voted a seat on the Security Council in 1993. Ambassador Karel Kovanda was a child of the Holocaust as his parents were German Jews. He worked out that the percentage of Tutsis in Rwanda was the same as that of Jews in Poland before the war. Kovanda telephoned an historian called Alison des Forges, a consultant to Human Rights Watch/Africa. Des Forges remembers the call because the Ambassador was at home; it was Saturday morning and she heard the sound of his new-born baby son. Kovanda said he had just read an article in a newspaper about Hutu extremists and although Rwanda was not high on his list of national priorities, he could not sit back and do nothing. After all he explained to her, human rights was the cornerstone of the Czech Republic's foreign policy.

Kovanda gathered some of the Council's non-permanent Ambassadors together and invited des Forges. There she described to them, over coffee in the Czech mission, the hours she had spent on the phone to friends caught up in the hell of Kigali. She told them about those already dead and those who were in hiding. She described the slaughter, and she thinks she used the word genocide. Kovanda said he learned more from her about what was happening that he ever did from the UN. In the first weeks, the focus of UN reports was on how to save the peacekeepers.

Kovanda said that UN officials neither informed the Security Council when the genocide started nor managed to describe it as systematic killing. The violence was depicted as an uncontrollable civil war, tribal in origin. The Secretary General's own report to the Security Council on April 20 described killings started by "unruly members" of the Presidential Guard. Added to UN reports was a diplomatic blizzard by Belgian diplomats, urging everyone that nothing could be done. Kovanda said that what was happening to Rwanda, happened to his own country before World War II. Non-intervention sent his country to its doom. "We were once abandoned by the world," he said.

Kovanda wondered why the US was doing nothing. During the dramatic US intervention in Somalia, they had airlifted 30,000 troops into a famine in a matter of days, proof that the only UN member to be able to save thousands of innocent lives by putting a large force on the ground in a distant place, quickly and efficiently was the US.

In Kigali, Dallaire dismissed the fine words in the Security Council as empty rhetoric. If ambassadors were really bothered, surely they would return to their capitals and get him some troops. The Czechs had an army, hadn't they, which some country could airlift? Dallaire was watching the scramble to leave. Within a week, every embassy in Kigali shut down and everyone was moved out; the French waited long enough to shred what looked like a ton of documents which quite obviously proved the close links between France and the Hutu extremists.

With white flags draped over white UN Toyotas, the evacuation of the ex-pats began. Belgium led the rescue attempts, relying on France to negotiate with the Rwanda army. Six hundred French paratroopers, assisted by UN troops, made armed sorties into Kigali from the airport on rescue missions. Their evacuees were badly traumatised. Some had watched neighbours beaten and hacked to pieces with machetes; all had been forced to abandon friends and colleagues. The UN left behind its Rwandese employees, certain militia targets.

A survivor recalled: " . . . we were told they could not take us. We pleaded with them, pointing out the danger. Some of the children were screaming. But they told us that they were forbidden from taking Rwandese out of the country . . . we were in so much fear that we were shaking and could hardly talk."

One of the last groups to go were Belgium nuns and lay workers who abandoned two hundred patients at a hilltop compound for the mentally ill. There were no illusions about the fate of patients or hundreds of Tutsi refugees camped in the compound. Most of the people were killed in large-scale massacres, people who flocked for sanctuary to hospitals and churches, schools and clinics. In a town called Kibungo 2,800 gathered in a church centre, and there followed a four-hour slaughter. Only about forty were left alive.

"I couldn't move because there were so many dead bodies on top of me . . . I saw my four-year-old son.. a spear had gone through his head . . . but when I touched him I realised he was still breathing. I saw corpses of my mother . . . one of my younger sisters", said another survivor.

In most of the large massacres, soldiers played a key role. Bus loads of troops turned up to seal exits. All the time, the militia found new recruits. Local government officials used the promise of inheriting the land of Tutsis.

"They told people that they would not kill them if they gave . . . money. Those who had money gave it to them. But they killed them anyway."

The bodies of the Belgian peacekeepers came home to full military honours on Thursday, April 14, 1994. The oldest was thirty-two. Belgium began two days of mourning and Willy Claes, Foreign Minister, announced the immediate recall of the Belgian force. He was blamed for not heeding warnings. The force had been too small, the situation in which the soldiers had found themselves, was absurd.

In Kigali, the second battalion of Flawinne prepared to go home, and its commanders tried to work out the least troublesome way to abandon thousands of refugees who had flocked to the UN-protected sites.

They tried to sneak away . . . We could not believe what they were doing, just abandoning us when they knew the place was surrounded by militia . . . some of the young men threw themselves on the road to prevent them . . . some Belgian soldiers took out grenades and people moved back from the road. As soon as the Belgian soldiers were out of the gate, the firing started . . . I could not do anything because I had my wife and baby,

said another survivor. The Belgian soldiers, disembarking from transport planes hours later, slashed their UN blue berets with combat knives. They were ashamed to be part of a bluff; ashamed to be part of what once had been the world's last, best hope.

Their evacuation gutted the force. Without the Belgians the rest were little more than sitting ducks, and Dallaire told New York that if the Security Council were not going to reinforce his troops, there should be immediate withdrawal. There was yet another harsh reality. There were thousands of Rwandese in hotels, in schools, and in hospitals in UN areas. These people depended on the UN for their survival. They could not be abandoned. Dallaire wanted the Security Council to authorise a token force to stay with him for their protection.

From their concrete balconies in the run-down hotel where they were barracked, his men watched. One of them was haunted by a murder, not yards away. " . . . he just held him by his shirt and started dragging him . . . and just raised his machete and hacked him on the head . . . after that he just rubbed his bloodstained machete on his buttocks, and then searched his pockets . . . we all screamed at this. Not long after . . . there was a tipper truck with prisoners from the Kigali prison who . . . had been detailed to collect bodies from the streets."

A survivor said: "The UN protects no one. They were sent to protect the security of Kigali. How can they protect the security of Kigali when they are doing nothing to protect its people."

Every evening Dallaire put his 2,000 men on alert to evacuate, and every morning he cancelled the order. He shouted at the indecision – these soldiers belonged to the Security Council, their lives were at risk. But the days of indecision accumulated, passing slowly.

In New York, the Council issued its latest statement. It was an appeal to all Rwandese not to commit further violence.

Rwanda's second city is Butare – an intellectual centre, where Tutsi and Hutu lived together for centuries, known for liberal traditions and ethnic tolerance. Butare was the home of the National University and the National Museum. While the killing went on in Kigali, refugees flooded to Butare for protection and for two weeks Butare held out. On April 19, a contingent of the Presidential Guard flew in and bus loads of militia arrived from Kigali. At dawn the next day, the road blocks went up.

The first targets were moderate Hutu and prominent Tutsi and the first many knew of what was happening was the sound of continuous gun-fire as executions took place all over the city. On April 21, the university campus was raided and students were dragged screaming from their dormitories and shot in the arboretum. On April 23, the university hospital was hit and hundreds were shot, among them a pregnant nurse accused of carrying a Tutsi baby. The massacres went on for seventy days and it is thought that in that time, 300,000 people perished.

Dallaire was once asked about Butare. He looked at the questioner with some disdain: "If I had the mandate, the men and the equipment, hundreds of thousands of people would be alive today", he said.

The Security Council met again on April 21. There were hours of debate, and again no decision. Two of the veto powers wanted evacuation: the US wanted a complete pull-out and the UK wanted a small force to remain. Too many of the non-permanent members wanted the troops reinforced. During an adjournment, a huddle of ambassadors developed in a far corner of the lounge outside the chamber, listening intently to Major-General Maurice Baril, the Secretary General's special military adviser. Baril hated contact with the Council; it was his least favorite part of the job. This time, there was no alternative. Baril and Dallaire came from the same French-Canadian brigade and Baril had been in daily contact with Dallaire since it started. Baril was the best person to describe the conditions in Kigali under which UN soldiers were living. That night, Baril read out loud the rules of engagement. There was no military commander in the world, he said, who would leave his army exposed in this way. Dallaire could hold out no longer. He was trying to feed 16,000 desperate Hutu and Tutsi fugitives who were being shelled and 2,000 soldiers who could not fight.

Later that evening, the withdrawal of UN troops from Rwanda was recognised as inevitable and the tired ambassadors struggled to agree one last point – whether or not to leave a token force. Dallaire requested a minimum 470 to help protect the thousands who had fled to a large stadium and local churches. Close to midnight, a resolution was agreed. Baril telephoned Dallaire to tell him that the council finally allowed the soldiers to leave. Dallaire could at last give the order to evacuate.

Within two days, the blue helmets were gone. Only Dallaire's token force remained, along with the Red Cross, whose employees were stunned by the UN's decision. Philippe Gaillard was deeply shaken. He saw six wounded women dragged from his Red Cross van and slaughtered on the spot; he witnessed seven people killed with machetes in front of the Red Cross emergency field hospital. Accused by Hutu extremists of only treating Tutsi, the Red Cross had fifty-five of its employees slaughtered. A survivor recalled: "I reached a place where a woman, who had recently been beheaded, was lying. Next to her were two men who had their throats cut . . . I smeared my face and body with their blood . . . Red Cross workers came to check if anyone was still breathing . . . they put me in an ambulance."

Rwanda's countryside was littered with dead. There were bodies floating down the current of the Kagera river. On the border with Tanzania where the Kagera is wide, the river was clogged with the bodies of men, women and children and babies. Laetitia Ugiriwabo was ten:

> Some people dressed in uniforms and carrying guns came into the church. They asked everybody to come out with their arms in the air . . . They made us sit in the sun and then searched people for money. They separated the boys from the women. They . . . removed baby boys from their mothers' backs . . . Then they macheted the men, including the babies right in front of us . . . they brought a tractor to take the bodies away.

The Presidency of the Security Council changes monthly in strict alphabetical order of country. For the month of April 1994 it was New Zealand's turn. The Ambassador, Colin Keating, like many of his countrymen idealistically considered the UN the only hope in an anarchic world – the UN could achieve what no single member could. But Keating was also a realist. He thought the only way to get the international community to do anything for Rwanda was to recognise officially that this was genocide. Everyone could see that plainly on the nightly television news. But were the UN's Security Council to admit genocide, then it was required under the Convention on the Prevention and Punishment of the Crime of Genocide of 1948, to prevent and punish it.

Keating decided to force the issue. At a Security Council meeting on April 28, 1994 he submitted the draft of a Presidential Statement. A Presidential Statement is weighty, it requires a unanimous vote. Keating's draft second paragraph was the following: "The horrors of Rwanda's killing fields has few precedents in the recent history of the world . . . the Security Council reaffirms that the systematic killing of any ethnic group, with intent to destroy it in whole or in part constitutes an act of genocide . . . as defined by international law".

Keating was already unpopular with the Big Five, those countries who wield veto-power, France, Britain, China, Russia and the US. They thought him irritatingly persistent about UN reform. He said the veto should be abolished, it was anachronistic and undemocratic. His Presidential Statement on Rwanda was therefore viewed by some of those on the Council as little more than a new irritation. It was late on a Friday night and everyone was tired. Most of the ambassadors were gone for the weekend, leaving their deputies in the chamber. Time was running out for Keating. It was the end of the month and in a few hours' time, his presidency was going to evaporate and next in line was Nigeria – a country which has no great respect for human rights.

None of the permanent five approved Keating's Presidential Statement. Sir David Hannay, the British ambassador, already said of an earlier version that were it issued as an official UN document, the Council would become a laughing stock. The French ambassador, Jean-Bernard Mérimée, wanted to know why the statement did not apportion blame evenly: he had information that the rebel army was killing civilians and wanted the fact included in Keating's draft. The Chinese, allergic as ever to any discussion of human rights, were also against.

Keating's last resort was UN gamesmanship. To almost imperceptible groans, Keating said he was changing tack and that he wanted to submit a Security Council Resolution. Under Council procedure, a Security Council Resolution requires twenty-four hours' notice. This meant that the Council would have to reconvene the following night, a Saturday. There would be press coverage and a public debate. Some Council members would not be willing to say in public what they said in private. They argued until the early hours and in the end accepted a typical UN fudge. A Presidential Statement was agreed which skirted the word genocide, but which did finally recognise massacre of civilians and blamed Hutu extremists. The Statement paved the way for a Security Council resolution which Keating submitted on May 1. This New Zealand draft demanded an immediate expansion of the UN presence in Kigali and provided a powerful mandate for the troops. The only support Keating was sure of was from Argentina, the Czech Republic and Spain.

It took another two weeks for the Security Council to authorise reinforcements. In that time, the voluntary aid agencies reported a doubling of the estimated death toll to 500,000 and compared the slaughter with the Nazi Holocaust and the Khmer Rouge killing fields in Cambodia.

On May 17 Alison des Forges was elated when finally 5,500 extra troops were authorised for Rwanda. She telephoned a friend, a Tutsi who worked for the US Embassy, who had been seven weeks in hiding with Hutu friends. She told him to hang on and she remembers that he pleaded for urgency. The next day the militia came and he was killed. They came back the following day for his wife and baby and killed them as well.

Des Forges was desperate to know how long it would take the new UN force to arrive. She telephoned Kovanda to find out, and he broke the news to her – that the Resolution really meant delay and there was little likelihood of troops arriving for another three months.

"I threw up my hands in horror," she said. "It was unacceptable: human lives were being lost. Why not tomorrow?"

Her answer lay in Resolution 918, the Resolution which authorised a 5,500 reinforcement. The Resolution avoided any mention of deployment. The Security Council had no soldiers. Even if it had offers of troops, there was no means to get them to Kigali. No country offered an airlift. Even if the Council were offered an airlift, it had no idea where the troops would go.

There was one plan: to airlift a standing brigade into Kigali, but the Americans were dead against this. It was not the UN way – far from it. Dallaire reckoned it was the only way to save lives. The US, on the other hand, wanted a smaller force to fly to neighbouring Tanzania to set up safe havens for the Tutsi. As a first step, a team of 150 UN observers should be sent to try to obtain the views of the warring parties. The Americans insisted that future troop departure depend on progress towards a ceasefire. An US ambassador told the Council that the US was hoping to create an achievable mission.

Dallaire replaced the receiver that night, knowing Rwanda had been completely abandoned. All the Resolution provided for immediately was 500 extra troops to secure the airport – and 150 observers. Not one Security Council member offered a thing. Dallaire compared it to the Alamo. It was the same indifference and bickering – and abandonment.

In one of his last reports to headquarters in New York, Dallaire wrote: "What we have been living here is a disgrace. We have no food, fuel, water. We have no operational vehicles . . . we have no spare parts . . . What is worse we have no sign of the situation getting better in the near future." A living hell surrounded them and his loyalty was taxed beyond reason. The UN was at the centre of a Holocaust, and yet the Security Council was incapable of helping its own.

"We were left to hang out and dry," Dallaire said later, "not by the Secretary General, not by the Secretariat . . . but by the international community." There were a few offers. A number of African countries said they had troops available. But their soldiers possessed little more than boots. In the UN Secretariat, dozens of requests for equipment were received from hard-up armies willing to serve but lacking the means. There were so many requests a grim joke did the rounds about how the UN could become a conduit for arms. In future peacekeeping, so went the punch line, the Third World would provide the soldiers and the First World the weapons.

In the last few years everything had changed. There was a huge increase in UN operations and the UN's Department of Peacekeeping was presently responsible for more and more troops. There were now 70,000 blue helmets in seventeen different trouble-spots around the globe. An army this size, belonging to a developed nation, would require thousands in support back home – in New York there were just about 300 coping with logistics for the UN soldiers.

The UN had no genuine peacekeeping headquarters, no adequate communications links, few planning staff, no timely intelligence, no adequate command and control operations room. But by mid-May, 1994, halfway through the Rwanda slaughter, the UN's Department of Peacekeeping was Rwanda's last resort. If they could find the right equipment, the Ghanaian battalion could go back in quickly. The battalion was the nearest available force, evacuated from Kigali, and languishing in an aircraft hangar in Nairobi. Ghana was willing on one condition: the troops were to receive protected vehicles, armoured personnel-carriers to help with a civilian evacuation.

Immediately, UN officials sent urgent requests for armoured personnel carriers to forty-four member states, those with spare military capacity.

Not one country wanted to touch it. And then, on May 28, an official from the Pentagon telephoned. There were forty-eight armoured personnel-carriers in storage in Germany. If the UN wanted them, the Americans would be willing to lease them for $4 million.

The US already owed the UN a billion in back dues but to a separate account. This was the only offer they had and UN officials started negotiations. They pleaded for urgency but every obstacle was in the way. The UN wanted the armoured personnel-carriers moved at once; the Pentagon insisted that until a lease was signed, and terms agreed, surplus equipment did not move an inch. Worse, once the lease was agreed, it was going to take two weeks to get the carriers to Uganda, to the nearest large airport. The Pentagon ended up organising its own transport to get the armoured personnel carriers from storage in Germany to Uganda at an extra charge of $6 million to the UN.

Later, when the UN was under a barrage of criticism for incompetence and waste in its procurement of equipment, it was found that a commercial contractor would have got the armoured personnel carriers to Entebbe $4 million cheaper.

Three months later, in August, 1994 the armoured personnel-carriers were still in Entebbe because no trucks which were large enough could be found to transport them to Rwanda.

The New World Order created at the end of the Cold War was publicly envisioned by Presidents Bush and Gorbachev and was supposed to be founded on the rule of law and the principle of collective security which was enshrined in the UN Charter. The use of military force by the Security Council, foreseen by the founders of the UN, was to be an essential element. So enthusiastic was the international community about the New World Order, that they gave the UN ambitious new tasks – nation building and peace enforcement.

President Bill Clinton endorsed this view and came to office committed to UN peacekeeping, promising to upgrade the size and professionalism of the UN headquarters staff. He wanted an international standing army, and US troops under UN command, to guard borders and protect civilians. After Somalia, Clinton lost his enthusiasm. In October, 1993 eighteen American soldiers under American command were killed. Clinton blamed the UN, but the greatest humiliation was TV newscasts of an American serviceman, dragged through the dusty streets of Mogadishu by a jeering mob. Some said this was the moment that the New World Order died.

The Council commissioned its own report on Somalia, and, after reading it, suppressed it. It outlined in graphic detail a UN mission completely out of control. The report described patchwork command structure, as unstable as it was dangerous. Besides the Americans, other national contingents refused UN command and followed orders from their own capitals. In Somalia, the Council lost its grip and the special report suggested that the Council consider UN compensation to hundreds of Somalia civilians injured and the relatives of those who died. Never again should the UN undertake enforcement action.

By April 1994 it was generally assumed that similar operations would not be tested again – not unless a major power took charge, as the Americans had during Operation Desert Storm.

After Somalia, the White House tried to fathom another strategy towards peacekeeping, and a Presidential Review Directive was published setting out a new peacekeeping policy. Months in preparation, the Directive bounced backwards and forwards from department to department. When it was finalised, it laid down conditions so weighty that it seemed to rule out any US involvement at all. In future US involvement would depend on whether or not US interest were at stake, whether or not there was a threat to world peace, a clear mission goal, acceptable costs, congressional, public and allied support, a working cease-fire, a clean command and control and a clear exit point. Rwanda failed every Directive. A reinforcement of the UN peacekeepers in Kigali was not relevant to American interests; it was not prudent; success could not easily be accomplished; and there was no likelihood of political reconciliation.

On May 25, 1994 at the launch of D-Day commemorations, President Clinton explained further. He said he wanted to work with others to restore the most difficult problems of the age, but the US could not solve every outburst of civil strife just by sending in her forces. "We cannot turn away from them, but our interests are not sufficiently at stake in so many of them to justify a commitment of our folks."

Only France offered an airlift of troops. France announced that it could not stand idly by; President François Mitterand said that every hour counted. France would send soldiers on a humanitarian mission to the south-west where Hutus were gathered, having fled the rebel army as it swept across the country. The Security Council grudgingly and narrowly accepted France's offer – Brazil, China, New Zealand, Nigeria and Pakistan abstained. The US Ambassador to the UN, Madeleine K. Albright voted for the idea. Albright thought the Council should be flexible enough to accept imperfect solutions, which this was. France, a military ally, was given a UN mandate to go in alone. It made a mockery of UN principle of multilateralism.

To dispel accusations of partiality, one of the first tasks by French troops was to rescue Tutsis encircled by Hutu troops on the Zaire border. A group of sick and frail men, they were some 400, the remnants of the 10,000 Tutsis from the region who had been hunted through the forests. There were few women and children among them, they could not run fast enough. With the French presence, a few survivors at last emerged from months in hiding, creeping out from under sheds, inside cupboards, attics. Some spoke of brave Hutus who sheltered them at risk to their lives.

The second great tragedy for Rwanda was the flight of the Hutus, incited by militia, and in fear of rebel reprisals. It was the fastest and largest exodus the UN had ever recorded. The horizon was black with people, a remote rural corner of Tanzania turned into a giant muddy camp. Hundreds of thousands of people settled on a barren plain surrounded by volcanoes. Thousands died in appalling suffering in filthy overcrowded camps, walking in a mud of choleric vomit and diarrhoea. Some died from exhaustion, others from starvation, cholera or dysentery. There were more than 4,000 orphaned children. In one camp, boys were paid by French troops to collect the dead, ready to be tipped in vast graves. Further north, the corpses sat among the living.

Here then was the direst of all human situations – the systematic elimination of an entire people. Genocide is the first, last and most serious crime against humanity, and its prevention the single most important commitment of the countries who join together as the United Nations. But fifty years after the UN was founded, it cannot begin to delay genocide. Its member states know no better than to use the UN as a camouflage.

The reason is in its past, in the beginnings of the union, in the layers of hypocrisy that over the history of the UN, destroyed the dream.

2. THE GOLDEN GATE

The United Nations began on April 25, 1945 and San Francisco looked glorious in the sun. There were flash-bulbs, red carpets and flowers. Like a Hollywood prèmiere, the words "United Nations" flashed in neon outside the cinemas. The billing was a golden moment in history: the Golden Gate would open upon a better, a happier, and a safer world.

Delegates from fifty war-weary nations had come together in peace to establish a New World Order, a rule of law that could prevent the inhumanities and the genocide that haunted every survivor's mind. Thousands crowded behind police lines to watch. The impact had been calculated carefully for months. Each delegation stepped out of sleek, black cars and walked into the Opera House for the opening session, to the piped tune of its national anthem. The Opera House had been transformed for the occasion. The stairs to the stage were garlanded in flowers. The stage itself was a parade of flags, floodlit against a background of grey-blue drapes, flanking four golden pillars at centre stage which symbolised the four freedoms that President Franklin Delano Roosevelt proclaimed in 1941: freedom of speech and religion, freedom from want and from fear.

The hopes of the world had come to rest on one great, theatrical event. To create the UN "look", politicians had summoned the Broadway designer Jo Mielziner, a man who would become best known for staging grand American musicals. When called so suddenly to government service in 1945, Mielziner was off-Broadway, staging a play named *Foolish Notion*. A man of great talent, he did not disappoint. His UN design was spectacular.

They brought the press in specially chartered trains, two thousand of them, because the world was not meant to miss a moment of this day. Reporters were welcomed with flags and flowers and promised they were going to witness the foundation of enduring peace and freedom for the peoples of the world. There was a more specific promise, too, the only honest and decent promise that could be made by a world that now knew what had happened in the Nazi camps: "Never again". A small screening room ran news reels of the recently liberated concentration camps, of skeletal relics, the piles of children's shoes, the piles of teeth pulled for their gold. While the United Nations conference was still going on, the Soviet news agency, Tass, broke the story of the exact process of the gassing and cremation at Auschwitz.

While war with its privation and rationing continued elsewhere and the world was short of everything, there were no shortages of anything in San Francisco. San Francisco became a diplomatic island of spectacular buffets, a luxurious sufficiency of petrol, enough cars, typewriters and telephones to make life workable. The bills were paid by the US, determined to make the conference work and deliver a charter that could stop war and save the world.

At the closing session President Harry Truman described the Charter as a declaration of great faith, a faith that war was not inevitable. "If we had had this Charter a few years ago – and above all, the will to use it – millions now dead would be alive. If we should falter in the future in our will to use it, millions now living will surely die." At the end, while the delegates stood and applauded, Truman opened his arms wide towards them. Afterwards, a band played the *Star Spangled Banner*.

The American selling of the UN idea has been called the most dramatic hard-sell huckstering in twentieth-century politics. In the State Department, the poet Archibald MacLeish, assisted by Adlai Stevenson, special assistant to the Secretary of State, used every conceivable means to win the support of the American people for the UN idea was almost an obsession with Franklin Delano Roosevelt. A film was distributed, *Watchtower over Tomorrow*, an uncritical summary of UN responsibility, and it was sent to groups around the country – to churches, women's clubs and civic groups. In New York, The League of Women Voters and the YMCA distributed pamphlets and sent out loud-speaker vans to stir up public interest. The Federal Council of Churches asked all Protestant congregations to observe April 22, the nearest Sunday before the conference opening as UN Sunday to pray for its success. This success, Americans were told, was a tribute to the memory of President Roosevelt who had died on April 12, just a fortnight before the conference opened. Harry Truman's first decision as President was that the founding conference of the UN would go ahead as planned. Its success could be dedicated to the memory of a great wartime leader.

It was to break with isolationism that the desperate attempts were made to sell the UN. There was a determined effort to exorcise the past of 1920 when the US Congress had elected to stay out of the League of Nations, and the Republicans had rejected President Woodrow Wilson's view of a New World Order. Many believed that the American abstention had been the reason the League had died. The UN would not suffer the same fate and President Roosevelt, in order to ensure Senate support, had named several prominent Republican Senators to the American delegation to San Francisco. The opposition of any more than one-third of the Senate could prevent American membership.

The original copy of the Charter was brought back from San Francisco to Washington by Alger Hiss, a senior State Department official who had organised the glittering conference. He flew from San Francisco with the Charter in a metal safe and he took no chances. The safe had a parachute and a label: "Finder! Do not open. Send to the Department of State, Washington". Hiss was proud; the Charter for which he had laboured so long and believed in so heartily, was now a reality.

When Hiss was ushered into the Oval office, he found Truman in his shirt-sleeves. The President asked him to sit down, have a drink. Truman enthused about his whisky: he said it was the oldest in America. Hiss thought Truman somewhat flippant and casual, and later told how Truman had failed to express similar enthusiasm for the contents of the metal safe, which Hiss had placed at his feet. The informality of the occasion disturbed Hiss. Hiss, an East Coast liberal and New Dealer was comfortable with Roosevelt. Roosevelt's New Deal had been the battle waged pre-war against the Great Depression when the Federal Government provided recovery and relief through programmes of price stabilisation and public works and tightened banking and finance regulation to benefit working people. There was huge public spending and higher taxes. Speaking some years later Hiss says that had Roosevelt lived to see his UN dream a reality, the UN story would have been different.

Hiss was Secretary General of the founding conference; his selection by-passed the State Department's Division of International Conferences because the assignment had come from Roosevelt himself at Yalta conference in February, 1945. After the San Francisco conference was over, it was thought fitting that Hiss deliver the Charter to President Harry Truman in Washington.

Truman may not have shown much enthusiasm for the document in front of Hiss but in Congress he began intensive lobbying and he spoke to virtually every Senator to drum up support. When the US Senate did ratify the Charter in July 1945 the vote was overwhelming, the critical support already won. The powerful chairman of the Foreign Relations Committee, Texan Democrat, Tom Connally, was ecstatic. Wearing his usual black string tie and preacher's coat, Connally told his colleagues that the Charter was the greatest document ever written – a star in the night. He appealed to Senators to erase the memory of 1919 when the League of Nations was slaughtered on the floor of the Senate. "Can you not still see the blood . . . ? Can you not see upon the walls the marks of the conflict that raged right here in the Chamber where the League of Nations was done to death?"

Another Senate Democrat, Claude Pepper, said that the UN grew from the prophecies of Isaiah and Micah. For the Republicans, their leader, Senator Arthur Vandenberg, said that the UN gave America a veto on war: it would give America the security that two world wars had proved it could not achieve on its own.

Only two Senators spoke against. One of them, William "Wild Bill" Langer of North Dakota, forever an isolationist, believed the UN to be a "cynical imposture bred by hypocrisy out of power politics". The other dissenting voice was Henrik Shipstead of Minnesota, who wanted to know how anyone could be so simple-minded as to believe that the new organisation would be more successful than the League of Nations, where in every major crisis the big powers had disagreed. The two Republicans were regarded as cranks.

The Charter was an American triumph. The US had paid for the extravagance of San Francisco and she kept the original copy of the UN Charter in her National Archives. An American philanthropist gave the land for the Secretariat building in New York City, and Congress loaned the money to build this thirty-nine floor headquarters. But to continue to view the creation of the UN as a glittering show, the huge enthusiasm it evoked was not much longer than a curtain-call.

Some famous names were bandied about for the UN's first Secretary General – including Dwight Eisenhower and Anthony Eden. But in reality, the most important attribute was not to be opposed by five veto-wielding members of the Security Council. These great powers, the Allied victors in the war, had more power than other UN member states. They retained their status within the Council by each having a veto, a special vote. The veto was considered recognition of a reality; the organisation could not be used against the will of any of the great powers and nor could any major decision be made without their concurrence. This applied to the choice of Secretary General. Scandinavia already assumed the role of honorary neutral and as anyone other than a national of a neutral country would fail to satisfy Washington or Moscow, the Norwegian wartime Foreign minister, in exile in London, a former trade union lawyer called Trygve Lie seemed to fit the bill perfectly. The decision was taken by diplomats representing the Big Five – the USSR, France, Britain, US and China – at an unscheduled meeting rapidly arranged in a suite in Claridge's Hotel, London, on January 29, 1946.

Lie was hardly a household name, although the American Secretary of State, once he had learned to pronounce the name "lee" and not "lie", would pretend differently when the time came to eulogize him upon his election. Lie himself was amazed. Although previously Foreign Minister, he admitted to a lack of experience in international relations which the job would need, and he admitted no expertise in the language of diplomacy, qualities he knew were important. How could he refuse? It was a challenge beyond his wildest dreams.

The British soon regretted the choice. Within a few months their diplomats were sending secret reports to London describing Lie as vain, touchy and sometimes tricky. They said he was small-town in outlook. He appeared to be in awe of the Russians, thought the French a bad joke and probably regarded the British as "governessy". And he was such a bad administrator that the UN was effectively leaderless. Lie, or so the British surmised, had been over-influenced by the

Americans in basing the structure of the UN bureaucracy on that of the US Federal Government. This had resulted in over-staffing, inefficiency and a hierarchical system that tied down scores of officials to make sure that staff complied with complex regulations and procedures. The UN's cumbersome and over-elaborate personnel and financial machinery "was based on the concept that everyone is out to defraud the management". Sir Gladwyn Jebb, the British Government's UN adviser, thought this might be a good system for a company like Standard Oil of New Jersey but it would not work in an international organisation. The UN was barely one year old when the Foreign Office concluded that it was in disarray. It risked becoming a talking shop.

Roosevelt wanted the UN headquarters to be in Hawaii and Churchill thought it ought to be in Morocco; it ended up on New York's East River, previously the home of abattoirs and slums. It was dominated by a thin, glass palace and its construction substantially improved neighbouring property values.

The UN's founders had left specific instructions. To staff this new headquarters, there would be created an international civil service and its members would serve the international community without fear or favour; to this end guarantees were written into the Charter. The founders were mindful of a tragic weakness in the League of Nations when the Fascist government of Italy had insisted on clearance for their nationals in order to prevent the employment of opponents to Mussolini. Nazi Germany and authoritarian Poland had also applied pressure to ensure that only their loyal citizens were employed by the League.

The UN Secretariat would be different. Its staff was to be bound by an oath of loyalty which would prevent its members from seeking or receiving instruction from any government. The member governments of the UN were bound by the Charter too, forbidden to seek influence within the Secretariat. The staff would be chosen by the Secretary General who was bound to secure the highest standards of efficiency, competence and integrity.

It did not work out that way. The Big Five found it more convenient to divide the bureaucratic spoils among themselves and they carved up the top jobs. The first Secretary General, who was to be the UN's chief administrative officer, fell in with the arrangement and soon Lie was giving away the middle-management jobs to middle-ranking powers. There were appointments through patronage and some countries used the Secretariat to dump unwanted bureaucrats.

Lie took to confiding in American diplomats about the pressure on him to give jobs away. He complained about being provoked by governments. The British were particularly persistent and were pushing hard for a deputy. Secretary General Lie believed the British intention was to plant a spy in his office to undermine him, someone who would report directly to the Foreign Office on what Lie did every day. The Secretariat was soon a shambles. Unqualified people were appointed on very high salaries and the bureaucracy became top heavy. There persisted a critical shortage of qualified people – financial experts, statisticians, archivists, historians and economists. As for other appointments not won through patronage, these members of staff were recruited rapidly and sometimes at random. There were too many applications to cope with; most of these letters, unanswered, were simply stored in crates.

In a nine-month period nearly 3,000 people were taken on, four times the number employed by the League of Nations. A third of them were Americans and many, inspired by a New World Order, had come from Roosevelt's New Deal.

Inevitably the UN Secretariat was not a happy place. The idealists and romantics wanting to restore a world devastated by war were quickly disappointed. The majority of the staff soon became disgruntled. Just eighteen months after the UN became operational the Staff Committee called a mass protest meeting to which the Secretary General, Lie, was invited. A big, burly man, he sat in silence while employee after employee complained about conditions. There were moans about New York's cost of living, which was spiralling. There were complaints about the food in the cafeteria; worse, the lack of job security and the low wages. The administration of the Secretariat was so chaotic that at times whole sections of employees were left for weeks with no pay.

"Most of us have left good jobs to come here," someone in the meeting said. "If money really is in short supply, why is your entertainment budget so high?"

Lie was fuming when he finally got to his feet, his face red. He proceeded to shout and bang the rostrum with his fists. They should blame the member states, who voted the UN budget, for their troubles, he said. It was not his fault. As Secretary General, he received his instructions from the member states who had told him to take stock and try to create a lean and efficient adminstration. As international civil servants, they owed their loyalty, obedience and discipline to the UN.

There was silence. The applause came later for the popular French interpreter, Jean-François Rozan, who stated that the Secretary General quite clearly had lost the confidence of the staff. The Secretary General had sat in furious silence and he vowed never to address the Staff Association again. Rozan was transferred to UN offices in Geneva.

By March 1947, the Secretary General had other preoccupations. The UN's stock was so low that when he met his senior officials at a meeting in his office on March 18, 1947, Lie warned that the UN was going the same way as the League of Nations and becoming laughable. He wanted his senior aides to come up with ways of making UN decisions binding on member states. Lie was contemplating resignation: governments increasingly ignored him and public interest and goodwill had been lost.

Lie concluded that his job was impossible.

In London at roughly the same time there were similar conclusions. Prime Minister Attlee's government ordered a discreet investigation to discover whether or not there was some way that Secretariat efficiency could be improved and the expense reduced. There were fears about the militancy among staff. As the mass meeting was taking place in March, 1947, a secret report had come from the British ambassador to the UN, Sir Alexander Cadogan. He described a number of starry-eyed, left-wing sympathisers among the staff who, "while doubtless well intentioned themselves, were apt to become instruments of intrigue in the hands of their more hard-headed colleagues".

More sinister, before the mass meeting the first strike at UN headquarters had threatened when chauffeurs employed there vented their anger after a sudden cancellation of payment for overtime. The UN's management had no option but to negotiate a deal with the Staff Association's ruling committee, narrowly averting a strike. The Staff Association worried the British.

The Association, which was not technically a trade union, was run by an elected committee dominated at first by French interpreters. They were determined that, in accordance with Charter principle, the UN should lead the world in progressive employment policies. The committee managed the removal of the words "colour" and "race" from UN employment forms which were based on those used in American government service. The association made successful representations for equal rights after two pregnant women were forced to resign. The committee lobbied for pay during sick leave and for more equitable salaries. But the reality of working for the UN was cut-backs in funding and staff dismissals. At first they thought that the Secretary General, who was after all a former trade union lawyer, would fight their corner. But they were wrong.

Some people put these problems down to teething troubles; others said that as international co-operation was for a greater good, it would never be easy. This was the world's greatest experiment. Alger Hiss, who as Secretary General of the founding conference believed that all his life. He thought that member states were sincere when they wrote and agreed the Charter and signed it in June 1945. After San Francisco and the disagreements between East and West, Hiss argued for diplomatic correctness at least. He never forgot the spirit of celebration that permeated the founding conference saying it was the kind of moment that made it impossible to believe that the great powers could not get along. Hiss believed for ever that the signing of the Charter was the greatest moment in the history of international relations.

There is no escaping Hiss's air of superiority. According to *Life* magazine in 1945, Hiss was in a class of his own. His prestigious appointment as Secretary General was the culmination of a brilliant young man's outstanding career. There was some truth in the slogan that the UN was the house that Hiss built in as much as he was there from the beginning. From Spring of 1944 he was a member of a team created by Roosevelt in the State Department to plan a post-war New World Order. During the same year he was Executive Secretary of the Dumbarton Oaks Conversations, which produced the Charter blueprint. Hiss was one of half-a-dozen advisers on the UN at Yalta, later becoming Director of the State Department's Office of Special Political Affairs, co-ordinating US policy on US-UN relations. He was appointed the US delegation's principal adviser at the first session of the UN General Assembly held in London in early 1946.

Hiss was suggested as a possible UN Secretary General. The young Soviet diplomat, Andrei Gromyko suggested that this bright young man would be a good temporary Secretary General – until such time as someone else was elected. Others said that Hiss was bound to be Secretary of State. He was a Harvard lawyer with Gary Cooper looks, a man of authority and ability. But hopes for post-war co-operation were fast disappearing. He was being secretly watched and followed by the FBI; the Secretary of State had placed restrictions on his access to confidential departmental documents. The FBI Director J. Edgar Hoover, for want of hard evidence against Hiss began to leak information to favoured journalists about his doubts; there were rumours that the loyalty of a high ranking American official was being questioned, and that the matter had been brought to the attention of the President. In secret meetings with agents, an FBI informer was claiming that Hiss had been a leading underground Communist whose unit "was not a spy ring", but whose task was to "mess up policy". In March 1946, when told about Hoover's concerns Hiss went to FBI headquarters and, in a meeting with an assistant director, denied membership of any Communist or Communist-front organisations. But the surveillance did not stop.

In February 1947 Hiss left government service. He became President of the Carnegie Endowment for International Peace. He was so engaged when the bombshell dropped. On 3 August, 1948 an FBI informer named Whittaker Chambers gave public testimony to the House Un-American Activities Committee, that Hiss had been in the Communist underground during the 1930s. The charges were an instant sensation and the case divides America to this day. As James Reston pointed out in the *New York Times* in 1949, many could not consider Hiss guilty because to do so would discredit the Roosevelt administration; others could not believe he was innocent because viewing him as guilty proved that Communism was the New Deal in a hurry.

Another part of the Hiss puzzle involves a Soviet defector. Igor Gouzenko was a cipher clerk who, while serving in Ottawa in September 1945, defected to the West. He exposed a major spy ring in Canada and his information led to other major Soviet rings being smashed. Communists and sympathisers were moved from sensitive government posts. Gouzenko gave valuable clues about the extent of Soviet recruitment; he claimed that the Soviets had a top-level agent in the US who, in May 1945, was an assistant to the Secretary of State, Edward Stettinius. When Gouzenko's information was linked with that supplied earlier by FBI informants, the bureau concluded that the spy was Hiss.

Liberals maintain that Hiss was a first martyr to the UN cause, wrongly accused by a diabolical gang which included a young Richard Nixon and J. Edgar Hoover, who loathed the East Coast, educated American elite. These men were convinced of Hiss's guilt, and claimed that he had exerted a Svengali influence on Roosevelt at Yalta. They accused Hiss of having drafted the section of the agreement that gave the USSR three votes in the UN General Assembly. Three large Soviet Republics, Russian, Byelorussia and the Ukraine were classified as member states.

The moment of his accusation, Hiss issued a writ for defamation. The US Statute of Limitations prevented an espionage charge and Hiss was accused of perjury for having persisted in denials under oath. His first trial resulted in a hung jury in July 1949. Congressman Richard Nixon, a California Republican who bore major responsibility for the indictment, explained: 'Members of the administration feared than an adverse verdict would prove that there was a great deal of foundation to all the reports of Communist infiltration into the government during the New Deal days'. On 21 January, 1950 Hiss was found guilty on two counts of lying to a grand jury about his ties to the Soviet Union and was sentenced to five years in prison. Hiss' conviction resulted in a bonanza for the Republicans.

Hiss was vilified in Conservative circles thereafter as the personification of the social philosophy that underpinned the New Deal. Richard Nixon, who continued to pursue him with vigour once said: "If the American people knew the real character of Alger Hiss, they would boil him in oil".

Hiss commented that he could not understand why so many had eulogised Nixon; Nixon was an unscrupulous, self-dramatising rascal, responsible for many nefarious acts. Others too were sure where the guilt was to be found. In 1984, President Ronald Reagan posthumously awarded Chambers, the FBI informer and Hiss's original accuser, with America's highest peacetime award, the Presidential Medal of Freedom. The President was said to admire Chambers' anti-Communist writing. Chambers viewed the Cold War as a death struggle between enlightenment and evil.

Hiss protested his innocence at every opportunity. and, years after the charges, by then a frail eighty-seven-year-old man, he heard what he took to be a final, public exoneration. After the dissolution of the USSR, Hiss had written to the KGB. In reply the Chairman of the Supreme Soviet Commission of the KGB archives, General Dmitri Volkogonov, declared that he could find nothing which substantiated spying allegations. Hiss tried once more for a pardon from the US Supreme Court. But few minds were changed. No statement had come from the GRU, the Soviet military intelligence and later Volkogonov retracted. Americans of the Cold War generation are as polarised as they were decades ago.

Hiss never wavered in his support of the internationalist cause; but he never knew what the UN became. He was incapable of hearing a word of criticism about the organisation; he never knew the extent of government manipulation of the system. He refused to hear about victims other than himself, other tragedies and other lives ruined. In the UN Secretariat on the East River two camps were trying to operate in a one-world organisation. Two diametrically different systems, Communist and Capitalist, were trying to adhere to the same set of rules within an international bureaucracy. Lives were lost and hundreds of careers ruined as a result of a Cold War fought in the ranks of the international civil service.

The reputation of the United Nations rapidly diminished. In March, 1949 came the arrest, in a blaze of publicity, of the first UN spy. The story had everything: espionage, surveillance and sex, and it was in the headlines, day after day. It was also a triumphant affirmation for the American right-wingers who had warned that the Secretariat was turning into a nest of spies.

The spy was Valentin Gubitchev, a handsome Soviet engineer, caught in a secret liaison with an American woman, one who happened to be an analyst working on Soviet security matters in the Department of Justice. It would end with Gubitchev returning to Moscow to a hero's welcome and his spying would become part of KGB history. The Gubitchev case was later scrutinised by students at the KGB teaching institute: identified as example number 101 it is reported in a textbook published by the Higher Advanced Intelligence School in 1956.

For America, the case was a milestone in quite a different way. The woman arrested with Gubitchev, Judith Coplon, was the first American civilian arrested for Soviet espionage and the arrests were a considerable coup for the FBI Counter-Intelligence Department in New York. It badly needed to make its reputation; up until then the section handling counter-intelligence was nicknamed Sleepy Hollow by fellow agents. In those early days, the more popular assignments in Manhattan were stocks and bonds and crime on the high seas.

In spite of all the fuss in the newspapers, the Gubitchev case was not quite as it seemed. When the news of the dramatic arrests reached the administration in Washington there was less than jubilation. As the State Department's file on the case reveals, Gubitchev had claimed diplomatic immunity after his arrest. As a UN employee he would not have immunity, but Gubitchev had a point. Because of a mistake by a US consular official in the US Embassy in Moscow, Gubitchev travelled to the US as Third Secretary on a diplomatic passport, not as a UN employee. A UN employee can be arrested and tried for breaking US laws or deported for violating residence privileges, a Third Secretary cannot. Only a few hours after the arrest there was a secret briefing in the US mission to the UN. The US Ambassador to the UN Warren Austin, was told that although FBI agents had witnessed three clandestine meetings, this time Judith Coplon still had government documents in her handbag and Gubitchev still possessed $125 in cash which the FBI assumed he was to give her. "We all agreed the agent in charge of this case ordered the arrest after an attack of nerves," Austin was told.

The case against Gubitchev was entirely circumstantial. There were serious doubts that a conviction could be obtained. The FBI confided to Austin they believed Gubitchev more a messenger than a spy, and that he was simply in place to pick up papers provided to the Soviets by American Communists. Washington became seriously divided. The Secretary of State, Dean Acheson, wanted Gubitchev deported immediately. A trial would be dangerous. There could well be retaliation against US citizens in Moscow. Acheson revealed a secret deal in which a Soviet spy was exchanged for three Americans, caught in similar circumstances. Acheson feared diplomatic embarrassment: the UN Headquarters Cornerstone ceremony was approaching and world leaders were due to visit New York.

Elsewhere, other considerations prevailed. Judith Coplon was a Justice Department employee and the Department felt strongly that an example should be made. A trial without Gubitchev would make it harder to convict her. Tom Clark, the Attorney General, argued with Acheson and later, in a telephone conversation with Warren Austin, Clark suggested that assuming the Soviet delegation allowed Gubitchev to sit through a trial the Americans would insist on his being deported immediately afterwards. Austin said he thought the Soviet Ambassador incapable of keeping his mouth shut about such a deal.

The President finally settled the arguments and on March 21, 1949, after a cabinet discussion in the White House, Truman gave a green light for a trial. As for the problem of Gubitchev's diplomatic passport, the Soviets would be told that Gubitchev had effectively given up his diplomatic status – the day he took the UN oath of office.

The woman who stood in the dock was in her late-twenties. A brilliant Barnard graduate, she became a political analyst in the Foreign Agents Registration Section of the Justice Department. Judith Coplon's job was to help to ensure that anyone acting for a foreign government in the US, in whatever capacity, complied with the law and registered with the authorities. During the war, during the hunt for Nazi front groups, this section grew. Coplon, taken on in 1945, specialised in the Soviet Union, an assignment that gave her access to FBI case reports about on-going investigations. Valentin Gubitchev appeared to meet her, as the KGB textbook teaches, quite by chance, in front of a painting in the Museum of Modern Art in New York City. Coplon was given the code-name Sima.

Gubitchev worked at the UN as an architectural engineer, the result of pressure on the Personnel Department by the most senior Soviet official in the Secretariat, an Assistant Secretary General named Arkady Sobolev. Sobolev's insistence on the employment of Gubitchev had become a joke because there was no opening for a man of Gubitchev's limited qualifications. Gubitchev spoke little English, but he ended up at the construction site of the UN's permanent headquarters on the East River, initially in the Buildings Management Division and later the Headquarters Planning Office, although no one was able to say with certainty what he did all day. The FBI interest in Gubitchev began – or so agents claimed – by decrypting KGB coded messages to Moscow. At one point there were eighty agents on the case. Coplon and Gubitchev were followed through New York subways, on to buses, up and down the avenues on round-the-clock surveillance. The agents were full of admiration for the couple's methods at throwing off potential tails with their professional evasion techniques.

In the summer of 1949, Coplon went on trial charged with stealing government documents. She pleaded not guilty. The prosecution claimed that Coplon, operating undercover, had provided secret information to the KGB for three years. When arrested, she was carrying thirty-four data slips about current FBI investigations into the Soviet penetration of government agencies. To the delight of Soviet embassy officials sitting in court, the Judge allowed the files on these investigations to be produced in evidence. The consequence was the exposure of FBI methods. Information on the FBI's techniques and how wide the agency cast its net were among the revelations. Anyone could come under FBI suspicion for the most remote reason. The files produced in the Coplon trial were an amalgamation of unconfirmed reports, gossip and rumour about alleged Communist and left-leaning sympathies of well-known writers and entertainers – including Dorothy Parker and the actor Edward G. Robinson. The files contained information about who read the *New Republic*, who supported the liberal politician Henry Wallace, Presidential candidate of the US Progressive Party.

Coplon defended herself vehemently. She said she was taking the data slips from the office as part of her research for a novel which she was writing called *Government Girl*. She told the court that one of the chapters in the book described a witch-hunt in which reports were prepared on thousands and thousands of people. Eventually everyone ended up reporting on everyone else. Coplon claimed that Valentin Gubitchev was her lover, that they met in 1948 in front of a Cubist painting. Just before the arrests, Gubitchev had finally admitted to her that he was married: he said he wanted to leave his wife and defect. The reason they had behaved evasively was the fear they were being followed by agents from the KGB.

The prosecution responded with evidence of another man in Coplon's life and Coplon was found guilty.

In November 1949 she stood in the dock again, this time beside Gubitchev. Also in court every day was Yuri V. Novikov, Second Secretary at the Soviet Embassy in Washington, who would be credited with having orchestrated the case for the defence. Novikov continually passed notes to Gubitchev's American counsel, Abraham Pomerantz. Novikov was watched taking copious notes while Russian-speaking FBI agents were questioned about investigative techniques and the internal administration of the bureau. Pomerantz questioned FBI witnesses about wiretapping and monitoring, asked about where the taps were located and which types of receivers were used, what form of written notes resulted and who had access to them.

The FBI Director J. Edgar Hoover in his book *Masters of Deceit*, wrote that although Novikov's audaciousness at spying knew no bounds, his brazenness reached a climax during the Gubitchev trial.

The jury, after deliberating for forty-eight hours found both Gubitchev and Coplon guilty on a conspiracy charge. Gubitchev, found guilty of attempting to obtain government secrets, was sentenced to fifteen years in prison. The Federal Judge, Sylvester Ryan told him: "You came here as emissary of peace . . . you violated your oath of office to the Secretariat of the United Nations of the world . . . you stand before the world accused of betrayal of all mankind . . . and with a smile on your face you stand here before me for sentence in defiance of all humanity." Then, to everyone's surprise, Judge Ryan announced that Gubitchev's sentence would be suspended provided he left the country immediately.

Coplon was found not guilty of passing government secrets to an unauthorised person but she received fifteen years for conspiracy. She appealed her sentence on the grounds that she was arrested without a warrant and that the prosecution depended on inadmissible wire-tapping evidence. During the appeal it emerged that FBI agents had wire-tapped illegally, lied about the fact at the first trial and destroyed some records. In December, 1950, Judge Learned Hand and two other US Court of Appeals judges reversed the Coplon decision on the grounds that the arrest of Coplon was illegal. The Government failed to show that its case was not based on illegal wire-tap evidence. The Appeals Court did not dismiss the Coplon indictment as guilt was plain. Although Coplon did not serve a prison term, the case fell into legal limbo where it has remained ever since.

When the trial was over the Soviet Ambassador, Yakov Malik, officially complained to the Secretary General about the threats to the independence of the Secretariat which had been so blatantly

exposed. Malik demanded to know how the official UN photograph
of Gubitchev managed to migrate in some queer way from his UN
personnel file into FBI hands. The Soviets expressed outrage at the
wire-tapping of senior UN officials and objected strenuously to these
breaches of the Charter which guaranteed the independence of the
staff and the UN's international status.

The Soviets must have been aware by then that wire-tapping was
the least of it.

The UN's most senior American employee, Assistant Secretary
General Byron Price was a blunt former executive news editor of the
Associated Press. He owed his appointment to the fact that he had
worked directly with the White House during the war as head of the
Office of Censorship. Price, a Washington insider, was the UN's most
powerful official, controlling the finance and the personnel
departments. He was unpopular with staff, not least because one of
his lieutenants was a Vichy Frenchman.

In June 1949, Price went to Washington to have lunch with
Secretary of State Dean Acheson. Price was keen to assure Acheson
that he would not tolerate spies in the Secretariat. Nor would he
tolerate American Communists although, of course the UN had to
accept Communist employees from Communist-dominated member
states. Price, pointing out that the UN was in no position to
investigate the backgrounds of staff, asked if the State Department
could provide an indication of the loyalty of the Americans the UN
employed, on a formal and regular basis. There was a receptive
response and by September of that year, a secret agreement was in
place – so secret indeed that all the information passed under the
agreement, from the State Department to the thirty-eighth floor of
the UN, was by word of mouth.

Between Price and the State Department a cover plan was devised
– necessary in that the agreement, a surrender of the independence
of the Secretariat to a member state, breached Article 100 of the
Charter. They agreed that lists of American employees' names would
be sent to the Assistant Secretary of State for UN Affairs, John
Hickerson, and returned immediately with a letter saying there were
no comments. In fact, intelligence information would be collected on
each individual and this information would be evaluated in
Hickerson's office. If an employee was suspect, derogatory opinion
would be transmitted to the UN. Each evaluation was usually one

word – "reject", "questionable" or "incomplete". The evaluation would indicate strong suspicion that staff were Communists or [even] there were a "likelihood . . . they were to become so".

The secret agreement was hardly surprising. Suspicions about Secretariat staff were nothing new. On October 6, 1948 the US Attorney General was in possession of a memorandum from Hoover; "Espionage Suspects Connected with the Central Secretariat of the UN or with the Delegation of the Member Committees of the UN". But the intentions went further than suspicion. The American Government wanted influence over Secretariat employment. In the National Archives in Washington is the proof of the increasing American pressure over who was hired, promoted or fired from the UN and who within the Secretariat secretly kept Washington informed. The National Archives reveal how Lie's Executive Assistant, an American called Andrew Cordier, a former history professor from Ohio, was warned on March 30, 1948 against giving a Secretariat position to a Polish diplomat. Cordier was told that the diplomat under consideration was an opportunist who took the line that Communists were "pretty reasonable people": the case should be called to the Secretary General's notice "on the same bases as the two previous occasions". Cordier was apparently most appreciative. On another occasion, Cordier was warned against an employee who worked in the UN's Social Affairs Department. A professor of international law he was under consideration for promotion. State Department officials concluded that although he was not an "outright Communist" and, although he had undoubted ability, there were doubts about his stability and opportunism. The professor, Enrique Sanchez de Lozada, mixed with those of a "liberal-leftist" persuasion – Sumner Welles, Lawrence Duggan, Henry Wallace and Nelson Rockefeller. He was said to have the "usual Latino disinterest [sic] in punctuality". After duly accepting the warning, Cordier responded that although it would be difficult to find another candidate, the professor would be eliminated from consideration.

Within the American intelligence community internationalism was soon equated with communism. Britain's deeply committed John Ennals, who helped to set up the World Federation of UN Associations and was its first Secretary General, was followed by the CIA in 1947 whilst touring Latin America on a trip to promote the UN. The World Federation was a people's movement to work for the

40

realisation of UN goals: it would "give expression to the wishes of the people on UN matters". Ennals' public meetings in Latin America were fully reported to the State Department; he did not "shy away from Communist support" and agents reported to Washington that his meetings were attracting Communist and left-wing groups. The British Foreign Office was also interested in an organisation which was in a position to affect popular attitudes towards the UN. The Foreign Office reported to Washington that they were somewhat uneasy about Ennals themselves: he was regarded by some as a "parlour pink".

The FBI's initial contact with the Secretariat was through an American employee, David Vaughan. Vaughan, an administrator, was the director of the Department of Conferences and General Services, which employed the largest number in the Secretariat and which was responsible for servicing all the meetings and employed secretaries, verbatim reporters, interpreters, editors, translators and precis writers. The FBI contacted Vaughan whenever its agents needed to make "discreet enquiries". Vaughan would locate American members of staff who could be interviewed without, as a 1949 memo reveals, the "alien members of the Secretariat" being aware of the enquiries. Vaughan once confided to an American diplomat that a UN employee, a Ukrainian called Feodor Parkhomenko, whose grand title was Chief of the Questionnaires and Territorial Reports Section of the Department of Trusteeship, was quite obviously an MVD (KGB) agent. Parkhomenko, Vaughan reported, never seemed to do any work while at the Secretariat and although only a medium grade officer, he was treated by members of the Soviet delegation and the Soviet nationals on the staff with great deference as he was beyond the ordinary powers of discipline.

By 1949 the FBI was actively investigating UN personnel and in early spring that year the first was summoned to appear before the House Committee on Un-American Activities. Trygve Lie was appalled. He tried desperately to have the hearing postponed so he could fire the employee concerned and asked the American Ambassador, Warren Austin, to help with the delay. Lie said he did not want it to appear that he had fired the employee because of the summons to the Congressional committee. Lie was dissuaded from such action only by a senior UN lawyer but he had already assured the American Ambassador that he wanted to get rid of "such people who bring public embarrassment".

The employee, Mary Jane Keeney, was a UN documents editor and economist. She was not surprised by her summons. By then she was almost used to FBI agents following her. Along with her husband Philip, she was well known to the Bureau. Its files went back to the late-thirties, when Philip Keeney, a librarian, was dismissed from the University of Montana for incompetence. He claimed he had been victimised for resisting censorship and for having organised a local chapter of the American Federation of Teachers. The American Civil Liberties Union fought his case and the Montana State Supreme Court ordered his reinstatement. During the war both Mary Jane and Philip received government security clearances: Philip analysed classified material in Japan and Mary Jane edited documents in Paris for the Allied Commission on Reparations.

In 1949 both the Keeneys were called to the House Committee. Philip pleaded the Fifth Amendment to all questions about Communist Party membership but he talked freely about the medical aid he helped send to Republican Spain during the civil war. He admitted meeting Earl Browder, head of the US Communist Party. Mary Jane denied under oath that she was or ever had been a member of the party but she was condemned nonetheless because of her connection with the Washington Co-operative Bookshop, believed by the FBI to be an outlet for Communist propaganda. Its members defended the shop as a place where bargain-hunting book lovers could meet and there were musical evenings, intellectual conversation. Keeney was confident in court. She said that her links with the bookshop were known to civil service investigators who had cleared her for government work in the war. Part of Keeney's FBI file was submitted in evidence to the House Committee. It detailed how in March 1946, on her return to New York from Paris after the war, she had been observed by FBI agents in a restaurant passing a manila envelope to a man suspected of espionage. He was followed and he took the envelope to the office of a left-wing publisher, Alexander Trachtenberg. The House Committee, whose members included a freshman Congressman from California called Richard Nixon, branded her a Communist Party courier. Keeney was defiant. On July 25, 1949 she issued her own press release through the UN to explain this incident as "innocent and trivial": she had simply brought to America books in French which were not available in America. The envelope contained a book by Gabriel Péri, French resistance martyr, a book published openly in France.

No sooner had the Secretary General weathered the Keeney storm than an anti-UN senator, a Democrat called Patrick McCarran from Nevada, held his own hearing. An anonymous witness was called to a Senate subcommittee who claimed that a Communist terror was gripping the UN Secretariat. His testimony was quickly issued in a press release. Trygve Lie was seriously alarmed by the anti-UN outcry.

In January 1951, three of the nine officers of the Staff Committee, the ruling body of the UN's Staff Association were dismissed. The Association's Presiding Officer was Benedict Alper, a Harvard-trained lawyer who was amazed the management would dare act in this way. Alper was outspoken. He was widely quoted as objecting to the UN Secretariat's "manifest injustices against women, blacks, Jews, and lower-grade income employees". Alper, a criminologist, was convinced a blacklist of staff existed of those who had openly objected to UN action after the invasion of South Korea. Alper claimed double standards – other invasions, China's into Tibet in 1949 for example, had been ignored by the Security Council. Alper, who was a founding member of the UN Staff Association, worked at the UN for more than four years. The reason given for his dismissal was that he was unsuitable for permanent UN employment. Also dismissed was the Assistant Secretary of the Staff Committee, an American called Raymond McGuire. McGuire had spearheaded a campaign against a proposal to contract out the work done by the UN's cleaners and portering staff. McGuire was frank with UN management; he told senior officials that if the plan went ahead it would signify that the UN sanctioned the low salaries and poor health standards which characterised such work in New York City.

Jeanne Picou was dismissed for "bringing the organisation into disrepute". During a Staff Association campaign against the Red Cross she was active in trying to stop the registering of donors according to race. A resolution had been adopted during a Staff Association meeting that staff would no longer contribute blood on UN premises if it was segregated. The Secretary General's office had defended the Red Cross and had argued that US servicemen in Korea had to be assured that the blood they received was not from blacks or Asians. The story was leaked to the press and within months the Red Cross removed racial origin from its donor forms throughout America. Picou was the Secretary of the Staff Committee and a former member of the French resistance.

The dismissals caused an uproar and an appeal was launched by the Staff Association to pay for legal advice to challenge the management through the Administrative Tribunal. This Tribunal, established by the General Assembly in 1949 despite strong objections from the American delegation, was the last resort for staff in dispute with management. It had seven members, no two of whom were nationals of the same country and only three of whom sat on any particular case. The Tribunal's decisions were final. A year previously, in July 1950, the Tribunal found in favour of sixteen Verbatim Reporters dismissed from the Secretariat and all were reinstated.

The appeal by the dismissed staff to the Tribunal was widely assumed to be a challenge to the Secretary General's power. Five members of staff appealed jointly – Jeanne Picou, Ben Alper, Raja Howrani, a press officer and Monika Kehoe, Staff Counsellor. The fifth was Mary Jane Keeney, discharged eighteen months after her appearance before the House Un-American Activities Committee because she did not reach "the high standards contemplated by the Charter". Another appellant was a Staff Counsellor, a psychiatric-social worker, outspoken about staff morale. Monika Kehoe was not given a reason for her dismissal but she was openly critical that two-thirds of the UN staff were employed on temporary contracts. "Insecurity hangs like a pall over the entire organisation", she once reported to management. Most members of staff "devote a large part of their time and energy trying to . . . ingratiate themselves with top-ranking personnel . . . gossip floods the corridors . . . (as) evidence of fear and uncertainty." Kehoe claimed to have been told that the UN required a counsellor with white hair, no university degree, and who would take care the "girls" on the staff had nice living-quarters.

The hearings, in summer 1951, lasted several weeks. The Staff Association was represented by a powerful advocate, no less than Telford Taylor who had been assistant to the US prosecutor at the Nazi trials in Nuremberg. In a carefully crafted case, he accused the UN of conducting a campaign of victimisation and intimidation; staff members were reduced to "fear-stricken nonentities". In the case of Mary Jane Keeney the management was said to have dismissed her for suspected Communist sympathies, the same reason was given as the cause for the dismissal of press officer, Raja Howrani. Howrani was a talented linguist and his job entailed writing UN news releases for Middle Eastern and North African press. He was much praised for his translation into Arabic of the Universal Declaration of Human Rights. Before joining the Secretariat, Howrani had been active in the Arab Friends of Ethiopia during the struggle against Italian Fascism and he helped to organise the Syria and Lebanon Friends of the USSR Society. These details were readily provided on his UN employment form and Howrani also told his UN employers how, in 1937, while teaching in Palestine, he had been deported by the British with the reason that he was "undesirable".

The UN's defence was conducted by the its most senior lawyers, who argued that none of these staff members had the right of appeal – none had permanent contracts. They argued that the Secretary General was not obliged to give reasons for dismissing non-permanent staff. The UN's General Counsel, an American called Abe Feller, a confidant of the Secretary General, argued that Lie needed broad powers to enable him to create an efficient administration which was a requirement imposed upon him by the General Assembly. The Secretary General was restructuring the administration and between January 1947 and July 1951 there were 635 dismissals. Neither Communism nor trade unionism played a part in any of these decisions.

It was a great test of the Administrative Tribunal and the ruling was a compromise. In favour of the Staff Association, the Tribunal noted that every employee, no matter what his or her contract, had the right to appeal. But only Keeney and Howrani won their cases. The officials of the Staff Council did not. Ben Alper, Jeanne Picou and Monika Kehoe, were deemed not to have expected to have their contracts renewed.

Keeney and Howrani, rather than accept reinstatement, claimed damages against the UN. While awaiting the outcome of his damages claim, Howrani, whose US visa had lapsed, was interviewed by the FBI. He refused to answer any questions. A few days later he was arrested by immigration officials and detained on Ellis Island. Howrani was bailed by UN staff on condition he leave the US within two weeks – time in which he had to sell his house, take his three children out of school and pack. Howrani left New York on the Queen Elizabeth on November 13, 1951 for his home in Syria, since 1949 under an army dictatorship led by Brigadier Adib Shishekly. In a last letter to staff, Howrani remained encouraging: "Do not despair concerning your legal rights . . . (though) they are seriously threatened they are not entirely gone . . . the UN is committed to the protection of legal rights . . . do not give up hope".

Mary Jane Keeney spent her UN compensation helping to finance an art film club in New York. A year later she was called before a Grand Jury and told the club was suspected to be a spy ring whose task was to plant Reds in the UN. She was subpoenaed once more by a Congressional Committee she was cited for contempt after pleading the Fifth Amendment. Keeney was found guilty but awarded a new trial on appeal. And in April 1955 she was found not guilty.

Not long after the Administrative Tribunal issued its ruling, a former vice-chair of the Staff Association's Committee – someone who had helped to organise the appeals – was told his contract would not be renewed. He was a Canadian called Lukin Robinson and the director of his department had requested he serve another two years in the Population Division which at the time was understaffed. Robinson joined the UN Secretariat in 1950 after a pressing invitation from New York. He had resigned his job in the Dominion Bureau of Statistics to do so. Robinson appealed to the Administrative Tribunal, claiming that the UN management sacked him because of his Staff Association activities.

The Robinson ruling proved to be a landmark and Robinson won damages and obtained a good deal of publicity. The Tribunal ruled that the UN had violated Robinson's right of association – a basic trade union right. The judgment referred to the Universal Declaration of Human Rights which the Tribunal declared "must prevail also inside the organisation's own Secretariat". The *New York Times* pointed out that the Robinson case was the first time the Declaration, which guaranteed free association, proved of "dollar and cents value to anyone".

For Lie, the outcome could not have been worse. He had been so desperate to win that he had tried to influence the appeal secretly. Lie told the then chair of the Administrative Tribunal, an eminent French international lawyer, Suzanne Bastid, that as the Canadian Government had wanted Robinson dismissed, then as Secretary

General he had no alternative but to comply. Lie hoped to persuade Bastid that Robinson not be reinstated. Years later Robinson said that the Canadian Government had nothing to do with his dismissal and he was convinced that he was dismissed from the UN to make it easier for purges still to come.

The UN's archives contain reams of documents about this period but many are closed to researchers. Among those inadvertently left outside the ban is a fascinating letter written to Lie in July, 1952 by his General Counsel, Abe Feller who went to Geneva to attend the Robinson appeal. He wrote to Lie that he was not confident of victory. "How do we state the reasons for the refusal to grant him (Robinson) a new contract? . . . we might be faced with the same situation as in the previous cases." One can only surmise that Feller was referring to the secret agreement with the US State Department and that Robinson, like the others who had been dismissed, had all secretly been given the thumbs down in Washington.

By 1952 Lie was of the opinion that the Administrative Tribunal was a nuisance. He told the senior officials he was considering creating a subcommittee to study its revision. Feller thought it would be a good idea if delegates were made fully aware of the costs of the Tribunal hearings.

Within the UN Secretariat, the circles of suspicion grew. There was increasing rumour of paid informers, secret dossiers and blacklists. Staff members were convinced the phones were tapped; there were fears about fraternising with fellow staffers from Communist countries, fears about sitting with them in the cafeteria or meeting them by chance in corridors. Guilt was by association. American liberals who worked for the UN were frightened of being called Communists; soon they were frightened of being called liberals. Witch-hunts have their own dynamic and Robinson was right: worse was to come.

3. PATRICK McCARRAN

The McCarthy period is a misnomer for, among the strange characters in US politics in the 1950s, another stood out – the virulent anti-Communist Senator, Patrick McCarran. He was organised and effective in his witch-hunting and was investigating Communists in government before Joe McCarthy. McCarran thought McCarthy had poor judgment and told him time and again not to distort the facts. McCarthy hit on the anti-Communism issue in mid-1950 half by accident, and it was more of a racket than anything else. For McCarran it was a crusade. McCarthy may be better known but McCarran's legacy was enduring.

McCarran thought loyalty the only quality that "counted in a man". He believed himself to be ideologically pure. The son of an Irish sheep rancher in Reno, Nevada, an immigrant frontiersman, McCarran had ridden horseback ten miles to school and supported his studies by working as a shepherd for his father, perfecting his Irish oratory. He made a name for himself from the Nevada divorce laws, acting for Mary Pickford in her 1920 Reno divorce which cleared the way for marriage to Douglas Fairbanks. McCarran became an expert in mining and water rights and after ten years at the State Supreme Court, became Nevada's Chief Justice. He was supported by mining and gambling barons among whom he remains a hero.

Today the McCarran ranch in the Truckee River Canyon outside Reno is owned by the eldest of McCarran's four daughters, Sister Margaret Patricia, whose staunchly anti-Socialist views – she thought Fabianism ruined Britain – were an influence of her father. (McCarran said that Sister Margaret was born a politician but God made her a nun.) Green shamrocks continue to dominate the wooden signs which threaten trespassers on the McCarran ranch. Some land is to be sold for a dog food factory but Sister Margaret keeps the place on as a shrine to her father: part of his archive is in a shed next to the house and protected, says Sister Margaret, by a rattlesnake. A much-weeded McCarran archive is held in the Nevada State Museum and indicates how much time McCarran spent on patronage.

Senator Patrick McCarran built one of the most effective State organisations ever; he worried about long absences from the State while he was power-brokering in Washington. It was a rule of his Washington office that letters from a Nevadan had to be answered the same day and such rules were not broken by McCarran's staff.

McCarran promised his constituents he would develop their State – and he kept his word. Nevada, with only mining and gambling, was highly dependent on federal projects and McCarran's twenty-one years in the Senate saw the Stead Air Base built near Reno, Nellis Air Base near Las Vegas and the atomic testing ground established in south central Nevada. McCarran was accused of representing only parochial interests to the detriment of the nation at large, but in Nevada elections are not usually based on national issues. Small and under-populated, Nevada has an equal voice in the Senate with larger and more highly populated States.

McCarran became Chairman of the Senate Judiciary Committee in 1933 and it gave him more power over jobs in the US Judiciary than anyone in Congress; he would have a say in the appointments of federal judges, marshals and US attorneys and this would give him the chance for patronage in his home State. He controlled laws effecting immigration, naturalisation and federal court procedures. McCarran had power within the appropriations network too: he was member of an appropriations subcommittee for the State Department and had a voice in the budgets of the Department of Agriculture, the Department of the Interior and the Armed Services.

McCarran is remembered for a piece of legislation which bears his name. In 1950, he created the Internal Security Act and passed it into law despite the veto of President Truman. The Act provided for the registration of all Communist-affiliated organisations, kept Communists from being employed by the Federal Government or from receiving passports, planned internment camps for subversives and saboteurs in case of war.

The McCarran legislation was already prepared by the time of the Korean war in 1950 and the war provided more favourable climate for it. The Act was based on the conviction that there was an international Communist conspiracy; that there were so many dangerous people in the US, there had to be a means of control. President Truman believed the McCarran Act mocked the Bill of Rights and that it would put government in the business of thought-control. But the Act got through both the House and Senate with an overwhelming margin. By 1950, McCarran had seen to it that no politician in Washington could afford to be lukewarm in his anti-Communism.

Life magazine used McCarran language: in 1950 they called him an unpredictable mustang. McCarran, in his seventies with a mane of white hair, made good copy. No one could predict his vote. McCarran was elected to the Senate in the Roosevelt landslide of 1932, but although a Democrat, he opposed many New Deal measures proposed by Roosevelt. He was only just elected when to the astonishment of his colleagues he attacked the New Deal and from that day on had the reputation as a maverick. He opposed national health insurance and federal aid to education and he fought "a drift to war" from 1939 until 1941. McCarran's power lingers on. He was the author of the McCarran–Walter Immigration and Naturalisation Act of 1952, provisions used by the American government to bar anyone from the US it wishes.McCarran was an isolationist and described the Democratic presidential hopeful, Adlai Stevenson, and President Dwight Eisenhower as "dumb men", being misled by "Eastern Jews and Commies".

McCarran said that the worst decision he ever made was to have voted in the Senate for the UN Charter. He tolerated it at first, said his daughter, because it was a popular idea which one did not easily oppose and in 1945, McCarran went to the founding conference in San Francisco. "The League of Notions", he would roar, laughing loudly. He concluded that the UN was an extension of the welfare state, whose founders intended to create a welfare world. "If the UN continues to be a cell from which Communism radiates, if they continue to give the support and encouragement to Communist activities, then in my judgment the UN should be removed from the Unites States of America," he said. McCarran was the first UN-basher, and would do more damage than any. "They teach that the UN flag should be put above Old Glory . . . enemies worse than those firing at your boys in Korea are undermining the home front."

The McCarran onslaught began in earnest in the UN's third year. In July 1948, the Senator organised a special hearing for a witness before one of his judiciary subcommittees. In a moment of high drama – the press were tipped to attend – the witness claimed that several hundred subversives, including Moscow-trained terrorists, were roaming America under the auspices of the UN. It was a startling allegation, made more so because the witness was a serving – and senior – government official. He was Robert C. Alexander, Chief of the Visa Division, the Department of Justice.

What Alexander really objected to was the recent agreement between the US and the UN which guaranteed the independence of the UN's headquarters. This agreement obliged the immigration authorities to allow entry to New York to anyone on legitimate UN business. Alexander considered it a back-door amendment to US immigration law. It caused his department extra work. In early 1948 two journalists working for Communist newspapers in Europe were detained trying to get into the US to write about the UN. The Secretary General had immediately intervened and the journalists were released. The UN's lawyer, Abe Feller, announced that the UN had the right to insist on entry for anyone it chose – delegates, UN staff and accredited reporters.

Alexander's testimony about terrorists under UN auspices obtained wide news coverage. An embarrassed Secretary of State, George C. Marshall, set up an enquiry which quickly reported the claims unsubstantiated, but Alexander kept his job. He was protected by Senator Patrick McCarran.

From this moment and thanks to his links with Alexander, McCarran had access to information in files kept in the State Department's Visa Division. Soon, investigators working for McCarran had lists of names: everyone allowed into the US on UN business whose visa had been queried. There was a list of every American working for the UN who was born in Soviet bloc countries.

Pompous, vindictive and power-grabbing, McCarran built the finest intelligence service on Capitol Hill.

In 1946, an American anthropologist called Jack Sargent Harris was enjoying a quiet life as Assistant Professor of Social Science at the University of Chicago when he received a telephone call from his friend, the future Nobel Prize winner, Dr Ralph Bunche, who asked him to come to New York to join the UN Division of Trusteeship. Bunche wanted Harris to help research living conditions in Africa and Harris was thrilled. He believed in internationalism, and believed that he could help contribute to the Charter's noble principles.

The Trusteeship Department and the Trusteeship Council were set up to transform and eliminate colonialism, the system under which one-third of the world's population lived. Among the powers accorded the Council was the right to visit those territories placed under UN Trusteeship and so, in mid-July 1948, Harris found himself in East Africa, a member of a mission of delegates and Secretariat officials to Ruanda-Urundi, under Belgian control, and Tanganyika, under British. Both colonies were former mandates of the League of Nations.

Harris helped write a report on the visit, a report which caused storms of protest. It condemned the British for the poverty of the black Africans in Tanganyika and advocated these people be given education and health care. The report contained a suggestion there be a tax on the export of diamonds to pay for these necessities. The Foreign Office was indignant. Britain did not accept the right of the UN to tell her how to discharge her responsibilities. In London the UN's report was considered no more than mischievous political propaganda. At the time, the issue of colonialism was as dominant in the UN as the East–West conflict and some countries were increasingly vociferous about how slowly the great powers were applying Charter principles. By the early fifties the member nations Egypt, India and Pakistan were busy organising an increasingly effective anti-colonial bloc which was beginning to enjoy the support of the Soviets. The Americans were basically anti-colonial, but torn by their close alliance with Britain.

Washington worried about the radical nature of the Department of Trusteeship, and particularly the influence of certain Secretariat officials within it. Jack Harris did not concern himself with Washington. He was too wrapped up in his work. In 1949, Harris met an Anglican priest named Michael Scott who had become the champion of the peoples of South-West Africa. Harris got on well with Scott. He admired the tenacious Englishman, and considered him something of a saint. It was largely thanks to Harris that Scott was able to appear before the Fourth Committee to plead the cause of the people – the first non-governmental representative to do so.

Scott was an extraordinary man. He was tall and gaunt and he wore the same threadbare suit, year after year. At the UN they formed a special committee to study his credentials and he gave them shabby pieces of paper which he collected from tribal chiefs and headmen. With diffidence almost, this troublesome man told them that the tribal leaders he represented believed the UN to be God's instrument of justice and freedom. "These people's fate", he said, "is for the UN to decide." The Rev. Michael Scott told the UN the story of a Paramount Chief named Frederick Maharero and other similar leaders of South-West Africa's people exiled from their own land. The scattered tribes were dispossessed of land, living on the edge of the Kalahari desert, and their peoples were dying through drought, disease and poverty. Scott told them the Chiefs were unable to come themselves, the South Africans refused them passports. Scott explained he was their messenger, sent to plead the sufferings of the peoples of South-West Africa.

Soon the UN committee knew Scott's story and how he travelled at risk to his life to meet the tribesmen of South-West Africa in the Veld. Scott had secret meetings with them by hurricane lamp, endured police harassment and death threats from armed white farmers. Scott, undeterred, consulted as many of the tribal elders as he could. The second time Scott left to go to the UN he was barred from the airport and had to find another secret way out of South Africa.

Once in New York, Scott was barred again and this time from speaking directly to the relevant UN committee. The colonial powers did not want to listen. For three years Scott was prevented from speaking; Britain and France were both against allowing him to speak, arguing South Africa was under no legal obligation to be answerable for South-West Africa. In reality, of course, these governments were frightened of precedent. If Scott were to be allowed to appeal directly, other trouble-makers would be encouraged: the Jamaicans would embarrass the British, and the Arabs from Algeria and Tunisia would indict the French.

These governments reckoned, quite sincerely, that the Charter did not justify petitions from individuals; such witnesses represented no people, state or nation recognised by international law. Scott returned each year to New York. He believed there should be no compromise on apartheid. The world's dependent peoples were a matter for international concern.

Most diplomats were busy with politics and procedure and took little notice. Scott wrote many letters to the Secretary General but his petitions were lost along with others in the growing ranks of steel cabinets in UN offices.

It was finally owing to pressure from India, Mexico, Guatemala, Pakistan, the Philippines and Haiti that a debate was held on whether or not to give him a hearing. Someone searched the files in the UN's archives to find the pieces of paper from the tribal chiefs. Eventually, by twenty-five votes to fifteen – and six abstentions – Scott won his victory. In November 1949, he became the first non-governmental representative to address a main UN committee and the room was packed to hear him speak.

Scott's appeal is remembered as spoken in the quiet tones of a sermon preached in the church of an English village. He very quietly told the dramatic story of the Herero, Ovambo and Bantu peoples, of how they were first the victims of brutal German rule. He spoke of how the Germans massacred them and stole their land. Scott reminded them of British rule which came later. After the First World War, the British promised them that their land would be restored. The promise was broken and after that the South Africans imposed a savage doctrine of white superiority and domination.

"Are we a cursed generation?" one of the Chiefs wanted to know. Scott read them a letter. "What are the United Nations thinking of us in South-West Africa?" it asked.

South Africa's delegate walked out before Scott's address began. In Pretoria, the Nationalist government declared that Scott's speech violated the Charter principal of non-intervention in the domestic affairs of nations.

Scott never let go. Scott wanted the Herero leader, Hosea Kutako, to come to the UN but South Africa refused to grant the necessary passport. So Scott again came himself. At the 1952 General Assembly, the South African delegate declared Scott's hearing to be an insult, maladroit and vindictive. Scott succeeded again in 1955 and this time the South African Ambassador and all Union delegates walked out of the General Assembly. That year, a first resolution was passed which condemned apartheid.

The South African government considered Scott an agitator and in 1952 tried to stop him getting a visa to enter the United States. Through secret channels Pretoria told Washington that Scott, "although not a Communist", was "nothing more than a troublemaker". The British Security services told the American Embassy in London that Scott was a former member of the Communist Party. By then both the FBI and the CIA had files on him but the American government was obliged to let him enter through the agreement which had been signed between the UN and the US government which allowed entry to anyone with an official invitation from the UN. Sympathetic delegates on the Trusteeship Committee simply invited Scott to attend their meetings. But America would become grippped in McCarthyism and in 1953 it took intervention from the Secretary of State John Foster Dulles to get Scott a visa, though he hated the Scott issue. At all costs he wanted to avoid public discussion, and the embarrassment over it.

Scott's American visa classified him an inadmissable alien. From his first visit to his last, the Americans confined him to a few blocks around the UN headquarters on the East River. He needed a visa waiver to enable him to stay in the General Theological Seminary, downtown on Ninth Avenue. He was banned from speaking in public, and needed special permission to accept an invitation from the Bishop of New York to preach in the Cathedral of St John the Divine. Scott was watched and followed by US government agents, and so were members of the Secretariat and the UN delegates who helped him. The liberal approach to dependent territories was pitted against the colonial powers who determined to minimise the UN's impact in their territories.

Jack Harris was a natural ally for Michael Scott. Harris, with his outspoken anti-colonialist views cut quite a distinctive figure in the UN Secretariat: he was handsome, always self-assured, and had intimate knowledge of African nation based on first-hand field studies. Only later would his colleagues learn that he was the former head of America's intelligence network in South Africa during the Second World War, recruited into the intelligence community by Ralph Bunche. Harris was one of the first secret agents trained by the Office of Strategic Services. After the war Harris was commended many times but he turned down an invitation to join the office's successor the CIA, partly because of promises which the US broke to certain of his contacts – people to whom he owed a debt of gratitude for helping him out of some difficult situations.

Harris was an academic and more suited, so he thought, to the life of an international civil servant, far away from espionage and treason. He intended to stay at the UN and he settled outside New

York City with his wife and young son and built the house of his dreams.

One day in the autumn of 1952, when Harris arrived home from work, his wife said that a man had arrived unannounced and given her a piece of paper. It was a subpoena and from that day on, Harris's life changed for ever. The all-American war hero found himself being denounced as part of the UN conspiracy to enslave America.

A few weeks later on October 24, 1952, Harris appeared as a witness before Patrick McCarran's Senate Internal Security Sub-committee, in a public hearing in the Federal Courthouse, Foley Square, New York. The subcommittee's mandate was espionage, sabotage and the protection of the internal security of the US. McCarran ordered that the hearings open the same day as the UN's General Assembly – it guaranteed maximum publicity. The hearings were mobbed. It was theatre, and billed as the unmasking of "UN Reds". No sooner had the gavel banged than Senators – all of them chosen by McCarran, most of them southern lawyers – fell over themselves to put the question which all had come to hear.

"Are you a member of the Communist Party, Mr Harris?" Harris invoked his constitutional right to silence. "I stand on my rights under the Fifth Amendment." Senator James O. Eastland, a planta-tion owner from Mississippi, would not accept that right. A year earlier, Eastland had distinguished himself during subcommittee hearings on the Distributive Workers in Memphis, by addressing their black President as "boy", and telling the union's lawyer to keep his mouth shut. His hatred of radicals found expression in ven-omous and violent outbursts and he told Harris that the real reason he refused to answer questions about political beliefs was because he had betrayed the American government. "You ought to make your country proud of you and fully, frankly and freely disclose whether or not you were a Communist . . . " Harris stood firm. "I have always tried to make my country proud of me . . . I have served her to the best of my capacity and ability. I was once at the door of death because of my country, more than once. I . . . uphold the Constitution of the United States, Sir, and that is my answer . . . " At the end of the second day, and after four witnesses pleaded privi-lege, Eastland announced to reporters that the UN was quite obviously part of a Communist conspiracy to dominate and enslave the United States.

Years later, Harris recalled with some amusement the difference between the closed sessions of the subcommittee which were quite businesslike and those hearings conducted in public. Only in public did the Senators shout, wave their arms and call him a traitor. When hearings were held without the public in attendance the senators were civil.

In June, Lie was asked what was happening: newspapers were speculating that there were some employees sacked from the UN because of subversive activity.

"I do not know anymore about these things than you," Lie lied. Asked if was the policy of the UN to terminate an American employee who had been found to be a member of the communist party, Lie lied again. "No", he said, "there is no such policy at all."

Asked if it was policy to fire anyone who appeared before a hearing, Lie answered: "My policy is to have good people."

Much of the questioning concerned a Communist cell in the Staff Association. At times, the subcommittee focused attention on officials in the UN "who might be Communists". But as the hearings progressed, it was obvious the Senators wanted more than just a cell, they wanted a plot. The Korean war had tremendous effect. "There is a conspiracy to destroy your country", Senator James Eastland told a witness. "Thousands of mighty fine young men have given their lives as a result of this communist conspiracy to dominate and enslave us . . . Give us information so that we can root out the people . . . in official positions . . . who would endanger the safety of the US."

Not all of them pleaded the right to silence. Ruth Crawford, a New Dealer who had worked in the US government's Department of Labor for eleven years, shocked them with her admission that she had been a party member seventeen years before. She refused to name names. Crawford was a public information officer for the International Children's Emergency Defence Fund, set up in 1946 for the millions of children in Europe who were malnourished and which became part of the UN system in 1953.

"I . . . think that every American citizen has the right to belong to any political party as long as that party is not subversive of the interests of this country . . . I have never apologised for joining . . . I never have, and I never intend to." Crawford was asked to resign her job at the UN. She refused. On January 7, 1953 Lie dismissed her. She was later reinstated by the Administrative Tribunal.

Another admission came from a UN cartographer who had initially joined the UN on loan from the State Department in 1946. Leo Drozdoff, just like Jack Harris, worked for the OSS during the war. He said he had been a party member fifteen years previously and it was not "entirely conventional but certainly not monstrous activity".

On October 23, 1952 the McCarran subcommittee took public testimony from Whittaker Chambers, the informer who claimed to have worked in the Communist underground between 1932 and 1938. This time he testified that a UN official called David Zablodowsky, director of the UN Publications Division, had been a fellow traveller at Columbia University. Zablodowsky testified that he had sympathy with Communism but had never been a member of the party. Chambers claimed that Zablodowsky had provided cover for an agent whose job it was to secure false passports for Russian agents. Zablodowsky, a former editor with the Viking Press and General Manager of Modern Age books, had served with the OSS in Washington during the war, later organising charts and other exhibits for the trials of the Nazis in Nuremburg. He admitted knowing Chambers whom, he said, he knew to be in the underground with J. Peters – the Head of the Communist Underground in the US. Chambers had asked him to help in some secret work against Hitler which had entailed handing an envelope to two men.

"In the middle of 1935 . . . I got terribly excited about Adolf Hitler and Nazism . . . I had more reasons perhaps than other Americans . . . I joined . . . the League Against War and Fascism." Zablodowky said he did not know the Communist Party dominated the organisation but he knew it was an active part. " . . . in 1936 there were very few people who were awake to what was going on in Germany and the Communists were among them . . . they made a great deal of it." Zablodowsky told Senators he had been a former President of the Book and Magazine Guild – which Senators reminded him had recently been expelled from the Congress of Industrial Organisations, CIO, for Communism. "That is right," he replied. "The CIO at that time did not mind . . . it now minds".

After two days of public testimony, the McCarran subcommittee issued a statement demanding the Secretary of State take immediate steps to "sweep American Communists and security risks out of the UN Secretariat". In so doing, these Southern Democrats handed fresh ammunition to the backers of the Eisenhower–Nixon Presidential ticket who just launched their anti-Communist campaign issue.

Thirty UN witnesses were called to McCarran and of those, eighteen invoked the Fifth Amendment in response to questions about past or present Communist Party membership. Some denied present membership but refused to discuss any possible past connection. Some said they invoked the Fifth Amendment to avoid trumped-up charges of perjury. All of them were advised to avoid use of the First Amendment, the guarantee of free speech. The Hollywood Ten, a group of screenwriters and directors, had gambled on the First Amendment – unsuccessfully. In 1950 the Supreme Court sent them to prison for contempt thereby upholding criminal penalties for proscribed associations and ending the prerogative of keeping silent about political views. Nonetheless, the Fifth Amendment was no less serious an option with its invocation of guilt.

The choices were hard. An American Communist who admitted membership of the Communist Party or any other proscribed organisation ran the risk of prosecution under State sedition or conspiracy laws and further interrogations to name names. Senators wanted associates past and present, the views of friends past or present, friends who retained radical views and those who abandoned them. A non-Communist – a liberal, a Socialist – ran the risk that someone else, another witness under rigorous questioning, could inadvertently supply circumstantial evidence. Non-Communists risked indictment for perjury. They faced a long process through the courts, an indictment based on circumstantial evidence, followed by one based on alleged perjury at a subsequent trial, a legal process which could go on indefinitely. Some of the witnesses were suspect because UN employment had brought them into contact with colleagues who were nationals of Communist countries.

By 1952, internationalism was a crime; anything less than America, "my country right or wrong", was widely considered nefarious subversion. The war in Korea had reached a stalemate, the Rosenberg spy case was in the headlines. By now the Federal government's Loyalty Program of 1947 was well under way: every government employee was subject to investigation for loyalty, a programme to investigate background, deeds and thoughts, designed to root out subversives or potential subversives working for the government. Congress appropriated $11 million for the first year of the programme and most of the money went to the FBI. The programme begun with fingerprinting millions on the Federal payroll.

There were more than 370 Americans in senior positions at the UN and, as international civil servants, they were exempt from this security programme. For US Senators, this posed a special difficulty. Time after time witnesses were asked whether or not they would put America or the UN first. Many of them tried to defend internationalism, and most notable among them was a man named Alfred Van Tassel, a senior UN economist who patiently tried to explain to Senators that internationalism did not turn people into traitors. "I consider I can be a perfectly loyal US citizen and a loyal member of the Secretariat . . . and I think I am both." Van Tassel took the Fifth Amendment. He told Senators that he believed Communist party membership to be irrelevant. The Secretariat employed all nationalities and people of every political complexion. In any event, neither political beliefs nor an oath to the UN made anyone less loyal an American citizen.

Van Tassel is forgotten. Had it not been for McCarran, he would have gone down in UN history as a distinguished pioneer, a hero to internationalists and environmentalists all over the world. In 1949, Van Tassel organised the world's first international conference on the environment. He invited to New York 700 scientists from fifty countries to discuss "the wasteful use of the world's natural resources". The reports of this conference sit on library shelves, gathering dust – *The Proceedings of the UN Scientific Conference on the Conservation and Utilization of Resources*, published in February 1950. In these pages the world's eminent scientists discussed deforestation and its effects on drainage and soil erosion, the problems involved with the control of water pollution, the possibilities of hydro-power and the conservation of marine life. The focus of the debate was under-developed countries and the conference concluded that if the world's starving were to be fed, the imbalance of wealth between the world's poor and those living in industrialised nations would have to be corrected. These scientists advocated that only worldwide education and the eradication of disease would help to improve the world economy. More radical was the idea that a world free from want was possible. To achieve it, scientists would have to be given a say in decision-making to ensure that discoveries and knowledge were put to proper use.

The UN is careless of its past. The conference is never mentioned and Van Tassel's work is wiped from institutional memory. The UN's environmental effort officially starts with the UN Conference of the Human Environment in Stockholm in 1972 which established the UN Environment Programme.

Van Tassel's vision was extraordinary, and alarming to governments who continued to work on the assumption that military might and economic efficiency should come before the welfare of citizens. But Van Tassel alarmed American investigators for another reason. He had a friend called David Weintraub.

David Weintraub joined the UN in 1946 as Director of Economic Stability and Development in the UN's Division of Economic Affairs, and he had stood at the heart of the American New Deal. He was a former Director of the National Research Project of the Works Progress Administration and, at one point, an assistant to Harry Hopkins, Roosevelt's closest adviser. New Dealers were early targets: in 1938 the House Committee on Un-American Activities warned that the Federal Relief Program was the cause of the government being peppered with "subversive and disloyal" employees. In Weintraub's UN Division most American economists were New Dealers, who with their continued enthusiasm for the Federal Relief Program, believed they had a duty to solve unemployment and to prevent the misery it caused. These economists did not believe that Depressions were inevitable: Roosevelt himself said that economic laws were not made by nature but by man.

Weintraub was exactly the kind of person the Secretariat needed.During the Second World War, Weintraub helped to organise America's worldwide programme for refugees, later he was Deputy Director General of the UN Relief and Rehabilitation Administration [UNRRA] which dispensed some three million dollars and took the constructive step of adding raw material and machinery to the customary food relief. UNRAA failed to last in a politically divided world and in 1946 the US decided to discontinue its contributions. When Weintraub had arrived at the UN he seemed to find a natural home; the Department of Economic Affairs was established by member states to fulfil the Charter's promise of social and economic progress for all. Weintraub believed that in order to fulfil that promise, the world should look carefully at the success of the Marshall Plan whereby massive American aid helped reconstruct parts of devastated post-war Europe. Weintraub considered it the most enlightened act of self-interest this century for the American need to stabilise and secure Western Europe was compelling. By 1951 the Marshall Plan was seen to have worked but a comparable system – a Marshall Plan for the less developed countries – was a revolutionary notion. The received wisdom was already trade, not aid.

Weintraub was summoned to the subcommittee in October, 1952. He denied membership of the Communist Party and did not resort to the Fifth Amendment. But they subpoenaed his sister Rose Alpher and she pleaded the Fifth. Weintraub was condemned. Six people working in his division pleaded the Fifth – and they all worked with him in the New Deal. Weintraub was condemned too because he knew Owen Lattimore, an academic at Johns Hopkins University, identified in 1950 by Senator Joe McCarthy as the top Soviet spy in the US. McCarthy, shooting from the hip as always, later retracted the accusation and five years later the government dropped seven counts of perjury against Lattimore. Lattimore, a Far East scholar and writer, and briefly President Roosevelt's adviser to the Nationalist Chinese leader Chiang Kai-Shek, was thought in some circles to have been responsible for "losing China to the Communists". That the "Reds swallowed China", was blamed on treacherous foreign policy, American failure to man the watchtowers, and no individual was blamed more than Lattimore. Lattimore it turned out, did some work under a temporary contract for Weintraub's UN division. Guilt by association passed easily.

Weintraub, responsible for a series of UN reports on world economic conditions, had seen his idea for aid for the least developed nations gather support among UN members – the younger and poorer states. In the early fifties India and Indonesia were lobbying for a programme for the world's poor, paid for through compulsory contributions charged on the industrialised member states. At the time, America's national income was almost half the world's. But the UN's Economic and Social Council, created along with the General Assembly and the Security Council was to become, in the words of one delegate, the wailing wall of lost illusions.

Weintraub's career came to an abrupt end. In the final weeks of 1952 he was named, along with thirty-seven others, a "UN Communist", in a press release issued by the McCarran subcommittee. Weintraub was defiant and put out his own statement in which he denied ever having been either a Communist or a spy, ever having engaged in disloyal or subversive activity. A few days later the McCarran subcommittee published a devastating interim report in which it described Weintraub masterminding a Communist cell in the UN, and accusing him of being the director of a plot to infiltrate it with Communists. The only evidence ever produced against him was testimony from an FBI informer who claimed to have heard his name in the Communist underground as someone who could get jobs in government for fellow travellers.

When in November 1952 the McCarran subcommittee recessed, Senator Eastland made a grab for the headlines and announced that most UN witnesses who appeared before them were not fit to represent either the US or the UN. They were not typical Americans, not people of high calibre and they should be removed from the UN.

"Let me make this crystal clear," the Senator warned. "No international body will be permitted to deprive or circumvent the US government in the control of its own citizens." In that, Eastland was absolutely right. The one person who might have protected the internationalists from the onslaught failed to do so, for the Secretary General, Trygve Lie, accepted Weintraub's resignation with relief. In reply to Weintraub's resignation letter, Lie praised Weintraub for his outstanding contribution to the economic work of the UN. All too readily, Lie hoped that Weintraub would succeed in overcoming "his difficulties".

Trygve Lie was having lunch in New York's Metro-politan Club when a messenger came in with an urgent summons to go to the telephone. That morning, Thursday November 13, 1952, the UN General Counsel, Abe Feller, had jumped from the rear window of his twelfth-floor Manhattan apartment into the courtyard below. His wife, Alice, said her husband ran through the rooms in a frenzy, shouting he was going to kill himself. She tried to hold him back from the window but he struggled free, hell-bent on destruction. There was a tussle and then he jumped.

Lie was closer to Feller than any other Secretariat official; " . . . hardly a day passed . . . when he did not come to see me. Whenever anything was up, Abe was there, alert, discreet, full of energy", Lie wrote in his memoirs. Lie arrived at the Feller apartment that afternoon, accompanied by his Security Chief called Frank Begley and stayed at the Feller apartment a long time. They supervised the interviews that

Alice gave to newspaper reporters. Begley told reporters that there was no question about Feller's own loyalty. Lie issued a statement later which claimed Feller's death was caused by the strain of defending UN employees against "indiscriminate smears and exaggerated charges". It was the one time Lie spoke out strongly against the purges. Feller's wife told the police her husband had suffered a nervous breakdown.

The news went worldwide and the Secretary of State, Dean Acheson, sent a message of condolence, as did Eleanor Roosevelt, a member that year of the US delegation to the General Assembly. The *New York Times* speculated that Feller was saddened by the defeat of Governor Adlai Stevenson, the Democratic candidate for President in the elections nine days before.

Abraham Feller was Lie's confident and adviser, a man Lie trusted more than any other, and his dramatic suicide was a terrible shock. Feller wrote his speeches, devised his policy, playing a key role in the crucial Security Council meeting in June 1950 when it had given UN troops to the US and its "Unified Command" when South Korea was invaded. For Feller the action over the invasion of South Korea was a turning point which had strengthened everyone's belief of the necessity of a UN army. In Korea, while the burden of the military efforts was borne by the US, fifteen other members also participated. Feller devised the arrangement which made the US the chief agent of the UN in the war; it also ensured for himself and Lie the continuing antagonism of the Soviet bloc.

Feller was the first American to be appointed to the Secretariat. He had come from UNRRA where he was General Counsel. and was an internationalist all his adult life. Feller published a book just before he died in which he outlined his belief that the UN was going through a critical stage. "The world is sick", was Feller's wry little joke, and yet the UN's enemies wanted to shoot the doctor. He argued that the world had got it wrong: the UN did not amount to an automatic guarantee of security. It was no magic machine. Its principal task was to try to hold the world together, to try to find the most practicable solutions to the world's problems.

"In these troubled years, when the world seems to be tearing itself apart, the concept of a community may appear as an ironic paradox", he wrote. In reply to the UN's American enemies Feller wrote that a nation's standing could not be measured only in terms of the size of its armed forces: a great power must have abiding moral standards, otherwise it would become the focus of hostility and fear. Feller was unshakable in his belief that the success of the UN was in the interests of its most powerful member state.

In a letter to a friend, one month before his death, Feller revealed his fear that the UN was not going to survive. Closer to the suicide, just three days before, Lie had announced his resignation, blaming the Soviets for his decision to leave and their hostile attitude to him because he supported UN action over Korea but, in reality it was the question of staff loyalty and the dismissals which led him to conclude he could continue no longer. Lie thought Feller a victim of the pressure imposed on the Secretariat by reactionaries and he wrote in his memoirs, "Although he felt as strongly as I that the UN officials who had pleaded the Fifth Amendment had betrayed their obligation and should be removed, he had a genuine sympathy for the victims of the headline-hunting investigations".

Feller may have died because he could no longer live with the effect of the purge on his colleagues. He knew some who were dismissed, and he knew some who were called before the McCarran committee. A few turned to him for advice. Perhaps Feller died because, as his FBI file reveals, he feared he was the next target. The last document placed on his file, two days before his death, is a report from an informer that Feller's face was familiar. The informer insinuates he might have known Feller "in connection with his work in the Communist party". He could not have been sure.

A few days before his death Feller was secretly interviewed by the witch-hunters. He was threatened with a subpoena. Feller was nervous about the Senate Internal Security Committee hearings. His daughter Caroline was a teenager at the time, but she can still remember her father's fears, and the conversations round the supper table about who had just been summoned.

That Feller was a target is not in dispute, although a *Daily Worker* editorial stated that it took a McCarranite to pin a leftist label on Feller. Feller first came to FBI attention in 1941 when he was with the Justice Department: his name had turned up on the mailing list for the Washington Committee for Democratic Action, an alleged Communist front. A year later Feller swore an affidavit for the House Committee Un-American Activities denying membership of the Communist Party but, after Feller was appointed UN General Counsel, J. Edgar Hoover himself had ordered agents to make a more thorough investigation. They found very little. Feller's FBI file is small.

The cold hand which reached Feller a few days before his death did not belong to the FBI but to Roy Cohn, an Assistant District Attorney, South District, New York. Cohn was the inspiration behind a Grand Jury which was investigating whether or not Communists had infiltrated the Secretariat. Cohn was ruthless and cunning, determined to make his name. He was at the start of a notorious and corrupt career, and he perfected his fearful talent on UN employees, preparing for the day he would become Senator Joe McCarthy's Chief Counsel. The jury was hand in glove with the McCarran Subcommittee. Cohn was in close touch with the McCarran interrogator, a lawyer named Robert Morris who would recall how Cohn gave him the names of UN employees to call as witnesses. They were having a drink in New York's Stork Club at the time and Morris remembers that he wrote the names on the back of an envelope. Morris exploited the procedure whereby Chairmen of Congressional Committees signed batches of blank subpoenas and gave them to counsel. All the witnesses called to the McCarran subcommittee were first called to the Grand Jury. Abe Feller knew exactly how it worked.

Years later Robert Morris claimed all witnesses called to McCarran were Communists. He believed that they were hand-picked for UN employment by Alger Hiss. Morris thought the subcommittee hearings a huge victory. "Everybody conceded . . . there must be something wrong with the UN when top officials can't even deny they are Communists."

Morris said that Senator Patrick McCarran and the FBI Director J. Edgar Hoover were determined to smash a Communist conspiracy within the Secretariat and had reached agreement that the FBI would give the Subcommittee information about UN people. This was done with discretion. The Chief Counsel of the Senate Internal Security Subcommittee, Morris, became the FBI liaison. He would meet the bureau's Assistant Director, Louis B. Nichols last thing at night in the FBI building in Washington.

As for Abe Feller, Morris recalled that he was "a big one". Morris could not remember whether or not Feller had been subpoenaed to appear. "I knew that he was in, in the shadows . . . you see we didn't get all of them . . . . I'm sure that if the thing had been prolonged a little bit more that we would have subpoenaed him". A friend of Feller, who saw him frequently in his last days, was Bernice Bernstein, wife of his best friend. She was sure Feller had already received a subpoena as Feller had confided in her husband. Feller thought it demeaning to his position to be called before a Senate Subcommittee. The Secretary General was trying to persuade Feller to weather the storm.

The Feller suicide was an embarrassment for McCarran and when the news reached the hearing room in Foley Square, there was an immediate adjournment. That day McCarran was on board a cruise ship on his way to Latin America in his capacity as chairman of the Senate Appropriations Committee to "find out where our money is going" in embassies in Brazil, Columbia and Venezuela. Reporters caught up with him on board the *Uruguay* and he gave an impromptu press conference at which he admitted that Feller had been subpoenaed. Morris was concerned enough to write a memo about it, in which he called the admission a slip-up. "I got there in time to correct the record . . . and the Senator told reporters he was mistaken . . . all the newspapers accepted this correction as a matter of fact . . . "

Lie's meeting with senior UN officials two days after the suicide was taken up with how to avoid further drastic cuts in the budget which delegates wanted to impose. He was told staff morale was at zero and agreed to a suggestion that supervisors should speak to staff to reassure them about the UN's future. Within days Lie received a visit from Roy Cohn and Senator Alexander Wiley. The meeting lasted two and a half hours and afterwards Wiley told the press that the Secretary General had agreed there was "no room in the Secretariat for any American disloyal to his own country". Wiley had warned that the forthcoming Congress would block funds for the UN unless there were security guarantees against espionage and subversion.

A year after Feller died, a small room in the Secretariat was dedicated in his memory. Lie came out of retirement to say a few words but no one mentioned the purges, everyone avoided any mention of suicide and, after that, Feller was forgotten.

Roy Cohn's Grand Jury convened for nearly a year and inter-viewed more than a hundred UN employees, but Cohn was frustrated. There was not one indictment.

Cohn decided he would help the McCarran Subcommittee where, unlike a Grand Jury, witnesses could be accused of subversion in public. It was still not enough to satisfy him and Cohn came up with the idea of publishing a report, calling it a Presentment – an obsolete legal word. The Justice Department was outraged. This was a dramatic departure from strict Grand Jury custom and practice and publication would be illegal. Cohn was told by Justice Department officials that this was tantamount to government by hysteria. Cohn, shortly to join McCarthy's staff, got his way; he claimed that the FBI Director J. Edgar Hoover helped pull strings in Washington.

The Cohn Presentment made some wild claims, not the least of which was to describe the Grand Jury's work as "probably the most important investigation ever conducted in the entire history of the United States". It described an "overwhelmingly large group of disloyal US citizens" who had infiltrated the UN and who were "posing a threat to the survival of democratic nations".

At the time, the anti-Communist newspaper, *Common Sense*, published a list of UN employees who were thought to be Jews. It claimed that the UN was a plot for world conquest and its editorial stated that there was no surprise that the UN flag used the same colour blue as the flag of Israel: "The Jewish plan for world conquest . . . is now well underway. There is every likelihood that the future world government will be the organisation presently known as the United Nations."

In one of his last acts as President, Harry Truman signed an Executive Order which was based on the Federal Loyalty Program of 1947 and which laid out procedures to investigate every American who worked for the UN or for any other related international agencies.

Within weeks, in a basement corridor in the UN headquarters American employees stood silently in line, waiting to be finger-printed. A handful of UN officials had been specially trained by the American Civil Service Commission to do the work. The Chairman of the Staff Committee objected. Trygve Lie told him that the finger-printing was none of his business. The fact that it was carried out in the Secretariat was a convenience which would save staff travelling to local police stations.

"If anyone wants to go and stand in line with immigrants and criminals . . . he has that choice," Lie said, and advised that all Americans on the UN staff should comply with the FBI.

Like all federal employees, every American member of the UN staff was required to fill out "Identification and Personnel Data" forms. The penalty for incorrect information was imprisonment.

Each employee had to provide all addresses, employment details and countries visited in the past fifteen years. All political and religious affiliations were to be revealed as were all relatives and their addresses.

The FBI was to conduct investigations on all Americans with senior UN posts – and on any of the more junior staff who aroused suspicion. This amounted to some 2,000 people at the UN and another 1,500 working for other international agencies. Immediately, as a result of filling in the form more than one hundred people were fired or left UN employment of their own accord. Eventually more than 1,500 were the subject of investigations by FBI agents. A special team of interrogators was sent to Europe to interview Americans working for the UN family of agencies.

Shortly after the fingerprinting began, Lie allowed FBI agents access to UN headquarters. He justified his decision to his inner cabinet by assuring them that UN operations would not be discussed – the FBI would only be asking questions about personal lives. Soon there was speculation that Lie had allowed the purge programme to extend to non-Americans. Five Europeans were suddenly dismissed, four said to be for political views and one for "morals" – homosexuality.

On December 11, 1952, the UN issued a press release in which the Secretary General expressed his greatest admiration for the way the staff kept its chin up during this time of trial – caused by a small minority. Meanwhile, in Washington a Republican Congress waited in the wings – after successive Democratic victories and threats were already made that unless watertight guarantees were given against espionage and subversion within the UN, America would withhold her UN dues.

In October, 1952, Lie dismissed every member of staff employed on temporary contracts, who had pleaded the Fifth Amendment. Those Fifth Amendment people with permanent contracts, such as Jack Harris and the environmentalist Alfred Van Tassel, posed a more difficult problem. Under the staff regulations, approved by the General Assembly, they could be discharged only for abolition of post, unsatisfactory service, misconduct, or physical incapacity. Lie suspended them and, in October 1952, banned them from entering the UN headquarters.

Years later Jack Harris, still angry at what happened, called Lie a big, blustering buffoon.

In October 1952, Lie was faced with a serious dilemma. He did not know what to do about American nationals who held permanent contracts and who received adverse reports from Washington. His General Counsel, Abe Feller told him that he had no power under staff regulations to get rid of permanent contract holders for being Communists. Lie decided to form a committee of international jurists to help him to decide. Quite a few distinguished and well-known men turned down his offer to serve. In the end they settled on Sir Edwin Herbert, a British solicitor formerly in charge of censorship in the Ministry of Information, Paul Veldekens, Professor of Civil Law at the Catholic University of Louvain, Belgium and William D. Mitchell who had been US Attorney-General under President Hoover.

Within weeks these three neatly solved the Secretary General's dilemma and ruled he could get rid of Fifth Amendment staff with permanent contracts because they had breached the staff rule that all international civil servants should conduct themselves in a manner befitting their status. Lie immediately gave the staff concerned one more chance to revoke their pleas and when each of them refused he dismissed them. But he gave them the severance pay to which summary dismissal did not entitle them, to help them over the difficult time they faced, "after all the publicity".

British diplomats were incredulous. A Foreign Office note records: "One can see what the possibilities are if one imagines that the UN headquarters were situated in Russia . . . it would be impossible to employ anyone but dyed-in-the-wool Communists." The ignorance of the American public about the issue was shocking as was the scantiness of evidence that any of those involved was a subversive. How could espionage be conducted in an organisation to which no member government entrusted any of its secrets? In his annual report on the UN, British Ambassador Sir Gladwyn Jebb described a discouraged UN staff which had lost all confidence in Lie.

So concerned was the British member of the UN's Administrative Tribunal, Labour Peer, Lord Crook, that he visited Lie accompanied by Sir Gladwyn Jebb, and a Foreign Office Minister of State, Selwyn Lloyd. Crook was blunt. He accused Lie of bowing to American pressure and advised he should review the Fifth Amendment cases. Lie was furious saying Crook should mind his own business. But Crook went on to warn Lie that if he continued to dismiss staff, the compensation awarded by the Tribunal could eventually reach a million dollars.

Unknown to the British, Lie recorded the conversation on a dictaphone and some weeks later tried to get Crook removed from the Tribunal because of his "bias". Lie told the Americans of the conversation with Crook.

Lie was by now desperate for sanction from the UN's member states for his actions. He prepared a lengthy report in which he tried to justify himself and submitted it to the General Assembly for approval. During the whole of February, 1953 he lobbied hard for support from member states. He talked about a smear campaign which he believed was organised against him by the Canadian politician, Lester Pearson, then President of the General Assembly. Though Lie had resigned three months earlier, he had agreed to stay until a successor was found. The Security Council was deadlocked in the choice of successor and Pearson was a favored candidate. Lie seems quietly to have hoped no one would take his place and that the Big Five would ask him to stay. Were this to happen, it would give credibility to his personnel policy.

The British, through informants in the Secretariat, believed that Lie was persecuting members of his staff to make himself acceptable to Washington and the new Republican administration. Sir Gladwyn Jebb, in a letter to Prime Minister Churchill, described Lie as a man of "indecisive character and eagerness to please". Jebb, dismissing UN gossip, told Churchill that Lie was keen to be relieved of his responsibilities before his reputation suffered further damage.

The Americans were no more complimentary than the British. Ambassador Henry Cabot Lodge, close to President Dwight Eisenhower, described Lie as jealous and paranoid. Lodge had the most amazing story to tell. Lie had asked him to talk to Pearson and to tell him that he must support the sackings of the staff. If Pearson did not support the sackings, Lie would ruin Pearson's chances of becoming the next Secretary General. Lie told Lodge that he was prepared to withdraw his resignation to stop Pearson.

A secret airgram to all US ambassadors worldwide was sent in February, 1953 containing a detailed history of the loyalty issue in the Secretariat. It was State Department priority and instructed all ambassadors to tell their respective host governments that the "elimination of subversive US nationals" from the UN Secretariat was imperative. Unless there were enough votes in the General

Assembly to approve Lie's sackings, Congress would withhold her financial contribution to the UN.

The State Department asked those ambassadors in India, Canada, the Netherlands, Egypt, Belgium, Sweden, Mexico and France to exert particular pressure; these governments were expressing the opinion that Lie's behaviour threatened the independence of the international civil service. But even the greatest ally, Britain, was causing problems. The British government seemed to think that Lie had overstepped the mark with his personnel policy. But both Henry Cabot Lodge, and Secretary of State, John Foster Dulles, remained determined about the issue. Dulles, a leading international lawyer who prided himself on his ability to present a complex case with great address confided to Lodge that he had started to collect material on Soviet imperialism and the conspiratorial character of the Communist Party for use in the forthcoming General Assembly debate.

Lie opened proceedings on March 10, 1953 with a long speech. It would be his last major address to the member states.

Lie outlined the problems he had encountered in creating the Secretariat and blamed the steadily mounting hostility between the superpowers. His work was hampered because there were such widely varying opinions on what constituted an international civil service. Lie said the Charter and the staff regulations were open to wide interpretation and Lie denied he was being pressured by America. He said the crudest pressure on his office was from the Soviets, whose control of their own nationals in the Secretariat was well known to everyone. The debate lasted a week.

Lie was heavily criticised with particular attack coming from Canada, Australia and the Netherlands. The Byelorussian delegate said Lie had turned the UN into a police station. But the most bitter speech of all came from the French ambassador, Henri Hoppenot who ridiculed Lie. Hoppenot said that action taken against UN staff for acts, associations, or affiliations before they entered UN service amounted to punishment for presumed intent. He said UN management was autocratic and that careers within the Secretariat were dependent on blind obedience. Hoppenot said UN employees were more than clerks: the primary, onerous and difficult responsibility of the Secretary General was to protect them from oppression.

Lie was furious. He rose to his feet and accused the French ambassador of an unnecessary and unfair attack. But only minutes before he got up to speak, Lie had received the news that the Big Five had finally found his successor, Dag Hammarskjöld of Sweden. Lie announced the news and then in a final swipe at his critics, said that the new Secretary General would need all the guidance, support and understanding they could give him – not the least when it came to matters of UN staff.

Dag Hammarskjöld took office on April 10, 1953. Lie stayed on for a while in New York but after a few months left for Norway, taking with him most of the documents from his office. He intended to write his memoirs. Afterwards, he was given a number of important government posts in Norway but he faded from international prominence. When he died in December, 1968 aged seventy-two his daughter, Guri Lie-Zeckendorf found in his wallet a small piece of paper. On it were the names of the five Americans officials of the Staff Association – Alper, Picou, Howrani, Keeney and Kehoe – dismissed in 1951. Why Lie had kept the list so long, she could not say.

Hammarskjöld was horrified at the magnitude of his task. He thought the UN in a hopeless state and blamed Lie's mismanagement. A liberal, trained in the Swedish school of neutralist policy, he told the British that he quickly concluded that his role would be to defend European interests and principles against extreme forms of Americanism. He gave the British the impression he was prepared to "fight to the death".

At Hammarskjöld's first lunch with the American Ambassador, Henry Cabot Lodge had explained that America intended to restore the UN's good name by eliminating "disloyal Americans" from Secretariat ranks. Hammarskjöld told Lodge that he would make up his own mind. Lodge responded by reminding Hammarskjöld of a case which needed a decision. Eda Glaser worked in the Security Council reference library and she refused to complete the questionnaire which all American employees were required to do under Truman's recent loyalty order. Lodge wanted the matter to be cleared up quickly. Glaser, born in Manchuria of Russian parents, a naturalised US citizen, recently pleaded the Fifth Amendment to the McCarran Subcommittee. Like Abe Feller, she had worked for the refugee organisation UNRAA but as a field worker, helping the thousands starving in Byelorussia and the Ukraine. She joined the UN shortly after her return. Glaser knew from experience that the Cold War had already began when one day in Minsk in late 1945 she was told a consignment of American tractors would not after all be delivered.

Hammarskjöld did take action on the Glaser case. He appointed a committee of senior officials to interview her. He sat in on the hearing. Glaser said she was allowed no legal representation. A few days afterwards, Hammarskjöld dismissed her – she had told the hearing that she pleaded the Fifth to protect her friends and Hammarskjöld considered she put loyalty to friends above loyalty to the UN.

Lodge gleefully reported to Washington the Secretary General's prompt action; here was an instance of good co-operation. Hammarskjöld obviously had a broad understanding of the internal security problems. He confided in the British that the questioning by FBI agents of non-American staff was intolerable, but nothing could be done until the investigations of the all American employees was complete. He said that he would resist at all costs American pressure to dismiss staff unless there was clear evidence of wrong-doing. Hammarskjöld claimed not to agree with action taken to dismiss the Fifth Amendment cases – although he considered the staff involved warranted further investigation. Then came the bombshell.

In early 1953, nineteen Americans, dismissed from the UN for pleading the Fifth Amendment, challenged the decision before the UN's Administrative Tribunal. Among them were Jack Harris and Alfred Van Tassel. A detailed and lengthy brief was prepared by a group of lawyers accusing UN management of breaching the Universal Declaration of Human Rights – denying UN staff the standards of freedom the UN sought to promote throughout the world. The UN stood accused of violating seven articles: equal protection against discrimination; the right to a full and a fair public hearing; the presumption of innocence; protection against punishment for offences not deemed penal when committed; the right to freedom of thought, conscience and religion, and the freedom to hold opinions without interference.

The former Secretary General Trygve Lie was accused of more than just a violation of grand principles, was accused of impugning the independence of the Secretariat by breaching Article 100 of the

Charter which laid down that no nation should try to select or to control international civil servants – a Charter principle. The lawyers pointed out that the Secretary General had resisted pressure from regimes in Poland and Czechoslovakia to sack their nationals employed by the UN before the Communist take-over.

By the time the lawyers came to prepare the case, the 1949 secret agreement between the UN and the US government was already exposed, revealed in testimony to the McCarran Subcommittee by a beleaguered official from the State Department, anxious to prove the concern within government about UN "subversives". To the lawyers who were representing the nineteen, it was clear that their clients had been dismissed as a result of the secret agreement. The Secretary General had injured the livelihoods and reputations of the nineteen who had been pilloried and pre-judged as disloyal. None was charged with or convicted of violations of US laws. In not one case did the Secretary General specify facts to show lack of competence or devotion to duty. The terminations were based not just on alleged political heterodoxies but that some members might favour such heterodoxies at some future date.

As for dismissing employees for pleading the Fifth Amendment, this was contrary to centuries of Anglo-Saxon law and in conflict with the decisions of the United States Supreme Court. Inference of guilt could not be drawn from its assertion. The Fifth Amendment was intended to protect freedom of conscience and belief. The charges of espionage and subversion were a cruel hoax to conceal the fact that the nineteen were dismissed because of radical conviction, sentiment and affiliation – fired for the very reasons that had drew them to work on such an experiment in internationalism in the first place.

The Administrative Tribunal handed down its judgment in August, 1953 and found that Trygve Lie had wrongfully dismissed staff with permanent contracts: only serious misconduct justified dismissal without notice. Pleading the Fifth Amendment did not amount to serious misconduct. But the tribunal found Lie was within his rights to dismiss those hired with temporary or fixed term contracts because under staff regulations, only he could determine whether or not their continued employment was in the interests of the UN.

Of those wrongfully dismissed, four determined to get re-instatement to the UN. Hammarskjöld refused to re-employ them.

He never fully explained why, only that it was "inadvisable from the points of view which it is in my duty to take into consideration".

Damages were awarded to eleven. The amounts varied between $6,000 to $40,000 and the total amount came to $179,000.

There was uproar. On hearing the news, the Vice-President, Richard Nixon telephoned the State Department to tell the Assistant Secretary for UN Affairs that the monetary awards were "catastrophic". Nixon said the tribunal totally overlooked Congressional and public opinion. Senator McCarthy announced that if the UN paid money to these "Communists", the US should pull out of the UN. Senator Alexander Wiley called for a "showdown" with the UN. Ambassador Lodge called the decisions deplorable. "The spectacle of . . . foreign lawyers interpreting . . . the Fifth Amendment . . . without any American representative . . . is in itself fantastic to contemplate."

Hammarskjöld's problems increased for it was up to him to find the money to pay the awards. There was no provision in UN accounts for damages to staff and Hammarskjöld had no alternative but to insert an item in the 1954 budget to be approved by a two-thirds vote in the General Assembly. Hammarskjöld confided in the British that he thought the amounts which were awarded were excessive, but he did not feel in a position to question them openly.

The State Department launched yet another campaign, and this time desperate to get enough votes in the General Assembly to block the payment of the awards. The British vote was vital for in its wake would come Commonwealth support. Unfortunately for Ambassador Lodge, the British had other ideas and told Lodge that if the payments were prevented, world regard for US leadership would be damaged. But Lodge was desperate. He told the British that failure to support the US in this vital vote would "seriously affect future Congressional consideration of matters such as exchange of atomic information, trade policies etc.". If the British sanctioned the "enormous sums paid to the Communists", Congress would know "who their friends were".

The British believed that if the payments were blocked, UN prestige would be harmed; if the payments were made, there would be an outcry in the American press and demands for cutting off American funding for the UN. Government law officers in Whitehall were convinced the awards could not legally be blocked. In the Foreign Office there were inevitable fears that this serious breach in the special relationship with America would be made public. The press would be told only that the matter was complex.

The British finally proposed a compromise with a suggestion that the International Court of Justice in the Hague be asked for an advisory opinion. Lodge would have none of it. He threatened a "situation in which the UN was without US funds". Lodge told Minister of State, Selwyn Lloyd that the Americans were in possession of certain evidence which might upset everything: Lodge was in possession of a recording tape of a conversation between Lord Crook and Lie in which it was obvious that the Labour Peer was biased.

The British were furious and a Foreign Office note blamed American hysteria about Communism, a minute records. "Until the current witch-hunting started, there was no suggestion that the presence of Communists or crypto-Communists among the UN staff constituted a danger to any State." Any concession over the awards would be a betrayal of conviction, a capitulation to the

frightened emotionalism which is already threatening the future of the UN . . . by its attempt to turn the organisation into a weapon in the cold war and which is now threatening the concept of an independent international civil service . . . essential to the success of . . . multi-national co-operation.

Hammarskjöld was absorbed with the problem, almost to the exclusion of everything else. In September, 1953 he came across Senator Joe McCarthy who was making an unscheduled visit to the Secretariat. The Senator walked up to him in the delegates' lounge and, accompanied by Roy Cohn, had joked that Hammarskjöld should not work too hard and get stomach ulcers. Hammarskjöld was worried that the purge was extending, that Dr Ralph Bunche was next on the list and that "minor cases involving morals charges" – homosexuality – would occur. He demanded an urgent meeting with the State Department and he met with Robert Murphy, Assistant Secretary for UN Affairs. Hammarskjöld told Murphy about the unexpected meeting with McCarthy. He said the majority of UN members did not share the US aversion for the Administrative Tribunal – it was, after all, a European concept. Murphy reminded Hammarskjöld of Congressional threats to UN funds.

Hammarskjöld eventually told the Americans that the moral authority of the UN and respect for international law was dependent on payment of the damages. The Americans began to sense that Hammarskjöld was resentful and feared the issue would soon be used by the Soviets in a campaign to get the UN out of America. There was a Soviet suggestion for a UN study into the surplus conference and office facilities in the old League of Nations building in Geneva.

Hammarskjöld tried to get American diplomats to back down and at one point told them that if money had to be spent to get rid of the political, morals and Fifth Amendment cases, as happened in private business practice in the US, it was a small price to pay.

Dulles and Lodge were unconvinced. They turned their persuasive techniques on the French with whom relations already verged on the delicate. The Eisenhower administration wanted France to ratify the Charter of the European Defence Community but the French government thought a European military community premature and wanted a *quid pro quo* – American finance to help their war in Indo-China.

In October 1953, when it was obvious that the French would vote for payment of the damages, Dulles sent a personal message to Georges Bidault, the French Foreign Minister. "We have been trying to be helpful to you in the UN . . . the US cannot willingly pay funds over to American Communists who presumably plan to devote these funds to the Communist party in America and thus attempt to overthrow the US government."

France, whose press was reporting the row, stood firm. Dulles sent a cablegram to Bidault, expressing his deep personal concern. Dulles said that as the UN's Administrative Tribunal was a creation of the General Assembly, it could be over-ruled by the General Assembly. Bidault replied he was doubtful of a change in the French attitude, telling Dulles he should be mindful of French public opinion. There had been furious anti-American protests in France over the death sentences for espionage recently carried out on the Rosenbergs.

In desperation Dulles instructed the American Ambassador in Paris to remind the French of a recent favour: the Americans had helped to prevent a debate in the Security Council on French repressions in Morocco and Tunisia, a decision which caused much soul-searching and was much criticised in the American press.

On November 19, 1953, there was a meeting in Washington between the French Ambassador, Henri Bonnet, and Dulles. Bonnet suggested that although their respective legal experts disagreed perhaps a way could be found to avoid an Assembly debate on the issue, such as a recourse to a UN committee. Dulles was tetchy. He said that France and other free countries were continually asking Americans for help and yet when asked to support America at no cost to themselves, they found it inexpedient.

The British, through their Ambassador in Washington, Sir Roger Makins, told the Americans they were obliged to vote for the payments: it was the Crown's highest legal opinion that the proper solution to the problem was reference to the International Court of Justice. The great benefit of this was the creation of a delay, allowing sentiment to cool. In reply, Dulles once more threatened the consequences of Congressional opinion – there was an imminent danger that the US might simply quit the UN.

Ambassador Lodge was at the end of his tether. He telegrammed from New York that that if the US ever behaved like the British, and suggested anything remotely like the World Court idea, "we would call down upon our heads the condemnation of all the people with beautiful and superior minds from one end of the world to the other". He recommended a last-ditch appeal to Prime Minister Churchill.

When the vote came, the British proposal was carried by a substantial margin and the Americans had to accept it as their best hope. In July 1954, the International Court of Justice rendered an advisory opinion that the compensation would have to be paid. Tempers had cooled by then. Although the US lost the battle to pay compensation, it kept the concessions over the screening of US personnel. For the next thirty-three years all Americans who wanted to work for the UN or any other international organisation were subject to a full loyalty investigation. The UN tacitly agreed not to employ anyone whose loyalty was questioned by the US government.

The programme ceased in June, 1986 after a successful appeal by a doctor who was refused clearance for a job in the World Health Organisation. A US court declared that Truman's Executive Order had been unconstitutional in that it violated the First Amendment rights of American citizens.

4. UNITING FOR PEACE

The British thought of pulling out of the UN in 1957 but timing was wrong. "Our unhappy experience of the UN in recent months makes it tempting to suggest that we might resign from it . . . " In a document described as a UN stocktaking, an Assistant Under-Secretary of State, Sir Ivor Pink, advised it would be unwise to leave the UN with one's reputation in tatters – one's previously "glorious reputation for wisdom, honesty, fair dealing and restraint". A foreign policy document records: " . . . . far from being able to pull the levers which direct the UN, we do not always know how they are being pulled by others".

Britain, a pioneer of international co-operation had fallen out with the UN after Suez. After the invasion in October 1956, Britain was pilloried before the world, an experience described by one diplomat like "a man with his back to the wall facing a pack of Afro-Asian jackals". There were new members in the UN by then. The Afro-Asian group of states was only one vote away from the third necessary to block General Assembly resolutions. The British ambassador to the UN, the dapper classical scholar, Sir Pierson Dixon, believed that this newly powerful bloc of States regarded the UN as an opportunity to "cut a dash in the world". These new nations considered the UN a way for the "backward and, in the past, more passive coloured peoples . . . to challenge the position of the white races whose greater vigour and advanced techniques have for the last 500 years made them the arbiters of the world". Dixon reported to the Foreign Office that the Afro-Asians looked on the UN "as a means of cutting us . . . down to size and entering into their rightful inheritance." Since Suez, wrote the ambassador, "the part played by the UN in the . . . crisis . . . has raised widespread doubts as to its usefulness . . . and its value to the interests of Her Majesty's Government".

The real Suez crisis was over oil – and the real value of Security Council Resolutions and whether or not any state would adhere to them.

Britain blamed the Americans for her humiliation in the General Assembly. Shortly before Suez, the State Department had come up with a new idea to try to bypass the Cold War deadlock in the Security Council. The idea had an appealing name – Uniting for Peace. It was a device to transfer consideration for the world's peace and security from the Security Council to the General Assembly. In the event of a veto-bound Council, when faced with a threat to peace, a majority of states would be able to call an Emergency Special Session of the General Assembly. The British were against the idea from the start and predicted that the idea would backfire once the Western majority in the General Assembly gave way when the new nations joined.

The Soviets argued that Uniting for Peace was an illegal attempt at Charter revision, violating the principle of superpower unanimity upon which the Charter was based. But there was nothing the Soviets could do about it and the American idea went forward.

There were no emergency sessions under Uniting for Peace until November 1956, when it was used over Suez not, as intended, to by-pass a Soviet veto but to override Britain and France who had just deceived the world with their invasion of Egypt. There was additional irony. Two days before the first planes flew over Suez, American ambassador, Henry Cabot Lodge, was planning to call an Emergency Session of the General Assembly to condemn the Soviet brutality in Hungary. Unusually, the UN became a hive of activity. In November 1956 the crises in Hungary and in Suez coincided and resulted in a series of round-the-clock meetings. The UN became the focus of the world as television cameras recorded the drama in the Security Council. There was life in a UN which many believed had ended and journalists hung on every word. But the diplomats themselves were stunned at the speed and implications of these events. In one crisis two of the five permanent members, clearly flouting their special Security Council trust, had collaborated with Israel, while continuing to engage in diplomacy at the UN to detract from undercover manoeuvrings. It was shameful. The British Prime Minister, Sir Anthony Eden, prided himself on his internationalist credentials: he called himself a man of peace, he had led British delegation when the Charter was agreed in San Francisco. In the thirties, Eden, as the Minister responsible for the League of Nations was identified with the League and its quest for disarmament. He believed in collective security. In the war years, as Foreign Secretary, he had argued that in the post-war era, the principles behind the League be maintained.

On October 30, 1956, Sir Pierson Dixon cast Britain's first veto – against a resolution drafted by her greatest ally, America. The resolution demanded that military action cease immediately and Israeli troops withdraw behind established armistice lines. For the urbane Dixon it was a difficult moment in a distinguished career. As he raised his hand he knew that along with international humiliation, the Anglo-American relationship was destroyed. Later in the General Assembly where America and the Soviet Union were united with Afro-Asian countries, Britain was condemned before the world. Dixon had warned Eden of the consequences of defying the world community, not least the threat of UN members to impose an oil embargo. As for the Secretary General, his position was strengthened. Dixon also told London: "We may find it inconvenient to have to deal with a Secretary General who will be elevated to the status of a Pope with temporal as well as spiritual powers". By now, Hammarskjöld was a world figure with increasing confidence and power.

The conflict between Arab and Jew, rooted in ancient claims of two peoples for a tiny Mediterranean coastline, was the first great test for the UN. It was a seemingly intractable problem, bequeathed to the UN by the British who were unable to keep order. In the end the conflict nearly destroyed the organisation.

Britain passed its responsiblity for the problem to the General Assembly in May 1947. The Assembly created a committee with eleven member states – Australia, Canada, Czechoslovakia, Guatemala, India, Iran, Netherlands, Peru, Sweden, Uruguay, and Yugoslavia. It comprised six diplomats, four jurists and one professor. It was not a talented group. Ralph Bunche, Top Ranking Director in the Department of Trusteeship became its special assistant and he characterised it as the worst group he ever worked with. He said the members were petty, vain and either vicious or stupid.

The Committee, known as UNSCOP, the UN Special Committee on Palestine, toured the Middle East and came up with a partition plan, with an economic union between Jewish and Arab States. The Committee did not detail the boundaries and gave no plans for Jerusalem, which was at the heart of the problem of Palestine; the city was sacred to three religions. The General Assembly created another committee to consider the report made by the first.

The vote for the partition of Palestine was made by all members of the General Assembly on November 29, 1947 at a meeting in a converted ice-rink at Flushing Meadows outside Manhattan. The Resolution split the land into two states, one Jewish, covering about fifty-six per cent, and one Arab. The resolution provided that Jerusalem would be an international zone administered by the UN as a holy city for Jews, Muslims and Christians. The Arabs denounced the plan and pledged to ignore it and the decision.

"The Charter is dead . . . all the consequences will fall on your heads, not on ours", the Syrian delegate, Emir Adel Arslan warned and the delegates of Syria, Lebanon, Iraq, Saudi Arabia, Yemen and Egypt filed out of the hall. The Arabs had wanted an advisory opinion from the International Court of Justice as to whether the Assembly had the right to partition Palestine against the wishes of the majority of its inhabitants but they lost the referral by one vote.

The Arab states were not alone in disliking the idea of partition. Some British and American diplomats considered it unworkable and unfair and there were warnings from the State Department that the plan would have to be implemented by force. But there was increasing public pressure – and increasing violence in Palestine. If the threat to prevent partition succeeded, the UN's greatest weakness would be exposed as the UN had no means to enforce its decisions. The Secretary General wanted UN troops to enforce it. But the UN had no troops; there was no neutral international armed force available to the Security Council. The Cold War had ruined any plans for a UN army. Lie tried to persuade member states that the partition decision should be backed with force but at a special session of the General Assembly in April, 1948 no offers of troops were forthcoming. The superpowers were unwilling to commit resources. The British absolutely refused to let their own troops take part. In Washington, the Department of Defense estimated that enforcement would need 100,000 US troops – and that would require partial mobilisation. Lie argued in vain that the Security Council was responsible: as Palestine was a League of Nations Mandate then the Council had both a moral and a legal duty. In the Assembly the New Zealand delegate, Sir Carl Berendsen said: "What the world needs today is not Resolutions, it is resolution." But his pleas were to no avail. Lie tempered his ambitions and proposed a small neutral force of some five to ten thousand men, not to enforce partition but to be a buffer force to keep Arab and Jew apart. This too met with stiff opposition and Lie concluded that the problems in the Middle East would destroy the UN.

On May 14, 1948, the day on which the British mandate was relinquished, the State of Israel was proclaimed by the Jewish authorities in Palestine. The General Assembly partition Resolution gave it international legitimacy. Although the new nation had no agreed boundary it quickly received wide international recognition. Within hours violence gave way to war. Neighbouring Arab states sent forces into Palestine in an attempt to crush the new state. Thousands of people were now homeless, some 750,000 Palestinian refugees. Israel was now in posession of more territory than allotted to it under the UN partition plan as well as Jerusalem which the Jews considered to be a fulfilment of Jewish history. The Security Council did little beyond calling for ceasefires and truces and it appointed a mediator, Count Folke Bernadotte of Wisburg, the President of the Swedish Red Cross and now Chief Repre-sentative of the UN. While its greatest weakness was exposed, a strength emerged.

Within two weeks of his arrival, Bernadotte, in a brilliant feat of diplomacy, managed a four-week truce and the guns stopped firing. To monitor and to ensure the peace would last the Security Council agreed to a small group of military observers to act as go-betweens. This was the start of peacekeeping and this mission still exists. The observers who made up the UN Truce Supervision Organisation (UNTSO) were unarmed, wearing national military uniforms but with a UN armband. Their job was to report and investigate complaints of ceasefire violations and they were dependent on the co-operation of the parties for their effectiveness. They had only jeeps, radios, maps and binoculars; they carried UN flags and their vehicles were painted white. This first group set a peacekeeping tradition: its members were late arriving, the build-up was slow and at one point Bernadotte threatened to resign if more observers were not forthcoming. In New York, Trygve Lie was lobbying too. He wanted one thousand UN civilian guards to monitor Jerusalem and forty were sent from headquarters as soldiers of peace but they had no training or discipline. They held a party their first night and their behaviour was so appalling that they were sent back to New York.

The peace was fragile; when the observers arrived the ceasefire lines were not yet drawn and there were violations by both sides. The observers were frequently under fire and some lost their lives. Though they numbered just a few hundred, too small a group to prevent confrontation in those days, the world had a better understanding of their role and did not expect them to solve the conflict.

Bernadotte was murdered by a Jewish terrorist gang on September 17, 1948. He was working to develop a long-term settlement. The assassination was planned by the Lohamee Herut Israel (Lehi) better known as the Stern Gang and the decision to kill Bernadotte was taken by three men of the central committee, Nathan Friedman-Yellin (later Nathan Yellin-Mor), Dr Israel Sheib (later Israel Eldad) and Yitzhak Yezernitsky (later Yitzhak Shamir) who became Prime Minister of Israel in 1983.

Bernadotte had been negotiating a comprehensive settlement which would include a solution to the thousands of homeless Palestinian refugees living in camps in desperate conditions. He had wanted the Security Council to insist with Israel on the return of some 300,000 refugees to their homes. The Israeli government ignored his pleas; only when the Arabs were ready to conclude a peace treaty would the problem of the refugees become part of a general settlement. Bernadotte wanted a special session of the General Assembly to consider the matter. It was his insistence on such a course which worried those who killed him. In an interview years later, one of the gang admitted that if Bernadotte had used his influence and the General Assembly had sat in special session, member states would have decided overwhelmingly for settlement of the refugee question. Bernadotte thus stood in the way of Jewish control of the whole of Palestine.

Bernadotte's successor was Ralph Bunche, a Director in the Department of Trusteeship promptly appointed by Trygve Lie as Acting Mediator. Bunche soon built a reputation for integrity but he was unable to persuade the member states to adopt Bernadotte's ideas. There was no scope left for mediation. The Security Council was weakened by the ambivalence of the US. Bunche, like Bernadotte, firmly believed that the real victims of the conflict were the refugees and their suffering a constant reminder of failure, but Bunche did not give up.

By 1949, through his perseverance, Bunche managed a negotiated armistice between Israel and her four Arab neighbours, as a first step. Congratulations poured in from all over the world. *Time* magazine, describing Bunche as "a Negro social scientist", said only his ability and patience kept the talks alive. To Bunche's surprise this armistice agreement became the status quo for eighteen years. Though Bunche had become a top-level executive he never lost his devotion to the Secretariat and when he was awarded the Nobel Peace Prize in 1950, he said it was a tribute to the international civil service.

In July, 1956, after Britain and the US withdrew pledges of finance for the building of the Aswan Dam, President Nasser of Egypt nationalised the Suez Canal and expelled British oil and embassy officials. Nasser signed a substantial arms deal with the Government of Czechoslovakia. Previously France and the US had monopolised sales to Arab countries. The West was concerned at Nasser's anti-Israeli rhetoric and, in British eyes, Nasser was demonic. On October 29, Israel, barred from the Suez Canal and angered by incursions of the Palestinian fedayeen across her borders, invaded Gaza and the Sinai peninsula. Britain and France, after a pretence at peacemaking and demanding the evacuation of all Israeli and Egyptians troops to ten miles beyond the Canal zone, attacked Egypt. The British bombed Egyptian airfields allowing the Israelis to secure what they wanted with no threat of attack from the air.

The Canadian Foreign Minister, and sometime candidate for the post of Secretary General, Lester "Mike" Pearson was shocked by the behaviour of Canada's ally and Commonwealth partner. He thought that what was needed was an international peace and police force which, unlike UN observers, would be armed. At the time, although no mention was made of it, Pearson's idea was similar to the plan put forward by Lie in 1948 following the partition of Palestine. Pearson believed that inter-national troops, under a UN flag, would be able to keep the borders between Israel and Egypt at peace during which time, political settlements could be found for both problems – Palestine and the Suez Canal. Hammarskjöld's initial reaction was cool. He reminded Pearson that Israel treated the UN truce observers with scant courtesy – but Pearson, a veteran of Commonwealth diplomacy, was not discouraged.

At the very moment that the Assembly voted in principle for this first international army, on 4 November, 1956, the news came from Vienna that the Soviet army was attacking Budapest with tanks and airplanes. Ambassador Lodge was given telexes from the Hungarian News Agency, (MTI), which had managed somehow to keep an open line to Vienna for almost seven hours. Lodge immediately requested a meeting of the Security Council and a few hours before dawn, as the Assembly adjourned its debate on Suez, the Security Council went into session on Hungary to hear Lodge read the dramatic appeals: "Help, help, help . . . The tanks are getting nearer . . . What is the United Nations doing? . . . We will hold out to our last drop of blood."

The Soviet Ambassador, Arkady Sobolev, tried to dull the effect by pointing to Suez and the illegal action of the British, French and Israelis. Sobolev blamed the Hungarian uprising on reactionary elements instigated by the West, and then cast the Soviet Union's seventy-ninth veto. The Americans called for an emergency session of the General Assembly on Hungary but not much else could be done. In Washington the possibility of UN police action to help the Hungarians was already discounted: the risk of all-out nuclear war was too high. No UN mandate would be forthcoming anyway. Washington recognised that the Soviet Union had taken a page from US policy regarding spheres of influence – two years earlier, in 1954, the US had organised and backed an invasion of Guatemala to overthrow a government considered pro-Communist. In any event, America and her European allies were weakened through Suez and were not prepared to propose anything stronger than censure.

Ambassador Sobolev's diplomatic difficulties over Hungary were matched by those of Ambassador Pierson Dixon over Suez. Dixon cabled Prime Minister Anthony Eden to tell him that at the forthcoming General Assembly meeting, UN member states would be "out for British blood". Dixon added: "I do not see how we can carry much conviction in our protests against the Russian bombing of Budapest if we ourselves are bombing Cairo". The British government, condemned at the UN, and with the Soviet Union threatening retaliation in the Middle East, was in a mess. There was a sudden and terrifying flight from sterling. The special relationship with America lay in ruins and Eden was faced with little alternative but to welcome the Lester Pearson peacekeeping lifeline.

The plans for the peacekeeping force, the UN Emergency Force known as UNEF, were put in the hands of the Secretary General and, with no precedent to help him, Hammarskjöld very quickly decided the principles underlying the structure, nature and functions of the force. Initially uncertain about its size or how it would be financed, he was certain that this pioneer force would not enforce peace. As he explained in December, 1956 in a message to UN troops in Egypt: "You are taking part in an experiment that is new in history . . . you are the front line of a moral force which extends around the world . . . Your success can have a profound effect for good . . . on the future prospects for building a world order of which we may all one day be truly proud."

The force was a model for all future peacekeeping operations and helped to ensure ten years of quiet frontiers between Israel and Egypt. It prevented violent incidents from escalating into major threats. Its creation was a turning point for the UN and its Secretary General. Hammarskjöld put his whole being behind the idea and within the Secretariat the creation of the force was considered a minor miracle, its logistical arrangements described as a "triumph of improvisation". With no agreement finalised between the UN and President Nasser, the first UN troops, one hundred Danes and Norwegians, arrived at a staging area in Naples. The force would eventually oversee the withdrawal of the British, French and Israeli troops and the clearing of the Suez Canal. In March 1957, when Israel withdrew her troops, these UN peacekeepers took their places along the Egyptian-Israeli Armistice demarcation line. UNEF was the first truly international army which everyone wanted to serve – there were twenty-one offers of troops. Ten contributing countries were chosen, providing 6,000 troops, and the first peacekeepers were Colombian, Danish, Finnish, Norwegian, Swedish, Indian, Indonesian and Yugoslavs. They wore, for the first time, blue helmets and they could fly only the UN flag. Aware of the mission's importance as a model, Hammarskjöld and Bunche defined the legal status of the force. Principles and precedents were set for the future. Peacekeeping needed patience, impartiality and an unlimited supply of goodwill.

For Hammarskjöld, the creation of UNEF had deep significance. This new mission was a fundamental responsibility. From now on the UN would be able to help the great powers remove themselves from situations they should never have entered in the first place. Within the Secretariat there was a new sense of purpose. Hammarskjöld's standing throughout the world improved and he earned the respect of world leaders.

British diplomats thought Hammarskjöld was becoming too powerful. As for the UN, the British concluded that its weaknesses outweighed its merits. The news department at the Foreign Office was given a brief that the British public be taught the real nature and limitations of the UN. A Foreign Office note records: "We must recognise the UN for what it is and teach the public to realise that its weaknesses outweigh its merits." Arguments could conveniently centre on the UN's double standards: while the Soviet Union flouted the Charter with impunity over Hungary, and successfully withstood international condemnation, the UK, France and Israel were forced to bow to the weight of world opinion over Suez. "We must avoid using the UN as a forum to discuss matters of serious concern to us ... " was the prevailing view.

Ambassador Dixon advised London to be cautious. It would not do to appear too cynical about the UN after the setback of Suez. "Our attitude, I feel, should be that the institution could not exist without us."

At a summit meeting with America in March 1957 in Bermuda, Britain left no doubt about her disdain for the UN. At the meeting it was hoped that Britain's new Prime Minister, Harold Macmillan would mend fences with President Dwight Eisenhower and repair the special relationship damaged during Suez. The British wanted the UN to be used with greater discretion and insisted that problems be kept away from it. Major international disputes would have to be dealt with between the US and the UK who would agree which policies to take to the UN.

It worried Eisenhower. He did not want the British to turn their backs on the UN. He desperately needed their help with his own difficult UN problem which risked destroying the organisation completely.

America's policy towards the UN was dominated by China from the moment the People's Republic was declared. In 1949, when Chiang Kai-shek's government was swept away by the Communists to Taiwan, he hung on to China's UN membership, occupying China's

Security Council and Assembly seats. At first, the British were keen for Chiang Kai-shek to remain at the UN: he had been an ally in the Second World War and was involved in early discussions which laid the UN's foundation. Chiang Kai-shek joined Franklin Delano. Roosevelt, Winston Churchill and Joseph Stalin as sponsors of the San Francisco Conference in 1945 and it was no surprise that China became one of the five permanent members of the Security Council. But the policy of excluding Communist China was hard to maintain for shortly after the People's Republic came to power, the British government offered diplomatic recognition. Furthermore, Chinese Communists were in charge of the most populous nation on earth – which was now excluded from the family of nations.

In Washington the mood was different. There it was argued that the Communists in Peking were illegally in control of mainland China and the rogue regime did not represent the true will and aspirations of the Chinese people. The Chinese committed aggression in Korea, destroyed the autonomy of Tibet, subverted governments in South East Asia and threatened Taiwan. Eisenhower had outlined the American position to China's UN seat in March, 1957 at the summit in Bermuda. He told Macmillan that if the Communist Chinese were ever admitted to UN membership, America would withdraw altogether – and kick the UN out of the country.

The terms of membership of the UN were laid out in the Charter. Membership was available to peace-loving States able to meet their Charter obligations. Admission or expulsion was through the General Assembly, on the recommendation of the Security Council which allowed the Big Five a veto, giving them the ultimate decision. There quickly developed two tests for UN membership, two theories about what the Charter really intended: one, only those States willing to honour high principles of international behaviour should be allowed to join, or two, as no member lived up to high standards, the only test of suitability was whether or not the applicant state was legally a state.

The Soviet bloc supported Communist China's membership and, angered that the Communist Chinese were not seated in the Security Council, in January 1950 the Soviet Ambassador, Yakov Malik, walked out of the Council chamber. In the following weeks the Soviets pulled out of twenty-one UN councils and committees and the Secretary General was not alone in thinking that the Communist bloc countries would pull out and form a rival world organisation. Lie supported membership for Peking and the UN's General Counsel, Abe Feller prepared legal arguments that the Communists were in a better position to fulfil Charter obligations than the exiled regime in Taiwan. The British announced it "extremely regrettable" that the Peking government, exercising power over 500 million people, was prevented from membership. The exclusion diminished the UN's authority. But the British were hypocritical and in private supported America.

In 1951 a secret moratorium was agreed between America and Britain whereby, if the subject of China's admission appeared on a UN agenda, both the British and US delegates would insist on a postponement to prevent a vote. The moratorium was agreed by the Secretary of State, Dean Acheson, and the British Foreign Secretary, Herbert Morrison. There were fears that the Soviets would skilfully play procedure and get the Chinese in through the back door. In the next two years the matter came up 135 times – and the Chinese Communists managed to slip into the family only once. They entered the less than influential Executive and Liaison Committee of the Universal Postal Union – which after an uproar of criticism reversed its decision the following year.

When North Korea invaded South Korea in 1950, China's chances were set back, but the issue reappeared in 1953 when the Korean Armistice was imminent. America feared that Britain would give way and allow the Communists entry. Congress took preventive action and included a rider to an appropriations bill that all US funding for the UN would be cut at once if the Communist Chinese entered the UN.

President Eisenhower was worried. He feared that the vote on Chinese membership could not be prevented for ever and so he asked the Congressional leaders to the White House to persuade them to lift the threat on UN funding. UN dues were sacrosanct; they were a treaty obligation under the Charter. In front of the Congressional leaders, Eisenhower made a plea for international co-operation. He told them that the UN was the world's only hope. William Knowland, the Republican Senator from California, was unmoved. Knowland told Eisenhower that the admission of Red China to the UN would violate his basic beliefs in freedom. Eisenhower had nothing but contempt for Knowland. He pointed out that every member nation must undergo defeats in the UN from time to time: it was a democratic organisation. Eisenhower warned that were the UN ever to be destroyed, NATO would break up too. "Where would we be then?" the President asked. He for one would no longer be able to fulfil his responsibilities for the country's security.

Later that day, June 2, 1953, Eisenhower wrote a brief memorandum which reveals a promise he made that day. In order to kill the amendment, Eisenhower assured the senators that America's allies would not use a Korean truce as an excuse for urging the acceptance of Red China into the UN. The President also gave his word that he would never be party to UN membership for China.

Eisenhower had created a problem because there were increasing doubts within the State Department about allied support. The British Ambassador to the UN, Sir Gladwyn Jebb, told Lodge in June, 1953, a month before the Korean armistice, that it was illogical for the Americans to oppose membership for the Communist Chinese. After all, the Soviet Union had a UN seat. Lodge's response was that it was the Chinese, and not the Soviets, who recently inflicted more than 50,000 American casualties in Korea. Lodge was as blunt with the French ambassador, Henri Hoppenot, telling him that the Americans would not dream of asking the French to get into bed with the Germans after a Franco-German war ended.

The Secretary of State, John Foster Dulles, feared the worst, convinced that the British were contemplating supporting Chinese admission. Dulles believed the French were also strongly tempted and he was desperate for both British and French support in the Security Council. Dulles believed that were the Chinese Communists admitted, the UN would be utterly destroyed. For the first time, America prepared to use its veto.

As it turned out, the British were supportive but the problem remained until the following year. In March, 1954, Ambassador Lodge told Dulles he was planning some dinners, receptions and "other entertainments" in order to establish friendly feelings with other member states at a time when "it does not appear that we want anything out of anybody". In fact, obtaining the support of the British to stop the admission of communist China was the priority. Lodge wrote:

> The UN at present is a marvelous vehicle for organizing the free world coalition in case World War III should ever come. It is only prudent to assume that World War III is a distinct likelihood . . . .If we have reached the stage in world affairs

where it is either we or they . . . it would be folly to weaken and vitiate this great potential organ for organizing the free world in case of war.

Dulles regretted that it was America, when the UN was founded, which had pressed the victorious allies to get Nationalist China a permanent Security Council seat after the Soviets contested her inclusion as a great power.

In June 1954, Prime Minister Churchill and President Dwight Eisenhower talked over the issue. Churchill, who was on a visit to Washington, said he understood the reasons the US could not abandon its loyal allies, the Nationalist Chinese. He thought perhaps they could consider two Chinas – one in the General Assembly and the Communist Chinese in the Security Council. Eisenhower was unimpressed. He said that if the Chinese withdrew to their own borders, if they released American prisoners captured during the Korean war, and if they "observed propriety in international relationships" he would consider whether or not to use his influence to obtain American recognition for the régime.

With the approach of the 1954 General Assembly and a re-doubling of the efforts of the Communist group of nations to admit the Chinese, Dulles and Lodge kept up the pressure. They worried about remarks made by Britain's Pierson Dixon at a dinner at the British Embassy in Washington. Dixon was heard to say he thought the Communists qualified for membership, and he was concerned about the American anti-Communist campaign. When Dixon's remarks were mulled over in the State Department, desperation set in and at one strategy meeting it was decided to take another tack and approach Sir Robert Scott, British Minister in the Washington Embassy and an expert on Far Eastern Affairs. Scott would be left in no doubt that preventing Communist China from becoming a UN member was of far greater concern than anything else on the agenda of the forthcoming General Assembly. There was something else Scott should consider – the very strong opinion in America that Cyprus be turned over to Greece.

Cyprus was the British Achilles' heel. It was the touchstone for British attitudes to all other UN matters for, almost at any cost, the issue had to be kept away from the agenda of the General Assembly. A campaign against British rule was under way. At the time, British rule was being challenged by partisans of Enosis, who wanted union with Greece, and the situation was complicated by the fact that almost twenty per cent of the population was Turkish. The British argued that Cyprus was not within the UN's competence, maintaining the fiction that discussion of Cypriot independence was prevented by Article 2 – non-interference in the internal affairs of a member state. No one had yet worked out whether Article 2 was breached at the point of inscription, debate or recommendation. Nevertheless, Article 2 stood guard while Greece exerted increasing pressure for a UN debate and was getting increasing support among UN members. Britain, whose occupation dated from 1878, had no intention of allowing the Cypriots to govern themselves. In 1954 Cyprus was a bargaining chip. Sir Robert Scott relayed Lodge's thoughts to London and a few days later Scott told the State Department there would be a British guarantee of support for postponement of the Chinese membership issue until the end of the 1954 Assembly. The linkage worked although the Americans were safer than they realised. On September 21, 1954, the General Assembly, by forty-three votes, with eleven against and six abstentions, approved a US resolution for postponement of the question of Chinese representation. The Cyprus issue stayed off the General Assembly agenda.

They were dreading the UN's tenth anniversary in 1955. The Secretary of State, John Foster Dulles, feared that the Anniversary Commemorative Meeting, in the razzmatazz of San Francisco, would become a propaganda battle between the superpowers. But, apart from a speech by Syria calling for the liberation of the French occupation of North Africa, it went rather well. The British privately thought it important to remember that the organisation had been over-sold to the Americans in 1945 and since they lacked experience in the League of Nations, the Americans had only latterly come to realise how little the UN was able to take the "weight of responsibility for world peace off American shoulders". The tenth anniversary might have been a flop or a propaganda victory for the Soviet bloc, derided as a junket, or allowed to assume the character of a prayer meeting but it was a good show. On the whole the speeches were moderate – apart from the Cuban who castigated the Soviets for the rape of the Baltic States. The speech of Vyacheslav Molotov, Soviet Foreign Minister, was interrupted by bursts of cheering which the British assumed was organised by the new Soviet

Deputy Foreign Minister, Nikolai Fedorenko, backed up by members of the audience, amongst whom the singer Paul Robeson was prominent. But even Molotov reaffirmed his faith in the UN.

For the first time since the UN was founded, the Cold War began to thaw. In July 1955 there was a summit in Geneva between US, Britain, France and the Soviet Union and the meeting had enormous effect on the General Assembly. Ambassador Pierson Dixon was astonished by the reasonable approach of the Soviet delegates. Ambassador Vasiliy Kuznetsov devoted considerable time and effort to sometimes rather embarrassing attempts at intimate consultation with the British and other delegations. Even Dulles's views of the Soviet Union shifted: he thought their delegates more tolerant. He moved to a position of co-existence and his speeches became less bellicose. But there was one Cold War problem which would not go away. At the top of the 1955 General Assembly agenda was the UN waiting list.

By 1955, nineteen nations had been waiting several years to become UN members – and all had been prevented because of the veto. The Soviets vetoed membership for the non-Communist applicants, and the Americans vetoed the Communist ones. Both superpowers were deeply and publicly committed to their positions. The countries excluded in this veto were Austria, Cambodia, Ceylon, Finland, Ireland, Italy, Japan, Jordan, North and South Korea, Laos, Libya, Nepal, Portugal, Vietnam, Albania, Bulgaria, Hungary, Rumania and Outer Mongolia. The applications of Albania, Outer Mongolia, Hungary, Roumania, Bulgaria and Viet Minh were twice rejected by the Security Council because of a lack of votes. There was no hope for progress and Secretary of State Dulles thought the issue was strangling the organisation.

Since the inauguration with fifty founding members, only nine states had joined; they were Afghanistan, Burma, Iceland, Indonesia, Israel, Pakistan, Sweden, Thailand and Yemen and thus, by 1955, a majority of the world's population was still outside the UN. The waiting list was causing a progressive deterioration in the UN's prestige. The log-jam could even result in states from under-represented areas such as the Far East and Asia setting up their own organisation. Already there were signs. The Bandung Conference in April 1955 provided a display of solidarity when twenty-nine of the world's poor and struggling countries, new to internationalism, met and determined to increase their diplomatic weight. Until this meeting there was no organised collaboration among Asian and African countries, neither inside nor outside the UN. In Bandung, Communist China's Chou En-Lai was a leading figure and the conference made colonialism a target.

The Eisenhower administration was facing a 1956 election, thus no one wanted a row over UN membership. Year after year in the General Assembly, American delegates condemned the Soviet satellite countries for violating human rights; if America allowed countries like Albania, Bulgaria, Hungary, and Rumania to join the UN, blocking the Chinese Communists would seem ridiculous. Doubts would be created about US opposition to international Communism. Not the least, UN membership for these countries would increase Soviet power within the UN system and worsen the problem of internal security in New York, where the FBI was constantly lobbying for more resources to keep up surveillance on Communist delegations. Congress posed problems of a different sort although it might be possible to persuade legislators to accept Communist satellites as members as long as Spain entered. There were strong objections from the Eastern Bloc to Spanish membership because of Franco's fascist regime. They mulled over various compromises, retrieving a Latin-American idea from 1953 whereby there would be a tit for tat, one Communist nation for a non-Communist one. A familiar solution was found in the creation of a UN committee named the Good Offices Committee on Membership consisting of three states, the Netherlands and Egypt, with Peru in the Chair. The Committee was to consult the Security Council informally to try to reach a settlement. But the US considered the Committee little more than a way to avoid the issue. The Peruvian chairman, Victor Andres Belaúnde, was prevailed upon, by the Americans, not to be in too much haste in finding a resolution.

A year later Secretary of State Dulles came up with an idea which allowed for non-member participation for those countries who managed to obtain a majority vote in the General Assembly. The Japanese, impatient after two years on the list, thought associate membership an insult. Japan said it would be rather like asking her government to ride in a second-class car which did not yet exist and for which plans were not yet drawn. The Italians agreed. The British declared the idea unconstitutional, a way for the General Assembly to seize power from the Security Council.

In truth, although certainly not for public consumption, the membership fiasco suited the British. An influx of new members would radically change the balance in the General Assembly and the anti-colonial vote would increase. The longer the admission of new members was put off, the better British government interests were served. "We must of course appear publicly to be working for universality", the British delegation recommended to London. "We are already suspected of cynicism and could easily be suspected of sabotage." Indeed, if the Minister of State at the Foreign Office Selwyn Lloyd's attitude was anything to go by, this was exactly right. In October 1954, in a conversation with one of America's chief delegates to the Assembly, James Fulbright, the Democratic Senator, Lloyd revealed that Britain wanted no further admissions to the UN – with the exception, perhaps, of Italy. Lloyd told Fulbright that it would be unwise to let "trouble-makers" in. Were Nepal allowed entry, her vote would be always under Chinese or Indian influence; Finland would be "under Soviet guns". Portugal was not that keen on admission because of her colonial problems. As for Ireland, Lloyd said she would be a "constant source of irritation and embarrassment to the UK". Lloyd said there were already too many small countries in the UN.

Lloyd reckoned without the gentle thaw in the Cold War. In Spring, 1955 there was a rumour of a Soviet change of heart, an indication that their objections to certain States might be relaxed – perhaps allowing entry for Japan, with whom the Soviets were still technically at war, and the former enemy States of Italy and Austria. The Americans tried nifty diplomatic footwork: delegates quickly revived non-member participation but suddenly they began to backtrack. The State Department feared that if the US were seen to be stalling on the issue, she would lose popularity.

Once more it was rescue by Canada. Canada's diplomats, circulating among her allies, ceaselessly worried about the damage caused to the UN by the waiting list. Canada, occupying a non-permanent seat in 1955, prepared a draft Resolution which proposed that eighteen States be admitted together – excluding, for the time being, the divided state of Korea. London and Washington were resentful. The British Foreign Secretary, Harold Macmillan, hoped the Canadians could be dissuaded but he feared they were likely to insist and he would have no choice but to support them. It was important that Britain should not be seen to be obstructing the entry of eighteen applicants, particularly since one of them was Ceylon – a staunch and faithful Commonwealth ally. Macmillan recommended support of the Canadian idea but insisted that Spain be added to the list. France, however, would not countenance UN membership for Franco's regime. Macmillan wanted France to support Spain's application, explaining that Spain would benefit from closer association with the free world. The *quid pro quo* for Macmillan was that Spain be invited to reconsider her attitude to Gibraltar, a Crown Colony over which Spain claimed sovereignty. British diplomats were told it should be made clear the British were not seeking to strike a bargain – although that is exactly what it was.

Apart from a divergence on Spain, France thought much the same as Britain: the French delegate said that his government was not at all anxious to see "fifteen new animals in the menagerie". Neither were the Americans. Secretary of State Dulles, much like Macmillan, was unenthusiastic about the Canadian package deal. But Dulles had recently visited Italy and Spain where the passionate desire for UN membership surprised him. Franco, much to Dulles's surprise, showed him a copy of the Canadian draft Resolution and told Dulles that the UN could have been a non-Communist organisation but, once a number of Communist states were in, a few more would make no difference. Franco said that the damage caused by admission for the Communist States would be offset through the membership of vigorous anti-Communist and Christian countries such as Spain, Portugal, Italy and Ireland. Franco reminded Dulles that Spain filed her application to join the UN at the behest of America and took it for granted she would be allowed entry.

The Americans dithered. Admission for the Soviet satellite countries would be bad enough; but the Canadians had included Outer Mongolia on the list which made US support for their draft impossible. Macmillan sympathised, for Outer Mongolia was a model satellite of the Soviet Empire since the 1920s. Outer Mongolia, nominally under Chinese suzerainty, was conceded to the USSR by the Western Allies at Yalta. Macmillan told Dulles the British would help all they could and that the British delegation would "go slow on the Outer Mongols". Macmillan told one American diplomat: "It is worth remembering that the Communist Chinese cannot look with much pleasure on the independence of Outer Mongolia. It is their Ireland . . . "

Support within the UN for the Canadian Resolution grew. The Latin-American states, together with the countries of Asia and Africa and most of the Europeans were, at least in public, in favour of admitting eighteen states all in one go. It looked as though the US, holding out against Outer Mongolia, would sabotage entry for everyone else. President Eisenhower, who was consulted on the issue in November, 1955, tried to see the way forward and said that the Soviet satellites on the list of eighteen were small nations. "We would be getting in Italy and Japan . . . look at the size of the population of Japan and Italy", he said to persuade Dulles.

All that was left was damage limitation and Allen Dulles, Director of the CIA, and brother of the Secretary of State, advised that the *Voice of America*, the worldwide short-wave radio service established and financed by the US government, and Radio Free Europe be given time to prepare for the announcement, to explain in vigorous terms why America had changed its mind about allowing Soviet Satellites into the family of nations. Dulles was shown the draft of a speech to be made by the UN Ambassador Henry Cabot Lodge which pointed out that UN membership was intended for the citizens of these repressive regimes, not for the regimes themselves.

On a Sunday morning in November 1955, in a hotel room in Geneva, Vyacheslav Molotov, the Soviet Foreign Minister, and Secretary of State, John Foster Dulles, tried to work out a trade over the waiting list. Molotov made the first move and said that he was willing to agree membership for Japan and Spain: he found it hard to understand why America was holding out against Outer Mongolia. Dulles told him there was no chance of UN membership for Outer Mongolia because it was not an independent state, but an occupied one. Despite this, he would make Molotov an offer; he would negotiate membership for Spain in exchange for two Soviet satellites in Eastern Europe. Molotov replied that the overwhelming sentiment in the UN was for admission for all eighteen on the list. The conversation ended without a resolution and so did the chance to solve the problem.

Dulles was aware that if Outer Mongolia were to be included, the Canadian Resolution would be torpedoed by the Nationalist Chinese veto in the Security Council. If this were to happen, the resentment against the Nationalist Chinese government within the UN would be so great that there would be a strong and determined attempt to expel the representative and give the seat to Peking. Dulles faced a clamour from all countries on the list – some of them had been waiting six years, and now their own admission depended upon whether or not Outer Mongolia were to be included in the Canadian package deal.

Lodge's gloom knew no bounds. The only alternative was for America to accept the terms and vote for all eighteen – and hope to persuade the Nationalist Chinese not to use the veto. His hopes were soon dashed. Wellington Koo, the Nationalist Chinese Ambassador, was a veteran of the League of Nations and he was unhesitating: if Outer Mongolia were proposed for UN membership he would use his veto. The Soviets heard about Koo's threat. They let it be known that should the membership of Outer Mongolia be vetoed, they in turn would veto the application of Fascist Spain.

Lodge's annoyance with the Canadians could only increase. This was their fault. The British concluded that the American delegation had lost its grip. The only possible outcome was to exert pressure at a higher level. President Eisenhower dictated an urgent cable to President Chiang Kai-shek. "Whatever may be our own national judgment, I feel that we cannot properly interpose a veto to block arbitrarily the will of the great majority." The President told Chiang Kai-shek that America had never been in favour of using her own veto over membership matters. To do so now would strengthen the Communist cause and damage American influence. Eisenhower asked the Chinese to abstain on the Canadian resolution and allow UN membership for the eighteen applicants. "I venture to make this personal appeal that our two countries should not seem divided in this matter."

In his reply Chiang Kai-shek pointed out that his Government had a duty to uphold the membership principles in the UN Charter. The regime in Outer Mongolia, detached from China, was a Soviet creation: in domestic and foreign affairs Outer Mongolia was under rigid Soviet control. Admission to UN membership would signify a recognition of its present occupied status which would preclude future settlement. Chiang Kai-shek warned Eisenhower of a Soviet change in tactics: the Soviets were banking everything, not on admission of the Communist Chinese puppet regime in Peking, but on the admission of their satellite, Outer Mongolia. Chiang Kai-shek told Eisenhower he would even accept four Soviet satellites into the UN – but never Outer Mongolia.

Eisenhower wrote another telegramme, more pleading than the last, but Chiang Kai-shek remained unmoved and stood on Charter principle. In Washington his Ambassador, Wellington Koo, was called to the State Department to be told that the two telegrammes from Eisenhower to Chiang Kai-shek were an extraordinary departure from diplomatic procedure. Koo was warned that his government was about to walk into a Soviet trap. If he used the veto against the Canadian Resolution he would have to accept the blame for UN membership deadlock. Koo said that once the UN yielded to blackmail its moral authority would be gone. The Americans told Koo they were at the end of their rope and the diplomatic mess could only get worse. A group of Congressmen – the Chairman and five members of the House Foreign Affairs Far-East Subcommittee – were visiting Taipei and they went to see Chiang Kai-shek at his home in Sun Moon Lake. Afterwards they cabled Secretary of State Dulles to tell him that the package to accept all eighteen states was a violation of the letter and spirit of the Charter. "If principles are to be abandoned whenever a majority believes it expedient, why should we have Charter or even constitutions?" The admission to UN membership of the Soviet Satellites would weaken the hopes and the will to resist on the part of the enslaved people behind the Iron Curtain. Respect for America would decrease. Already her power was dwindling alarmingly throughout the Middle and Far East. The Congressman told Dulles that what was morally wrong could never be politically right. As for the possibility of a Nationalist Chinese veto in the Security Council: "History may well record its veto and steadfast adherence to the UN Charter as its finest deed."

You could almost hear the laughter from the Soviet delegation, enjoying the spectre of America, unable even to control the protégé in which it had invested so much of its wealth and reputation. The Soviets quickly announced support for the Canadian package allowing admission to all eighteen countries: Soviet diplomats let it be known that they would never relinquish support for the admission to the UN of Outer Mongolia.

In desperation, Ambassador Lodge turned to the Canadians. He tried to persuade them to drop the application of Outer Mongolia from the list. Paul Martin, Canadian lawyer and later statesman, who led the initiative, refused. In Washington, Dulles met the Canadian Chargé d'Affaires, and gave him an extraordinary dressing down. Dulles blamed the Canadians for not first consulting America, for failing to think through the consequences of their all-eighteen-or-nothing Resolution. Dulles said continuing US mem-bership of the UN was at stake. He pleaded for delay.

The Security Council met on December 10, 1955 when the Nationalist Chinese submitted thirteen draft resolutions of their own

– each recommended the admission of an applicant – Italy, Japan, Spain, the Republic of South Korea, Vietnam, Cambodia, Laos, Portugal, Ceylon, Jordan, Libya, Austria and Ireland. In turn, the Soviet Union submitted its own eighteen Resolutions, but insisted on a vote for each, followed by an immediate vote in the Assembly: the Soviets were suspicious of a double cross whereby the Eastern Bloc countries would be voted through the Council only to be voted out by the Western majority in the Assembly. The West too suspected a plot. The Soviet Resolutions put Albania and Outer Mongolia before Spain in the queue. The Security Council adjourned in chaos.

At the next meeting three days later, the Chinese Nationalists resubmitted their Resolutions; there was an immediate Soviet veto. Another Resolution which recommended membership for all eighteen countries was vetoed by the Chinese. There was a corporate moan of despair from the chamber. The Soviets retaliated, casting their veto against all western candidates. The Canadian package deal came crashing to the ground.

The next morning, the Soviets asked for an urgent meeting in a side room and their Ambassador suggested a compromise. He proposed a package of sixteen countries – all those on the Canadian list, apart from Japan and Outer Mongolia. Their applications could be deferred. And so the deadlock was broken. Sixteen countries were recommended for admission by the Security Council and that same evening the General Assembly endorsed the decision.

The Japanese were stunned. In Tokyo there was bitterness and indignation, and fears that as a result of such humiliation the Government would fall. The Foreign Minister, Mamoru Shigemitsu, was blamed for relying too much on US help and there were rumours he would leave office. The Socialist opposition blamed Japanese stubbornness in government dealings with the Soviets; at the time negotiations over renewal of diplomatic relations between the Soviets and the Japanese were taking place in London. To save face, the Japanese Foreign Office announced that Soviet action in the Security Council was a way of increasing pressure on Japan over the Kurile Islands which were ceded to the USSR at Yalta – and which the Japanese claimed as their own.

In Moscow there were many congratulations while in Paris in the Quai d'Orsay there was pessimism. From now on the balance of power in the General Assembly would shift towards the under-developed and anti-colonial countries and it would be impossible for the French and other countries with African possessions to deny them self-government without coming under very heavy attack – an attack which would bring together the anti-colonial and Soviet countries. It would become increasingly difficult for the French to hold back the tide and deny self-government for their African possessions. Earlier, during the General Assembly in the autumn 1955, France walked out after a one-vote majority put Algeria on the agenda, and the delegation returned only after a hasty compromise and removal of the item.

As for the British, Ambassador Pierson Dixon thought congratulations were in order. Cyprus was successfully kept off the Assembly agenda and, moreover, a new alliance was forming in the UN – the European group to which Dixon reported was under British leadership. Dixon told London that British support for the Canadian Resolution was seen as statesman-like and far-sighted. The Commonwealth continued united.

Dixon reserved his criticism for the Canadians and he called Paul Martin, who pushed the all-eighteen idea, messianic. He said that Martin had totally ignored his pleas for caution, and had behaved like a man playing a hunch at a gambling table. Martin took the line that everyone was bound to give way in the end – hardly the behaviour one expected from Canada, given their traditional policy of keeping in line with America and with Britain. Dixon accused Martin of gambling on Russian unpredictability which, as it had turned out, saved him. Dixon believed that America and France were the real losers on the membership issue, the Russians the winners. The Soviet campaign to woo the uncommitted States with "smooth words and assumed friendliness" had been a certain success, especially with the Arabs.

In Washington there was only despair, for this had been a spectacular diplomatic defeat. Throughout the 1955 General Assembly press criticism had been ferocious and both the State Department and diplomats in the US mission in New York had been condemned – for incompetence, for wavering, quibbling, and clumsy diplomacy. Behaviour over the UN membership issue was described as cowardly. The delegation had blundered into a Soviet trap and over-reacted to right-wing domestic pressure. Diplomats were seen to zig-zag aimlessly while Russia held close the ace of Japan. The Americans were left with the deuce of Outer Mongolia. Lodge was roundly criticised for voting against inscription of the

Cyprus question on the Assembly agenda, for having argued that Cyprus was isolated from other colonial issues. America was accused of putting military expediency and old ties with Britain above ethical and legal requirements. America was losing power while the Arab-Asian groups were forming a bloc supported by a growing defection by the Latin-American countries.

The membership fiasco led America to question her UN role seriously. The only cause for congratulation was the success in keeping out the Communist Chinese. Another fourteen years elapsed before America lost the vote and China was admitted to the UN.

The British optimism expressed by Ambassador Pierson Dixon in 1955 was short-lived. By 1957 the British undertook UN appraisal and of paramount concern was the changing role of the Secretary General. Hammarskjöld had taken the office of Secretary General from one of international administration to world statesman. They were wary of his increasing power and in secret began to look for his successor. They thought Lester Pearson, the Canadian statesman who came up with the idea of the first international peacekeeping force, to be a good choice but they soon faced the reality that the Americans, and even the French, were in favour of keeping Hammarskjöld.

British diplomats gave up the search, kept their reservations to themselves and on September 26, 1957 the General Assembly unanimously re-elected Hammarskjöld to a second five-year term. Hammarskjöld was not surprised. It was obvious that the Big Five dare not risk conflict over a successor. As to whether or not he should accept, he had no choice. His guidance was from a higher authority than the Security Council. He was prepared for this burden. Although seen as remote and inaccessible by many, Hammarskjöld was popular among the staff. He was particularly well liked by the peacekeepers; the blue berets appreciated his presence when, as was his custom, he visited them at Christmas. Later, when the Hammarskjöld myth developed, there was a conviction that his term of office was a bright and shining moment, like the presidency of John F. Kennedy, though he served for more than eight years.

The British were never enthusiastic about him. In 1955 Ambassador Dixon predicted that Hammarskjöld ran a serious risk of burning his fingers over some controversial question.

Hammarskjöld increasingly played a leading political role and held press conferences at which he expressed himself fairly freely. He organised private Security Council lunches each month at which he would raise matters as he wished with members.

Hammarskjöld's own ideas about his role were made clear in his acceptance speech after re-election in 1957. He said that the Secretary General possessed the right under the Charter to act without the guidance of either the General Assembly or the Security Council for his duty was, with the Charter as his guide, to try to ensure the world's peace and security. It was a turning point. Hammarskjöld had endowed the office with the power to act independently. Some time after his acceptance speech, he spoke of preventive diplomacy: he would be available as a neutral representative of the UN which would allow him to negotiate quietly within the framework of the Charter. By the end of 1957 Hammarskjöld had reversed the original concept upon which the UN was based – that of collective security by the great powers. In its place was the UN as third party.

Hammarskjöld, working from his thirty-eighth floor Mount Olympus, became "Mr UN" and was widely considered a man of greatness. His physical energy and his profound learning were much admired. He travelled all over the world – there were few nations he did not visit, few Heads of State he did not meet. For Hammarskjöld, Africa was a special challenge. He toured the continent in late 1959, visited twenty-four countries, territories and regions. He believed the development of Africa to be the international community's greatest test. Only with help from the UN did Africa stand a chance of survival. He wanted to keep the emerging African nations from the Cold War and wanted aid channeled through the UN – not given bilaterally in order to exert influence.

In May, 1960 Hammarskjöld wrote to the Prime Minister of Somalia, Abdullah Issa, about his country's imminent need for UN assistance. Hammarskjöld was planning to visit Mogadishu after the country's independence in July. An uprising in the Congo changed his plans.

Within weeks of its independence on June 30, 1960, the Congo had exploded into civil war. The size of Western Europe, it was a country rich in minerals which over the years had brought tremendous wealth to its Belgian masters. But the Congo was ill-prepared for the challenge of freedom: there were no trained personnel or technicians for government and no infrastructure and yet the likelihood of trouble in this new country was never adressed.

Serious trouble occurred almost at once, when, on July 5 the armed forces mutinied because of the failure of the new government to Africanise the officer corps: there were 1,000 Belgian officers in the 25,000 strong Armée Nationale Congolaise. Civilians fled in panic and Europeans were killed by mutineers. Many fled the country leading to a breakdown in public services. Thousands of Belgian airborne troops were flown in to protect the white population. The violence intensified and resulted in a mass exodus of all embassies and virtually all the country's administrators. Law and order collapsed. On July 11, the richest province of all, Katanga, broke away and came under the control of Moise Tshombe who seconded Belgian officers to lead his provincial army and it seemed as though European control of the Congo was set to continue and independence circumvented. In desperation, the weak Congolese government asked the UN for help to get rid of the Belgian troops of which there were now around 10,000. There was fierce fighting between the Belgians and the Congolese Army. Ralph Bunche, the Secretary General's special representative in Leopoldville, wired Dag Hammarskjöld in New York saying that in his opinion only the force of a third party could save the situation. They needed a UN army. British Prime Minister Harold MacMillan was of the opinion that the best hope of excluding Communist influence in the Congo was to rely on the UN.

The UN operation for the Congo was the largest so far and was christened ONUC – the Organisation des Nations Unies au Congo. Bunche was convinced that the only way to restore calm was the withdrawal of Belgian troops and their replacement by UN troops. Both superpowers voted for it – Britain, France and Nationalist China abstained. With almost unbelievable speed, never matched by the UN ever again, Hammarskjöld assembled the world's largest international army – more than 20,000 soldiers from eighteen countries who had to be transported and equipped. It was a tremendous challenge and extraordinarily efficient. The first UN troops arrived in Leopoldville thirty-six hours after the Resolution was voted through the Council. The war in the Congo was a forerunner of the troubles which confronted the UN some thirty years later in Somalia and Yugoslavia.

The Congolese government was in disarray with two unpredictable leaders. Prime Minister Lumumba was courted by the Soviets, and President Joseph Kasavubu by the Americans; both were caught in a power struggle and both had different ideas about what the newly arrived UN force was supposed to do. Hammarskjöld and Bunche laid down the principle that the UN would not try to influence the outcome between the factions. The Belgians stalled, refusing to remove their troops from Katanga. The Belgian military presence compounded the fears of the already suspicious Lumumba and he wanted the Belgians out and the UN troops to crush the secessionists in Katanga. When this failed to happen, he asked the Soviets for help, for transport planes and trucks. Moscow met his requests. But disagreements with Congo's Head of State, Joseph Kasavubu, led to Lumumba's dismissal in September. Later that month, with the help of American agents, Colonel Joseph Mobutu, in an army coup, took over the country. Mobuto closed all Soviet Bloc embassies whose personnel, under UN escort, were taken to the airport and flown home. It was little more than two months since the UN intervention had been authorised.

The civil war in the Congo turned the 1960 General Assembly into a circus. By the time the Soviet Premier Nikita Khrushchev arrived in New York in September, Soviet diplomats were openly hostile to Hammarskjöld whom they accused of having done the colonialists' dirty work. The Khrushchev visit is remembered for his banging his shoe at Prime Minister Harold Macmillan, but he made UN history in a much more fundamental way. In a speech lasting two and a half hours, Khrushchev called for the removal of the UN from America. He wanted the post of Secretary General abolished and replaced by a troika, a collective executive body of three representing the West, the Socialist States and the non-aligned.

Later on Khrushchev made another and more abusive speech, personally attacking Hammarskjöld, telling member states that he would have to go. There was no room in the UN for a man who violated the elementary principles of justice. People believed that the onslaught was a Soviet bid for the friendship of the UN members, all sixteen new African States. It was a way for Khrushchev to prove to the Communist world that he could bend the Western-dominated UN to his will.

Hammarskjöld was defiant and said that by resigning he would be throwing the UN to the winds. He would not compromise the office of Secretary General. His own speech was dramatic:

> I have a responsibility to all those member states for which the
> organisation is of decisive importance . . . It is not the Soviet
> Union, or indeed any other big power which need the UN for
> their protection. It is all the others. In this sense, the organ-
> isation is first of all their organisation and I deeply believe . . .

He did not finish. His words were drowned in a wave of applause, a
roar of approval throughout which Khrushchev, who remained
seated, pounded the table with his fist, a broad grin on his face.

But applause was one thing and, in fact, in the winter of 1960
there were few delegates willing to speak in his defence and
Hammarskjöld's prestige and acceptability deteriorated as Third
World leaders – Nehru (India), Tito (Yugoslavia), Sukarno
(Indonesia) and Nkrumah (Ghana) tried to find a compromise
arrangement for the Secretary Generalship. Hammarskjöld could
no longer mediate between East and West. Adding to the gloom was
bankruptcy. Despite the massive operation established by the UN in
the Congo, the only provision for its financing was, at the Secretary
General's suggestion, a voluntary fund of $100 million. Four months
after the collection began, no more than $13 million was pledged by
member states. This non-payment built one more fault-line into the
UN system.

The Congo crisis overshadowed all other events and, in attempts to
keep the Cold War out of Africa it was impossible to avoid hostility:
the actions of the UN troops created a storm of criticism and abuse,
and the UN was accused of either showing too little vigour or of
exceeding its authority. In January 1961 Patrice Lumumba was
kidnapped and with two of his associates was taken to Elizabethville
in Katanga province and murdered by Tshombe's soliders. The
murder was widely assumed to have been encouraged by CIA agents
whose orders were to get rid of a Communist stooge. There was
uproar and a violent demonstration in the Security Council's public
gallery. The murder was a crime for which the Soviets held
Hammarskjöld responsible. It was a critical turning point. The
Soviets argued that the UN should have protected Lumumba
against his Congolese enemies, even though he voluntarily left the
UN-protected residence in Leopoldville to drum up support

elsewhere. In February, 1961 the Soviet Union withdrew formal recognition of Hammarskjöld and labelled him an accomplice and organiser of the murder.

Hammarskjöld's most quoted defence was a lecture to Congregation at Oxford University on May 30, 1961 in which he described how the Charter laid down basic rules of international ethics to which all members should be committed. The Charter was the first step towards an organised international community. "As in national life, the principle of justice must be considered applicable in international matters . . . one standard valid for the strong as well as for the weak." The UN's Secretary General should never compromise the UN's aims and principles.

By the Spring 1961, the Soviets realised that there was no support for replacing the post of Secretary General with a troika. Neither were the Africans nor the Asians too keen. The Prime Minister of New Zealand, Walter Nash, was instrumental in persuading the Indian Premier Jawaharlal Nehru against the idea. The President of Ghana, Kwame Nkrumah suggested three deputy Secretaries General. The idea never materialised. As the 1961 General Assembly approached, it was clear that without a dramatic change in world affairs, Hammarskjöld would never be re-elected. In the Secretariat, action was paralysed as Hammarskjöld awaited renewed Soviet insults.

In August 1961, in conformity with a Council Resolution passed in February which turned the peacekeepers into peace enforcers, the UN troops began to round up mercenaries. The Resolution authorised the UN to take all appropriate measures to prevent civil war, including "the use of force, if necessary, in the last resort". It called for the withdrawal of all foreign military personnel and political advisers. Mercenaries were the backbone of Tshombe's army. Tshombe was armed from Europe with hundreds of seconded Belgian officers in addition to mercenaries. He remained hostile to the Congo's Central government and to the UN. On August 28, a UN operation for evacuating foreign military personnel was begun and UN troops rounded up several hundred Europeans. A series of terrorist attacks by Tshombe's forces created a wave of 35,000 refugees who looked to the UN for protection stretching the mission's already meagre resources. There were attacks against UN personnel, arson at a UN garage and sniping at UN soldiers. The UN resumed the rounding-up of mercenaries but the lightly armed troops had no means of countering Tshombe's forces. Heavy fighting ensued in which the conduct of the UN troops was constantly criticised: their force was depleted and several governments had withdrawn contingents. Among the remaining troops there was no unity between the different nationalities. Lack of command led to loss of control between soldiers from Sweden, Ireland, Ghana and Tunisia, some of whom had no military experience. Against this background of mounting violence Hammarskjöld, determined to silence the chorus of criticism, decided that he himself would meet Tshombe to obtain a ceasefire and to unite the war-torn country. Because of the fighting he flew to Ndola in Rhodesia, now Zimbabwe, to meet with the breakaway leader. Brian Urquhart, who was to become one of the best-known UN officials, believes that after meeting Tshombe, Hammarskjöld would have resigned.

Hammarskjöld was killed on the way. The news of the plane crash came over the radio in New York on Monday morning, September 18, 1961. There was silence in the Secretariat. "Never before has this house been so full of quiet sadness and never before have we had so little to say to each other," a member of staff wrote.

Hammarskjöld's plane, a DC-6B owned by a Swedish company operating under charter to the UN, crashed near Ndola while turning to its landing approach. All four engines were developing power at impact. The aircraft's wheels and flaps were lowered but the plane brushed the trees of the forest four miles west of the airport; its left wing eventually touched the ground, it cartwheeled and disintegrated in a ball of flame. The assumption that the Secretary General had been murdered was immediate. The Soviets thought that Tshombe, supported by the British and by Sir Roy Welensky, Prime Minister of Rhodesia and Nyasaland, was probably to blame. A UN Investigation Commission reached no firm conclusion. The damage to the aircraft was extensive. Only a small percentage of it was scientifically examined and there was little forensic evidence owing to lack of expertise. The enquiry concluded that neither mechanical failure, pilot error nor sabotage could be ruled out. But suspicion remains. Radio contact with Hammarskjöld's plane was lost just before its landing but no search was undertaken until the following morning. No systematic investigation was made of the wreckage, security at the site was deficient and there was an extraordinary degree of carelessness in the investigation. A Rhodesian enquiry conducted four months later by the Governor-General, the Earl of Dalhousie, quickly concluded the accident to have been owing to pilot error.

Rumour and conjecture continue and the most likely conspirators are considered to be Katanga's white mercenaries who hated the UN. Ndola was the launch pad for mercenaries into Katanga and in UN headquarters there were fears about holding a meeting there. If peace negotiations had been successful the mercenaries would have been out of work. Several former mercenaries have claimed that they shot Hammarskjöld although they have alleged preposterous circumstances. In 1992, thirty-one years later, two former UN officials, George Ivan Smith and Conor Cruise O'Brien, claimed publicly they knew the accident to have been murder and that at the time of the crash there was talk of two aircraft in the sky. The two revealed that European industrialists, who controlled the resource-rich Katanga province, sent an aircraft to intercept Hammarskjöld before he met Tshombe so they could attempt to persuade him that continued white control was imperative for Africa's stability. A warning shot was fired to divert his plane which caused it to crash. In 1992 such certainty made some impact. In Stockholm a retired Swedish diplomat was appointed to look at the claims which he later dismissed for lack of evidence.

The 1961 General Assembly began with a one-minute silence and the first meeting was set aside for tributes to Hammarskjöld. His *Annual Report* became his political testament. In it he outlined two views: either the UN was a conference machinery served by a Secretariat or it was a dynamic instrument which itself sought reconciliation. He believed in the latter, thinking that only a dynamic organisation could meet the needs of a world of increasing international interdependence. The UN was more than the sum of its parts – it possessed an elusive spirit.

On 28 September there was a memorial service for Hammarskjöld and the other victims killed with him. It was held in the General Assembly and took the form of the UN day concert in which Hammarskjöld had always taken the greatest interest. When it came to the customary address of the Secretary General, they broadcast the address he made the previous year and the Assembly members sat like stone: "No matter how deep the shadows may be, how sharp the conflict . . . we are not permitted to forget that we have too much in common . . . too much that we might lose together . . . for succeeding generations, ever to weaken in our efforts . . . "

It had been Hammarskjöld's idea to have Beethoven's *Ninth*

Symphony performed each October 24. Hammarskjöld believed it appropriate because the symphony reflected the Charter; like the Charter the symphony was an enormous confession of faith in the "victorious human spirit and in brotherhood". Although the symphony opened with dark threats and harsh conflict, a single human voice is raised in rejection. There is eventually reconciliation and joy and a dreamed kingdom of peace. The final hymn of praise was a reaffirmation that the struggle for a peaceful world would endure.

5. THE RED BOOK

The UN was devised in the summer and autumn of 1944 at a lavish American country house, Dumbarton Oaks, on a beautiful private estate near Washington DC, far away from the war. Before settling down to the arduous task, the diplomats and officials decided to go to New York for an evening's entertainment. To no one's surprise, the un-smiling Andrei Gromyko, leader of the Soviet delegation, turned down the chance but the others had a thoroughly good time; they started with an excellent dinner and then went to the Radio City Music Hall to see the Rockettes. Afterwards the distinguished group was taken back-stage to meet the chorus girls. A Soviet general made a quick speech of thanks and said he thought this must be true democracy. Gladwyn Jebb, then a counsellor at the British Foreign Office would remember it all in his memoirs; he thought that the Rockettes were intelligent and charming.

At Dumbarton Oaks the meetings were not without acrimony but over several months a blueprint for peace was agreed. It was here that the allied powers, representing Russia, Britain, China and America came up what they hoped would be a watertight system of security to ensure world peace. Along with a General Assembly open to all there would be a Security Council which would have restricted membership and it was the Council which would have prime responsibility for international security, a crucial element in the planned New World Order. The Council would be empowered to take enforcement action. It would determine threats to international peace and would require governments to put at its disposal a UN army, with troops and airpower provided by member states. It was agreed at Dumbarton Oaks that the Allied-powers would retain their status within the Council by each having a veto, a special vote. The veto was considered recognition of a reality: the organisation could not be used against the will of any of the great powers. The guarantee of peace was based on the combined military powers of the wartime alliance.

The veto power caused many problems during the long hours of debate at Dumbarton Oaks. Andrei Gromyko wanted broad use of it and insisted that it be applicable to the Council agenda; he wanted to be able to prevent discussion of a dispute and was absolutely insistent that great power unanimity be inviolable. If a matter of peace and security were to be discussed against the wishes of the great powers the relationship among them would be exposed to strain. The Americans were unconvinced. Restricting the freedom of discussion in the Council would make a farce of the UN idea. No consensus was reached on the question. Neither was there agreement over Gromyko's demand that membership of the UN be given to sixteen of the Soviet Union's Republics. At Dumbarton Oaks, although no one seems to have doubted that the Soviets were sincere, it appeared as though they were not quite as sincere as everyone else. Afterwards, Stalin was enthusiastic enough to announce that nine-tenths of the post-war security problems were solved at Dumbarton Oaks in a spirit of unanimity. President Roosevelt announced that the proposed UN was the major objective of the war.

The following year the unanimity was gone. The UN's founding conference in the spring 1945 was overshadowed by the deterioration in the Soviet-American relationship. The United Nations Conference on International Organisation, which took place between April 25 and June 26 in San Francisco almost collapsed. Not everyone was ready to blame the Russians. There was some considerable shock when America insisted that Argentina be admitted as a founding member; Argentina was a Nazi ally, a military dictatorship. The magazine *Time* was outraged at America's gall, accusing Truman of playing a power game in Latin America as amoral as Russia's in Eastern Europe. I. F. Stone wrote in *Nation* that some members of the American delegation at San Francisco seemed to be using the conference to organise an anti-Soviet bloc. In defence of the decision the Secretary of War, Henry Stimson said that it was hardly asking too much for America to have her own region, if

Russia were "going to take these steps . . . of building up friendly protectorates around her".

The most bitter issue was over Poland. The war-time alliance was fracturing about the very country over which Britain and France had gone to war in 1939. Poland was not represented at San Francisco and the argument between East and West was who should sit in Poland's empty conference seat. The Soviets wanted the government which had been set up in Warsaw to come to San Francisco, the pro-communist Polish Committee of National Liberation, and a Soviet creation. The US would not issue an invitation to this government and was continuing to insist on free Polish elections in accordance with the Yalta agreement of February 1945. Poland was a special ally and merited special treatment. At Yalta, Roosevelt had been conscious of America's Polish electorate: there were an estimated seven million Americans of Polish origin. Polish pilots were revered by the British; they were among the heroes of the Battle of Britain. A Polish army had fought in the war as part of the British armies. In London there was a Polish government-in-exile.

In Poland itself power over the people had moved directly from the German Nazi army to Soviet control. Over Poland the Soviets would not budge. The Soviet Foreign Minister, Vyacheslav Molotov, insisted that the Warsaw government be invited to San Francisco otherwise he would withdraw the Soviet delegation altogether.

Molotov arrived in San Francisco straight from a first meeting with Truman who had assumed office only days before after the unexpected death of Roosevelt on April 12, 1945. Molotov would remember the first meeting with Truman; he said later that he had never in his life been "spoken to like that". Truman gave Molotov a lecture; he was in possession of reports from Warsaw of the arrests of anti-Communists, deportations and shootings. Truman had been adivsed to take a harder line with the Soviets. The Secretary of the Navy, James Forrestal, had warned the President that the Soviet intention in Poland was to spread the grip, to overrun Eastern Europe. Truman assured Forrestal he would tell Molotov "in words of one syllable" that unless the Russians stopped dragging their feet over free elections in Poland, in accordance with Yalta, then the Senate would refuse to ratify the UN Charter.

Stalin's response came the very next day. "Such conditions must be recognised unusual [sic], when two governments – those of the

United States and Great Britain – beforehand settle with the Polish questions in which the Soviet Union is first of all and most of all interested and put the government of the USSR in an unbearable position trying to dictate to it their demands". Stalin considered the interests of the Western powers in Eastern Europe unwarranted interference; he believed in a mutually agreed sphere of influence worked out with President Roosevelt and Churchill at Yalta. On May 3, sixteen Polish underground leaders loyal to Polish leaders in London who had gone to Moscow to negotiate, were arrested by the Russians but in San Francisco they papered over these ugly cracks. The Secretary of State Edward Stettinius began to stress the fundamental unity upon which the work at San Francisco was firmly based. It was clear that sometime during the UN's founding conference Truman realised that were the US to refuse to budge over Poland it would be the end of the new UN. So, in the end, delegates in San Francisco agreed a motion affirming the hope that a new and representative Polish government would soon be formed. Some said this was the start of UN hypocrisy. Anthony Eden thought the wartime alliance all too obviously unravelling, but, as British Foreign Secretary and chairman of the British delegation in San Francisco, he kept such thoughts to himself.

The UN was created against a background of acrimony. Even while the set designer was choosing the right shade of blue for the UN stage, American negotiators realised that the New World Organisation would not be capable of doing what it was set up to do, to enforce world peace. The interest of the Soviets in the idea seemed to be on the wane. Molotov was not even going to attend San Francisco using the pretext of a meeting of the Supreme Soviet. It was only after the US Ambassador in Moscow, Averell Harriman, spoke to Stalin that Molotov changed his mind and went to the founding conference.

Although there was substantial agreement at Dumbarton Oaks, at San Francisco the debate continued about the power of the veto. Gromyko dug in his heels. At San Francisco Gromyko was the acting Chairman of the Soviet delegation and he remained convinced that the veto must be used to prevent debate of an issue of international peace and security. They settled it in Moscow. Harry Hopkins, who had been Roosevelt's senior adviser was sent on a mission of reconciliation and, on June 6, 1945, at the last of several meetings with Stalin, Hopkins raised the issue. At first Stalin did not grasp the question and after a few moments Stalin turned to Molotov to say he did not think the point significant. Stalin said that the American view should prevail. Stalin quite clearly did not understand the issue which had not been explained to him. This meeting was considered further proof of the lack of interest by Stalin in the New World Order. Apparently, Stalin's hopes for the post-war world lay outside the UN.

At Dumbarton Oaks, the UN's architects gave extraordinary powers to the Security Council. The Council was to command the obedience of every UN member state; every UN member was under an obligation to accept a Council ruling, even when decisions involved the use of force. Of eleven Council members, amended to fifteen members in 1963, six would rotate every two years. The other five would be the permanent members who alone had a veto. No important UN action could be initiated without the Big Five.

If at San Francisco the great powers believed that the smaller powers would accept this arrangement, they had a rude awakening. A total 12,000 amendments to the Charter blueprint were submitted; sailors had to be drafted to collate them. An anti-veto campaign was orchestrated by Australia's Foreign Minister, Herbert Vere Evatt. Evatt was indefatigable. He resented the power retained by the permanent members and gave up only when it was clear that without the veto, there would be no UN at all. Evatt even sought a compromise and suggested that the General Assembly be given the right to recommend issues to the Council for discussion. Evatt found himself up against Gromyko's disdain. Gromyko described Australia, New Zealand and Canada as "rude nations who made themselves look silly with their torrent of words against veto power". Gromyko turned aside the pleas of both major and minor delegates looking for a way to concede some power to the Assembly. Gromyko told everyone who lobbied that should the Australians get their way, the Soviets would refuse to sign the Charter. The Earl of Halifax, a member of the British delegation, was so impressed with Gromyko's obstinacy that he told Gromyko that he finally understood how the Soviets held Stalingrad.

It was high noon. In Moscow on June 19, Ambassador Averell Harriman told Stalin that some power would have to be devolved to the General Assembly and that if the Soviets continued to hold out, then the Americans would go ahead and sign the Charter without them. The Soviets eventually compromised on a face-saving formula whereby the Assembly could make recommendations on a dispute, unless that dispute was already under active consideration by the Security Council.

In the end Stalin probably thought that membership of the UN was the best option and it was a way to avoiding the stigma of non-participation. The UN would be an ancillary instrument of Soviet foreign policy; it was after all only a facade covering the domination of the world by the superpowers.

The Charter of the United Nations was officially and unanimously adopted on 25 June, 1945 when, after taking the vote, the delegates and audience had risen to their feet and cheered. The Charter treaty was signed the following day and brilliantly coloured flags of fifty nations draped from gilded flagpoles were the backdrop for the ceremomy. The Charter was in hand-tooled blue leather and the new emblem of the UN rose behind the glorious scene in a sky of pale blue.

Some of those present believed that UN was created on illusion. Others believed it a plot. The US was foolish to accept that the Soviets would co-operate. Others thought the UN could help to bridge the East-West gap. Some thought international co-operation was now a certainty. Soon everything changed.

On August 6, 1945 two days before the US formally deposited its instrument of ratification, America dropped the first atomic bomb on Hiroshima, South Honshu Island, Japan. Within a minute nearly 100,000 were dead and another 100,000 injured and thousands dying slowly from radiation poisoning. The bomb destroyed three-quarters of the city and perfected the World War Two barbarity of the mass killing by bombing civilians as part of the conduct of war. While the founding conference of the UN had been taking place in San Francisco, back in Washington there were discussions about where to drop the bomb.

In June, some of the Manhattan Project scientists had asked that a demonstration be given to the UN; they wanted the bomb placed under UN authority and that America should consider using the bomb only on UN approval. This was rejected. The bomb would be useful not just in the defeat of Japan but would intimidate the Soviets. A month before the Charter was signed, the Secretary of War, Henry Stimson, advised Truman that if the proper use of the weapons could be solved, "we should then have the opportunity to bring the world into a pattern in which the peace of the world and our civilisation can be saved". The New World Order was not designed by diplomats at San Francisco but by scientists working secretly in Chicago, Oak Ridge, Hanford and Los Alamos. The UN's founding conference was compared to the preparations some little girls might make for a tea party.

There were good intentions. Three weeks before the bomb was dropped the Truman administration debated about whether or not to tell Stalin. Two days before the first atomic test took place in July 1945 he was given a bare outline and told that the US had developed a powerful new weapon, though Stalin probably knew as early as 1942 about the work being done in the US nuclear research laboratory. Russian diplomats were told that America planned to place control of atomic weapons in the hands of the UN.

The notion of international control was old as the bomb itself and many scientists working on the Manhattan project had discussed the formation of an international agency to control the weapon to avoid a weapons race between nations. A month after the bombs were dropped, a petition signed by sixty-four scientists was given to Truman urging him to share the secret. The scientists believed that since the weapon had evolved from the application of widely known scientific laws, given time, any industrial nation would be able make the bomb. Stimson, who from the very beginning supervised the project, warned President Truman that "thoroughgoing rights of inspection" would be needed and "international control as we have never heretofore contemplated". Stimson cautioned Truman that hanging on to secrets was dangerous; the US should offer to stop all work on the nuclear weapons as long as any similar projects were halted elsewhere. All nations should agree a mutual arrest in further bomb construction and agree to collaborate on the development of atomic power for peaceful purposes.

Others thought differently. The new Secretary of State, Jimmy Byrnes, recently appointed by Truman, believed that too much emphasis was placed on the views of the scientists, and in April 1945 told Truman that the bomb might well put America in a position of power at the end of the war. The Joint Chiefs of Staff and others in the Pengaton had no faith in UN control: it would be handing over the country's most powerful weapon to an unproved organisation whose success depended on Moscow. The Secretary of the Navy worried about trusting the Russians: they were "Oriental" in their thinking. He wanted the UN to appoint America as world trustee of atomic information: in return Washington would only use the bomb according to directions from the UN. The idea never came to fruition. On October 8, 1945 Truman announced that the Atomic bomb would not be surrendered: it was the only means of countering Russian strength in Europe. Truman said that possession of the bomb was a sacred trust which the US would respect until such times as international control could be achieved. The President was partly persuaded that Russian spies had penetrated the Allied atomic project. As for the Allies, the British and Canadians urged him to discuss international control. In London, Prime Minister Clement Attlee's Cabinet believed that only an effective UN could control the use of the weapon.

At a summit meeting in November 1945, President Truman, Clement Attlee and Canada's Mackenzie King adopted a plan to create a special UN commission which would devise enforceable safeguards for the application of atomic energy. The commission, comprising the Big Five together with Canada, would investigate the best way of ensuring the elimination of all atomic weapons. A committee of inspection would have the right to look at any laboratory engaged in atomic research. It sounded fine, but it was cautious and made no mention of America's existing weapons. On that score Truman said that no country would give away the "locks and bolts necessary to protect a house" unless the community were stable and the police force reliable. The Soviets retaliated with a forceful declaration which accused the US and Britain of forming an anti-Russian bloc. Nonetheless, Jimmy Byrnes, on a visit to Moscow, secured agreement from the Russians that a UN Atomic Energy Commission be created.

The very first Resolution which the General Assembly passed on January 24, 1946 was to create a UN Atomic Energy Commission. It was the peak of international co-operation and it was down-hill from then on. The Commission was intended to be under the direction of the Council. It was to formulate and submit to the Security Council plans for eliminating atomic weapons, setting up regulations and safeguards, and assuring the use of atomic energy for peaceful purposes only.

The first meeting of the Commission was held on June 14, 1946 when the US submitted a plan providing for an international authority which would exercise a monopoly over the ownership, production and research for peaceful purposes of all atomic material. Atomic weapons would be prohibited and a system of inspection would be instituted. But only when adequate controls were in place would the US destroy its stockpile of weapons and turn over to the international authority the secret of the scientific process. Under this plan the US would decide when it stopped manufacturing the bombs and the proposal was viewed as cynical without the slightest chance of acceptance by the Soviet Union. The Soviets had their own ideas. They wanted the destruction of all existing weapons – before the discussion of control. Andrei Gromyko flatly rejected an earlier American suggestion that this particular UN commission be exempt from the great power veto.

The debate dragged on. The Soviet Union's rejection of the US plan came as no surprise; nor did America's rejection of the Soviet Union's plan and soon it was too late for co-operation. By the end of 1946, the great powers gave up on trying to find a foolproof scheme for controls and from now on the discussion was mostly rhetorical. In 1949 the Soviets tested their own bomb which was between three and six years ahead of Washington intelligence estimates. The result was a decision to increase the US stockpile of atomic bombs. Early in 1950 the Soviets walked out of a Commission meeting, part of the general Soviet protest demonstration at the failure to admit the Communist government in Peking to the UN.

For the UN it was bleak. The Joint Chiefs warned Truman that increasing Russian expansion was the greatest threat to the US and that the US should not place undue reliance on the UN to guarantee peace and security. In Canada, in February 1946, twenty-two suspects were arrested under suspicion of having stolen information on the atomic bomb for the Soviets. The FBI Director, J. Edgar Hoover, told a Senate Committee that the Russians had managed to obtain secret information on the bomb. "There is no doubt", *Time* magazine commented, "that Russian Communism holds a peculiar attraction for some scientists and technicians." A further warning came from Moscow itself. At the end of the month a US Chargé d'Affaires at the American embassy, George Kennan, wrote a long appraisal of the motives behind Soviet behaviour. Kennan had been posted to Moscow in the 1930s and did not forget the fanatacism he had seen then. Returning to Moscow in 1944, he found himself at odds with the American policy of co-operation with Stalin. In February 1946,

Kennan was asked by the State Department for his opinion and he composed an 8,000-word telegram in which he warned that Russian nationalism, under the cloak of Marxism, was more dangerous than ever and predicted Russian expansion would be America's greatest diplomatic headache. Peaceful coexistence between the capitalist and socialist camps was impossible because the Soviets were determined to use all their power to strengthen the Socialist camp, and to weaken the capitalists. The Soviets believed that Capitalism would eventually collapse. Kennan wrote that Stalin was the last in a long succession of "cruel and wasteful Russian rulers" who needed increasing military power to guarantee security for a weak régime.

The reaction to the Kennan memo in Washington was in Kennan's own words, "nothing less than sensational". President Truman read it, and the State Department sent Kennan a message of commendation. The memo crystallised their thinking; Forrestal insisted the Kennan document become required reading for thousands of serving officers. It was a milestone. There would be tougher attitudes.

The Security Council's first complaint was against the Soviet Union and it involved neither Poland nor the division of Germany, but Iran and her oil wealth. During the war, Soviet troops were stationed in northern Iran to protect the oil fields – and to stop the strategically located country from falling into the hands of the Nazis. British troops were stationed in southern Iran and Allied control provided a guaranteed route for American supplies into Russia. The agreement under which both the British and Soviet troops were stationed provided that both Allies would respect the independence of Iran and would withdraw six months after hostilities ended. The British prepared to withdraw in the summer, 1945. The Soviets did not and, in November 1945, they were suspected of trying to retain control of the province of Azerbaijan in northern Iran where a liberation movement was receiving Soviet support. On January 9, 1946 an American diplomat in Tabriz, the capital of East Azerbaijan, warned that unless there was energetic action to remove the Soviet troops, "Azerbaijan must be written off".

Oil was the issue. Before the British withdrew her troops, Britain and Iran agreed to set up a joint Anglo-Iranian oil company to exploit oil exploration in the south – Iran produced more oil in 1945 than the rest of the Arab nations together. Stalin wanted a similar oil concession but the Iranian Government, under Western pressure, refused. Middle East diplomats believed the Soviets were after both security for their adjacent oil region from which they drew eighty per cent of their oil, and also wanted a share in Middle East oil. The West had fabulous holdings in Iran, Arabia and Iraq. For the US, the failure of the Soviet Union to withdraw from northern Iran was a serious strategic problem; the US wanted no great power established in the Persian Gulf, in range of her petroleum development in Saudi Arabia. When the Russian pull-out from northern Iran failed to materialise at the end of 1945, it was assumed by both British and the US embassies in Tehran that the Soviets were aiming eventually for a secure outlet on the Persian Gulf – and complete control of Iranian oil. Sir Frank Roberts, the British ambassador in Moscow, warned that the Soviet Union considered the Middle East rather like an artichoke, whose leaves were to be eaten one by one.

In northern Iran the Soviets were assisting the revival of the Persian Communist Party and supporting Turkish-speaking Azerbaijani minorities against the Tehran government. Under the protection of Soviet occupying forces, a local Azerbaijan left-wing government was established which increasingly disputed Iranian control. In December 1945 Stalin was warned by Jimmy Byrnes that unless Soviet troops were withdrawn Iran would complain to the UN, and America was bound to support her.

The crisis got to the Security Council eventually, but not without opposition. The Secretary General, Trygve Lie, thought discreet diplomacy would have been preferable and bilateral negotiations between Iran and the Soviets were not yet exhausted. The British thought it unwise to have open discussion at the UN about a matter which was nothing more than a failure of the Big Three – the US, USSR and Great Britain – to agree. Britain tried to persuade Iran not to go to Council with her complaint but Iran, through Ambassador Jussein Ala, declared the prestige of the UN to be at stake. After all, the UN was created to protect small states against aggression.

At its very first meeting the Security Council dealt with procedural matters. The meeting was held in Church House, close to Westminster Abbey on 17 January, 1946. Two days later, the Council received the complaint from Iran. At subsequent meetings the Council turned into a theatre for the Cold War, a place for East-West brawling. For the Soviets, the accusation against her submitted by

Iran betrayed the spirit of great power unity which lay behind the UN's creation. The Soviets maintained that in accordance with the Charter member states should settle disputes by direct negotiation – the Soviet Union was perfectly willing to do this over Iran.

These first Security Council meetings crystallised Soviet attitudes and, in his memoirs, Gromyko described what happened as a "murky wave of anti-Soviet feeling". The Soviets answered the Iranian complaint by countering with complaints of their own, and wrote to the Secretary General about the continuing presence of British troops in Greece. The Soviets pointed to the plight of the Azerbaijani who wanted autonomy from a bourgeois, landowning dictatorship. There was poverty, widespread malaria, and a fifty per cent infant death rate. The two per cent landowning class was corrupt.

On January 30, 1946, the Security Council adopted a resolution noting the readiness of the parties to seek a solution by negotiation. However, against Soviet wishes the issue remained on the agenda and the Council called for regular reports about the progress of these bilateral negotiations. On February 19, 1946, the newly appointed Prime Minister of Iran, Qavam es Sultaneh, flew to Moscow to ask the Soviets to conform with the wartime treaty allowing both Soviet and British troops in Iran and said that in accordance with it he wanted Soviet troops withdrawn. The Prime Minister wanted an early March deadline. Stalin made his own demands. He wanted automony for both Azerbaijan and Kurdistan and he wanted oil concessions, as requested in 1944. The Prime Minister pointed out that the consitution of Iran proscribed automony and said that he feared that if Azerbaijan were to be granted automony, other provinces could follow and the central government would lose control. He recalled an Iranian law which forbade discussion of oil concession to a country whose troops were on national territory. Stalin was angry and within days there were reports of Soviet reinforcements into northern Iran to which America's response was the strongest diplomatic rebuke for years; Washington declared that she could not remain "indifferent" to these troop movements.

On March 4, 1946, on the day that the wording of that message was approved, President Truman was preparing to go back to his home state, Missouri, fulfilling an earlier promise to accompany the former British Prime Minister, Winston Churchill, who was to receive an honorary degree from Westminster College, in Fulton. Churchill was to make an acceptance speech on March 5. The first part of his speech concentrated on the UN, called for the World Organisation to become a reality and not a sham, a force for action and not merely a Tower of Babel. The UN should equip an international armed force immediately. "I propose that each of the Powers and States should be invited to delegate a certain number of air squadrons to the service of the world organisation. They would wear the uniform of their own countries but with different badges." Churchill said he had wished to see this done after the First World War. Yet it was only Churchill's central stark comment which everyone remembered: it described an Iron Curtain across the continent of Europe, "from Stettin in the Baltic, to Trieste, in the Adriatic". In grand prose, he told his Fulton audience that a "sad and breathless moment" had been reached in world affairs. Churchill spoke of the League of Nations. "In those days there were high hopes and unbounded confidence that the wars were over, and that the League of Nations would become all-powerful. I do not see or feel that same confidence or even the same hopes in the haggard world at the present time." There would be no prevention of war or a successful UN without an alliance of the English-speaking peoples, a successful relationship between the British Commonwealth and Empire and the US, the only means by which the UN could achieve its full stature and strength. "Beware, I say; time may be short." Communist fifth columns were everywhere and were a growing challenge and peril to civilisation. Churchill described a Red Russia out to conquer the world. "If we adhere faithfully to the Charter of the UN and walk forward in sedate and sober strength seeking no one's land or treasure . . . the high-roads of the future will be clear . . . ", was the end of the speech.

There was speculation that the harsh, anti-Soviet address was to test the American public's response to a get-tough policy but Truman denied advance knowledge of the speech. However Truman's hearty applause on the podium was seen to be greatly significant. Churchill was worried about America's inertia in the face of a Soviet threat to Europe. The speech was not greeted with much enthusiasm in America. The initial popular reaction was that it was inflammatory at a difficult time of post-war adjustment to new power relationships. UN supporters believe that Churchill's suggestion for a special alliance between Britain and the US had cut the throat of the UN and when Churchill passed through New York ten days after the speech, he was picketed by protesters shouting: "Winnie, Winnie, go away, UNO is hear to stay". At the UN there was dismay. The Secretary General wanted the speech repudiated and he visited Britain's Foreign Minister, Ernest Bevin. Bevin would not help for, though he would not admit it publicly, he believed that what Churchill said was true.

The Iranian problem continued to worsen relationships. On March 6, 1946 the State Department was told that heavy Soviet troop movements continued in the direction of Turkey, Iraq and the Iranian capital. Byrnes reported: "Now, we'll give it to them with both barrels".

At the next Security Council meeting, Andrei Gromyko announced that the evacuation of Soviet forces, in accordance with the wartime agreement with Iran, had begun and that total withdrawal would be achieved in five to six weeks. He requested the item be struck from the agenda. His request was turned down, so, declaring he would not take part in the ensuing discussion, on March 27, 1946 he left the chamber – the first time a representative walked out. With the Soviet delegation absent, the Council agreed on a US suggestion that the Secretary General discover from Tehran and Moscow the state of their negotiations about troop withdrawals. Within five days Lie reported that the Russians appeared ready to leave. The Council decided to postpone further discussion, but the US insisted that the item stay on the agenda to keep pressure on Moscow, a symbolic move which was much resented by the Soviets because the Iranians, on 15 April, formally requested that their complaint be withdrawn. The West argued that as long as a threat to the peace persisted it was a legitimate subject for Council attention.

An ensuing wrangle over whether or not the Iranian issue should stay on the agenda was long and complicated and it proved that the Council's own agenda had become symbolic – another problem in the international community's lengthening list. At one point the Secretary General intervened and backed the Soviet view; but the US viewed his behaviour as beyond his authority and became more suspicious than ever about his possible Soviet leanings. As for Gromyko, he was greeted with exasperation. Britain's Ambassador at the time, Sir Alexander Cadogan, complained to London that Gromyko dominated everything. He was the centre of attention "for the swarming photographers, the centre of comment for the journalists and the centre of irritation". Cadogan said that more progress could be made if Gromyko would only stop using the Council's time. They were dancing continually to a Slavic tune.

This first Security Council confrontation was a shock for the Russians. The UN was an irritant and they were embittered by fights in the Council and felt their previous concerns about their minority position to be justified. From now on they would resort to the veto. As for Washington, the withdrawal of Soviet troops from Iran was seen as a success for the State Department's increasingly firm handling of relations with the Soviet Union. The principle of containment, now the cornerstone of American foreign policy, first enunciated by Kennan, was working. But no way was found to tackle the basic problems in Iran, its impoverished people, its unrest and the clash for oil and control. There were no constructive proposals.

When the Secretariat was established in 1945 the Soviet Union did not have anyone to send to New York, and the Soviets failed miserably to take up their quota of Secretariat jobs. In Moscow, there was no one qualified to go: no diplomats or Foreign Service officials with adequate English or international experience. The majority of the Soviet Foreign Ministry's experienced staff had been murdered in the 1930s, thousands of them shot or disappeared in Stalin's purges.

Stalin was suspicious of diplomats. He believed the purpose of a foreign ministry was to take account of the game of nations. There were no permanent friends, only permanent interests. Other tasks could be carried out by his unique network of Communist Party members and secret agents. Even after murdering the brightest and best of the Foreign Service and replacing them with middle-ranking officials, Stalin continued to believe that the diplomatic corps was a nest of spies. Within the ministry the slightest slip led to death or a lifetime within the Arctic Circle.

Professor Grigori Tunkin remembered arriving for work in 1939 at the Foreign Ministry in Moscow and finding it eerily empty. When Tunkin began his career there were only three specialists left in the Ministry's Treaty and Legal Department: one specialist in public international law, a second in private international law and an economist. "All the rest", says Tunkin with no obvious emotion, "were thrown away."

Tunkin ran this department between 1952 and 1965. Like him, most colleagues joined the Ministry inexperienced in the ways of diplomacy. Everyone was conscripted. "I did not want to join the Ministry. I worked in the Academy of Sciences writing a history of state law. I was quite content. I had to join the Ministry because I knew three languages." Andrei Gromyko, the world's longest serving Foreign Minister, was conscripted in this way, originally trained as an agricultural economist.

Today there is a monument to the lost diplomats in Moscow, in the Stalin–gothic Foreign Ministry building which dominates Smolensky Square. The memorial, commissioned after the New Thinking sometime in 1989, is in a corner of the massive lobby, among its shining marble and polished brass. It consists of a rough white marble slab with an ugly crack. Underneath there is an elegant wooden plinth bearing a large book with a red leather cover which contains all the names of those who were purged by Stalin though for many entries the date of death is unknown. On the cover of the book are the words: "To the Memory of Workers of the Diplomat Service – Victims of Repression 1930-1940 and at the Beginning of the 1950s".

The Soviets were unprepared for an international co-operation. Maxim Litvinov, the Deputy Commissar for Foreign Affairs, admitted as much to Iverach Macdonald of *The Times* in June 1945. He said that the actual conduct of Soviet diplomacy was so clumsy that foreign countries had every right to be suspicious. The British Embassy in Moscow agreed. British diplomats considered the Soviet Government extremely badly informed.

The lack of qualified staff from the Soviet bloc was further indication to an already sceptical West that the Soviets did not care for international co-operation. There was speculation that the Soviets might one day pull out of the UN altogether and Western diplomats watched anxiously for clues about whether it was likely. Indeed, so frequent were the rumours of Soviet withdrawal that some thought it amazing that the USSR continued her UN membership. Particularly current were rumours between 1949 and 1952, a period which saw a deterioration in Soviet–UN relations. Indeed, in 1949 the Soviet Union and the satellites began to disengage: the Soviet Union, the Ukraine and Byelorussia left the WHO, Czechoslovakia withdrew from the Food and Agricultural Organisation and in 1950 both Poland and Czechoslovakia abandoned UNESCO. By the time of the historic and dramatic walk-out of the Soviet Ambassador from the Security Council on 10 January, 1950, over the question of Chinese Communist representation, plans were well underway for the creation of a World Peace Council which was deliberately played as an alternative. The Soviet Peace Campaign was designed to be a mass movement of the rank and file. It would represent the "We the Peoples" of the Preamble to the Charter, rather than "ruling circles" which ran the UN. The Secretary General, Trygve Lie, thought Soviet withdrawal almost certain and believed that an alternative UN comprising the Communist states was in preparation. But Stalin stayed, even after he concluded that the UN was an "instrument of aggressive war", even when the UN waged war against Communists in Korea.

Soviet diplomats deny that a complete withdrawal was ever on the cards but confirmation is lost to research for only the Kremlin's archive can reveal the truth. Perhaps the Soviets wished it to be known that they might leave; the threat was a way of showing that even though they were in minority, their views should not be ignored.

Although the public perception was of a Secretariat peppered with Soviet spies, initially the Soviets were so under-represented in the Secretariat that it was an embarrassment. In 1955, with a potential quota of nearly 200 staff jobs, there were only nineteen Soviet nationals and it was not until 1960 that Moscow determined to do something about it. A campaign got underway, introduced by a Soviet woman called Zoya Vailiyevna Mironova, newly appointed to the Secretariat. She was a former chemical engineer and had risen in the party, becoming Deputy Mayor of Moscow. Mironova was successful in that within a few months of her appointment a UN committee of experts was created to try to solve the problem of under-representation. The committee confirmed that whereas the West held seventeen Under Secretary General posts, the Socialist bloc had just one. At middle-management level, known as D2, the West held eighty-three per cent of all available posts. In the Department of Economic and Social Affairs five out of seven directors were from America. Mironova submitted a list of more than 600 candidates to the UN's personnel department which came back with the riposte that only thirteen of these 600 people were adequately qualified for UN work. In 1962, three UN officials spent two months in Moscow with the sole purpose of interviewing candidates proposed for UN work by the Soviet Government. Not one was considered qualified. The Department of Personnel complained of being hampered by a lack of real knowledge about the employment market in the USSR. There were frequent misunderstandings between UN officials and the Soviet authorities. While Moscow stressed the Charter requirement for a wide geographical spread among UN employees, senior UN officials continued to insist that a geographical requirement was less important than the Charter principle of having a staff which was efficient, and was competent – and free from Government pressure.

The Soviet campaign to acquire UN jobs had only slight success: by the end of the 1960s the percentage of Eastern European nationals within the Secretariat had risen only slightly – from 6.6 to 11.8 per cent and by then the UN had 127 member states. Mironova set a precedent. Although many countries exerted pressures of various kinds on the Secretariat, the Soviet Union would go particularly far. Of all the great powers it became the most active in pressing the claims of its nationals, and sometimes even of nationals of other Eastern European states to appoint and to promote.

The year Mironova began her campaign for jobs in the Secretariat was a watershed in the history of the Soviet attitude to the UN. It was 1960 and during the Congo operation there was not a single expert from any Socialist state among the top sixty-five officials. This evident lack of Soviet representation was a major theme of Khrushchev's broadside against Dag Hammarskjöld, and a major dispute between the great powers. In many ways the Congo was the last straw. When Khrushchev came to New York and screamed and shouted and banged his shoe in September, his actions were hardly surprising. By then Soviet diplomats were in the habit of calling the UN the West's convenient tool: an organisation which invariably put capitalist interests first. The Soviet attacks at the General Assembly in 1960 were ferocious, insulting and abusive. Soviet antagonism went deep. They believed that international law was rigged and that the International Court invariably ruled in favour of the capitalists. Prime Minister Harold Macmillan recalled how Khrushchev flouted the high standard of decorum which was traditionally maintained in international assemblies. More serious, Macmillan worried about whether or not the Russians intended to leave the UN, destroy it or try to bully it into subservience.

Khrushchev was not always so scathing. The overall impression in 1959 when he first appeared before the General Assembly was of positive support. In his first speech to the world community Khrushchev made a surprising and dramatic proposal for general and complete disarmament. On his return to Moscow, Khrushchev initiated a significant reduction in the Soviet armed forces. Hopes soon evaporated. In early 1960 an American high-altitude reconnaissance plane was shot down over Russia. The U-2s deep penetration into Soviet air space and the explanation that the plane was a weather research aircraft gone astray infuriated Khrushchev and so did the failure of Soviet efforts to have the Security Council condemn the US for the U-2 flights – to have America labelled an aggressor nation.

Khrushchev pressed on with the disarmament theme and when he returned to New York the following year he relaunched the idea of complete disarmament. "Never forget the appeal the idea of disarmament has in the outside world," Khrushchev said on board the *Baltica,* on his way to New York. "A seductive slogan is a most powerful political instrument." But once he got to New York he found that the Congo dominated. "I spit on the UN," Khrushchev would yell to his assistant, Oleg Troyanovsky bringing the latest news from Africa where he believed that the UN was doing dirty work.

The Congo remained a bitter legacy, for the Soviets maintained that the sole result of UN–Western meddling in the Congo was the insane President Mobutu and his reign of terror. Mobutu treated the country as his personal property, sustained by Western interests. He was the man to whom the phrase "He is a bastard, but he is our bastard" specifically applied. The Soviets were out-manoeuvred. "All we wanted", someone in the Khrushchev entourage remembered years later, "was a share of UN control."

When the peacekeeping force for the Congo was first created in July 1960, the Soviets approved the Security Council Resolution which authorised the Secretary General to take necessary steps to provide the Congolese government with "such military assistance as might be necessary", until that government should be able to meet their tasks fully. The resolution was tough enough for the Soviets who wanted the Belgian troops rapidly expelled and mild enough not to be vetoed by Belgium's ally, France. But the Resolution was ambiguous and the Soviet ideas over what the UN force should do were soon different from everyone else's.

The Soviets believed that the sole purpose of the UN presence in the Congo was to put down the rebellion in break-away Katanga, and oust the pro-Belgium Moise Tshombe and his backers who were in control of the enormous profits the province produced. Katanga was uranium-rich: it was an economic exploitation machine controlled by foreign advisers, mercenaries, the Union Minière du Haut-Katanga, and of enormous benefit to the financial interests of Belgium, Great Britain, France and Western Germany. Tshombe was a puppet of the white colonial world. The failure of the UN to get rid of such a bandit was considered in Moscow to be the greatest example ever of the West's use of the UN for its own political ends.

Within only weeks of the peacekeepers arriving, the Soviets were portraying Hammarskjöld and Bunche as American-run colonialists. "In the UN there continues to dominate a group of Western powers, numerically small in terms of population and the most reactionary in terms of its political goals," an editorial in a Soviet magazine, *Kommunist*, noted in 1961. When Hammarskjöld pulled back the one Russian UN official operating with the UN force, it was insulting. Years later, in his biography of Ralph Bunche, the UN's Nobel Prize winning peacemaker, Brian Urquhart wrote that the official, Mikhail Potrubach, was caught trying to copy some of Bunche's code cables – and at the time Bunche relied on the American embassy for his communications to UN headquarters.

Khrushchev maintained the only permissable use of UN troops was to punish aggression. The Charter provided that the Security Council was the only source of legal authority for military intervention and under the Charter the UN was to co-ordinate enforcement action aided by a Military Staff Committee. To allow the Secretary General to assume command of UN troops was illegal under the Charter. Moscow considered the post of Secretary General to be solely administrative: it was unlawful to transform him into an international statesman. In this, the Soviets were consistent. President Roosevelt believed the position the "most important in the world" and thought the title should be the world's "moderator". The Soviets always opposed it, and wanted the Secretary General to be elected only for a two-year term.

Khrushchev's demand for Dag Hammarskjöld's resignation and a troika to run the UN was an idea basic to Communist philosophy. Khrushchev said that although there were neutral countries, there were no neutral men. Impartiality was impossible in a bipolar world.

The Congo was a major test of the authority and independence of the Secretary General. The Soviets targeted his civilian chain of command and suspicions were made easier in that Hammarskjöld relied on American officials.

Dag Hammarskjöld tried to appease Khrushchev. Early on, in July 1958, he may have succeeded for the Soviet leader suggested that Hammarskjöld be invited to a superpower summit. But during a visit to Moscow in March 1959 Hammarskjöld apparently blotted his copybook: during a dinner he talked of Boris Pasternak and of his own role, as a member of the Swedish Academy, in awarding the Russian author the Nobel Prize for Literature. Khrushchev angrily asked how the prize could possibly be given to someone so totally rejected by the Russian people. Such hostility was exacerbated by Hammarskjöld's oft-stated opinion that the UN could fill the vacuum left by the colonial powers, plus his stance on Laos in 1959 when the Security Council received a plea from the Laotian government about Communist infiltration from North Vietnam. Hammarskjöld proposed that he go to Laos, an initiative which Moscow announced it would veto immediately. Hammarskjöld went without seeking the Council's authorisation, receiving instead a personal invitation from the government of Laos. Hammarskjöld said that the visit was part of his general responsibilities as Secretary General. For the Soviets this contravened the Charter. Hammarskjöld's behaviour effectively eliminated the notion of collective security by the great powers.

While condemning the UN, Khrushchev tried to shatter the US hold on it in another way and suggested the UN headquarters leave America. He made strenuous objections to security investigations by the US intelligence services on American employees which he felt damaged Secretariat independence and he said that the Secretariat would be welcomed in the USSR where there would be a guarantee of full freedom and security for everyone, regardless of political or religious convictions. In June 1961 he returned to the theme and proposed that the UN move to Vienna and, during the summit there with President John Kennedy, it emerged that the Soviets had already explored with the Austrian authorities the possibility of such a move. Khrushchev demanded a complete reorganisation of staff in to better reflect the increased economic and military potential of the Socialist bloc. Future recruitment to the UN system should be on the basis of tripartite equality of Western, Communist and neutral blocs. "It is clear", said Khrushchev, "that no international organisation can survive in our days if it caters to the tastes and interest of one group of states."

6. BANKRUPTCY

The Soviets lobbied hard to abolish the post of Secretary General after the death of Dag Hammarskjöld. They wanted a troika instead – three officials representing the power blocs. The Americans were steadfastly against this idea and President John F. Kennedy outlined objections in his first speech to the General Assembly on September 25, 1961. Kennedy told them that even a Russian three-horse carriage did not have three drivers, going in different directions. A troika would require amendment of the Charter – and that required the agreement of all five veto powers which made the proposal unlikely. Meanwhile the UN had to replace Hammarskjöld and although there was an early front runner – U Thant of Burma – the permanent members continued to argue about the nature of the Secretary General's power and influence.

The Soviets wanted change, a more equitable balance at the senior levels of the Secretariat. They were smarting from their lack of control during the Congo operation when Dag Hammarskjöld's closest advisers were Americans – Andrew Cordier and Ralph Bunche. When accused of Western bias, Hammarksjöld's usual response was to describe both Bunche and Cordier as experienced international civil servants with proven ability. Yet the Congo Club, the small group which regularly met to discuss the crisis, consisted of Bunche's deputy Cordier and a Briton, Sir Alexander MacFarquhar, a special adviser on civilian operations. MacFarquhar was a veteran of the Indian Civil Service and he eventually became the UN's Director of Personnel. The Soviet's most senior UN official within the Secretariat was excluded.

As the Big Five struggled to replace Hammarskjöld in the last weeks of 1961, others pushed for radical change at the top of the UN. The Prime Minister of India, Jawaharlal Nehru, in New York for the General Assembly, thought the Secretary General should have an advisory body but some thought that such a body, representative of member states, was unlikely to agree on anything. The President of Ghana, Kwame Nkrumah, a leading spokesman for newly independent Afro-Asian member states, wanted three deputy Secretaries General. This too, was rejected and there was no alternative but to proceed with the election of a new Secretary General.

U Thant, a quiet Burmese diplomat, had bided his time and resisted all attempts to enmesh him in agreement and compromise. He believed that the imposition of a staff structure would reduce the Secretary General's authority. He refused to commit himself, one way or another. After his election as Secretary General he chose eight advisers, each with the rank of Under Secretary General – one each from the USA, the Soviet Union, India, France, Brazil, the UAR, Czechoslovakia and Nigeria. There were two Communists out of eight senior appointments – instead of two out of six as the USSR had hoped – and U Thant received a frosty welcome. The day he was sworn to office, Ambassador Valerian Zorin announced that the Soviets only agreed to his appointment for the sake of the UN and the urgent need for a decision. A further insult was the Soviet insistence that U Thant serve out what remained of Hammarskjöld's second term. His title would be "Acting Secretary General". America supported U Thant partly to defeat the troika campaign. But there was more to the election. By 1961 the size of the UN had nearly doubled from the original Charter 50 to 100 member states. There were new forces at work: a radical and angry constituency was forming which resented the industrialised Old World and U Thant was one of its champions. The first Secretary General from the Third World, U Thant thought the Cold War was a passing phenomenon. Of much greater urgency was world poverty. He considered the divide between the rich and poor nations was morally wrong and politically intolerable. The West's leaders could not for ever postpone telling their constituents the truth – that progress for the world's poor could not continually be delayed. U Thant is credited with coming up with the term "Third World" and changing the derogatory "under-developed countries" to "developing nations". His election is easily explained.

The superpowers were keen to seize the initiative. President Kennedy had already proposed a concerted programme for the economic and social development of the poorer nations. At America's urging, the UN declared the sixties to be the First Development Decade, with a goal of at least five per cent annual growth for developing nations and when the 1961 Assembly was over, member states unanimously endorsed a suggestion that U Thant prepare proposals for speeding up economic and social development. His report, submitted in 1962, was based on the belief that the climate was favourable for a concerted attack on under-development. The objectives in the report were never attained and, anyway, as far as public opinion in the West was concerned, the test of the UN and its Secretary General lay elsewhere.

U Thant's first unsolicited appeal for peace was made a few days after his election and it achieved no more than prove his lack of power. In early December, 1961 India was preparing to invade the Portuguese colony of Goa a tiny province on the west coast of India which had been colonised by Portugal. Portugal, under the dictatorship of the aging Antonio de Oliveira Salazar, steadfastly refused decolonisation. India's approaches were rebuffed. As a result, Indian public opinion became increasingly hostile towards Portugal, resulting in pressure for the Portuguese to leave Goa. This intensified by 1961. Prime Minister Nehru spoke of terror and torture in Goa against the people by the Portuguese rulers; shots were fired from a Portuguese island at Indian fishing boats. Nehru announced that the situation was intolerable and Indian troops were preparing to invade and building up on the border. In the Security Council Portugal accused India of violating Portuguese territory. Goa had been Portugese for almost 450 years and the enclave was an integral part of the nation. Portugal asked for international observers to be placed on the border between India and Goa. U Thant sent appeals to both Nehru and Salazar but at midnight on December 17-18 about 30,000 Indian forces invaded Goa. The Security Council met in New York the same day.

Among Western delegates India was not overly popular; India was a shining light for the world's newly independent states and Nehru was fond of lecturing the old world on different and more honest international standards of conduct. Within UN circles India had a reputation for smugness and the West was irritated by Nehru's preaching about international morality and his country's non-violence tradition. For the West, the invasion of Goa mocked all this. On December 18 India was accused in the Security Council of violation of Article 2 (4) which forbids the use of force. While the West condemned India the non-aligned group stood in defiant support. This was a colonial issue and Portugal was defying the UN's Declaration on Decolonisation. A resolution by the US, Britain, France and Turkey deploring the use of force was vetoed by the Soviet Union whose delegate accused America of double standards, recalling the botched and covert American attempt to invade Cuba in the recent Bay of Pigs disaster. The American ambassador, Adlai Stevenson, in an emotional speech, said failure to take action to stop the aggression against Goa was a drama which could only end with the death of the UN. "I was . . . present at the birth of the UN," he told the Council and he got carried away and departed from his prepared text. "The League of Nations died, I remind you, when its members no longer resisted the use of aggressive force . . . we have witnessed tonight an effort to rewrite the Charter, to sanction the use of force in international relations when it suits one's own purpose. This approach can only lead to the disintegration of the UN." No one questioned the depth of disagreement between Portugal and India, he said, but if the UN Charter meant anything, states were obligated to renounce force and seek a peaceful solution. These were fine words. It was left to the representatives of Ecuador and the Taiwanese Chinese, to point out that India and Portugal were both guilty of a violation of Charter principle: while Portugal denied Goa self-determination, India was guilty of taking the law into her own hands.

By the time the Security Council's deliberations ground to a halt, the occupation of Goa was complete. As usual, it was the fault of the UN, rather then the Security Council. The *New York Times* condemned India's unjustifiable aggression, and demanded less reliance on the UN and more on Western strength. The criticism was nationwide. In Omaha the UN was described as "bankrupt and tottering", in Atlanta the UN had been "clubbed to its knees" by India. In the Senate, Thomas Dodd, a Republican from Connecticut, asked whether or not the UN was worth saving. The Goa crisis reinforced the perception of UN powerlessness – it could not act, even against a middle-sized aggressor. In the State Department the conclusion was that the UN should be regarded as simply another place for politics – with limited uses.

On December 21, 1961, Stevenson gave a press conference in which he said that the UN faced virtually insuperable life-and-death problems. There could only be one law. "It is painfully evident that we have neither used as well we might the existing procedures for peaceful settlements and the peacekeeping machinery of the UN . . . This is not an organisational problem . . . it is a problem of will." On Goa, he said: "What has happened in the last week is a warning to all of us."

In Goa the Portuguese authorities had surrendered within thirty-six hours of the Indian invasion and there had been little loss of life. The Indian parliament unanimously passed a constitutional amendment declaring Goa to be part of the Indian union. All the Portuguese who were detained during the invasion were returned to Portugal.

The omens for the new Secretary General were promising at first. After his role as a useful intermediary in the Cuban Missile crisis in October 1962, U Thant was elected to a full five-year term, losing the prefix "Acting" from his title. The Soviets, who only months previously wanted the office abolished, were so grateful to his help in the Cuba crisis that Khrushchev wrote him letters which began "Dear U Thant". The two had met in the summer, 1962 and had a long *tête à tête* at Khrushchev's Black Sea dacha.

U Thant believed the crisis to have been totally unnecessary. The Cuban–US relationship had been the subject of Security Council dicussions and started in January 1961 when the US broke off diplo-matic relations. In December 1961, Fidel Castro publicly announced that Cuba had become a Communist state. The US instigated a full economic and political blockade against Cuba. Cuba was increasing-ly isolated in the Western hemisphere. There were attempts at mediation both at the UN and at the Organisation of American States but the talks were ineffective and unproductive. However, two weeks before the revelation of Soviet missile bases Cuba had said that were the US to give proof that it would not carry out aggression against Cuba, as it had done in the Bay of Pigs fiasco in 1961, Cuban army and weapons would be unnecessary. U Thant believed that the US should have taken advantage of this. U Thant recalls, "it . . . made President Kennedy's ultimatum unnecessary . . . [the ultima-tum] only brought the world to the brink of a nuclear war." In U Thant's judgment, Cuba was fully within its rights to ask for and receive missiles and bombers from a big power, in the same way that Turkey, Pakistan, and Japan, countries on the border with Communist countries had done. "Did Cuba build these missile sites just to demonstrate to the Americans that the Soviet Union had the same right as the US in building offensive missiles and bomber bases in any country that wanted them?" he asked. The only difference was that while these countries received their arms openly from the US, the Cubans were receiving theirs in secret. The Cuban missile crisis was a spectacular blunder of international diplomacy and U Thant found it hard to believe that the US was prepared to plunge the world into a nuclear holocaust.

President Kennedy's ultimatum was broadcast on the evening of October 22. He was unequivocal, accusing the Soviets of having been deliberately deceptive and provocative. His unswerving objective was to end the nuclear threat to America. Kennedy recalled the lessons of appeasement in the thirties and announced the immediate imposition of what he called defensive quarantine, a naval and air blockade around Cuba to stop all offensive military equipment. There would be an intensification of the surveillance of Cuba itself. "I call upon Chairman Khrushchev to halt and eliminate this clandestine, reckless and provocative threat to world peace . . . I call upon him further to abandon this course of world domination." Kennedy urged the Soviets to withdraw the missiles. U Thant immediately sent identical messages to both Khrushchev and Kennedy to plead for moderation, self-restraint and good sense, and urged that they enter into negotiations immediately.

In New York on Thursday, October 25, Adlai Stevenson received instructions to tell U Thant that the US hoped Khrushchev would keep his ships out of the quarantine area for a limited time to permit discussion. U Thant said he would transmit those views and he confided to Stevenson that the Soviet ambassador, Valerian Zorin, had not liked U Thant's recent speech to the Security Council. Zorin had wanted a strong condemnation that the American blockade of Cuba was illegal. U Thant said legality be damned; the powers were playing nuclear poker and he was trying to avert the explosion. After passing the message to Khrushchev, U Thant contacted Kennedy and appealed to the President to instruct US vessels in the area to do everything to avoid confrontation. U Thant wanted to go back to Khrushchev with the message that Kennedy was willing to do everything possible to avoid confrontation.

U Thant's quiet diplomacy allowed the Soviet Union to back down and confrontation was avoided. Twenty-five Soviet ships, strung out across the Atlantic and bound for Cuba turned away from the blockade and stayed outside the interception area. The immediate danger passed. The next set of negotiations was conducted directly and secretly between Kennedy and Khrushchev.

U Thant received a joint letter of thanks from both the US and Soviet Ambassadors for his efforts. It was the only high point.

U Thant had inherited a bankrupt Organisation and he believed that lack of finance was the UN's most serious internal crisis. The Soviets pinned the blame on Dag Hammarskjöld for the huge expense of the Congo operation. During one acrimonious meeting, Hammarskjöld had received a humiliating and public dressing-down by Soviet delegates about the Congo's considerable and continually increasing costs. In its first six months the Congo cost the UN almost as much the entire bill for the Secretariat. Within a year, UN expenditure tripled. And while the Congo operation grew, so did the reluctance of member states to pay for it. Those poor and developing countries, finding it hard to pay their regular dues, were faced with a sudden and extra burden and began to complain. In December 1961, to meet their complaints, a special scale was introduced by majority vote in the General Assembly which reduced their contribution and increased the burden on middle-income members.

More fundamental than reasons of poverty was a refusal by some states, for political reasons, to pay for peacekeeping. In 1956, thirty countries failed to contribute their share of the cost for UNEF, the UN Emergency Force sent to Gaza after the Suez war, a buffer to keep the peace along the Egyptian-Israeli border. They argued that the aggressor nations in the Suez war – Israel, France and Britain – ought to be liable for the costs of the peace. Other member states, including the Latin-Americans, insisted that the cost be borne by the permanent members of the Security Council who, after all, armed with their veto power, were responsible for peace and security.

The main problem was that two of the permanent members were among the non-payers. Both France and the Soviet Union objected to UNEF on consitutional grounds – that it was authorised by the General Assembly and not the Security Council. The peacekeeping force on the Israeli-Egyptian border was created under the Uniting for Peace resolution – the US way to by-passing the deadlocked Security Council. It was the General Assembly which apportioned the costs for UNEF and both France and the Soviet Union considered this illegal. France feared a loss of sovereignty. She argued that if the Assembly were given financial authority over its members it would become a super-state: France believed that those in favour of UN forces should pay for them.

President Charles de Gaulle considered the Congo an expensive mistake. In Paris the UN had no priority; the French hostility was a reaction to the Afro-Asian campaign in the General Assembly against the brutality of French colonialism in the North African territories. The Soviet objections to the Congo peacekeeping mission were constitutional. The Soviets maintained UN troops in the Congo were under the illegal command of the Secretary General, inconsistent with the basic principle of veto power. The Soviets demanded there should be strict observation of the Charter. Only the Security Council could create such missions and the strategic direction for UN forces should be in the hands of a Military Staff Committee provided for in Article 47 of the Charter.

All this left the thirty-eighth floor struggling to pay the bills and, while fears increased about meeting salaries, the Controller, Bruce Turner, borrowed money from the UN's Children's Fund, UNICEF. The bankruptcy reached absurd proportions with no solution forthcoming from member states. Those who refused to pay continued to do so. In December 1961, for the want of any other solution, the General Assembly asked the International Court of Justice in The Hague for a ruling, requesting an advisory opinion on whether the costs of these peacekeeping forces came under "normal" expenses, which all member states were under an obligation to pay, or were "special" expenses. In the interim and to keep the UN solvent, Washington formulated the idea that the UN should issue bonds to raise some cash. The bonds, worth $200 million, with twenty-five years to pay, would bear interest at two per cent. It was a desperate measure. The bonds were to be offered to member states and would be serviced out of the regular UN budget. More than half the member governments bought UN bonds but had the US not taken the lion's share, the scheme would have failed. It was only a partial success. The Soviets were disdainful of the whole idea and, together with France, argued that bonds were no more than a back-door way of financing illegal peacekeeping.

In July 1962, the International Court handed down a weighty judgment, 308 pages, on whether peacekeeping expenses were normal or special. The court argued that there was no distinction between the UN's administrative and operational costs. In other words, paying for peacekeeping was legally binding on everyone. The Soviets and the French still refused to pay and, by now, America was footing the bill for forty-five per cent of the UNEF and the UN force in the Congo. America already contributed thirty per cent of Secretariat costs and was by far the biggest contributor to the UN family of specialised agencies, plus the UN programme to help the refugees in camps in Palestine, the UN Relief and Works Agency and UNICEF.

A working group was set up by the General Assembly to discuss the crisis but it was quickly deadlocked and reached no conclusions. A year went by and the debts mounted. In June 1963 the Assembly asked the Secretary General for a feasibility study for a UN Peace Fund, financed voluntarily.

The peacekeeping deficit reached $112 million, money owed to member states for their troop contributions. The bigger the deficit, the greater the reluctance of countries to provide troops. In 1964 the Soviet Union's total arrears reached $60 million. U Thant warned: "Time, if I may say so, is rapidly running out". The Americans reached the same conclusion. There were limits to both Congressional patience and the depth of the American purse.

In March, 1964 the Johnson administration called the Soviets' bluff. The UN Ambassador Adlai Stevenson met Ambassador Nikolai Fedorenko to tell him that at the forthcoming General Assembly the Americans intended to enforce Charter Article 19. It was no mean threat. The Charter stipulated that a country owing two years' arrears would automatically lose its voting right in the General Assembly. The financial emergency now became a constitutional one. The Secretary of State Dean Rusk carried the same message to Congress where a vociferous lobby in the Senate was insistent that the Soviets not be allowed to get away with non-payment. In testimony to Congress Stevenson pledged that Article 19 would be applied: peacekeepers fulfilled an essential function and it was the duty of the UN minority to co-operate with a majority decision. The House of Representatives unanimously endorsed the administration's tough stand. Adlai Stevenson had testified before the US Senate and pledged that Article 19 be applied against the Russians. Stevenson was keen to reduce Senate reluctance about America's own huge contribution. "We shall be extremely stubborn about this."

Moscow was equally determined. There was nothing in the Charter which provided for either the Congo or the Middle East operations to be inescapable obligations. The costs of these forces were not, in the words of the Charter, "proper expenses". The Charter made it quite clear that only the Security Council could institute military operations. Moscow argued that were the Soviets to pay, it would signify tacit recognition of the legality of the peacekeeping forces. Ambassador Fedorenko pointed out that during the Korean war in 1950, the US did not insist that member states were to share all the costs.

While both Moscow and Washington resorted to convoluted legal arguments, everyone else believed the UN would close. If the Soviets were to be deprived of the vote they would leave the UN and take the satellites. The result would be a UN in which America and the other Western states were outnumbered by post-colonial and developing countries who would expect America to meet all the bills. In the State Department there was a secret hope that an immediate confrontation could be avoided; perhaps the Soviets might make a voluntary contribution – without prejudice – but nothing came of these hopes and so they postponed the General Assembly using the American Presidential election as an excuse, although previous elections had never delayed the opening. During the election and after Lyndon Johnson's landslide victory, desperate back-room negotiations continued.

No one really wanted a head-on collision but the Americans were determined to invoke Article 19. There was no doubt in anyone's mind that, when the Assembly opened, America would contest the right of the Soviets and her allies to vote, because of the arrears in their contributions, and risk the Soviets leaving altogether. So the diplomats decided that to avoid collapse of the UN, they would have to find a means by which votes could be avoided. The Secretary General thought one way round it was a no-objection procedure, and U Thant urged that the Assembly reach decisions by consensus or by acclamation, that is, without a vote. It would not solve the bankruptcy but it would avoid confrontation between East and West which might well destroy the UN. For the no-vote Assembly to work, every UN member would have to acquiesce. A new electronic voting system was just recently installed in the cavernous Assembly hall and there were jokes that world diplomacy had become unbalanced.

On the morning of December 1, 1964 U Thant opened the Assembly proceedings with a plea for a no-objection procedure, the first test of which would be the annual vote for the President of the Assembly. It worked. The President, Alex Quaison-Sackey of Ghana, was appointed by acclamation. They went on to admit three new members – Malta, Malawi and Zambia – and the Assembly managed to agree budgets and resolutions after laborious discussion, without a formal challenge to the non-voting arrangement. Where there was no consensus, the matter was shelved. Even a serious procedural problem like electing the non-permanent members of the Security Council was dealt with – there was a secret ballot with names filled out on scraps of paper and dropped into an empty box of Kleenex tissues in the Assembly President's office.

At no time did Washington force the issue. She could have called a roll-call vote at any time, yet she did not. The Indian delegate complained that the UN was paralysed, the Assembly's authority weakened, the future of the organisation endangered. There was considerable irritation with the superpowers and when the Assembly adjourned it was hoped things would improve in 1965.

Instead the new year brought new crisis. On February 16, when the Assembly reconvened, the Albanian ambassador, Halim Budo, rose to his feet, raised a yellow pencil above his head as a signal to speak and they all knew this was it. Albania announced that American blackmail of the UN membership had gone on long enough. Furthermore, he continued, US threats to deprive the Soviets of their vote was a bid for US control of the UN and as a result, all member nations were deprived of a vote. Budo demanded an immediate roll-call vote to decide whether or not the General Assembly should return at once to normal procedures. From that moment, Albania, stubbornly independent, whose own alliance had swung from Russia to China, refused to budge. Budo, it was said, was probably acting on behalf of the Communist Chinese.

The President of the General Assembly, using his only escape, adjourned the meeting. The delegates would now discuss the crisis in more comfortable surroundings – the bars, clubs and restaurants in New York.

On February 18, when the Assembly reopened, Budo, in the face of every private and public entreaty, pressed his claim. Interrupting an opening statement by the President, he called a point of order. The

President, Alex Quaison-Sackey, tried to stand firm and told Budo he would be allowed to speak later. Budo rushed to the podium. He attempted to make himself heard by shouting into a dead microphone and only the veteran Ambassador, Jamil Baroody of Saudi Arabia, managed to intervene and persuade him to sit down.

Ambassador Adlai Stevenson tried to speak, enraging Budo further, who started shouting again. Budo demanded the meeting abide by procedure, and he shouted "Rule 73" which allowed a delegate to challenge the President. He wanted a roll-call about whether or not the General Assembly should cease consensus and return to decision by a three-quarters majority vote. Adlai Stevenson, once it was quiet enough, announced that as the vote which Albania demanded was procedural, Article 19 of the Charter did not apply. The US would not raise any objection to a procedural vote. Thus Budo's challenge misfired and a majority of states in the General Assembly voted to continue with the no-vote arrangement. Budo was left telling them that he took pride in the fact that the machinations of the great powers had failed to intimidate one country at least.

The General Assembly drew to a close and later, in August 1965, Stevenson's successor to the UN, Supreme Court Judge Arthur J. Goldberg, announced an American climb-down; it was clear that the General Assembly was unwilling to apply Article 19 and in that case the US was unwilling to frustrate the consensus. They turned to a time-honoured solution and set up a committee, the Special Committee on Peacekeeping Operations, comprising thirty-three member states, which was to find ways to overcome the debt crisis.

The basic problem remained. In continuing their policies of non-payment the Soviets and the French, as permanent members, helped to establish a principle that any State could refuse to pay for something it did not agree with, almost with impunity. America warned that if members were allowed to decide which UN assessments they would pay for and which they could not, she herself would reserve the right to do the same. The financial crisis prompted hard questions about peacekeeping and there would be disagreement on its cost for ever. Subsequently in spite of all the controversy over paying for peacekeeping in 1964, the Security Council, faced with a war in Cyprus, created another force. It went under the ungainly acronym of UNFICYP – the UN Peacekeeping Force in Cyprus. Like all other peacekeeping forces, this one lived hand to mouth and its creation was a continuing nightmare for those responsible for its finance, shared between members through voluntary contributions. As for command and control, the Security Council kept a tight grip on it and, ensuring Council supremacy, authority for the force was initially given at only three-monthly intervals. The Soviets did not challenge the idea. When the vote for peacekeepers in Cyprus was taken, the Soviet Union abstained.

When U Thant was appointed, the Congo crisis was getting worse. One month after Hammarskjöld's death, in October 1961, the Central Congolese government began a military campaign to retrieve mineral-rich Katanga, which remained in the control of Moise Tshombe. The Congolese government troops were increasingly undisciplined, with detachments frequently on the rampage and killing peacekeepers: in November, 1961 thirteen Italian crew members of two UN aircraft were brutally murdered after the sight of white men in uniform led government soldiers to assume that they were hated mercenaries, in the pay of Tshombe.

In New York, the Afro-Asian group clamoured for the Security Council to rethink policy and the Soviet Union demanded decisive measures against mercenaries. The pressures were overwhelming and on November 24, 1961, the Security Council for the first time in the crisis authorised the Secretary General to use force to remove foreign mercenaries from Katanga. Britain and France abstained on the Resolution. Both governments predicted bloodshed and the day after Resolution 169 was passed in the Council in New York, Tshombe called the Council's bluff. In a large gathering in Elizabethville in the breakaway province, Tshombe declared: "U Thant will launch a war on our territory . . . Katanga fighters arise in every street, not one UN mercenary must feel safe in any place whatever." Tshombe's soldiers began to harass the UN troops. Up until now the peacekeepers were frequently insulted and spat at but, a few days after the rally, two redoubtable members of the Secretary General's staff were dragged from a dinner party and badly beaten. One of them was Brian Urquhart and the other was an Australian, George Ivan Smith. Urquhart was taken away and held hostage for a few hours. From then on peacekeepers were murdered frequently. In London, Macmillan thought that there were insufficient and unsuitable soldiers in the UN force. "The UN army consists (with the exception of the Swedes, who have not fought anybody for two hundred years, and of the Irish, who will fight anybody) of a queer lot. The chances of being a survivor if you are wounded in this war are said to be slender. You are likely to be killed . . . either by the backward races of Congolese or by the advance guard of civilisation represented in the UN army." Macmillan recorded in his diary than an Ethiopian soldier shot a Swiss banker in Elizabethville.

Tshombe, as always when fighting started, was elsewhere. He left the capital at the first sign of trouble. It allowed his thugs, his extreme elements, to take over. Mercenaries established roadblocks. They prevented the movement of UN troops. They cut peacekeepers off from their only lifeline which was the airport. U Thant was told of a plan to cut off the peacekeepers in Elizabethville and force them to surrender as hostages to Tshombe. U Thant believed the choice was clear: he must re-establish freedom of movement for UN troops if it meant going to war to do it. The UN had substantial military power including fifteen jet fighters, among them Swedish Saaba and Indian Canberra bombers. But its force was far from disciplined and it lacked cohesion. There was no Military Staff Committee to advise and the command and control was weak and confused. The Ethiopian contingent, Brian Urquhart recalled, was paranoid and dangerous and no one left with any credit. There was indiscriminate shooting by UN forces, extensive civilian casualties and about eighty Katanganese were killed and, among the UN forces, twenty-five killed and 120 wounded.

The news of the fighting brought a violent reaction in the Western media. Headlines screamed about the increasing casualties, alleged rapes by UN soldiers and of unnecessary ferocity used by the UN forces. There were fears that the UN was about to take over the control of Katanga. UN member governments were critical. Every move the UN made was questioned and criticised, matched years later when UN peacekeepers went into former Yugoslavia. Great Britain, France and Belgium, whose financial interests in the Tshombe's province were enormous, called for an immediate ceasefire. The French government issued a statement which claimed the action undertaken by UN troops in the Congo was in breach of the Charter. France and Belgium were the principal importers of copper from Katanga. Great Britain owned about forty per cent of the stock of the vastly rich Union Minière du Haut-Katanga. Macmillan thought that the Secretariat was committing follies through ignorance and inexperience.

The UN troops pressed on and by December 15 they were in almost complete control of Elizabethville. A negotiated ceasefire followed. Tshombe, realising his weak position, signed a declaration that accepted the authority of the central Congolese government. He pledged to try to ensure the implementation of all Security Council Resolutions. But it did not end there. Once more, while making every promise, Tshombe was lying. He maintained total independence for Katanga and so exasperated was U Thant that in July 1962 he broke with diplomatic nicety and called Tshombe unstable and his government in Katanga run by clowns.

A month later U Thant put forward a peace plan which he called his Plan of National Reconciliation. It was an American idea which involved drafting a constitution for a Congolese government to represent all provincial groups and for the unification of the military and police. U Thant gave Tshombe a ten-day deadline to accept the division of Katanga mineral profits fifty–fifty with the Congoloese government and he was backed by the Kennedy administration. Washington believed that the Congo was the crucial test of American intentions in Africa and wanted a quick settlement. The moderate and shaky regime in Leopoldville was to be strengthened against Soviet attempts to gain a foothold. If Tshombe did not accept the plan, the next step would be economic sanctions. On the last day of the deadline Tshombe gave his formal approval to the plan. But Katanga continued to recruit mercenaries and stockpile arms and, as Brian Urquhart later recalled, negotiating with Tshombe was like trying to get an eel into a bottle.

By October, impatient that only the US and the West Germans appeared willing to comply with sanctions, U Thant began to talk privately of placing forces in Katanga to protect Union Minière installations from Tshombe's threats that if the UN troops attacked he would destroy everything in the province, a scorched earth policy. U Thant determinedly began plans for a UN force of increased strength with more jet fighters and additional troops and Washington pleaded with him to slow down. U Thant was continuing to line up support for economic sanctions. France made it clear she would not participate, and Britain was hesitant, but both West Germany and a new government in Belgium agreed to comply. Belgium however, laid down conditions: they wanted it to be clear that were Tshombe not to yield, economic sanctions were designed to work, even without the support of France and Britain. The State

Department devised its own plan. It wanted economic experts from the International Monetary Fund to determine how much of the wealth from Katanga should be due the Central government of the Congo. Without a share of Katanga's revenues no government could hope to achieve financial stability. Tshombe wanted more than a fifty–fifty split with the Congo government of Katanga profits.

At the end of November, the US and Belgium formally threatened Katanga with severe economic sanctions. First the international postal and telephone communications would be cut, then there would be a boycott of copper, followed by a blockade of all imports and exports. Rail lines would be cut and none of this was likely to be achieved without heavy fighting. U Thant requested a boycott by key mineral purchasers unless duties were paid to the Leopoldville government, and he appealed to Brussels to freeze all foreign exchange earnings of the Union Minière. U Thant warned that if Katanganese troops tried to prevent the UN by force, then UN troops would fight.

By mid-December 1962, another round of fighting between the Katanganese Gendarmerie and UN soldiers seemed inevitable. A team flew out from the Pentagon to assess the UN's needs, and Washington told her allies that the Soviet Ambassador in Leopoldville was on the prowl, offering the shaky Congolese government military assistance. U Thant obtained more jet fighters from Sweden, Italy and the Philippines, and a Norwegian anti-aircraft battery and he prepared to go to war.

On December 24, 1962 the Katanganese rebels downed a UN helicopter and began to fire on UN positions. Four days later U Thant gave the order that the UN should remove the Katanganese Gendarmerie and all mercenaries from Elizabethville should clear all Katanganese roadblocks and establish freedom of movement for the blue helmets throughout the Province. He flatly rejected a call from Tshombe for a ceasefire and new negotiations. When Tshombe threatened total destruction of all Union Minière installations if the UN forces launched an offensive against them, U Thant repeated his demand for the UN to have freedom of movement throughout the province.

Both Britain and Belgium warned U Thant to back down. Their ambassadors told him that their governments had information that Tshombe would resist. They warned that if the UN pressed forward, the Union Minière installations at Jadotville, including a huge cobalt processing plant, and another mine at Kowezi, would be destroyed. What happened next is open to doubt and the subject of much speculation. U Thant maintained that his next step was to send orders from New York to Stanleyville that UN troops should not press forward towards the mining towns. For some reason, perhaps the UN's antiquated communications system, the message apparently did not get through, for by January 3, 1963, the UN had captured Jadotville. When the blue helmets entered the mining town the mercenaires had fled and the UN solders were welcomed by the staff of the Union Minière.

On January 21, with the last remaining Katanga stronghold under UN control, Tshombe announced he would end the secession. Two weeks later U Thant told the Security Council that the UN mandate in the Congo was fulfilled.

The UN troops left the Congo at the end of June 1964, but an extensive programme of assistance continued: the UN supplied thousands of experts which provided the backbone of the Congo's administration – lawyers, magistrates, teachers, agricultural advisers, airfield controllers. Although remaining fearful for the Congo's future, U Thant declared ONUC's operation to have been a success. Were it not for the presence of the UN, the country would have shattered into pieces. The UN prevented a full-scale civil war, engineered by powerful forces from outside, from spreading in the region.

The public perception of the Congo operation was of a UN disaster. Brian Urquhart, the UN official most closely concerned, could not understand why the public remained so ill-informed of what the UN had really achieved. The Congo operation was a peacekeeping success and the UN averted a possible Soviet-US clash in the heart of Africa. But the operation led to a UN financial crisis and the consequences of the Congo were huge. Afterwards there was widespread agreement that the organisation should never again become involved in such an exercise, as the UN could not help but sink into the quagmire of local Congolese politics. Initially invited in to evict the Belgians, the UN stayed on to end a civil war which meant that the public perception of the UN's aims were confusing and complex. Lessons like these were forgotten in later years.

Dag Hammarskjöld had once confided in U Thant that he never received as much hate mail on any issue as he had on the Congo. U Thant, in his intriguing though overlooked memoir describes his own experiences of a hate campaign waged against him over the Congo. In his book, *U Thant: View from the UN*, published in 1976, U Thant describes how Tshombe, awash with money from the valuable mining interest in Katanga, had bought the most effective "writers of propaganda" New York had on offer. The New York-based Katanga Information Office, with its plush suite of offices, was run by a man called Michael Struelens, a well-known public relations guru whose Katanga-financed anti-UN campaign rankled with U Thant. Struelens sent out dramatic accounts of what was styled Katanga's fight for self-determination, which resulted in the West's influential media being persuaded of UN incompetence. U Thant was particularly concerned about a newspaper report, published in December 1961 which claimed that a million dollars was deposited in a Zurich bank by Tshombe for use by Struelens in New York – a report no one denied. The UN's own efforts at public relations were puny. U Thant described how often the press suppressed, ignored or distorted facts about the UN, particularly when discussing what the UN could and could not do.

U Thant had every reason to be concerned about the image of the UN for its inability to do anything about the Vietnam war lost it the support of a generation and more; in the sixties, in the vocal and extraordinary anti-war movement the UN had no role. And yet for U Thant the war caused his deepest agony. His outspoken views about the war so antagonised President Lyndon Johnson that he exploded saying that he wanted to get rid of "that little yellow bastard in New York". U Thant firmly believed that there could be no decisive military solution but his attempts at quiet diplomacy were torpedoed in Washington. A series of misunderstandings elicited little response and he felt ill-used by the Johnson administration. Washington lacked wholehearted confidence in him and U Thant was told that his initial peace plan was one of twenty-five similar efforts by mediators to engineer talks between Hanoi and Washington.

The Vietnam war was not officially on the agenda of either the Security Council or the General Assembly and U Thant believed that the UN would never have a role in South-east Asia until the admission to the organisation of Communist China. The American policy of keeping mainland China out of the UN was disastrous. As for North Vietnam and South Vietnam – neither country was a member of the UN. Like the People's Republic of China, they had no dealings with it. The problems of Vietnam had always been dealt with elsewhere, by a Conference of Western nations, convened in Geneva in 1954.

This by-passing of the UN was a problem which had always bothered Hammarskjöld and he warned that trying to solve major issues outside the organisation would build up a false view in people's minds concerning the role of the UN itself.

U Thant believed that the Vietnam war was the most murderous and barbarous of the age, a war in which men had accepted slaughter without thought or question. In one memorable press conference, U Thant told correspondents that if the American people knew the true facts and background of developments in Vietnam, they would agree that further bloodshed was unnecessary. After that Stevenson had a meeting with U Thant to tell him that the UN's prestige in Washington was at an all-time low. This message was relayed to U Thant on the eve of sustained bombing of the North.

U Thant disputed the American view of the war. He argued that this was not a case of Communist aggression, but a struggle for national independence. Even if the aims of US policy were right, the conduct of the war was immoral. One did not have to be a pacifist in order to condemn the napalming of villages. Unless the hostilities ended, Vietnam would cease to exist and a war between Washington and Peking was inevitable. U Thant repeatedly demanded Washington stop the bombing of North Vietnam; on the thirty-eighth floor of the Secretariat there was fear and loathing of Johnson. U Thant believed deeply that the Vietnam war poisoned the world of international diplomacy and it lowered international morality.

U Thant's relationship with the Secretary of State Dean Rusk was a disaster. U Thant said that he was never spoken to in the way Rusk spoke to him. As for Rusk, he could not bear U Thant's name and was patronising and sarcastic about him, accusing him of trying to end the war only so he could win the Nobel Peace Prize. "Can't you keep U Thant quiet?" Rusk once privately asked Ralph Bunche.

By the end of 1967, the UN was so alienated from Washington, that the then US Ambassador, Arthur Goldberg, complained that there was no communication between the US mission to the UN and the President.

The relationship between the UN and the US was never worse

and U Thant's every effort to mediate the Vietnam war was rebuffed. But he maintained his demands for negotiation, and in the end his own approach was taken up with ultimate success by Henry Kissinger.

On December 2, 1966 U Thant accepted another five-year term and such was the hypocrisy of the Big Five that, though they despised him, it would have taken a miracle for them to agree a successor. Ambassador Goldberg reported to Washington that the UN might collpase if U Thant and his principal aid, Ralph Bunche, were to retire and President Johnson wrote to him to ask him to stay and even visited the UN to ask him to remain in office. There were rumours that U Thant gained concessions from the permanent members but he always denied them. The war in Vietnam remained a source of anguish. Years later he said that the only reason he accepted another term was because he could do more to stop the war from within the UN, than from without.

As it turned out, no sooner was U Thant eulogised for staying on than he was pilloried before the world. In May, 1967, U Thant withdrew the UN peacekeepers on the border between Israel and Egypt, a decision which gravely damaged his authority. The Six Day War followed and he was accused of a diabolical bias against Israel, destroying what little credibility was left the UN. Afterwards neither the Secretary General nor the UN was ever the same. U Thant was described as having acted out of an innate weakness in character which made him unable to meet the needs of the office. A *New York Times* editorial stated that U Thant had "used his international prestige with the objectivity of a spurned lover and the dynamism of a noodle". There was a belief that Nasser had been bluffing when he demanded the force be removed and that if U Thant had argued with him, Nasser would have climbed down but satisfied his constituents at home.

If the UN were out of focus after the Congo, its image was shattered at the end of the Six Day War. After the decision to withdraw the peacekeepers there was speculation as to whether the organisation would survive. In the House of Representatives the crisis was described as the end of the UN dream. U Thant's justification for the decision to withdraw UN troops was lost in a storm of outrage.

The blue helmets in the UN Emergency Force were among the most successful in history. For more than ten years, from their precarious observation posts along the 300-mile Israel-Egypt border these peacekeepers had kept the peace. The force was small, just 1,800 soldiers and lightly armed, yet so successful it was taken for granted.

Late at night on May 16, 1967, the Commander of UNEF, an Indian General named Indar Jit Rikhye, received a surprise visit from the United Arab Republic's Chief of Staff, General Mohamed Fawzi, who handed Rikhye a letter. (The United Arab Republic was the name given to the short-lived union between Egypt and Syria proclaimed in 1958 and ended when Syria seceded in late 1961 although Egypt kept the name until 1971). The letter contained a request from Egypt for the UN troops of UNEF to be withdrawn immediately for the "sake of [their] complete secure" [sic]. Rikhye was told that the UN troops would have to immediately withdraw from two places, including the base at Sharm El Sheik which controlled access to the Gulf of Aqaba. Rikhye immediately contacted the Secretary General and, in New York, U Thant summoned the Egyptian Ambassador to tell him Cairo should clarify its intentions. U Thant told the Ambassador that UNEF's presence had been negotiated directly between Dag Hammarskjöld and Nasser and that any request for its removal should come through the Secretary General, not the force commander. U Thant cabled Rikhye to tell him to stay put but Rikhye reported that Egyptian troops were taking over UN positions. U Thant immediately protested to Egypt.

The next day two of the largest UNEF troop contributors, India and Yugoslavia, pulled out their soldiers. Both countries told U Thant they would not allow their soldiers to serve in a force against the will of Egypt. U Thant's legal advice said that once a government withdrew its consent to the presence of peacekeepers, the Secretary General had no choice but to pull out the troops. U Thant felt that the safety of the peacekeepers was his responsiblity. The force was falling apart. U Thant quickly called a meeting of the Council's advisory committee, established by Dag Hammarskjöld when the force was created in 1956. U Thant told its members that the UN troops were in imminent danger. If there were to be a recurrence of fighting between Israel and Egypt these peacekeepers could do nothing. The UN would not even be able to feed them: the lifeline to the blue helmets was an Egyptian militiary airport. U Thant said

1

1. Andrei Gromyko on the
stage at the Opera House at
the founding conference of the
UN at San Francisco in June,
1945. Gromyko, Acting
Chairman of the Soviet
delegation, thought that the
delegates from Australia, New
Zealand and Canada made
themselves look silly as they
tried to drown the right of the
veto in a torrent of words.
(UN Photo)

2. Senator Pat McCarran,
Democrat, Nevada. The first
of the UN-bashers. McCarran
said the worst decision he
made in his life was to vote for
ratification of the UN Charter.
"They teach that the UN flag
should be put above Old
Glory", he said. McCarran is
on a visit to General Franco in
1949. (Nevada Historical
Society)

2

3

4   5

3. February, 1951. Three members of the UN Staff Association, Marjorie Zap, Lukin Robinson and Ben Alper (far right) present to Maurice Pate, Executive Director of UNICEF, a cheque for $14,000 raised by UN staff. Within a few months all three Staff Association members were purged in a first wave of dismissals from the Secretariat. (UN Photo)

4. Jack Harris, American secret service agent during the Second World War, and one of America's foremost anthropologists, who was hired to work in the UN Department of Trusteeship. Branded a traitor in 1952, Harris moved to Costa Rica and became one of Latin America's most successful entrepeneurs. (Courtesy: Jack Harris)

5. The elegant Alger Hiss, (right) considered by some to be the father of the UN conspiracy to rule the world. Hiss organsied the glittering founding conference at San Francisco and believes that had President Franklin Roosevelt lived to see his UN dream realised, the story of the organisation would be very different. (UN Photo)

6

7

6. A workshop for peace according to UN press releases, the Secretariat on New York's East River is shown here lit for the first time in December, 1950. But by now it is already considered to be a nest for spies. (UN Photo)

7. Secretary General Trygve Lie, the first occupant of the office on the thirty-eighth floor of the glass and marble UN Secretariat, New York.

8

8. Abe Feller, UN
General Counsel in
August, 1950 with
Yugoslavia's ambassador
to the UN, Dr Ales
Bebler who is presenting
his government's
instrument of ratification
to the Convention on
the Prevention and
Punishment of the
Crime of Genocide.
(UN Photo)

9. The UN's first
Secretary General,
Trygve Lie of Norway
with Abe Feller. Feller
was questioned by the
witch hunters in
November 1952 and
committed suicide a few
days afterwards. Feller
was afraid the UN would
not survive and that the
world would tear itself
apart. (UN Photo)

9

10. Dag Hammarskjöld, Secretary General designate arrives in New York from Stockholm on April 9, 1953 to be told by the incumbent, Trygve Lie that he is about to take on the most impossible job on earth (UN Photo)

11. U Thant of Burma, Secretary General, 1962–1971. He infuriated President Lyndon Johnson with his outspoken criticism of the Vietnam War. (UN Photo)

12. Kurt Waldheim of Austria was Secretary General between 1971–1981. In the Second World War he had been one of the best informed German Army intelligence officers in the Balkans, but there was never one word from him, not a scintilla of remorse or compassion for the suffering of that time.

13

15

14

13. Nikita Krushchev at the speaker's rostrum addressing the General Assembly on Septembr 23, 1960. Later in the day the Soviet Premier caused a storm by banging a shoe to interrupt Prime Minister Harold Macmillan. According to a well-placed eye-witness Krushchev had both his shoes on at the time.

14. Mikahail Gorbachev on December 7, 1988 making his historic speech to the General Assembly in which he outlined a revolutionary vision for international relations with the UN at the heart of a New World Order. He said the planet's survival depended on a balance of interests between states.

15. Secretary General Javier Pérez de Cuéllar aboard a helicopter leaving Beirut during a diplomatic mission to the region in June, 1984. A model diplomat, Pérez de Cuéllar won the confidence of the world's powers and pariahs and left office in some triumph.

16. A proud President of Peru, Fernando Belaunde Terry greets Javier Pérez de Cuéllar whom he had helped to elect Secretary General in 1981.

17. Boutros-Boutos Ghali became Secretary General in 1992 and he warned that the problems of the next ten years would be mainly in the countries of the Third World: the problems of refugees, hunger and drought. (UN Photo)

16   17

18. The UN headquarters in Sarajevo on a road known a sniper alley, in April 1994. A group of teenagers made the placards. (Kevin Weaver)

19

20

21

19. Kibumba Camp near Goma in July, 1994. There were 500,000 Hutu refugees from Rwanda in this camp. The volcanic lava made the digging of graves impossible. These bodies were about to be covered in earth. (Kevin Weaver)

20. Somalia, October 1992. A young girl is dragging her brother to his feet after being refused entry at a Baidoa feeding centre. The famine had reached such proportions that only the very worst cases could be admitted. (Zed Nelson)

21. and 22. Canadian Blue Helmet, Major General Romeo Dallaire, Commander UN Forces in Rwanda. "A living hell has surrounded us", he wrote in his last report to UN Headquarters. Of the abandonment of the blue helmets in Kigali by the Security Council he said it was the Alamo.
(Courtesy Major General Romeo Dallaire

that the usefulness of the force as a buffer had been eliminated. The Ambassador from Canada, George Ignatieff, insisted that U Thant call on the General Assembly immediately. U Thant told him that the decision on whether or not the troops were to be removed was his, and his alone, and the meeting ended.

Cairo formally requested that UN troops be withdrawn from the border with Israel. U Thant, that same day, May 18, ordered the UN's emergency force to withdraw. Ralph Bunche wrote the order which called for an evacuation with dignity, befitting a force which had won such widespread admiration. Bunche had worked closely with Hammarskjöld on its creation and supervision and he was certain that in similar circumstances Hammarskjöld would have acted in exactly the same way; there was no sensible alternative. Bunche believed there was never any doubt about the right of the Egyptian army to be present on any part of Egyptian territory should the government wish to assert that right. After all, Israel never agreed to the stationing of UNEF on Israel's side of the line, and their right to take this position was never challenged either by Hammarskjöld or by the General Assembly. U Thant warned the Security Council that the situation was more menacing in the Middle East than at any time since 1956 and then on 22 May, Egypt closed the Strait of Tiran to Israeli shipping and cargo. In New York the Security Council began a week of inconclusive debate.

It was Bunche who woke U Thant in the early hours on Monday 5 June to tell him that war had broken out. The Israelis had destroyed most of the Egyptian, Syrian, Iraqi and Jordanian air forces and radar bases, eliminating any Arab attack from the air. Israeli ground forces moved simultaneously against Egypt, Syria and Jordan. By June 12, Israel's armies had captured all of Jerusalem and the entire West Bank of the Jordan River, breaking the blockade of Aqaba, and took control of Gaza, the Sinai peninsula and the Golan Heights in Syria. The Security Council, in an emergency session, managed a call for a ceasefire. The General Assembly also in an emergency session, denounced the unification of the Old City of Jerusalem with the Israeli sector and called for humanitarian aid to help Palestinian refugees.

The war was perceived as the fault of a spineless Secretary General. U Thant was described as a sinister figure who finally exposed the depths of his anti-Jewish prejudices.

On the thirty-eighth floor there was a deep sense of failure. For Bunche, it was the end of his life-time's work and, for a time, the end of UN peacekeeping. Later, the Egyptians claimed that U Thant himself had decided to withdraw the force. President Johnson accused U Thant of failing to play for time. In the US Senate, U Thant was described variously as a "frightened rabbit" and someone who "violated canons of courage, good sense and responsiblity". He was attacked in the General Assembly by the Israeli Foreign Minister Abba Eban who asked what use was a fire brigade which vanishes from the scene as soon as the first smoke and flames appear. Lord George Brown in *The Sunday Times* came close to accusing U Thant of having started the Six Day War. "To everybody's surprise, and certainly to President Nasser's, the Secretary General promptly recalled the force. I shall never understand how he was advised to come to this ill-considered and . . . totally unecessary and unexpected decision." The paragraph was not repeated in Brown's subsequent memoirs.

U Thant's defence was contained in a thirty-four page report, submitted to the General Assembly, which described how the peacekeeping force had disintegrated following Nasser's withdrawal request. But his critics failed to accept that UN troops could not enter or remain in a country without that country's consent and failed to understand that peacekeepers were not armed as a fighting force.

In his memoirs, Brian Urquhart writes graphically about this period of UN history. Urquhart believed deeply that it was hypocritical and escapist nonsense to blame U Thant for the Six Day War. Urquhart wished U Thant had chosen to call a meeting of the Security Council under Article 99, which allows for the Secretary General to bring to the attention of the Council any matter which he considers may threaten the maintenance of peace. U Thant would then have been able to pass the buck, for a deadlocked Security Council, neutralised by the Cold War, would have been incapable of making any decision at all. The US was unlikely to restrain Israel, which was armed by France, and the Soviet Union would have been unwilling to restrain Egypt to whom she had sold new weapons. The permanent members were glad to have a Secretary General prepared to make a decision which they were incapable of making themselves. If U Thant had resisted Nasser the position would have been even more difficult.

U Thant dismissed the criticism but he was never the same again. Urquhart says the crisis broke both him and Ralph Bunche. "We all labored under a crushing sense of failure," he wrote. U Thant believed the UN to have been weakened. Its strength depended upon enlightened public opinion and that had gone. The viciousness was partly owing to U Thant's stance on the Vietnam war; many of those against him in 1967 were at the same time advocates of a hard line in South-east Asia. Some of the criticism can be traced to the State Department where hawks promoted a racist image of U Thant as a crafty Oriental wearing a mask of virtue. In Washington, U Thant was considered to be a tool of Third World revolutionaries.

A year later when the Soviets invaded Czechoslovakia, U Thant was attacked again, this time for timorousness. When he proposed an Assembly Resolution condemning the American bombing of North Vietnam, he was accused of playing politics, of abandoning all pretence of adherence to any principles. The UN's critics pointed to the continued lack of a settlement in Cyprus, failure of the UN to do anything about the Nigerian civil war over the secession of Biafra, and of not making an impact on the white regimes of Southern Africa.

In one of his last press conferences on September 16, 1971, U Thant said that the office of Secretary General was developed through trial and error. No clear-cut policy illuminated a Secretary General's path and he lacked the first-hand sources of information upon which governments based their plans. The Secretary General faced the conflicts of the present and the problems of the future with vague or non-existent directives, yet there was a widespread public belief that a Secretary General could solve problems which defied the collective wisdom of 127 member governments. The UN would become what its founders intended only when its member states abided by the rules. U Thant's last words to UN correspondents constituted a warning about the increasingly grave threats to the planet which he considered to be so serious they deserved a place of their own in the Charter: the problems of population growth and pollution which threatened humanity. These great humanitarian emergencies the UN was not equipped to meet and were matters of greater import-ance than monolithic Communism. "Great problems usually come to the UN because governments have been unable to think of anything else to do about them. This applies equally to the Middle East and to the environment. The UN is a last-ditch . . . and it is not surprising that the organisation should often be blamed for failing to solve problems which have already been found to be insoluble."

U Thant believed the world, in many respects, to be in the Middle Ages. "There's too much self in all national policies . . . too much dread of the unknown." As he left office, U Thant said that his successor should be a man who would look to the future; his successor's nationality was far less important than integrity, competence and impartiality. The new Secretary General would need an assailable conviction in the importance of human dignity and value.

U Thant's health was failing and before he left office he was in hospital for five weeks. He returned on December 6, 1971 by which time Ralph Bunche had died after a lengthy illness. U Thant was continually ill in the last years of his life, suffering from stomach ulcers. Cancer was diagnosed soon after his retirement but he bought a magnificent mansion in a small picturesque town in upstate New York, received a generous publisher's advance and proceeded to write his memoirs. He lived in some style with a swimming pool, a Cadillac with a driver, and his colleagues were happy to see it, feeling that he earned it. When he died three years later, in November 1974 at the age of sixty-five, he had just finished his memoirs. U Thant lay in state – the only Secretary General ever to do so – in the Secretariat building. His coffin was draped with a blue UN flag.

When U Thant retired in 1971 the press speculated that the UN needed a firm hand, a more dynamic personality to give the organisation a dramatic image. A new Secretary General would enable the organisation to revitalise itself under the leadership of a stronger man.

Close to the deadline of December 31, 1971, the Security Council came up with the nomination of a man well known in the rarified circles of international diplomacy – the Austrian ambassador, Kurt Waldheim.

7. REFORM

The UN's fortunes did not change just because of a new Secretary General. The year 1971 was marked by another major event when the People's Republic of China took her seat as a permanent member of the Security Council. The seating of the Communists and the ousting from the UN of the Nationalist Chinese was considered a great defeat in Washington. As a result a group of Senators tried to reduce America's contribution to the UN and a long debate about how much America should contribute to the organisation ensued. "Seldom have so many important people argued so heatedly about so little money", one UN official noted dryly. Although America paid about thirty per cent of UN running costs, the amount was a pittance. The entire cost of the UN family, including its regular budget, peacekeeping and the economic and social programmes and the cost of the agencies all over the world amounted to $900 million which was slightly more than 10 per cent of New York City's annual budget. Furthermore, New York made money by hosting the UN, the world's largest diplomatic community.

The Chinese soon demonstrated their new commitment to internationalism when Premier Chou-En-Lai offered to increase Peking's own contribution.

By the time of the vote in the General Assembly in October 1971 the Nixon administration had already softened its anti-China policy; there had even been talk of a two-China policy – Security Council admission for the mainland Communist government while the National Chinese government on Taiwan was allowed to keep a seat in the General Assembly. But the policy shift in Washington by no means was transformed to a change in tactics at the UN and by the autumn 1971, the usual vote-grabbing and arm-twisting was taking place – the Americans trying hard to garner enough support so that when the member states voted whether or not to admit Communist China, admission could be prevented, as in previous years. Just as the lobbying began came the news that Nixon's adviser on national security, Henry Kissinger, had paid a secret visit to Peking. From then on it would be difficult at the UN. America could hardly continue to argue prevention of membership – but she did. Ambassador George Bush was as determined as his predecessors to prevent membership and there was furious diplomatic persuasion all round. In the end, his efforts came to nothing and Bush and his team were out-manoeuvered.

Bush had been appointed a year earlier by President Richard Nixon and the posting, shortly after Bush lost a Senate race, was considered a consolation prize. Once in New York, Bush had little chance of forming a strong policy of his own, at least not with Henry Kissinger in the White House. But Bush would be remembered more fondly in the mission than most others who took the job.

That night, as the China vote approached, a Maronite Lebanese named Jamil Baroody, the Ambassador from Saudi Arabia, criticised for buffoonery by the West and famous for his long and irrelevant speeches, proposed an adjournment for dinner. There was a sigh from the American delegation. If the Assembly adjourned and the delegates left, some would certainly fail to return and the anti-China vote could suffer. Baroody got his way, and the Assembly adjourned.

Predictably, when the Assembly reconvened after dinner, the People's Republic of China was admitted to UN membership. Afterwards, Bush left the Assembly hall muttering about Saudi Arabia's "unguided missile": he thought he might have won if the Assembly had not adjourned. But since Kissinger's visit, Bush's position had been untenable. Some said that for the sake of consistency Washington might have spared Bush the job of trying to obtain enough votes to keep out the Communists. Bush later found out that neither Kissinger nor Nixon ever expected him to win the vote to stop China's membership anyway. And so Taiwan was ousted from the UN and the following year in 1972, Nixon visited Shanghai and officially recognised there was only one China. Taiwan never lost the ambition to get back in: in 1995, in a flamboyant gesture, the Nationalist government offered the cash-starved UN a billion dollars in return for membership. The then Secretary General turned down the offer and that said the only way forward was for the Nationalist government to engage in dialogue with Beijing.

Everyone knew that when Secretary General Kurt Waldheim took over, the Secretariat was in disarray; delegates frequently complained about a bureaucracy out of control. Waldheim's predecessor U Thant had recognised the need for more rational planning, and in one of his last reports, in August 1971, he had admitted: "We have all long been aware of the need to put our house in order". Thant was particularly concerned about the number of documents the UN produced, which "all but overwhelms".

By 1971 reform was the buzz-word and the idea that something should be done found a champion in Ambassador Jamil Baroody. Reform became his personal crusade and he determined that the new Secretary General should be under no illusion about what lay ahead. When Waldheim took office, there was a report from Baroody waiting in the in-tray. Baroody had conducted his own investigation of the Secretariat and had spent time chatting to employees at every level. He concluded that the UN was overstaffed, that it lacked discipline and that it supported wasteful and redundant programmes in the field. Baroody said that even staff admitted there was not enough work to go round. Many of them were bored, "as is evident . . . in the cafeteria". Baroody suggested an immediate staff cut. They could abolish the Council for Namibia which was no more than a sop to pacify the African member states and leave troops under the command of the Organisation of African Unity to liberate Namibia from South African oppression. All the Council for Namibia had ever achieved was to give the impression that some diplomatic solution was eventually possible. Baroody thought immediate savings could also be made by cancelling seminars on human rights – which were mostly of academic value.

For other delegates, the single most irritating aspect of Baroody's behaviour was that he did as he pleased. His backing from King Faisal was total and in return, Baroody supervised Faisal's US investments and the education of his sons. Diplomats grew weary of Baroody's lectures on democracy which did not even exist in Saudi Arabia neither did they relish a lecture on the West's unstable hunger for wealth – two weeks after Saudi Arabia tripled the price of its oil. One American wag thought the UN and Baroody were complimentary, the one deserving the other. Sometimes there were discreet complaints to Faisal about his ambassador but such attempts were met with either obstinacy or anger.

Baroody's ideas for a new UN included a committee of international bankers and lawyers who, together with the heads of world-wide corporations, would contribute to a fund of $500 million to pay the UN deficit. After all, business corporations had an interest in stable markets. Baroody told everyone that if the major powers spent less on defence, there would be more money to run the UN.

Even though reform was the buzz-word, when Kurt Waldheim arrived on the thirty-eighth floor he insisted it be redecorated, recarpeted and with a few exceptions, restaffed. Appearances became all important.

Waldheim also wanted an appropriate residence and immediately instructed a UN official, David Vaughan, who ran the UN's Office of General Services, that a search be made. Waldheim's own idea was an apartment on Fifth Avenue with at least five bedrooms and enough room for two maids. Vaughan was instructed to find two or three possibilities and then arrange for Waldheim's wife, Cissy, to visit. There was sniggering among the staff at this: the yearly allowance for a Secretary General's residence was never more than $25,000 – U Thant had lived in a small house in a leafy New York suburb and a Fifth Avenue apartment was quite clearly way beyond the UN's means. The monthly maintenance charge alone would cost at least $2,500. Vaughan reported to Waldheim that there was nothing available. An apartment would cost close to one million dollars. Vaughan confided in a colleague that he was at a loss.

It was a UN benefactor who eventually solved the problem. Through the United Nations Association of America, a powerful UN support group, a sumptuous four-storey town house was donated to the UN. It was ideal: a Georgian-style brick house in the heart of New York's most prestigious address, Sutton Place, with gardens and a river view. It had marble floors, servants' quarters, a library, a sitting room with eighteenth-century panelling, even a lift. It was on loan to the UN at a nominal rent, and the UN would pay for its upkeep and maintenance. The Waldheims would clearly live in style and Cissy Waldheim met Vaughan's staff to inspect dishes and silverware currently in stock at the UN headquarters to see if there were anything she could use.

While the house was being prepared for them, the Waldheims

stayed in a New York hotel and, when the time came to move, one of Waldheim's most senior staff members was put in charge. He received an instruction to take particular care of the wardrobe cabinets on rollers. Labourers did the packing. There seemed no end to the extravagance. Waldheim insisted on having two chauffeurs, one for his wife. Only one slight problem arose over whether or not the UN should pay for Waldheim's wife to travel with him. The sum involved would be considerable as Waldheim travelled nearly all the time, for he loved the pomp and ceremony, and in his first year visited seventeen countries. Waldheim's Chef de Cabinet, an Indian official known as C.V. Narasimhan, "C.V.", tried to discover a precedent. Thant's wife never took part in anything to do with the UN. Hammarskjöld lived alone, but the first Secretary General, Trygve Lie had travelled with both his wife and daughters at UN expense. The UN Controller of finance, mindful of the costs of first-class travel, eventually came up with a compromise – the UN would pay for Cissy if the visit were in response to an official government invitation. Somehow or another it always turned out to be one.

Waldheim's first meeting with his senior officials was on February 15, 1972 and he was bullish, telling the assembled Under Secretaries-General that his main concern was to re-establish the world's confidence in the UN. It was vital that the public know why the UN was able to effect certain things and not others. "A great job of public relations is to be done."

Waldheim, however, seemed more preoccupied with his own image. At his second meeting he complained that distorted rumours were doing the rounds: there was talk about the reconditioning of his private bathroom. The note-taker at this meeting dryly records: "He cited several other rumours of the same nature and explained the true facts". Waldheim was worried about what the press would think. "It may seem", he said, "as though I am over-exposing myself, but it is very important to inform the people." He ordered new directives be sent to the UN's world-wide network of information centres. Instead of waiting for journalists to come to them, the staff in these centres should keep up good relations with the local press. The UN's information policy of neutrality should be changed: there was no reason why the UN should accept criticism and the organisation should defend itself. A Consultative Panel on Public Information was constituted.

Waldheim realised that reform of the Secretariat was a common preoccupation among delegates and he announced that he was going to streamline and rationalise the UN. "I have definite indications that there are some officials with very little to do," he told his cabinet. They would be put to work. Why, for example, was the UN's Secretary General given a pile of newspapers to read each evening? From now on a daily news summary would be prepared to spare him this chore.

Waldheim was obsessed with what he called administrative tidiness and he insisted that letters addressed to the Secretary General and the UN must be answered within three weeks – and in as positive and friendly a way as circumstances permitted. On the thirty-eighth floor the bureaucracy became more structured: agendas were prepared for the bi-monthly cabinet meetings, as were lists of the participants in order of seniority. C. V. prepared a detailed background guidance for every one of Waldheim's meetings, covering every conceivable point. "You may also wish to refer" or "your colleagues will, I am sure, be interested to know" were phrases Narasimhan used time and time again in numerous memoranda. While Waldheim went on jaunts abroad, it was C. V. who ran the UN. As for fundraising for the bankrupt organisation, Waldheim decided to dispatch one of the leading lights of the non-aligned members, a man called Ismat Kittani, a former Ambassador of Iraq, now a UN Assistant Secretary General, to tour the oil-rich states of Qatar, Kuwait, the United Arab Emirates and Saudi Arabia bearing a letter begging for money.

The chronic condition of the Secretariat bureaucracy was of less concern to delegates from the Third World who had chronic economic problems of their own. The poorer member states considered the General Assembly the one place for public debate about how the UN was falling woefully short of its Charter promise for a better life for all. The poor southern nations, with two-thirds the world's population, saw the UN as the principle agency through which they could seek redress of grievances. The poverty gap widened and delegates talked of the urgent need for a new world economic order. Their shaky economies were damaged by the sharp rise in oil prices in 1973 and a global recession led to demands for control of unstable money markets, an end to the volatility in world commodity markets, which contributed to their insurmountable problems. The Third World wanted control over their natural resources and an end to grinding poverty.

The first UN sponsored development decade in the sixties did raise the annual average growth of the developing countries by five per cent but the gap between rich and poor continued to widen. A second development decade was launched in 1970 but it was an ambitious plan which achieved nothing, overwhelmed by the huge increases in oil prices in 1973. The West went through its worst economic crisis of the post-war years with inflation and unemployment, while the Third World debts increased. A continuing population growth exacerbated the problems. In 1974 the UN sponsored a World Population Conference which showed a measure of concern; officials within the Secretariat prophesised a doubling of world population over the next thirty-five years which would put an intolerable burden on the world's life-giving systems. The Conference, in Bucharest, was not a great success and did not result in international consensus. The focus of the debate shifted once again, this time to the structure of the world's economic system, with a developing militant demand for a redistribution of the world's wealth.

In 1974 a special session of the General Assembly was summoned at which a manifesto for change was submitted. The manifesto called for the possible expropriation of multinational corporation properties, the right to restitution for past colonial exploitation and for aid with no strings. The motion called for a just and equitable relationship between the raw materials the Third World exported and the price of the products it imported. The motion provided for subsidies, preferential trading agreements and a 0.7 per cent of gross national product to be spent by the industrialised states to help the Third World. The ideas came from the Group 77, a coalition formed in 1964 to promote the economic interests of semi-industrialised and poor countries. The Group 77 typecast America as the villain of neo-colonialism.

On December 12, 1974, the General Assembly approved, by a large majority, the Charter of Economic Rights and Duties of States. It succeeded only in polarising the UN and caused rage in the chancelleries of industrialised states. This New World Economic Order was nothing less than a demand for the wealth redistribution administered through the UN. American diplomats pointed out that the proposals would increase the dependence of the developing countries and benefit only a fraction of the people. Furthermore, the

West's wealth was legitimately acquired; what was needed was for the industrialised countries to strengthen the world economy. The Third World elites who put their names to the order were less committed to equality in their own countries, where dictatorships ensured that their own poor were silent.

In 1975, a year after the adoption of the Charter for a new world economic order, a special session of the Assembly was convened to discuss Third World poverty. The *New York Times* reported that the leaders of the Third World came to New York more like serious labour leaders rather than revolutionaries and Washington's attitude was more accommodating. At the special session, in the longest speech ever made to the Assembly by a US ambassador, one hour and forty-five minutes, America's new envoy, a Harvard Professor, Dan Pat Moynihan, offered a Marshall Plan for the Third World. The Secretary of State, Henry Kissinger, was due to have given this momentous news but he was delayed in the Middle East, trying to finalise an agreement for the Sinai. The speech, written by Kissinger and read by Moynihan began: "We assemble here this week with an opportunity to improve the condition of mankind." The speech proposed loans of up to $10 billion and an international investment trust. "We know that the world economy nourishes us all," Moynihan read. "We know that we live on a shrinking planet." In the debate there were fewer ideological rants but the realists pointed out that the State Department would have a hard time selling the plan to Congress. In any event it would be up to future international conferences to deliver the promises made at this one.

In Paris in December, 1975 the Conference on International Economic Co-operation laboured over the issues of raw materials, energy, development and finance. The Conference was inconclusive and eventually it became deadlocked over whether or not the developing countries should benefit from debt relief. The Conference ground to a halt in the early summer, 1977 and from then on the New International Economic Order [NIEO] remained little more than an abstraction. The General Assembly could assert important principles and even create an impression that something was being done but it failed to modify views. It was a talking shop where charges could made and then denied, a forum for parliamentary diplomacy and in the end it served to distract from the urgent realities of constructing a more just world order. From now on America would resort to union-busting tactics.

Waldheim thought that the UN was suffering from what he called "institutional inflation" and he told the member states at the General Assembly in 1978 that they were holding: " . . . too many gatherings, conferences and sessions . . . the result is that few and fewer people listen to the speeches, even among the representatives of Governments, let alone the press or the public."

Waldheim pleaded for fiscal restraint but nothing stopped the relentless slide into chaos. In each Waldheim *Annual Report*, he gave an honest appraisal of the gloom. They were written by and large the Under Secretary General, Brian Urquhart, and, although no one paid much heed to them they remain an extraordinary record. They bluntly point out that the UN would be more effective if only the member states would develop the habit of respecting UN decisions. "It is not enough to use the UN as a last resort in critical situations or as a repository for insoluble problems", one report noted. Waldheim worried that UN would collapse. He pleaded with delegates to cut the number of committees and conferences, pleaded for a reduction in the number of reports which were requested by the General Assembly. The production of one UN page cost $300. A half-day committee meeting at headquarters cost $7,300. Waldheim was increasingly critical. "The UN services can no longer carry the steadily increasing load. It is sometimes easier to call a conference, or even to found a new institution, than to confront a complex problem directly."

The pleas were unheeded. In 1979 more meetings were held than ever before and Waldheim warned they were losing public support "without which we shall not achieve the great objectives upon which mankind's future prosperity – even survival – may depend". A year later he moaned about the lack of interest in the UN. "There is almost no general knowledge of its capacity or importance as a balancing factor, as a safety-valve or in conflict control. As the memories of the Second World War fade, there seems to be less and less comprehension of the necessity of building . . . the framework of a working world community capable of withstanding the storms and facing the common problems of an uncertain future."

By now Waldheim's Secretariat and the member states were on a collision course, each blaming the other for the mess. The member governments began to believe that perhaps the problem arose because of faults in the basic structure – the conclusion secretly reached by the British Government in 1947. The first General

Assembly Resolutions on the concentration of resources dated from 1948. In a 1961 report a Committee of Experts noted member states' discontent with an increase in expenditure. Ever since the sixties there had been various attempts at reform; it was a permanent item on the UN agenda and the subject even developed its own UN-ese. But expansion continued; between 1963 and 1968 there was a fifty per cent increase in reports, conferences and commissions.

In some desperation the diplomats formed a police force. It was easier for some to believe that corruption was the root of the problem and they wanted their own "A team".

Within the Secretariat there was trepidation at the prospect. This was the first time outsiders were allowed in and quite clearly the General Assembly no longer trusted the impartiality of officials in the Secretariat. It was a fearsome creation and its name, the Joint Inspection Unit, was bizarre. It was given more power than any other department within the UN and its investigators could commandeer any document, from anywhere in the system, make on-the-spot checks without notification and were to be accorded co-operation at all levels.

The idea was French, first proposed by her ambassador in 1966 during the financial crisis which was splitting the UN apart. The French argued the unit's creation a necessity. France was desperate at the time, behind in her payments for peacekeeping, refusing to contribute to operations created by the General Assembly, arguing they were illegal under the Charter and only the Security Council had the right to authorise UN missions. Because of her debts, France was seen as a delinquent nation and blamed for the very crisis she was trying to solve. Peacekeeping was breaking the UN's back and France was refusing to pay her share. So, as the General Assembly approached, France wanted it known that she might consider contributing in other ways. Once assured that spending was under control, France might save the day by paying into a special survival fund which had just been created. It was an urgent matter. Very soon the UN's controller would not have enough money for salaries. France wanted some effective and administrative changes within the UN itself.

It took two years for the unit to become operational and it was finally constituted in 1968. The Secretary General, U Thant, declared it an expensive and quite unnecessary luxury.

The Joint Inspection Unit was based on the French Inspection des Finances which reports to the Cour des Comptes; in France there is total jurisdictional and administrative control over the state budget. The UN's version would monitor efficiency, the proper use of funds, methods of work, personnel policy. The unit was to come up with some solutions for the UN's long-term financial problems, but more than this, the unit would be able to scrutinise the UN's economic and social programmes in the Third World.

In 1968, the first eight inspectors were chosen. They were nationals from France, the UK, the USSR, the US, Argentina, Yugoslavia, India, and Tanzania. As it turned out, the founding group was revolutionary and its first main concern was how to make the UN more responsive in the developing countries: its early recommendations stressed the urgent need for development programmes which were more effective and in its first report it isolated a terrible faultline, the failure of the UN's Economic and Social Council whose role under the Charter was to co-ordinate and supervise the UN family. This Council, created alongside the Security Council and the General Assembly, was designed by the UN founders to find solutions to world poverty, help to end human rights abuses and ensure fundamental freedom for all. Few would argue that the council had failed to restrain what was uncontrollable anarchy in the system. The Council, originally comprising eighteen member states, was later enlarged to fifty-four. Its members were elected by the General Assembly.

The promise of a better life in greater freeeedom pre-dated the Charter, dating from January 1942 when the allies resolved to bring about the fullest collaboration between all nations in the economic field. Roosevelt wanted the expansion of production and trade and the elimination of discriminatory and restrictive economic policies. Cynics believed that the concern for economic well-being which led to the creation of the Food and Agricultural Organisation in 1943, was the bait for people hungry and oppressed in enemy-occupied countries. But a reluctance to take up the challenge promised in the Charter was evident by 1946, when it came to deciding the make-up of commissions to advise the Council on development. Instead of appointing experts and independent advisers, government officials took over. The commissions, instead of becoming the brains trusts, were unprovocative.

By 1969 when the JIU came to look at the system, the inspectors found that although the UN had embarked on a great economic task with larger agencies than had ever existed, the wartime dreams were no more than glib promises of a brave new world. The JIU discovered that within the UN system there was no overall policy or plan to help the world's poverty-stricken millions. Its report suggested that a start could be made if all projects undertaken by UN agencies in the field were to be combined and rationalised, which would effect huge and immediate savings. There would also be a subsequent increase in morale; a feeling that all aid workers, bureaucrats, officials and experts were part of a team, engaged in a common effort.

In the first year the inspectors travelled widely to UN outposts in developing nations, and what they found was truly shocking for it was rapidly obvious that each part of the UN system was busy sponsoring its own project – with no reference at all to anyone else. The Third World governments were the last to be able to determine priorities.

The inspectors soon learned a harsh lesson. The first law of internationalism seemed to be do not attack the "warlords", the powerful directors of the UN's various agencies. Here the inspectors unearthed a more appalling fault: those who ran the FAO, UNESCO and WHO and the other agencies were not keen on co-ordination. After all, what on earth would happen to their constitutional positions? There were many and various attempts at putting the UN right. In 1969, an enquiry into the how aid money was spent, commissioned by the UN Development Programme, concluded:

> The question must be asked who controls this machine? So far, the evidence suggests that governments do not, and also that the machine is incapable of intelligently controlling itself. This is not because it lacks intelligent and capable officials, but because it is so organized that managerial direction is impossible. In other words, the machine as a whole has become unmanageable . . . as a result it is becoming slower and more unwieldy, like some prehistoric monster.

The UN family is the subject of more studies and reports than any bureaucracy in history. In the US alone, the government watchdog, the General Accounting Office, looked at dozens of different UN activities and dating from 1969 its first report concluded there were substantial management problems, a lack of adequate audit and evaluation.

The General Assembly's reponse to increasing criticism about a lack of managment was to create yet another layer of bureacracy and in December 1974 set up a small group of high-level experts. These experts produced a report, "A New UN Structure for Global Economic Co-operation", which was wide-ranging and proposed major change. Its members recommended immediate reform. The Assembly's response was again the creation of another committee, an Ad Hoc committee to consider "relevant proposals". Next a working group was created and an increasing number of proposals for change were submitted. The "problem areas" were identified and were similar to those which the group of experts had identified a year earlier. The conclusion was an urgent need for co-ordination of the system. The Ad Hoc committee discussed it for several years and there the matter rested.

In 1976 the UN's own Board of Auditors spoke out. The Board, appointed by the General Assembly, consisted of three members, each one an Auditor General of a member state. They held a three-year term of office, with powers to look at efficiency, the accounting system, financial control and general management. In 1976, the board members were from Canada, Ghana and Bangladesh and they concluded there to be a dreadful lack of leadership in the UN, a startling and outspoken gesture by auditors. The auditors revealed that too many officials had too much financial responsibility; too many had power over how money was spent and were not required to report to the UN's Controller. No changes were made. Three years later the board had cause to complain again of inadequate financial direction.

As for the Joint Inspection Unit, it continued with its work and was increasingly ignored. One inspector, an American, produced a report which called for a limit in the production of documents, particularly annual surveys and statistics, most of them reproduced in the UN's five official languages – Chinese, English, French, Russian and Spanish with Arabic added as an official language of the Assembly, the Security Council and the Economic and Social Council. The inspector believed that they had reached the point of absurdity. He had discovered that each UN delegate was faced with daily reading amounting to almost 750 pages. The annual saving on documents could amount to $4 million a year; further savings could be achieved if the General Assembly session were cut by two weeks.

Each year, the General Assembly took note, with much appreciation, of the work of the Joint Inspection Unit. The Unit's recommendations were rarely, if ever, implemented. There developed a widespread belief that the UN was beyond help. The patient was moribund and there was the greatest difficulty finding a diagnosis, let alone a cure. UN member governments were not capable of creating an efficient international administration. There was not sufficient international co-operation to reform the UN. The UN was too useful for member states who could blame mismanagement and inefficiency for their own lack of political will.

Dag Hammarsjöld's dreams of a truly independent civil service remained a dream for while some complained about management deficiency, others likened the Soviets who worked in the Secretariat to insidious termites determined to undermine the ideals upon which the UN was based. The Soviet grip on its nationals was of iron. One notably tragic case involved Alicja Weselowska, a Polish member of the UN staff who was arrested by Polish authorites in Warsaw, in 1979, en route to a UN assignment and was convicted on charges of contacts with foreign intelligence. No evidence was produced but she was sentenced to seven years in violation of the rights and immunities granted international civil servants. The Secretary General at the time, Kurt Waldheim, was finally induced to make an appeal to Polish authorities, to no avail. The Weselowska case was not unique. Another staff member Liviu Bota from Rumania who went home on leave never returned to his job as previously in Geneva. The UN's Staff Union published a list in November, 1988 of the names of UN staff who had been executed or disappeared: a full list had been prepared by the UN Staff Union's Committee on the Security and Independence of the international civil service. Every employee from the Eastern bloc was pressured by his or her government: none was employed in the Secretariat without the express wish of his or her government and it was a particular tragedy that these habits were later adopted by authoritarian regimes from the Third World.

The focus was on Soviet bloc citizens who made use of the UN Secretariat in New York which was the most useful watchtower in the West. This was confirmed by Oleg Kalugin, Soviet Intelligence General, former head of the KGB's foreign counter-intelligence department and who worked at the UN as a KGB agent for a time. The Soviets always denied espionage at the UN and pointed out that there was no such thing as a UN secret. The real value of Soviet Bloc staff at the UN was their freedom, as international civil servants, to travel within the US, to collect information, make contacts and give messages. The UN allowed the KGB a library on US soil. "We love libraries," Kalugin said and when it came to technical information, the Soviets made the utmost use of the UN's extensive library in the Secretariat building.

The Secretariat as a nest of spies was described years later when the US Senate Select Committee on Intelligence published a report about how the Soviets were subverting the Secretariat. The Reagan administration made it an issue and shortly after publication of the report in 1985 imposed restrictions on Secretariat staff who were nationals of the Soviet Union, Afghanistan, Cuba, Iran, Libya and Vietnam. From then on, staff from these countries wanting to travel outside a twenty-five mile radius of the Secretariat building would have to book their tickets with the American government. The Secretary General, Pérez de Cuéllar, took exception to it, saying that the new regulations were incompatible with the Charter because they discriminated against staff on the basis of nationality and they would have to be applicable to everyone. Within UN committees diplomats argued for hours about the travel restrictions which were part of a toughening attitude towards the UN by the Reagan administration. In early 1986 in sharp rebuke to a Soviet ambassador, a UN ambassador, Joseph Verner Reed, replied: "In the words of President Reagan, you ain't seen nothing yet".

The proof of the Soviet Union's nefarious behaviour had already come from a defector, the highest-ranking Soviet official ever to come over to the West. He was Arkady Nikolaevich Shevchenko, appointed the most senior Soviet official, an Under Secretary General. During his final years in the Secretariat he spied for the CIA and gave the Americans secret cables which passed between the Soviet Mission in New York and the Foreign Ministry in Moscow. Shevchenko, one of an eminent group of Soviet diplomats, had graduated from the State Institute of International Relations in Moscow where he specialised in disarmament, a fashionable subject during the time of Nikita Khrushchev. Shevchenko's career was also helped by his friendship with Andrei Gromyko, which assured his promotion. After his defection Shevchenko wrote a book, *Breaking with Moscow*, in which he described a Gromyko briefing in April, 1973 in preparation for his posting to the UN. Gromyko told him to be vigilant about the West deviating from the Charter. It was inadvisable to attempt a good relationship with Secretary General, Kurt Waldheim. No great benefit would come from it. Shevchenko was advised to spend time on relations with the Chinese and their allies.

In the Secretariat, Shevchenko headed the Department of Political and Security Council Affairs although, as he told Congress in October 1985, the Soviet government considered him more an ambassador than an independent civil servant. His department was nicknamed The Gulag. Shevchenko says that for the first few years at least he behaved to type and insisted all documents within the Department pass through his hands. He encroached upon the responsibilities of other departments in order to defend and promote Soviet interests.

Like Kalugin, Shevchenko described the Secretariat as the fulcrum of the KGB operation against the West and said that the Soviets had managed the most thorough penetration of the entire UN family. It was ideal for collecting scientific and industrial know-how. Shevchenko's testimony to Congress and his book were of huge value to both the CIA and the FBI. The latter complained frequently that funding to keep tabs on the largest diplomatic community in the world was never enough; Shevchenko's evidence was invaluable in persuading Congress to vote more funding. Shevchenko's memoir describes all Soviets, both UN employees and the delegates, as lazy, drunk and inefficient. He claims that at least half were agents of the KGB or GRU. When Congress decided to restrict travel in 1985, it was a first step. A few months later in March 1986, the US ordered a thirty-eight per cent reduction in personnel serving in the Soviet Mission to the UN. The Ukraine and Byelorussian mission were to be similarly reduced.

Previously, actions taken against staff from the Eastern bloc were secret. They could be thrown out of the Secretariat at any time, the victims of any number of secret agreements reached between the US authorities and the office of Secretary General. Sometimes they were recalled by their own governments, returning home with no publicity or fuss – and to uncertain futures. Staff from the Eastern bloc had no defence when accused of real – or imagined – breaches of US law and many left the Secretariat with no obvious explanation. Others went on home leave and when they applied for a visa to resume UN duties, the US refused. The Secretary General was sometimes informed by letter that there was a clear violation of the employee's international status – a euphemism for espionage – and only rarely did these letters contain a bare outline of fact. Some went on home leave and were arrested by their own governments and either disappeared or were thrown into jail.

No accurate figure can be given for the numbers of international civil servants expelled. Neither is information available about staff from the Eastern bloc lured into the FBI, or CIA defector nets and who subsequently lost their jobs and sometimes their lives. The only certainty is that the Cold War damaged the international civil service for ever.

The international civil service was far from that envisaged by the UN architects who in 1945 had enshrined guidelines and principles for staff in the Charter. How far removed from these ideals one of the Joint Inspection Unit inspectors was to discover. The UN, so he realised, was a bureacracy with no recruitment policy, poor management, and no career development. The staff was inadequately trained and less and less suited for the work required. The responsibility lay with member states who lobbied and cajoled and sometimes paid for appointments for their own nationals, often relatives or friends of those in power.

Maurice Bertrand, the French Inspector, and a founder member of the unit, pursued the staff problem for his entire seventeen-year career. Appointed in 1968, a Senior Counsellor at the Cours des Comptes in Paris, it took him two years to write his first damning indictment of UN absurdity – the ridiculous appointments, the bartering for jobs – and in the years which followed, Bertrand did more than criticise, he wanted reform. In 1976, four years after the publication of the report, Bertrand prepared a timetable, anything to goad the delegates that something had to be done urgently about the corrupt personnel practice. But nothing happened. In public, when asked, Bertrand described it as "extremely bad". There was, he said, a "laxness that prevails in this matter . . . which would seem to put a premium on mediocrity". Bertrand could not understand why the international civil service could not be of the highest quality. The situation was impossible to justify.

Bertrand left the unit in 1985, the year of the UN's fortieth anniversary, and he commemorated the occasion with a last report which could best be described as a UN obituary. His final word was that there was no one with a clear idea of what the UN amounted to. Here was a bureaucracy throwing out a smokescreen to conceal its true nature. It had its own language, a barely comprehensible bureaucratic language of good intention. This allowed it successfully to manage to disguise a complete lack of determination. Some of it was hilarious. Bertrand found one UN project described to "develop administrative infrastructure in the various development sectors in developing countries". "One may wonder", Bertrand wrote, "whether this . . . has any relationship to the facts of life".

Bertrand's report became a UN classic and those who could not obtain one among Secretariat staff made free use of the photocopiers. The episode was tragedy comedy because Bertrand had written the most widely read report by the staff the UN ever produced for the reason that Bertrand was the first and only person ever to describe the UN labyrinth, with all its extraordinary and unnecessary institutional complexity. Bertrand had found, in one developing country, thirty different UN organisations and programmes. Each was independent, and each channelling aid. Each had different methods, and each had a different theory. The average project involved the employment of two to three experts, each costing $100,000 a year, most under-qualified and unacquainted with the countries whose problems they were trying to solve. Each project, which would be examined in committee after committee, was created in confusion.

"The way in which the mill operates becomes much more important than the flour it produces," Bertrand wrote. The UN delegates, sent by their governments, trying to learn the UN machinery, were obliged to follow the most trivial matters of administration. Countless impenetrable documents and reports littered delegates' desks, lacking analysis and precise conclusion. It was difficult to see how such a situation could be rectified by better management methods. As for the past efforts to try to co-ordinate the system, there was nothing to show but fifteen years of useless effort. Nothing could ever correct the structural shortcomings, nor the fact that the staff of the UN lacked adequate training and were grossly under-qualified. Everything the UN produced, its reports and its opinions, and all its projects in the field were mediocre. The UN could not even run its own publishing enterprise for the books which the UN produced about itself were neither profitable nor efficient, nor even interesting.

Bertrand believed that even if all the UN's faults were to be corrected, the organisation would still be incapable of carrying out its essential mission of peace, protecting human rights and ensuring world development. The very concept was at fault. The UN was utopian, founded before co-operation between states was sufficient to sustain it. Only in very few areas did co-operation ever achieve consensus. After all, there were different levels of consensus in different fields of interest, in transport, communications, and some humanitarian efforts. A basic revision of the entire idea was imperative.

Bertrand told them that it was too much to expect that in a politically divided world, the 159 states could negotiate usefully to try to solve some of the world's problems. There was far too much self-interest. The amounts given for aid were assessed according to the degree of emotion stirred up in public opinion: aid to the poorest was first and foremost a means of exerting influence. As for the bank loans handed out to the Third World, these were to the more advanced to take over markets. Bertrand had come to believe passionately that something had to be done. The UN was not addressing the world's most urgent needs. Three-quarters of humankind urgently needed an organisation which was capable of helping overcome their historical handicap, to close the gap between rich and poor nations. The five permanent members of the Security Council did nothing more than widen the gap, ensuring that the world's conflicts generally took place in countries which were poor and underprivileged.

Bertrand retired from the UN believing that reform was impossible. The diplomats would maintain the status quo because they believed they contributed to international co-operation. Increasingly, it was not so. Indeed, so unimportant was the UN system, that it was given only 6.5 per cent of all development aid spent world-wide. As for what it spent on peace and security, that figure was only one-tenth of a day's world expenditure on arms – or $243 million as opposed to $800 billion. Bertrand suggested starting again. He wanted an Economic Security Council, which would invite developing countries to the negotiating table. Each delegation would include an economist and a Minister of Finance. The main UN agencies would be reorganised under the authority of a commission, comprising independent people of distinction. It was unlikely. None of the diplomats wanted to relinquish power.

Within days of publication of Bertrand's last report, a senior UN official was quoted as saying that Bertrand was out of touch with the realities of the institution. As a result of the report, the General Assembly set up a commission of enquiry into the Joint Inspection Unit. A year later it reported that the unit wasted its efforts. It had attached too

much importance to elaborate evaluation systems. It should have spent
its time limiting spending and increasing productivity.

The next impetus for reform came in 1986, an idea from the
Japanese, proposed by their Foreign Minister, Shintaro Abe. By
1986 Japan was growing bolder and with her booming economy, her
financial commitment to the UN was large. There were rumours she
was after a permanent seat on the Security Council, a natural
extension of the principle of no taxation without representation.
Japan belonged to no large voting bloc and had a low visibility in
international diplomacy but she was second only to the USA in her
UN contribution, with none of the UN's top jobs.

By 1986 the UN was sliding further into bankruptcy. A hostile
Congress in Washington was loathe to allocate money to a wasteful
and corrupt international bureaucracy and the American debt was
growing daily. The UN's stock was never lower in Washington and
the Senate, mindful of the hostile Third World majority in the
General Assembly, wanted more control over the budget. The
organisation was in itself in jeopardy. The West was weary of being
the major contributors to an organisation which was ineffectual;
more than half the UN members contributed 0.01 per cent each to
the UN budget. The Third World was disillusioned too, admitting
defeat in attempts to build a new economic order.

In 1986 the Japanese, declaring that the organisation was
undergoing a crisis of confidence, offered to pay a group of
international management experts to make it more efficient. The
General Assembly jumped at the chance but instead of a group of
outsiders they chose insiders from eighteen countries from all
regional groups, former officials and diplomats, knowledgeable
about the arcane UN bureaucracy. They called it the "High-Level
Intergovernmental Group of Experts to Review the Efficiency of the
Administrative and Financial Functioning of the United Nations"
and thankfully it became known by the shorter title, Group 18.

For eight weeks during the summer of 1986, Group 18 studied
documents, records, balance sheets and statistics and the eventual
report was explosive. It described an inflated bureaucracy,
diplomats holding useless meetings and conferences, commissions,
committees and working groups. They found a top heavy administration which lacked adequate qualifications. High salaries gave
cause for serious concern. The UN was required by member

governments to produce more paperwork than it was possible for any one member state to study.

Group 18 called for drastic economies. It wanted an immediate reduction in the use of consultants, which ate up $8 million yearly. There was to be an immediate cut in top jobs by twenty-five per cent and a fifteen per cent cut in staff overall. There must be an instant reduction in travel costs. "As a rule first-class travel should be limited to the Secretary General," the report dryly noted.

The report blamed Pérez de Cuéller, then Secretary General, for a lack of leadership, accusing him of caving in to pressure from member governments wanting Secretariat appointments. This practice should cease. The Secretary General must adhere strictly to the Charter. He must hire nationals from developing countries and should promote more women.

In one vital area Group 18 failed. It did not come up with a solution to give Congress more power over the UN budget. Group 18 was meant to have come up with a formula. Unable to alter the Charter principle of one nation one vote, the Group had concentrated instead on trying to find a way for the US to have more of a say in the committees whose role was to scrutinise expenditure before it got to the vote in the General Assembly. There was a complication. Because of the elephantine bureaucracy set up by the member governments, a programme and its costs were never considered at the same place at the same time by the same diplomats. One set of diplomats made decisions on priorities, a conference on human rights or a study on disarmament, and another quite different group made a decision on cost.

At the last minute, Group 18 suggested a pivotal role for an existing committee of twenty-one, small by UN standards, which included representatives from the major donors and would ensure co-ordination of planning and budgeting and UN work. This small committee would be a gatekeeper, receiving the budget a year in advance and giving an opinion on its size.

At the General Assembly in the autumn of 1986, a gathering ostensibly concerned with apartheid, drugs, terrorism and war, the dominant theme became UN reform. The Third World grumbled about it, and its ambassadors said the new budget process was a convenient way for the West to extend its great power veto. The campaign to persuade them otherwise turned into a jamboree, as

Western ambassadors connived and contrived to get enough support for the reform package to be voted through. There was meeting after meeting and debates and discussion on tactics and strategy, as diplomats cajoled and persuaded. Many of the African delegates who attended that year did not really know what was at issue; they lacked instructions from their home governments. The US determined, dispatched a diplomat to tour the African continent to stress the importance of the issue. President Ronald Reagan wrote to the Heads of State of key African governments about the need for reform and his speech to the Assembly that year was written with reform in mind. Reagan told them the UN faced a critical hour. This was not about cash but credibility and there was an urgent need to restore the organisation's status and effectiveness. "And you have my word for it: my country, which has always given the United Nations generous support, will continue playing a leading role in an effort to achieve its noble purposes."

On the last day of the General Assembly the reforms were voted through, and there were sighs of relief. They had reformed the UN and satisfied American demands for more power over the budget. A new and pragmatic blueprint would re-establish the viability and credibility of the UN.

Reagan telephoned Pérez de Cuéllar to offer his congratulations and at the final assembly session, the American Ambassador to the United Nations, Vernon Walters, said it had been a great day for his country, the UN and mankind.

In one sense it was historic but the claims that the changes in the budget process had established consensus decision-making were way off mark. The new budget process depended solely on the will of the delegates to agree and it remained to be seen whether it would ever work. If the major donors decided to use the system unreasonably or if the Third World tried to force through UN expansion, they would be back where they started. Nonetheless, they rose from their seats believing the UN's problems were over.

There followed a reduction in staff, the trimming of budgets, and the cancellation of some meetings. As for the rest, it continued as before. Group 18 was another missed opportunity. The member governments had simply stalled for time. The financial constraints and squabbles about paying for UN operations continued as before and impinged on effectiveness. The debt to the UN rose to more than a billion dollars from all member countries but the lion's share was owed by the US.

Group 18 was followed by another vain attempt when a group of Nordic countries decided to try to relaunch the UN organisation in the late eighties. The Nordics wanted restructuring of development programmes and, like the Joint Inspection Unit before them, identified a shameful lack of co-ordination of UN agencies in the field. The Nordics suggested that the agenices merge into a single Development Assistance Board. They pointed to the urgency for action; development was a priority at a time when ethnic conflicts were breaking out, the numbers of refugees increasing and weapons proliferating.

The Nordic project was handed to Pérez de Cuéllar in May, 1991 and presented to the General Assembly five months later. Everyone agreed that the time had come at last to avoid dupliction and waste. But negotiations on implementation of Nordic recommendations led nowhere.

When the Cold War came to an end there was renewed hope that the UN would reform to meet the challenge. But the seismic changes made no difference; the grandiose expressions of faith in the UN by the permanent five failed to translate into action over the UN's blatant inadequacies. Instead the five gave the UN new responsiblities: peackeeping operations multiplied even though management back at headquarters was faulty. The five were no more willing than before to commit themselves to matters which did not affect their immediate interests. The UN's bureaucracy was a convenient excuse for failure, an excuse which left the five unaccountable.

Various attempts continued to make the UN more efficient. In 1994 the General Assembly appointed a retired chief executive officer of Price Waterhouse, Joseph E. Connor, as Under Secretary General for Administration and Management to try to undertake a radical streamlining. Also appointed was a German diplomat, Karl Theodore Paschke, as Under Secretary General for Internal Oversight Services to look for waste and fraud. The improvement of the UN was also discussed in 1995, the UN's fiftieth year by the world's richest countries, known as the G7 at a summit meeting in Halifax, Nova Scotia. The G7 comprise the US, Japan, Germany, France, Britain, Italy and Canada. Not much time was spent on detail. The countries could agree only that the UN ought to be more efficient, less costly, better managed and more accountable.

8. MISSION ACCOMPLISHED

On First Avenue the shining black traffic was stuck in place by the usual parade of diplomatic limousines as Presidents and Prime Ministers came to the world stage, the stars of diplomacy who would join the cast of thousands for scheming and gossiping. But this year the self-assured razzmatazz was misleading. This was 1981, the year the British first voted against the UN budget, expressing her "profound dissatisfaction" with the way money was spent and calling for rational and controlled slimming. America also demanded financial realism. The UN could not do everything about every problem for everyone. The West gave notice that spending money on Charter commitment would have stricter limits.

The Third World was unimpressed and Algeria confidently declared no member nation had the right to call for zero growth while the aims of the Charter remained unrealised; and Cameroon told the assembled delegates that if all member states were to disarm and co-operate on an international economic order, there could easily be a drastic reduction in UN expenditure. Their wit misfired. The UN was on serious notice to change.

The UN's response was sluggish, for reasons that are all too familiar. In any event, the issue was not the nature of the UN, or how it might be reformed. The issue in 1981 was who would be Secretary General.

Waldheim wanted an unprecendented third term. In November 1980, a year before his second term expired, he had started to use the slogan "Think of the Alternative". Ministers and diplomats dreaded his handshake for Waldheim had one matter on his mind.

At the October Security Council lunch hosted by Spain he was stopping ambassadors on the steps of the residence and preventing them leaving, holding up a queue of limousines. He started travelling too and rushed from capital to capital, twenty-four countries in just nine months, at UN expense, in an attempt to lobby support. Five years earlier, when China had reluctantly withdrawn the veto on his second term, Waldheim had promised them he would help to elect a Secretary General from the Third World the following time. He broke that trust when his campaign started. In 1981 his chances looked bleak; this time – for once – the Third World was united behind one candidate.

Salim Ahmed Salim, Foreign Minister of Tanzania, was an intelligent and debonair man who knew exactly how to work the cumbersome UN system to advantage. He had spent ten years as UN Ambassador and his special skill was his use of UN agendas; Salim Salim knew how to promote what the Third World wanted. He was the choice of the fifty-one-nation Organisation of African Unity, endorsed by the League of Arab States and all the Foreign Ministers of the non-aligned. His campaign had direct appeal to them all. Salim Salim maintained that either the international community continued to give priority to the East–West conflict and stuck with Waldheim, or it could elect a Secretary General attentive to Third World poverty and global development. The Soviets did not care to oppose him although they thought him unpredictable and too friendly with Beijing. The Soviets assumed that the Americans would organise the opposition for them and how right they were, for there was just one single incident in Salim Salim's past which guaranteed him the American veto. When ten years earlier the moment had come for the admission to the UN of the People's Republic of China, Salim Salim had danced a triumphant jig right in front of a humiliated US representative to the UN, Ambassador George Bush. It was the kind of diplomatic incident – personal, small, grating and publicity grabbing – which America never forgave.

The voting for Secretary General began. In each of sixteen ballots in the Security Council, Salim Salim was vetoed by the Americans while the ambassador from Moscow, Oleg Troyanovsky, simply abstained. Troyanovsky thought privately that Waldheim, like an old shoe, fitted the best.

The Security Council was trapped in a constitutional crisis, stymied by the relentless ambition of Waldheim and the sheer determination of Third World delegates. There was speculation that Waldheim's term might be extended or a caretaker appointed. Brian Urquhart's name was bandied about but nothing could hide an awkward reality: the Security Council was faced with the humiliating prospect of telling the General Assembly that no Secretary General could be found.

The campaign turned wretched. The President of the General Assembly, Ismat Kittani of Iraq, warned the corridor talk was growing distinctly racist. He called a private meeting with both candidates and Kittani later remarked that this meeting was the only time Waldheim and Salim Salim ever spoke to each other – then or since. On the official press release, and only there, the meeting was a "very friendly and cordial exchange of views".

The Americans had their own preoccupations. Their new Ambassador, Jeane Kirkpatrick, the neo-conservative academic, hired by her friend President Reagan, was alienating her colleagues. Kirkpatrick, unlike other US ambassadors, did not circulate in the delegates' lounge. She refused to do the essential and informal business of diplomacy, and she was gratuitously truculent with those she considered her inferiors. She lacked finesse. Worse, her manners reflected American policy. Washington was no longer interested, it seemed, in building any international constituency. Kirkpatrick, forthright and outspoken, quite clearly had nothing but disdain for the UN. She believed it exacerbated conflict. The UN was no more a reflection of the real world than a football match was a reflection of the drama of life. Some Europeans blamed her inexperience but career diplomats in the American mission knew otherwise: her impatience with bureaucratic routine, her disregard of State Department wisdom, her coterie of conservatives from Georgetown University all indicated that there was a cold gale blowing against the very idea of international co-operation. The Helms Amendment in Congress, intended to cut America's contribution, was but one example for, with the Reagan administration's blessing, Congress adopted an amendment to the Foreign Assistance Act which could deny aid to nations who took anti-American positions in the General Assembly.

No one imagined that the Security Council would give a lead when it came to a choice of Secretary General. Through monthly alphabetical rotation, the December Presidency had fallen to Uganda whose ambassador, Olara Otunnu, was impressive, young and talented – the youngest ever, at thirty-one, to hold the Presidency. Otunnu was clever enough to endear himself to the UN's elder statesmen but, up until his arrival in New York, his only political experience was leading student activists against Idi Amin. He was the last man anyone expected to make UN history.

Olara Otunnu had other ideas. The young diplomat went to sound out the Chinese Ambassador, Qing Ling. Ling was adamant that Waldheim would not get the job again. There seemed no chance that Beijing's position on vetoing Waldheim would change. Otunnu found that Ambassador Kirkpatrick was just as obdurate about Salim Salim. Each veto was deliberate, and unchangeable. Otunnu, unhesitatingly, went directly to Kurt Waldheim. He asked if Waldheim would mind withdrawing from the race, for just a few days. Such a brief time on the sidelines, he promised, would not be prejudicial. Indeed, it would enhance his stature and might help his campaign. Otunnu assured Waldheim he could call for a Security Council ballot at any time he chose. Otunnu said he would be giving Salim Salim the same message

It worked. Waldheim was sure that it was only a matter of time before the Chinese abandoned their veto; he was sure of victory. After all, he had visited Beijing that summer and the Chinese had praised his objectivity. Otunnu nodded, politely. That evening, during a diplomatic supper, Otunnu made the same case discreetly with Salim Salim. Within a few days, Salim Salim requested that for the time being the Security Council take his name from subsequent ballots. Otunnu knew that both candidates were assuming that the other seven contenders would draw vetoes from one ambassador or another on the Security Council.

Next, Otunnu talked to them all – the Big Five and those on the Council in the non-permanent seats, the German Democratic Republic, Ireland, Japan, Mexico, Nigeria, Panama, Philippines, Spain and Tunisia. To each ambassador he gave a copy of the curriculum vitae of the seven declared alternative candidates. He explained his sole purpose was to test the ground and he announced that at the next meeting of the Security Council not even the interpreters would be allowed. Otunnu would ask each Ambassador simply to mark "encourage" or "discourage" against each candidate's name. The five permanent members would be given the same list but would mark – anonymously – anyone who drew a veto.

Afterwards Otunnu waited until he was alone to look at the voting slips. Of the seven alternative candidates, Sadruddin Aga Khan had the most positive votes, but he was too Western not to draw a Soviet veto. Otunnu smiled. In second place was a Peruvian diplomat, Javier Pérez de Cuéllar, with an extraordinary advantage: no veto was marked against his name.

Otunnu at once called an informal meeting of the Security Council to announce the results of his straw poll. They had, he said, two options: either they waited until after lunch before passing into formal session or they went into the chamber and passed directly to a vote. He believed that if they chose to wait they risked whispers and rumours, press leaks, another frenzy of lobbying, and further damage to the reputation of the UN. They immediately filed into the Security Council and voted: Javier Pérez de Cuéllar of Peru was the new Secretary General. The Council stood in a gesture of self-congratulation and loudly applauded itself for managing to make a decision. China was delighted to save face; Beijing's news agency announced a Third World victory. The Americans were relieved to have a professional, quiet diplomat in office who would maintain Waldheim's careful impartiality in all the balances of the Cold War, but who was just sufficiently Third World. Indeed some believed Ambassador Kirkpatrick to have put Otunnu up to it. Otunnu was pleased: he was widely tipped to be the next Secretary General, when it was the turn of the African bloc.

The celebration inside the Security Council was nothing compared with the jubilation in Lima where the President of Peru, his Ministers and Pérez de Cuéllar were full of self-congratulation. They had pulled off a tricky campaign, all the while successfully denying that anyone was doing anything so improper as campaigning at all. Naturally, they saw the vote as a triumph not for internationalism nor for the future of the UN, but for Peru. Keeping their secrets, the Peruvians managed to construct a wall of legend. As for Waldheim and Salim, their gloom knew no bounds.

The election of Javier Pérez de Cuéllar became a myth. Ostensibly, this was a story of a quiet and unassuming career diplomat with no special influence who had been plucked from obscurity by a desperate Security Council. He was the perfect choice. He stood at the intersection of two world conflicts – a man from the Third World, acceptable to both the more and less developed nations, a member of the non-aligned bloc who was acceptable to both the East and the West. In the mess which was the 1981 General Assembly, Pérez de Cuéllar was a welcome compromise.

In fact, Pérez de Cuéllar of all of them, was the one Secretary General about which the least was known.

The official history states that Pérez de Cuéllar was surprised by his success. While the vote took place in New York he was in a beach house outside Lima, with a library, but no phone. No doubt he was pursuing one of his hobbies: writing poetry, collecting coins and listening to classical music. It was a version of Olympian detachment, and it was thought to be the proper behaviour of a diplomat with a distinguished career in the rarified world of international diplomacy.

"I didn't seek this job," he told the New York Times, "and it's important that everybody knows I won't seek another term, so that I can be independent enough to win the trust of the members and still speak out in defence of the Charter when I think this will be useful."

Time and time again Pérez de Cuéllar returned to this theme, most notably in a keynote address at Oxford University in 1986, just a few months after his second term was confirmed by a grateful Security Council.

> Impartiality is . . . the heart and soul of the office . . . [which] must remain untainted by any feeling of indebtedness to governments. I attach the greatest importance to this point. However impeccable a person's integrity may be he cannot . . . retain the necessary independence if he proclaims his candidacy and conducts a kind of election campaign, overt or covert.

The truth is that in Pérez de Cuéllar the Security Council had elected a fiercely and desperately ambitious man who was skilled in the art of nineteenth-century diplomacy. When the time had come for the crucial vote, contrary to the official version, he was sitting quietly in a comfortable Lima apartment along with two men who had campaigned so hard for him to succeed. When the call came his wife, Marcela, took it and immediately passed him the telephone. He turned to the room and said:"Ten minutes ago in New York I was elected Secretary General of the United Nations".

Later that day Pérez de Cuéllar took another call from New York, from a man named Celso Pastor de la Torre, the man's whose friendship paid off so admirably. Pastor de la Torre, one of Lima's most skilled political operators, had been sent to New York a few months ago as Special Envoy of the Peruvian Government to be Pérez de Cuéllar's behind-the-scenes operator. He had been in daily contact with the Foreign Ministry in Lima. That night he said to Pérez de Cuéllar: "Mision cumplida" – mission accomplished. Pérez de Cuéllar apparently said to him: "Toscanini's conducting was masterly".

In the rise of Javier Pérez de Cuéllar to the ultimate accolade at the UN, there are three vital elements – the international tensions which made it possible to elect him, the domestic politics in Lima which made him Peru's candidate, and the deliberate and sometimes dubious campaign which brought the two together.

In the end, Pérez de Cuéllar's success depended on one unlikely event. Peru, ruled for years by a rich elite, had suddenly found itself with a government with a passionate identification with the Third World. After centuries, the rich, white oligarchy had given way to serious-minded international ambition and a voice for the poor, diseased and suffering population. In Lima, General Edgardo Mercado Jarrin, responsible for Pérez de Cuéllar's first major diplomatic posting, would look back on Pérez de Cuéllar's extraordinary career and put it down to an uncanny knack of being where it mattered when it mattered most.

The rise of Pérez de Cuéllar had everything to do with his unofficial place at the heart of a Third World elite. But his international prominence depended on the left-wing military coup of Velasco, a general who in 1968 proclaimed a revolution on behalf of Peru's Indians, and who promised to break the domination of the elite, smash their links with the exporters, bankers and American investors.

There had been attempts at change before in the early sixties, when Fernando Belaúnde Terry tried to appoint qualified and younger men to his government but his initiatives were blocked. The economic decline continued; debt and inflation soared and a secret and wilfully generous deal between his government and the International Petroleum Company (IPC) brought him down – IPC was a subsidiary of Standard Oil of New Jersey and long benefited from ridiculously low taxation.

This time, the left-wing junta's actions were effective and millions of acres were seized from the ruling class. Most industries, including sugar plantations, were expropriated and turned into workers' co-operatives. There were sweeping agrarian reform laws passed to free the tenant labourers and to redistribute land throughout the country. The junta began to nationalise the banks. Its first action, however, was to send troops to occupy the IPC oil refinery at Talara. This was a particularly dangerous step. Any further attempt by Peru to refinance her foreign debt would now be blocked; foreign aid would be cut. There was every possibility that the US would try to destabilise the junta, lest it set a precedent for neighbouring countries. As never before, Peru needed allies and help from the international community.

It was not an easy task, particularly for a country without international standing. Neither would it be easy for Peruvian diplomats, schooled in the ways of elitism, to admit that the junta's revolutionary policies were realistic. In the living memory of the Foreign Ministry international relations were dictated by America. All their own expertise lay in negotiation with neighbouring states over border disputes.

All this created huge problems for the new Foreign Minister, a general named Edgardo Mercado Jarrin who had spent years in the army, but although he readily admitted a lack of experience in foreign relations Mercardo Jarrin was regarded the most intellectual man in the new government. Mercardo Jarrin was lucky to find one man in the ministry to rely on, Javier Pérez de Cuéllar. At the time, Mercardo Jarrin thought it a small miracle that a crisis in the diplomatic corps was averted and he later credited Pérez de Cuéllar with providing stability when it was most needed.

Peru's new radical policy, boldly proclaimed throughout the international system, quickly changed her relations with the Eastern bloc. Trade missions from Eastern Europe appeared weekly while, in Lima for the first time ever, diplomatic relations were established with the Soviet Union. A two-year trade agreement was signed and soon they would have to find Peru's first ambassador to Moscow. Edgardo Mercado Jarrin, suggested someone too close to the previous regime and was told to provide an alternative. When Mercado Jarrin consulted Pérez de Cuéllar, a solution soon presented itself. Pérez de Cuéllar discreetly offered his own services.

Pérez de Cuéllar made the most of the opportunity. Whilst he was ambassador in Moscow he won Soviet help for Peruvian industry and Soviet finance for the construction of an extensive irrigation project. A year after his appointment the Soviets granted Peru $30 million in credits to purchase Soviet machinery. And he laid the groundwork for Peru's eventual purchase of Soviet military equipment – the only Latin-American country, other than Cuba, to buy arms from the East.

Velasco's revolution brought Peru prestige. Around the world her diplomats successfully presented her government as a model for rapid economic development and social change, emphasising opposition to both capitalism and Communism. Peru became a leading and militant voice of the Third World. Peru promoted the idea that only increased development would lead to economic security for the poorer nations. Development was the only way to overcome weakness and poverty, a theory long expounded by the UN's Economic Commission for Latin America.

As for the UN itself, everyone knew that a country's image was made or destroyed in New York, and in the Peruvian Foreign Ministry it was assumed that whoever was appointed UN ambassador would have a profile and influence former ambassadors could never have imagined.

Pérez de Cuéllar, two years after his appointment to Moscow, was sent to New York to be Peru's UN representative. Within a matter of months he was voted President of the non-aligned Group of 77. In 1971 the Group of 77 held its Congress in Lima which was a major source of prestige for Peru. When, in 1971, Kurt Waldheim stood for Secretary General, there were rumours that Pérez de Cuéllar would be an obvious Latin-American candidate.

By all accounts the years which followed were exciting. Pérez de Cuéllar represented his country at a crucial moment. Peru defied Washington. Peru refused to continue sanctions against outcast Cuba. Peru voted to admit the Communist Chinese against all Ambassador George Bush's pleadings. Peru was close to China. She recognised the government of the People's Republic and was given a twenty-year, interest free $42 million loan by China. Peru, awarded a non-permanent seat on the Security Council in 1973, helped to write a resolution which called for neutralisation of the Panama canal. Thirteen nations rallied round and on March 21 forced the US to use its veto against the Resolution.

Pérez de Cuéllar was the prophet of these causes. He was the man who allowed a poor and dependent Peru to see herself in the middle range, with power alongside Canada, say, or Sweden. At the East River headquarters of the UN there was a school of thought that the dramatic change in Peru's foreign policy was due in large part to the dogged persuasion of Pérez de Cuéllar, an impression which would survive the ultimate fall of the Peruvian junta.

Velasco's economic success did not last. Peru would struggle as the windfall export price boom of the early seventies faded and Velasco policies led to an outflow of capital. Food output deteriorated, there was an investment strike and capital flight. Increased borrowing abroad financed a larger bureaucracy and increasing military expenditure. By 1975 there was a severe balance of payments crisis. The junta became an unstable military dictatorship suppressing strikes with violence and Peru turned its guns on the people to satisfy the International Monetary Fund that the country was secure. The officer corps gave up, hopelessly divided about what to do and, in 1980, the military handed the sick and ailing country back to civilian rule.

Pérez de Cuéllar was gone by then. In September 1975 he joined the UN, and was appointed one of Secretary General Waldheim's diplomatic trouble-shooters, given the unenviable job of Permanent Representative to divided Cyprus and for the next two years he spent considerable time in shuttle diplomacy in the Mediterranean.

In Lima, the years of the left-wing military junta were not easily forgiven or forgotten. In time, Pérez de Cuéllar's ardent espousal of the Velasco cause would come close to ruining his glittering career. His links with the junta would be a source of some embarrassment. After all, the best his friends ever managed to offer as proof of his distance from the junta was that Pérez de Cuéllar had refused to hang a portrait of Velasco above his desk in the Moscow Embassy.

In Cyprus Pérez de Cuéllar moved beyond his reputation as a skilled ambassador for he had joined the international elite. The appointment was a way for Secretary General Kurt Waldheim to say thank you, to show his appreciation for Pérez de Cuéllar's recent presidency of the Security Council. Pérez de Cuéllar happened to be in the chair when in July 1974 Archbishop Makarios of Cyprus was ousted by a coup. With a speed not normally associated with Council procedure, its members managed to pass eight Resolutions in ten days calling for restraint and ceasefire. They voted an increase in the UN peacekeeping force on the island which provided a buffer between Turkish and Greek protagonists.

There is no doubt among diplomats operating in this twilight zone that Pérez de Cuéllar's work was impressive. In Cyprus, with no special credentials to try to solve the deep-rooted problems, he managed to persuade the leaders of the Greek and Turkish communities to talks. It was a victory achieved through a process of ceaseless, hidden activity and some of his colleagues believed him to have been born to it. He possessed a legendary patience. " . . . it is not easy to be confident of achieving early progress: the longer it lasts . . . the more obstructions come to the surface", he wrote to Waldheim on the situation in Cyprus when he arrived. He was not a man to give up. No meeting was too long, no point of protocol too delicate. For a number of years, Pérez de Cuéllar regarded his achievement in Cyprus to be his greatest diplomatic success.

Soon, at home too, his reputation was restored and he returned in December 1977, after two years making his mark in Cyprus. Pérez de Cuéllar left the UN to become Peru's ambassador to Venezuela. But Waldheim got him back, offering him one of the half-dozen senior positions – Under-Secretary General for Special Political Affairs. In April 1981, Waldheim entrusted Pérez de Cuéllar with the conflict in Afghanistan – the superpower battle following the Soviet invasion.

When he returned to the Secretariat, Pérez de Cuéllar's old friend Fernando Belaúnde Terry was back in Peru's presidential palace. Belaúnde Terry had relied on Pérez de Cuéllar in the early sixties in Belaúnde's first presidency when Pérez de Cuéllar was Director of Political Affairs in Lima's Foreign Ministry. Belaúnde Terry had been ousted in the Velasco military coup, bundled out of office in his pyjamas, but was now returned to power. Through the calculation of ambitious people who chose their friends with a view to the future, or else the instinctive neutrality of a proper civil servant, Pérez de Cuéllar kept in touch with Belaúnde Terry during Belaúnde Terry's years of exile and, with Belaúnde Terry back in power, Pérez de Cuéllar was confident he now possessed the one vital ingredient necessary to make him Secretary General: with an old friend as President, he could count on government support.

Belaúnde Terry says that what impressed him about Pérez de

Cuéllar was that he was always meticulously prepared. Belaúnde first worked with him in the sixties, during his first presidency, when Pérez de Cuéllar would take part in weekly Foreign Ministry briefings. Belaúnde remembers how straightforward he was, and how, every time he introduced a new member to Lima's diplomatic corps, he would always detail the politics, culture and history of the country concerned. He was pleasant to deal with, impartial, frank and phlegmatic: and he never gave his own opinions, was never judgmental.

Pérez de Cuéllar's bid to become Secretary General of the UN began in April 1981 when, quite unexpectedly, he resigned his UN post. There was consternation on the thirty-eighth floor. Pérez de Cuéllar had only recently returned from Kabul where, as the Secretary General's high-profile Special Representative for Afghanistan, his diplomatic skill had been put to its greatest test. In his resignation letter, Pérez de Cuéllar wrote to Waldheim that he was "recalled by the Government of Peru", and "I have particularly appreciated this opportunity to work closely with you and to benefit from your profound political insight and understanding, which I have greatly admired". He hoped their warm friendship would continue.

For a week Waldheim tried to get him to change his mind. "I have depended upon your outstanding diplomatic skills and your discerning judgments." The two agreed Pérez de Cuéllar could leave New York in May but would make one more trip to Kabul in August before relinquishing his UN responsibility. This agreeable relationship between them did not last. In the autumn, Pérez de Cuéllar, Waldheim's chosen envoy to Kabul, twice publicly refused to travel to New York to partake in the General Assembly debate on Afghanistan. Pérez de Cuéller dared suggest to a Waldheim aide that a UN statement be issued which should read: "Ambassador Pérez de Cuéllar has informed the Secretary General that owing to a number of commitments which required his presence in Lima . . . he was unable to come to New York on the dates on which the debate would take place". Waldheim soon heard rumours that Pérez de Cuéllar was after his job. He grew angry, telling anyone who would listen that Pérez de Cuéllar was plotting and that he had lied to him. Waldheim claimed that when Pérez de Cuéllar resigned from the UN he had assured him he would not compete with him for the job and here he was, going behind his back. Waldheim accused Pérez de

Cuéllar of using the Secretariat as a stepping stone, making cynical use of his UN appointment to oversee the UN's delicate efforts in Soviet occupied Afghanistan.

Waldheim's mistake was to underestimate the forces that would deal, conspire and lobby. The Peruvian campaign to get Pérez de Cuéllar elected would make amateurs of everyone else, including Waldheim and the Austrian government bankrolling his own candidature. In Lima an entire department in the Foreign Ministry was dedicted to the effort, headed by the Foreign Minister himself, a lawyer named Javier Arias Stella. From an apartment nearby, so he could disclaim it later, Pérez de Cuéllar discreetly helped make the vital decisions about which governments were to be approached, which letters had to be written. The President of Peru was told which approaches to make at the highest level. At UN headquarters in New York a special envoy kept in daily contact: Celso Pastor de la Torre, Belaúnde's brother-in-law who had masterminded the recent Presidential election. He was a former ambassador to Washington who had the distinction of having represented his country at the World Bank and the IMF.

The campaign team was the best Peru could offer – and it would make only one serious mistake.

Pérez de Cuéllar returned to Peru alone after resigning the New York job and nobody met him at the airport. Just by chance a journalist bumped into him in the noisy arrival hall and asked what he was doing in Lima, of all places. Pérez de Cuéllar said he had come home because he was about to be appointed ambassador to Brazil. Pérez de Cuéllar asked that the journalist keep the news to himself for a few days. The journalist was somewhat taken aback.

When the news broke a few days later, it seemed to some that the nomination for Brazil was a demotion. A few in the Foreign Ministry saw the point. It was only a matter of weeks before the first visit to Lima by a Brazilian head of state. Pérez de Cuéllar must have the highest possible profile. Secretly mobilised were the diplomatic resources of Peru. But no sooner did the grand and private campaign get started, it was thrown into disarray. The powerful President of the Peruvian Senate, Javier Alva Orlandini, who belonged to Belaúnde Terry's party but was at odds with it, managed to persuade the necessary two-thirds of his colleagues to refuse to ratify Pérez de Cuéllar's new appointment to Brazil. It was a double blow for the Foreign Minister, Arias Stella who a few days before had called Alva Orlandini to his office to have a friendly chat to explain the importance of the appointment to Brazil.

Arias Stella was convinced that Alva Orlandini understood what they were planning. Instead, what Arias Stella now faced was the embarrassment of public statements by some senators who objected to Pérez de Cuéllar because of his close links with the left-wing military junta – although the rumour mill stated that for Alva Orlandini it was a matter of honour. Pérez de Cuéllar had been linked, years before, to the woman who married Alva Orlandini. The rumours said she had been madly in love with Pérez de Cuéllar and married the senator on the rebound.

The confusion grew. The Foreign Minister resigned and an enraged President appeared on national television to refuse the resignation. The following day, in what must have been his lowest point, Pérez de Cuéllar resigned from the diplomatic corps after more than forty years, his career apparently in ruins. He kept his immaculate calm and expressed suprise at the interest the press was showing. He denied newspaper reports which claimed he had read the decree at General Velasco's swearing in ceremony: he said the decree was read by General Fernandez Maldonado and that he himself was no more than a functionary.

Pérez de Cuéllar certainly knew enough about the state of Peruvian politics to understand that the refusal to send him to Brazil was owing to deep splits in Belaúnde Terry's Acción Popular party, a manoeuvre to damage the President and the Foreign Minister. His grand ambition had fallen foul of Alva Orlandini's hatred for Velasco, and Alva Orlandini's suspicion of new city-slickers in government. Alva Orlandini, a lawyer from a white landowning family in the north, was determined to defend rural interests against all these subtle, well-mannered international diplomats. Arias Stella returned to the Foreign Ministry after two days. "Now", he declared, "we are going to demonstrate who is against the country and who for it." Arias Stella called a strategy meeting. They would carry on and behave as though the failure to nominate Pérez de Cuéllar to Brazil never happened. Arias Stella had one all-important asset – the presence in New York of Celso Pastor de la Torre, the sharp gentleman with his crocodile-skin shoes and monogrammed shirts, as rich as he was elegant, and a founder of Belaúnde's Acción

Popular Party. Pastor de la Torre was determined that a Peruvian should obtain the world's highest diplomatic prize.

The first formal announcement that Javier Pérez de Cuéllar was available came from Arias Stella, and the candidate himself immediately and characteristically denied it. When it came to the office of Secretary General, Pérez de Cuéllar said: "There are no candidates".

Celso Pastor de la Torre was confident. He believed he could control the damage done to the campaign by the Peruvian Senate's inconvenient vote. He planned an announcement and slipped into a conference room which was packed with journalists and TV cameras waiting for Waldheim. Pastor de la Torre's aides followed him in, armed with photocopies of Peru's official notification to the President of the Security Council that Pérez de Cuéllar's name be added to the list of contenders only if Salim Salim should, for some reason, retire from the race. Until then, Peru would continue to maintain support for the Third World candidate.

Pastor de la Torre expected some awkward questions about the snub over Pérez de Cuéllar's appointment to Brazil but there was none. His speech about how Pérez de Cuéllar was the official candidate of a newly elected democratic government would have to wait. Only a handful of Argentinean diplomats tried to stir things up, campaigning for their own candidate. But nobody cared much about a minor political incident in Peru. In New York, no one thought Pérez de Cuéllar stood a chance.

In Lima the campaign team held strategy meetings, and there were frequent disagreements with the candidate himself who steadfastly refused the suggestion he go to New York and campaign himself. He told them the last thing he needed to do was to visit the toxic bureaucracy on the East River. A visit would do untold damage. It was better to remain obscure, and not make statements, take controversial decisions, or answer questions particularly about something as contentious as Afghanistan. They argued with him but Pérez de Cuéllar always shook his head. He did not need to go to New York for he knew exactly what was happening. His eyes and ears were right there, on the thirty-eighth floor with Emilio de Olivares, the charming Peruvian aristocrat, who happened to be one of Waldheim's executive officers. Olivares was happy to keep Pérez de Cuéllar abreast of events and he would be amply rewarded for his trouble. He would remain Pérez de Cuéllar's closest personal adviser, particularly on the more delicate matters of personnel.

As for the manoeuvrings among the delegations, Pastor de La Torre was increasingly optimistic. Although some would seem supremely qualified for the job, each of the other candidates had a handicap. Firstly, there was Prince Sadruddin Aga Khan, who had just completed his widely acclaimed stint as UN High Commissioner for Refugees with an Iranian passport, a Harvard education and living in Switzerland, thus too much Western influence. The Argentinean diplomat, Carlos Ortiz de Rozas, would suffer with the French who were concerned at Argentina's appalling record on human rights. The immensely qualified Shridath Ramphal of Guyana, the Common-wealth Secretary General, had the misfortune to come from a Third World country counting itself Socialist – ensuring an American veto whilst Ramphal's position in the Commonwealth would attract a veto from the Soviets. There were several Latin-American candidates and as a group the Latins had acquired the reputation of being a bit quick off the mark, a bit too eager to put forward their candidates while Salim Salim was still in the race. This did not go down well with the Africans who considered the Latin-American group damaging to the tactic of wearing down Waldheim's resistance with a united front. African hostility would rule out Carlos Julio Arosemena Monroy of Ecuador, Santiago Quijano Caballero of Colombia, Dr Jorge Illueca, Foreign Minister of Panama. In any case, none of them had a high profile in international diplomacy; nor had Rafael M. Salas of the Philippines, Executive Director of the UN Fund for Population Activities nor Radha Krishna Ramphul, UN Ambassador for Mauritius. Carlos Oriz Rozas and Alejandro Orfila could not even count on the support of their own governments. Of the other contenders, only two – the Venezuelan diplomat Andres Aguilar and Pérez de Cuéllar himself – had experience of both the Secretariat and the problems on the UN's agenda. Aguilar had been deeply involved in the lengthy Law of the Sea negotiations. Aguila was familiar in UN circles. He had American support, since Washington wanted to improve relations with Caracas, and he was rumoured to be in good standing with the Soviets. Pastor de la Torre argued that Pérez de Cuéllar was far better qualified.

The only name which really worried Pastor de la Torre was Olaf Palme, a former Prime Minister of Sweden rumoured to be about to throw his hat in the ring, but a discreet conversation with Qing Ling, the Chinese Ambassador, with whom Pastor de la Torre had built a friendly relationship, confirmed that the Chinese would veto him.

With this variegated field of candidates, the campaign strategy was obvious. There was no point wasting time in lobbying votes from the non-permanent members of the Security Council, who might be swayed by their own special interests or enthusiasms. What mattered most was the elimination of the veto. And while Javier Pérez de Cuéllar remained above it, Pastor de la Torre was free to stage the very model of a campaign for power in international diplomacy.

Celso Pastor de la Torre had high hopes for his first meeting with Oleg Troyanovsky. The Soviet ambassador was short, raucous and funny: once, when a visitor in the public gallery of the Security Council had thrown red paint on him, he was heard above the uproar to tell the American ambassador that he would sooner be red than dead. Troyanovsky was popular. He spoke English with no sign of an accent: his father had been Soviet ambassador to the United States before the war.

The formalities over, Pastor de la Torre set out Pérez de Cuéllar's attributes, which might well be described as English – his reserve, his diplomatic skill – but Troyanovsky had rudely interrupted. This was nonsense. There was nothing "English" about Pérez de Cuéllar. He was a Peruvian. Troyanovsky had done his homework. Troyanovsky glared across the table and jabbing his finger at the suave Pastor de la Torre, said that in one recent meeting a Peruvian delegate accused his country of actually using chemical weapons in Afghanistan.

"No one is interested in Afghanistan or Kampuchea," Pastor de la Torre quickly retorted. There were far more important considerations. Pastor de la Torre feared the veto and he tried to keep up the momentum. In turn he recalled Pérez de Cuéllar's years as Peru's ambassador to Moscow when the ground work was laid for the USSR to supply arms to Peru, not just during the years of Velasco's radicals, but also while Belaúnde held power. The USSR had agreed a substantial loan to finance the massive Olmos project to irrigate the Peruvian desert on the north coast. Besides, Pérez de Cuéllar had played an important role in the Velasco regime, indeed, was recently punished for it by the Senate. Troyanovsky recovered his diplomatic manners, but he did not change his mind. He explained that the Soviets were happy for Waldheim to stay because of his impartiality between the East and the West. In Soviet experience this was not a quality which past Secretaries General had possessed in great measure.

The meeting ended.

In New York the Security Council remained at stalemate. The Tunisian President for November, Ambassador Taieb Slim, lobbied his own idea, calling it "step aside": the two main contenders would withdraw to allow other candidates to be considered. Absolutely no one liked the idea at the time although, in December, when Otunnu had taken over, they grabbed at the chance. Some called it a trap to provoke vetoes against the alternative candidates. It would strengthen the chances of Salim Salim. Waldheim certainly read it that way.

Waldheim was optimistic. His team of Austrian campaign advisers, four ambassadors and seven assistants, had assured him that the lifting of the Chinese veto was now only a matter of time and Waldheim had let it be known he wanted another vote taken in the Security Council.

At the next meeting, however, the vetoes held, both against Waldheim and Salim Salim. There were eight rounds of voting and the only change from the first to the last vote was that Waldheim's support was eroding. There was speculation that he might, after all, step down. Even members of his campaign team were voicing doubts about his position. No one relished having to tell him that he might have to make an honourable exit, for that was the last course of action on Waldheim's mind.

Pastor de la Torre went about his business, talking to the permanent members of the Security Council. He found the British delegate, Sir Anthony Parsons, pompous, but it was no more than he had expected. It was part of the tradition of British diplomatic reserve for Third World diplomats. Parsons refused to confirm that a recent chat between the Peruvian Prime Minister and Prime Minister Margaret Thatcher in London had convinced her that Pérez de Cuéllar would make a suitable Secretary General. Pastor de La Torre did not press the point.

When he saw Jeane Kirkpatrick at the American delegation, she was cautious. He could not know the State Department had already dismissed Pérez de Cuéllar as a nonentity. He believed her assurance that the National Security Council had not yet made up its mind. Indeed, towards the end of November, Pastor de la Torre was cautiously optimistic. There was talk in the Secretariat that Pérez de Cuéllar was the candidate of the UN establishment – the bureaucracy naturally welcomed his low-key approach. They said he would "fall out of a boat and not make waves".

The rumours were welcome but they were beside the point – the vetoes were the main worry. Pastor de La Torre worked hard, particularly on the Chinese. At his very first meeting with Ambassador Qing Ling, he found that the Chinese were worried that during a recent Security Council meeting two of the Third World members had broken ranks and voted for Waldheim. Pastor de la Torre assured Qing Ling that Peru had only good intentions: she would remain a loyal member of the Third World and he stressed that Pérez de Cuéllar was only in the race should Salim Salim withdraw. Slowly, the two men developed a diplomatic closeness, and their meetings grew more relaxed and more confiding. Qing Ling admitted that although the Chinese veto against Waldheim would never be lifted, they had decided to scrutinise the list of other candidates – just in case Salim Salim stood down. The Chinese were afraid of a procedural coup in the Assembly, a vote to extend Waldheim's term of office and, rather than see Waldheim confirmed for another five years, they were contemplating the possibility of a split term between Waldheim and Salim. By this point in their friendship, Pastor de la Torre was confident enough to advise Qing Ling that the Chinese should make it clear they would not, under any circumstances, tolerate an extension. The private influence grew.

Pastor de la Torre's most relaxed meetings were with the French delegation. He flattered them for their reputation as Kingmakers, a sobriquet earned after they had formally proposed Dag Hammarskjöld in 1953. He grew confident enough to propose a plan to their Ambassador, Luc de la Barre de Nanteuil: he should try to persuade Salim Salim and Waldheim to withdraw.

At that point, Otunnu, the bright and young Ugandan who was December's President of the Security Council, announced that he would have a solution to the stalemate within fifteen days. In Lima, the reaction was sceptical, but Pastor de la Torre was alarmed. He saw danger in the restored relations between the Latin American and African groups, fearing that an alternative Third World candidate might emerge who had not made the *faux pas* of Salim Salim, and would not face a veto from Washington. When Salim

Salim withdrew from the election Pastor de la Torre was sure the Chinese had put him up to it, in order to show Waldheim as the cause of the embarrassing deadlock. When Waldheim withdrew Pastor de la Torre had even more reason to worry. He no longer grasped what was happening, and he was not alone: the African group convened an emergency meeting to interpret events. The main candidates had gone, and it was assumed by almost everybody that all the other names would be struck down by a veto from one or other of the Big Five.

In early December, Pastor de la Torre heard one more rumour. Ambassador Troyanovsky had been overheard to say that there was one candidate the Russians would not veto, and that was Javier Pérez de Cuéllar. Pastor de la Torre did not dare believe his luck, since Troyankovsky had not told him any such thing. He decided that if the Russians really did decide that they had no particular objections to Pérez de Cuéllar, and the French also approved, the British seemed to have no strong feelings either way and the Americans were still undecided, then the action of the last remaining permanent member of the Security Council was vital. The campaign needed China.

With the approval of the Foreign Minister, Arias Stella, Pastor de la Torre had a further meeting with Qing Ling. They discussed the campaign on the East River and the delicate question of China's debt to Peru: more than $100 million, due for purchases of fishmeal and copper, outstanding for two years. Sometime after this meeting the Chinese decided not to oppose the election of Pérez de Cuéllar.

For President Belaúnde the election of a Peruvian Secretary General would mean recognition for his government's record of democracy and human rights. As his country slid into chaos it would be a brief respite. Peru's economy was further deteriorating. Pérez de Cuéllar, ignoring the reality of his own campaign, wanted it known that no international civil servant would campaign for office. If diplomacy had been involved in his election, then diplomacy was by its nature secret. He would insist for ever on the legend of his immaculate election.

Six years later, just after Pérez de Cuéllar gratefully accepted a second term, Pastor de la Torre published a short and somewhat conceited account of his role in the 1981 election. He called the book *How a Peruvian was Elected Secretary General* and although it left out some of the more contentious detail it was a fair account which circulated widely in New York – thanks to UN photocopying machines. It confirmed what many had suspected: that no one was elected Secretary General without some sort of campaign, whether secret, overt or carefully diplomatic.

This effrontery, this unofficial information, seems to have infuriated Pérez de Cuéllar, or at least his friends were furious. His Executive Assistant, Alvaro de Soto, publicly challenged Pastor de la Torre's account in a long article for Lima's principal weekly magazine, *Caretas*. He denied almost everything. He said Pérez de Cuéllar had always been reluctant to take high office. He recalled how in 1971 he had telephoned Pérez de Cuéllar to let him know that Kurt Waldheim had been chosen Secretary General and that Pérez de Cuéllar had sighed with relief that the burden had not fallen on his own shoulders. De Soto denied Pastor de la Torre's contention that there were "immense obstacles" facing Peruvian diplomats during the nomination. He made fun of Pastor de la Torre's grandiloquence. He insisted that Pastor de la Torre's only assignment in New York was to confirm that Pérez de Cuéllar was available for office, and that Pérez de Cuéllar had been elected solely because of his "exceptional suitability", and qualities recognised long before. The argument continued in print for some weeks. De Soto's last shot was to assure his readers that had Pérez de Cuéllar known the book was in preparation, he would have been only too happy to correct Pastor de la Torre's "errors of fact".

When the UN was created in 1945 the American State Department laid out a few guidelines about how the Secretary General was to be chosen. Policy-makers insisted that the selection was a most serious undertaking and warned that any compromise solution would be disastrous. In order to find the right candidate, a systematic review would have to be undertaken of "the men of public affairs of all countries", to ascertain experience and ability. The UN's Secretary General should be a

man of broad interests, demonstrated intellectual ability, and should have experience in administering large organisations. He needs to be both a statesman and an organiser. He should have qualities of moral leadership and the ability to inspire . . . his writings and speeches should reflect a real understanding of international affairs . . . he should be progressive on economic and social questions, and should be free of racial or class intolerance . . . he should be relatively young, not more than fifty-five years of age.

Lie welcomed Hammarskjöld to the UN by telling him he was to inherit the most impossible job on earth. As far back as 1949 Sir Gladwyn Jebb wrote that the Secretary General could not possibly be the administrative director of the UN and the world diplomatic saviour as the Charter required. The burden was too great – and this at a time when the UN had a mere fifty members and a staff of 3,000.

Ever since the UN's beginning the selection of Secretary General, filled with intrigue and power politics, has made a nonsense of any procedure. Certainly during the haphazard election of Pérez de Cuéllar in 1981, the great powers did not look for either leadership or independence. These were the last attributes hoped for. Pérez de Cuéllar was typical of the old-boy diplomatic network which chose him. Yet from this apparently hopeless situation emerged a Secretary General who would preside at a time when there were serious attempts to close the UN down. He would see it transformed from the fringes of international power-broking, to its centre. When after the Cold War ended the great powers decided they might well need a UN, it was largely thanks to him there was a UN left to use. Pérez de Cuéllar was elected in 1981 simply because he believed himself to be supremely qualified for the UN job; he was probably right.

9. A CESSPOOL

At first Javier Pérez de Cuéllar was considered a reasonable choice, a man who was so keen not to give offence that he was said to be in the Waldheim mould. He was grey and two-dimensional, a diplomat's diplomat but who would have the experience to rise to the needs of the hour if necessary. The questions of how radical he might be arose only when his first *Annual Report* appeared and which was unusually candid and critical. It condemned the behaviour of member governments, and exposed their appalling record at abiding by the UN Charter. Pérez de Cuéllar said that during his first year in office the UN had been rebuffed time after time in the very situations where it mattered. There was an appalling litany of unsolved disputes: the war over the Falkland Islands, the Israeli invasion of the Lebanon, the Israeli bombing of West Beirut, the massacres of the Sabra and Chatila Palestinian refugee camps by Christian militiamen, the blood soaked Iran–Iraq war – all these conflicts would have responded to international solution.

"We are perilously near to a new international anarchy," he warned. There was an alarming successsion of international crises and he blamed governments for failing to come to terms with the harsh reality in the less developed countries. "We have poverty of a vast proportion of the world's population – a deprivation inexplicable in terms either of available resources or the money and ingenuity spent on armament and war." The UN had ceased to play a meaningful role, despite all its resolutions about development, self-government for black South Africans, self-determination for Palestinians. Pérez de Cuéllar blamed the Big Five for they had special rights and responsibilities and they ought to reassess their obligations to the Charter. They were, after all, bound by international law. He offered to meet with them to discuss their problems. "Institutions like this are not built in a day . . . they require constant constructive work and fidelity to the principles on which they are based." He spelled out his ambition: agreement among the five permanent members, for without it the UN would never work.

Pérez de Cuéllar's first year was disagreeable. The financial crisis was no nearer solution and he was unable to pay the UN's commitments to member governments providing troops for peacekeeping. Three months into his first term, in April 1982, the British ambassador, Sir Anthony Parsons, told the Council that an Argentinean fleet had left for the Falklands Islands. Pérez de Cuéllar's Under Secretaries General thought it inexplicable that the British, knowing how unstable the Argentinean junta was, had taken no serious steps to protect the islands. The war which ensued was described by Brian Urquhart as two bald men fighting over a comb. "If ever there was a war that should have been avoided, it was this one", Urquhart remarked. Pérez de Cuéllar came out of it well. He was much praised for his attempts to mediate. However much this new Secretary General bumped against the limits of the job, his private diplomacy was conducted in an orderly and straightforward way. Diplomats were beginning to speculate about how much a skillful Secretary General could accomplish.

When Pérez de Cuéllar assumed office, the UN was about to enter a period that it would barely survive. The critical impact was the continuing hostility between Arab and Jew. The cause was the homeless Palestinian people and the General Assembly's majority view of their right to self-determination. The "inalienable right of the people of Palestine" had advanced significantly in international diplomacy and in February, 1982 the UN Commission on Human Rights reaffirmed the rights of the Palestinian people to establish a full independent and sovereign State of Palestine and to return to their homes and property. Later on an emergency special session of the General Assembly called on the Security Council to compel Israel to rescind the annexation of the Golan Heights and declared that Israel's occupation of this land was null and void. The Assembly believed that the annexation extended Israeli law, jurisdiction and administration over a territory which it had captured from Syria in the 1967 war and that it was illegal. The Assembly called on all states to cease dealing with Israel. The Reagan administration was unreservedly pro-Israel and the US Ambassador to the UN, Jeane Kirkpatrick, described the Assembly pronouncements on Israel as miserable: the Assembly was denying history and inflaming passions. In early 1982 in New York there was renewed anti-UN hysteria from one of New York's tabloid newspapers, the *New York Post*, which climaxed a month after Pérez de Cuéllar's arrival with the headline, "*Post* Readers Tell the UN to Shove Off". The *Post* claimed that a telephone poll of readers had jammed the telephone lines at the newspaper with a total 54,000 callers ringing to say the UN should get out of town. A five-day poll revealed only 38,000 calls in favour of the UN staying on. Mayor Ed Koch led his own attack. "The UN is hypocritical and cowardly," he declared adding with perfect New York arrogance that if the organisation left the city, no one would hear from it again.

Mayor Koch was not alone in thinking that the Middle East was the centre of political life at the UN. The UN itself, upon whose decision the partition of Palestine was based, became a weapon to be used in Middle Eastern political warfare. The hardening of positions at the UN strengthened all extremists and the UN became part of the problem. Israel considered the UN with contempt and hostility and accused member states in the General Assembly of accepting Arab warfare and the hatred of Israel as inevitable. Israel claimed that the Arabs did not want to solve the Palestinian refugee problem, wanted to use it as a weapon against Israel. The General Assembly had been providing for the Palestinan refugees since December 1949 with the creation of the UN Relief and World Agency for Palestine refugees in the near East (UNRWA). This agency initially helped some 750,000 Palestinians who fled from the Jewish State and the war in 1948. In 1982 the number of refugees reached two million and UNWRA attended to their health, education and welfare. Israel was not prepared to allow any of the refugees to return and the Arab world was resolved not to resettle them. The UN dealt with the symptoms.

It was not always hopeless. In November 1967, after the Six Day War, the Security Council, in a rare show of unanimity and after hours of wrangling, voted Resolution 242, which was intended to secure a permanent settlement. It was based on the premise of a return by Israel of occupied land in exchange for peace. The Resolution mandated the ending of belligerency, the respect of sovereignty and freedom of navigation in all international waterways of the area. The rights and territories of each state had to be guaranteed by demilitarised zones. But in spite of this paper peace, the Middle East continued to cost thousands of lives and millions of dollars. It was a war of attrition – air raids, sporadic artillery outrages on civilians and terrorism, in which the superpowers restocked the weapons. In October 1973, war broke out again when Egypt and Syria attacked Israel and there with fears of escalation, drawing in the superpowers, like the Balkans in 1914. But they stepped back from the brink. As a last resort the Security Council passed another Resolution which called for an immediate ceasefire – and negotiation under Resolution 242. Resolution 242 became a benchmark for a solution.

Another UN peacekeeping force was created, put together by Brian Urquhart, comprising troops from Austria, Finland and Sweden and later Poland, the first East European country to provide troops. UNEF II as it became known, the UN Emergency Force, was a considerable success. The peacekeepers made a reality of a ceasefire and arranged prisoner-of-war exchanges. Later, in May 1974, the UN was given another role in the Middle East when Kissinger managed agreement between Israel and Syria for a UN presence in the Golan Heights to provide a buffer zone. The UN Disengagement Observer Force was to oversee an agreement for a limited armaments zone where there would be regular inspection by UN observers but there was no comprehensive settlement. The stateless Palestinian refugees were frustrated in their hopes of a homeland had survived for years in refugee camps.

With the creation of the Palestinian Liberation Organisation in 1964 there had been a rebirth of Palestinian nationalism. For the refugees the PLO symbolised the refusal to accept defeat. The PLO's charter pronounced armed struggle as the path to liberation, and called for an end to the state of Israel. In October, 1974 the Arab states recognised the PLO as the sole legitimate representative of the Palestinian people. In 1974, the General Assembly affirmed the inalienable rights of the Palestinian people to self-determination, independence and sovereignty. The following month, in September, the Chairman of the PLO Executive Committee, Yasser Arafat addressed the Assembly and was welcomed as a head of state and was the first person, apart from Pope Paul VI, not representing the government of a UN member state allowed to do so. Arafat, who wore a gun holster under a windbreaker, was given a euphoric welcome. The President of the Assembly that year, Abdelaziz Bouteflika, Algeria's Foreign Minister, a leader of the Group of 77, ordered from the storeroom the armchair used when the Pope had come ten years before. The West considered that such courtesies to a "terrorist" were an unforgivable outrage. Israel believed that the General Assembly had sanitised and glamorised the PLO and member states had given the PLO a mandate for terror. The PLO dominated all Arab policy at the UN in New York.

After the Arafat visit, the Assembly voted to grant the PLO observer status with the unprecedented right to participate in sessions of the General Assembly. Israel objected that the PLO represented "nobody but some 10,000 terrorists bent on the destruction of Israel". The PLO had entered the UN system; UNESCO had given the PLO observer status and the International Civil Aviation Organisation had followed shortly afterwards, a decision which was totally incomprehensible to Israel in view of the fact that aviation was a chief victim of PLO terrorism.

At the time of the Arafat visit to New York, there were plans by the the non-aligned states to eject Israel from the UN. It was intended that Israel become a pariah like South Africa and its policy of apartheid. There were increasing challenges to Israeli legitimacy. In early August 1975, the Organisation of African Unity passed a resolution requesting all members to "reinforce the pressure exerted on Israel at the UN . . . without losing sight of the possibility of eventually depriving it of its membership . . . ". This was fairly moderate and was seen as a sign that perhaps African and Arab resolve was changing; Libya thought moderation the result of American agents having infiltrated the Organisation of African Unity. Ghana, Liberia, Senegal and Sierre Leone voiced profound qualms about the Arab strategy. In 1975 the Committee on the Exercise of the Inalienable Rights of the Palestinian People was established by the Assembly. The Third World was strengthened by the Palestinian issue and the oil-based financial strength of the Arabs. The threat to expel Israel from the UN was a serious matter. The American Secretary of State Henry Kissinger warned in July 1975 that suspensions or expulsion would "threaten the survival of the General Assembly itself".

That November, his words began to seem like prophecy. Resolution 3379 sponsored by Somalia, Cuba and Libya stated "that Zionism is a form of racism and racial discrimination". It was passed by the General Assembly by an overwhelming majority. Such a formal condemnation of Zionism was a stepping stone to the next objective: the expulsion of Israel.

The Resolution had surfaced in the UN's Third Committee – the Social, Humanitarian and Cultural Affairs Committee as part of the UN's Decade for Action to Combat Racism and Racial Discrimination. The Third Committe was known to the international diplomats as the Women's Committee, for it was where most women delegates had previously served, including Eleanor Roosevelt and Shirley Temple Black. Some even more sexist delegates thought its nickname derived from the fact it never achieved anything. Resolution 3379 reached the Assembly floor on November 10. In a long and passionate speech the Israeli Ambassador, Chaim Herzog, told delegates that the day was the anniversary of Kristallnacht when, thirty-seven years earlier, Hitler's jack-booted thugs launched a co-ordinated attack on the Jewish community in Germany, burning synagogues and desecrating books and holy scrolls. "It was the night", Herzog told the silent hall, "which led eventually to the crematoria and gas-chambers . . . to the most terrifying holocaust in the history of man." Herzog said that Resolution 3379 was born of a deep, pervading anti-Semitism and it amounted to the first organised attack on an established religion since the Middle Ages. "Zion came to mean the Jewish homeland, symbolic of Judaism, of Jewish national aspirations . . . Zionism is to the Jewish people what the liberation movements of Africa and Asia have been to their people." How sad that a group of nations, many of whom were recently freed themselves from colonial rule, should deride one of the most noble liberation movements of the century. With Resolution 3379 what was at stake was not Israel, but the fate of the UN, "which has been dragged to its lowest point of discredit by a coalition of despotisms and racists".

No minds were changed by the Herzog speech. The Ambassador for Dahomey replied that as long as the Palestinians continued to be persecuted, Zionism would be condemned with the same vigour as apartheid. It was not normal for the Jewish people to expel the indigenous inhabitants of a country with the benefit of an "over-equipped and over-fed superpower". The Arab League would continue to defend the resolution claiming that Zionism was an exclusivist, nationalist political ideology. Zionism was racist in its treatment of non-Jewish peoples. Discrimination against Arabs living in Israel was rampant and the Palestinians in the Occupied Territories were denied the most basic civil rights.

The Resolution passed on a roll-call vote, with seventy-two in favor, thirty-five against and thirty-two abstentions. Of those voting for the Resolution, fourteen were Communist countries and thirty-six were countries with Muslim majorities. Of the non-Communist Europeans, Cyprus and Malta supported the Resolution. Malta was said to have been wanting finance from Libya while the Christian government of Cyprus needed Arab help against its Muslim secessionist minority. Regimes in Latin America supported it, Cuba and Guyana, and votes in favour came from Brazil, Mexico, Grenada and Chile. India also voted for the resolution as did Saudi Arabia, Uganda, Iraq, and the Sudan.

The American ambassador, Daniel Moynihan spoke to the Assembly after the vote was taken and his speech was an early indication of the damage the Resolution would cause. Moynihan believed there was not another issue in all of America's post-war history which brought forth such unanimity of American public opinion. To attack Zionists was to attack Americans. The Resolution "reeked of the totalitarian mind, stank of the totalitarian state". Moynihan told delegates they had committed an infamous act, and had unleashed upon the world a great evil. They had given anti-Semitism the appearance of international sanction. "The General Assembly today grants symbolic amnesty, and more, to the murderers of the six million European Jews." Indeed the UN had taken itself, step by step, to the point of declaring that Zionism was Nazism. Moynihan told them that during a previous UN debate there had occurred an argument over the definition of racism; during this debate the Soviet Union had declared that racism was merely a form of Nazism. "Sentence first, verdict afterwards", as the Queen of Hearts said. But this was not Wonderland. This was the real world with real consequences. Zionism could not be racist for there were Jews of every race, colour, descent. The population of Israel included large number of non-Jews, among them both Arabs of Muslim and Christian religions. The idea that Jews were a race, rather than adherents of a religion, was invented not by Jews but by those who hated Jews. The Resolution debased the language of human rights and distorted the very concept of racism.

How would the small nations of the world defend themselves when this language no longer had meaning? The Resolution would have terrible consequences.

Moynihan later wrote a book about his UN experiences and claimed that the Soviets were using Resolution 3379 to destroy peace in the Middle East. At the time, Israel and Egypt, with American sponsorship, were moving towards something like accommodation and the Soviets, expelled from Egypt, would not have it. "The object of the Resolution", Moynihan believed, "was to spoil these relations." Moynihan believed the true genesis of "Zionism is racism" to have been Soviet propaganda in which racism is applied to nationalist movements.

Moynihan was misinformed. At the time most people thought that "Zionism was racism" first appeared in a UN document at the Women's year conference in Mexico. But Zionism had been linked to racism, even identified with it in many UN debates; in 1968 in the Security Council, Iraq described Zionism as a classic example of a racist settler regime with the people of Palestine as the colonised.

Later, Sir Ivor Richard, the British Ambassador, and a sparring partner of Moynihan, expressed the view the Americans contributed to their own defeat on Resolution 3379. Richard said that the Europeans managed to avoid reacting to the vote in purely ideological and emotional terms. He did not see the UN as a forum in which to argue political ideology and much of his own time at the UN was spent trying to prevent rows. "Whatever else the place is, it is not the OK Corral and I am hardly Wyatt Earp."

The Resolution did more to alienate America from the UN than any other event in UN history. So extreme was the reaction that some felt obliged to come to the UN's rescue. Kissinger warned of the dangers of ignoring some of the UN's benefits. *New York Times* columnist Anthony Lewis wrote that the US was in no position to talk of moral standards – a superpower which dropped 500,000 tons of bombs on Cambodia was in a rather doubtful position to lecture about morality. On the tenth anniversary of the Resolution in 1985 Jeane Kirkpatrick said that more than any other act its passage symbolised the death of the UN dream. Indeed, more than anything, the resolution contributed to the inablity of the UN to play any role at all in mediation in the Middle East. Worse, it threatened the organisation's financial stability. In 1979, the Republican Senator from North Carolina, Jesse Helms, added an amendment to the

Department of State Appropriations Bill which prevented American money for UN programmes of technical assistance. The effect was to prevent payment of the entire US contribution; no one could tell with certainty which part of the sum went for which programme.

Helms told his colleagues on the Hill that UN technical assistance was an attempt to soak the rich; it was an international tax imposed on the American people. America's allies objected. Congressional action was "parsimonious". The restriction was illegal. But Helms was undeterred. He wanted more control over the American contribution.

The Helms amendment was signed into law in the midst of a Congressional budget marathon, during a long and arduous attempt to reach adjournment. It was passed without discussion and some members apparently had not known for what they were actually voting until some weeks later. The wording of the Helms amendment was innocuous, the term technical assistance not easily appreciated and any budget cut in a time of fiscal austerity was welcome. The White House was appalled. President Jimmy Carter immediately issued a statement that the action would lead the US into violation of a treaty obligation and he was quick to recall that over the years the US consistently opposed the Soviet Union's withholding of its contribution to UN funds.

On 1 January 1979 when part of the US contribution was due, no payments were forthcoming – neither could any money be paid until the amendment was repealed. In the State Department repeal became a priority. A special task force was created and although the Department was prevented constitutionally from lobbying, it used UN support groups to convey how damaging the amendment really was. The UN Association of America, the League of Women Voters, the Council of Churches and professional organisations, even the American Public Health Association, were sent background materials on what the amendment would do to the UN system, on the threats to the International Atomic Energy Authority's development of nuclear safeguards, the World Health Organisation's efforts to control disease, the Food and Agricultural Organisation's early warning system on crop and food shortages and how it was trying to combat swine fever and foot and mouth disease. The Helms amendment would cripple the agencies. How could such vital programmes be funded through voluntary payments? In health care there had to be long term planning.

It took months of persuasion but the State Department was eventually successful: the Helms amendment was defeated on August 15, 1979 – by six votes. No one was to know that this was but an opening skirmish – and a rare victory. The assault on the UN was just beginning.

Like the appointment of Moynihan, the appointment of Jeane Kirkpatrick in early 1981 indicated a shift in American policy towards the UN. The Reaganites were never fond of the organisation. Under a tabloid headline, "Jeane: 'Marxist' UN Wars Against US" in December 1982, she was quoted as berating what she called a new class of international bureaucrat wanting global socialism. Kirkpatrick said that the UN was advancing a Marxist ideology based on the assertion that all poverty was the fault of the rich. She said that the UN worked to harass and restrict US corporations around the world. She described the UN as an "iron triangle" comprising Third World radicals, ideologically sympathetic UN bureaucrats and Western non-governmental agencies – the thousand associations, philanthropic and pressure groups attached to the UN as lobbyists. This was before the US pull-out from UNESCO and she warned that the US would quit if corruption in the agency continued, but first Washington should try to understand the destructive ideology at work in the UN itself.

Kirkpatrick took no prisoners. She condemned all her predecessors, accusing them of having frittered away US influence within the organisation. Persistent incompetence was the reason that the America came to seem the enemy whereas the Soviets were in fact the principal contemporary colonial power who did not respect national independence and territorial integrity. As for development help in poor countries, it was an American invention.

Kirkpatrick became the personification of the Reagan revolution in New York. People on the thirty-eighth floor and at the US mission across the street found it hard to become accustomed to her style. How unlike her Democratic predecessors – Donald F. McHenry and Andrew Young, sensitive to Third World sensibilities, and William W. Scranton, respected for finesse – she was. "I'd rather be in Philadelphia," she stated at the end of 1982, openly admitting to hating being at the UN. She compared it to "death and taxes". She told an interviewer that she was intensely unhappy and had nearly resigned. "I was a woman in a man's world," she would recall. "I was an intellectual in a world of bureaucrats." She determined that US success would depend directly on cutting through bloc voting patterns. She closely watched Sir Anthony Parsons during the build-up to the Falklands War, noting how skilfully he cut through the normal bloc voting and used the Commonwealth alliance to get a Security Council Resolution to underpin Britain's future action. Parsons won admiration all-round for the Resolution; at the time he was not even sure he would get American support after Kirkpatrick told him she would try to block any effort to bring the Falklands question to the Security Council.

The cold winds from Washington were turning glacial. In early 1982 in the first of a series of studies about the UN, the right-wing Heritage Foundation asked whether the US taxpayers "benefited" from the $10 billion which was "invested" in the UN. The Foundation called on the US Government to consider relocating the headquarters outside the US; it wanted a White House review to determine whether or not it would be worth pulling out altogether. An idea born of liberalism, the UN had been criticised from the start. Now the intention seemed to be to destroy it altogether.

The Heritage Foundation was established in 1973 as a tax-exempt research institute dedicated to the principles of free competitive enterprise. An initial benefactor was Joseph Coors, the multi-millionaire Colorado brewer. At first the Foundation was involved in issues like textbook selection. By 1982 its scale had grown and it had a budget of $10 million, a staff of ninety and a network of some 450 research groups. Its publications programme was impressive. For an average press release Heritage reached 7,000 Congressmen, administration officials and journalists and spent nearly two-fifths of its budget on marketing its products – a bit more than on researching them. Its ambition was to reverse any decline in US influence and its bias against the UN was steadfast. It chose the UN as one of four areas of study, which helped put the UN at the centre of the right's political agenda.

Heritage, uncomfortable with what its directors perceived to be a liberal bias in the media on the East Coast, directed its resources in reaching the other America – the thousands of news outlets in the rest of the country. It was here that Heritage shipped its studies and press releases, Heritage claiming a success rate of an average 500 stories per mailing. The press releases were readable and punchy with vivid quotations, particularly useful for hard-pressed news editors. Heritage concentrated on trying to show how US interests were not served by the UN and suggested that the US might be better off pulling out and forming a new organisation limited to like-minded states. In this way the democracies would be able to challenge the anti-democratic rhetoric of the Soviet Union.

As a tax-exempt organisation, Heritage was forbidden by law from political propaganda or otherwise attempting to influence legislation. Heritage President, Edwin J. Fuelner, said, "We don"t lobby. We do the research part . . . anybody reading one of our studies could arrive reasonably at a different conclusion from the one stated by our people in the conclusion of the paper." But Heritage material about the UN promoted the notion that the UN was increasingly hostile to the US, Western democracy and free enterprise. Heritage's Senior Vice-President and Director of Research, Burton Yale Pines, believed that the UN, UNESCO and almost every other international organisation had been turned into an anti-America and anti-West lynch mob. Pines believed that "a world without the UN would be a better world". During two Reagan administrations Heritage was believed to be the most influential think-tank of the New Right. Jeane Kirkpatrick spoke of "My friends at Heritage, who did some good and valuable work on the UN and who I often worked with in their research and analysis."

Heritage claimed that the American pull-out from UNESCO in 1984 and the British withdrawal a year later were great coups. The other agencies were not of such great interest. Two of the largest were headed by Americans: William Draper, the Administrator of the UN Development Programme, UNDP, which had the largest budget of all but was financed through voluntary contributions, ran it like an American corporation. UNICEF's Executive Director, James Grant, had made UNICEF a household name and it was therefore untouchable. Grant promoted simple methods of child health in poor countries; he led the fight for immunisation for all at a time when fourteen million annual child deaths were from five or six preventable diseases. Grant believed that the success of nations should be judged not by their economic or military strengths but by the well-being of their people.

UNESCO was always different. The UN Educational, Scientific and Cultural Organisation had developed from the wartime Conference of Allied Ministers of Education, organised by Britain and the

International Institute of Intellectual Co-operation. The founding conference of UNESCO had been in London in December 1945 with thirty-four founding member states and the newly adopted constitution's opening lines, drafted by Archibald MacLeish read: "The Governments of the States Parties to this consitution on behalf of their peoples declare: that since wars begin in the minds of men, it is in the minds of men that the defenses of peace must be constructed . . . ". Its constitutional purpose was "to advance knowledge and understanding through all means of mass communication". Its first Director was the distinguished British biologist Julian Huxley and UNESCO was to give fresh impulse to education and to maintain, increase and diffuse knowledge. To rational First Worlders in the forties this seemed unproblematic; but the Communist Second World did not think Western knowledge always so politically innocent and the Third World countries, as they joined the UN, came to resent being patronised by all-knowing white men. Besides the means of accomplishing such nebulous ambitions proved problematic. Trouble started in the second half of the fifties with an alliance of developing countries who had joined UNESCO after decolonisation. These countries had their own views of what UNESCO should be doing and a larger share of the budget was devoted to training, technical assistance and practical aid for the developing countries. UNESCO like the UN itself, was split by the East–West and the North–South divides.

In 1982 the US Congress turned its attention to UNESCO, spurred by the Heritage Foundation which accused UNESCO of being actively hostile to a free society. The central crime was the 1975 New World Information and Communications Order, an Assembly Resolution promoted by the Third World which sought to redress the balance between the information rich and the information poor. The issue was as old as the UN itself: the General Assembly once characterised freedom of information as "the touchstone of all freedoms to which the UN is consecrated". In 1950 the General Assembly established a Sub-Commission on Freedom of Information and the Press to study the means of protecting news sources and to study measures to promote the dissemination of "true information". At the same time, the UN's Economic and Social Council began work on an International Code of Ethics designed to lay down a "standard of professional conduct" for those engaged in the dissemination of news. But all these bold intiatives foundered.

The Sub-Commission held five sessions, failed to reach agreement and disappeared without trace. The draft code of ethics was sent to national and international professional associations but the answer was no more than a deafening silence.

From the beginning UNESCO was concerned with the rights and the responsibilities of the mass media and there was a halcyon period in UNESCO when action was taken to help the developing countries build up news media: help was given to develop news agencies in Asia for example. In the seventies UNESCO began to pick up proposals which had been discussed and shelved at the UN in the early years. The objective was "the establishment of a New World information and communcation order". In 1977 UNESCO created an International Commission for the Study of Communication Problems headed by Sean McBride, Irish journalist and statesman. The Commission heralded a new era in space communications with global dissemination, the increasing pervasiveness of television and the dominance of four or five world news agencies to be discussed. The developed world owned ninety per cent of the world's communications and world news reflected western preferences and needs. Heritage thought the New World Order on freedom of information called for the control of world news.

Heritage had a major role in the American pull-out from UNESCO although supporters did try to prevent it. A commission was established with sixty Nobel and other laureates representing America's scientific and cultural community. UNESCO supporters defended the agency's basic philosophy that freedom and the improvement of the human condition could not occur in countries where ignorance was widespread. The commission of scientists accused the US government of misusing its UNESCO membership and pointed out the obvious decline in the qualfications of delegates America was sending to UNESCO meetings. UNESCO's headquarters were in Paris and America was using it as a way to thank campaign contributors and party drudges. Other delegates were more seasoned in the art of international diplomacy; no wonder America's influence had waned. The commission realised that in spite of frequent denunciations of Israel at UNESCO meetings, Israel was staying in.

To both the supporters and the detractors of UNESCO, one problem stemmed from the activities of the agency's Director General, the Senegalese Amadou-Mahtar M'Bow, elected in 1974.

His first term of office was fairly quiet although he was clearly authoritarian and he surrounded himself with sycophants. This deprived him of wise advisers who may have helped to spare his worst mistakes. In November 1984 Amadou-Mahtar M'Bow was exposed in the French newspaper *Le Monde* in a two-part series which described nepotism, cronyism and his extravagant lifestyle. *Le Monde* remarked on M'Bow's desire be to become Secretary General of the UN and hence his frequent pronoucements on events in the Middle East and other world crises. An inability to carry on any real conversation in English was a disadvantage. M'Bow, whose power base was the Soviet bloc and developing countries, saw himself as a champion of the poor and oppressed, an advocate of the New World Order which would establish equitable distribution of the world's wealth and knowledge.

There was loathing of Heritage in the Secretariat. Many staff members wanted Pérez de Cuéllar to stand up forcefully for the UN. Heritage press releases about UN matters were often riddled with inaccuracies. Brian Urquhart counted at least forty errors in one study which he described as full of distortion and outright mis-statement. But Pérez de Cuéllar was not easily persuaded.

As for the UN's first line of defence, its own Department of Public Information tried to be helpful at first. Its staff pointed out the various inaccuracies in Heritage. At the time, the Director of the Department of Public Information was a Japanese official named Yasushi Akashi, later to head the UN's massive operation in Cambodia, and afterwards become the Special Representative for former Yugoslavia. His early UN career was in the UN's Department of Public Information and, in 1983, confronted with the Heritage campaign, Akashi decided to visit the think-tank's headquarters in Washington. He said he wanted to explain the historic bonds between the US and the UN but, back in New York, UN officials blamed him for giving Heritage too much significance.

Traditionally the UN never answered back. There was a time when the office of Secretary General would not even write to the *New York Times*. This principle was established during the McCarran purge when the Assistant Secretary General in charge of Public Information was a Chilean named Benjamin Cohen. Once, after one of McCarran's more outrageous statements, Cohen had pleaded with Secretary General Trygve Lie to speak out and defend the organisation. Lie had refused saying that the UN must stay out of American politics. He believed that the Charter was a strong instrument of peace and hardly needed any defence. In the US, Lie said, the heritage of isolationism would continue to be a factor for some time to come. At the same meeting with senior officials in March, 1952 Lie had been told about a violent public campaign against UNESCO taking place on the West Coast of America; UNESCO was accused of attempting to modify textbooks in an anti-American direction. Cohen told him there was a feeling that the UN was promoting Socialism.

The UN continued to rely on friends and allies to defend its cause but by the time Pérez de Cuéllar became Secretary General they were few and far between. In the mid-eighties it was left to Stephen Lewis, Canadian UN representative, to give a rousing speech in New York in April 1985 about the UN's malevolent critics. "They pretend to be dispassionate, analytic, concerned", he said. "Poppy-cock. Folderol. They are, by and large, neo-isolationists in their views of the world, and they are made up of the Heritage Foundation and others of their ilk." He also called them philistines.

Heritage promptly deplored Lewis's interference in American internal affairs and called upon the Canadian Government to sack him. But the Canadian Prime Minister, Brian Mulroney, quickly came to Lewis's defence. "When he speaks, he speaks for the Government of Canada and I thought he spoke well." The former Australian Prime Minister, Gough Whitlam, who had been Australia's Ambassador to UNESCO, called Heritage "sinister". Whitlam described how Heritage influenced the British pull-out from UNESCO by wining and dining British journalists while talking about the evils of UNESCO. Whitlam described a dinner at the Garrick Club in London and said the cultivation of the media was effective. In October 1984, there were questions in the House of Commons and a sudden spate of newspaper stories about UNESCO – a subject rarely mentioned in the British press – which contained some of the arguments and information used in the US about how corrupt the organisation had become. Later the allegations of Heritage influence were confirmed by the House of Commons Foreign Affairs Committee, which wanted Britain to remain a member. In November in an unprecedented show of solidarity, all thirty-eight Commonwealth High Commissioners sent Prime Minister Thatcher a letter to support Britain's role in UNESCO but

Britain's answer to that was official notice of withdrawal. Afterwards the interest in UNESCO by the media and in the House of Commons subsided as rapidly as it had erupted.

The move by Britain was uncharacteristic and unsettling. Whitlam said American hustlers had used the British press and the House of Commons to stampede the government: Britain would never have withdrawn from UNESCO if the US had not already done so. UNESCO was deprived of thirty per cent of its budget and the participation of two founding member states. It was a first step towards the break-up of the UN.

In New York the UN relied on its strongest support group, the United Nations Association of America. Its President was Elliot Richardson, a former American Attorney General, and he said that Heritage propaganda was shoddy sensationalism at is worst and that its accusations bordered on the libellous. One company, McDonnell Douglas – which is probably the only company in the world to celebrate UN Day as a paid holiday – took out advertisements in *New York Times* with a photograph showing an empty Turtle Bay, the name of the East River bank where the UN headquarters are situated. In the photograph the Secretariat building is missing and the text is apocalyptic: " . . . stop the UN and you give the Four Horsemen – War, Famine, Pestilence and Death a clear chance to ride unfettered over most of the world".

The advertisement suggested that everyone write a letter to Jeane Kirkpatrick at the US Mission to tell her "how you feel about the UN".

At this time, Pérez de Cuéllar was busy elsewhere. He quietly lobbied and cajoled for his notion of a united Security Council, which often seemed naive, a fantasy. The Americans would certainly never agree. In 1983, Charles Lichenstein, an American ambassador and an old CIA hand, told a Soviet delegate that if the UN felt it was unwelcome in New York, "We will put no impediment in your way . . . and we will be at the dockside bidding you a farewell as you set off into the sunset".

He made the remark during a meeting of the Host Country Committee, whose task was to sort out the problems which arose between the national interests of the US over visas and the security and living arrangements for diplomats living in New York, plus the needs of the international community to which it played host. This was an uneasy relationship at best. The committee's deliberations were never amicable but by the early eighties there developed slanging matches between diplomats from East and West. The point which so enraged Lichenstein was whether the Americans had the right to prevent the Soviet Foreign Minister, Andrei Gromyko, from landing at one of New York's civilian airports. Gromyko was due to attend the forthcoming General Assembly but Washington told him to land at McGuire Air Force Base instead. The Soviets complained that the ban was illegal and, on September 19, 1983, appealed the decision to the Host Country Committee accusing America of an "insulting" campaign which breached the Headquarters Agreement signed with the UN in 1947.

Charles Lichenstein, furious, upheld the full force of the ban. "Normal conditions ceased to obtain [sic] when the Soviet Union shot down a civilian airliner with the loss of 269 lives", he said and the committee room fell silent. Two weeks previously a Korean civilian Boeing 747 airliner, KAL 007, had been shot down over Soviet territory on its journey from Alaska to Seoul, hundreds of miles off course, by Soviet missiles from an interceptor jet. Everyone on board was killed. President Reagan's first statement on the tragedy called it a "massacre". The attack on the jet turned into a major propaganda advantage for the US. Lichenstein characterised the Soviet action as a heinous crime and claimed that the Soviet pilot had the airliner in his sights, clearly identified as civilian, prior to launching the missile. When the Americans brought the issue to the Security Council, they staged a television drama for the world. Ambassador Kirkpatrick spoke in front of five video screens, erected in the Council chamber; Oleg Troyanovsky, the Soviet ambassador, resolutely kept his back to the screens. Kirkpatrick told the Council: " . . . violence and lies are regular instruments of Soviet policy . . . we are dealing here not with pilot errors but with decision and priorities characteristic of a system". But at the end of the day. A motion condemning the Soviets was bound to fail: Kirkpatrick had only seven of the fifteen Security Council members willing to vote with her. But the impact on American opinion was as dramatic as Washington had hoped. In the New York press Mayor Koch called the UN a cesspool.

With the press baying for a statement, the US Mission blandly announced that Lichenstein's remarks about waving the UN goodbye did not represent administration policy; the remarks about the UN quitting America were made in response to deliberate provocation. Some hours later, a White House spokesman, Larry Speakes, announced dryly that Lichenstein's comments reflected the ambassador's personal views, though he defended the denial of landing rights for Gromyko.

By 1983 the US had exercised its Security Council veto five times as often as the USSR and the atmosphere in the General Assembly was the worst in living memory. For the first time for twenty-seven years the Soviet Foreign Minister Andrei Gromyko did not even attend.

In the Secretariat they talked about "the omen", an incident which had occurred in 1985, during the celebrations for the UN's fortieth anniversary. A white dove released by Javier Pérez de Cuéllar's glamorous wife Marcela left her outstretched arms and flew skywards for only a brief moment before it fell dead at her feet.

The story seemed fanciful, even laughable, but it did happen, not during the fortieth celebrations, but during a UNICEF ceremony and in front of hundreds of children. The date was immaterial: the story simply served as proof that the UN was doomed. The headquarters building deteriorated around them, the Secretariat was grimy with unwashed windows and empty offices had broken-down equipment piled in the corners. Officials came to believe that the organisation would grind to a halt and then eventually the salaries would cease. Their grim speculations were not far from the nightmare predictions on the thirty-eighth floor.

The anti-UN campaign was unabated and American debts to the UN continued to mount. Those members of staff old enough to remember said it was worse than the McCarran purges; nowadays the very principles which underpinned internationalism were under attack. The American Congress no longer considered the UN an indispensable component of American foreign relations and some members of the Reagan administration let it be known that under certain circumstances the US might withdraw from the UN altogether. The Americans were accused by the Soviets of trying to break up the UN; in return, American delegates accused the Soviets of using it for spying.

The view of the world from the thirty-eighth floor is not the same as the view from elsewhere. In these cool comfortable offices there are political alliances which by their nature remain secret for ever. But what was increasingly obvious to anyone working there in the mid-eighties was that Pérez de Cuéllar was more and more trusted by Moscow. At the funeral of Soviet President Yury Andropov, who died in February, 1984, Pérez de Cuéllar was treated as a low-level Foreign Minister. Thirteen months later, in March 1985, at the funeral of Konstantin Chernenko, Javier Pérez de Cuéllar was the centre of attention. Immediately after the ceremony and pomp, he was ushered into a meeting with Mikhail Gorbachev and met the new General Secretary of the Communist Party in the presence of an interpreter only. All previous Secretaries General had been treated with disdain.

At this first meeting the fifty-four-year-old Soviet leader and the Peruvian diplomat measured each other's strengths. Gorbachev wanted to know about the Secretary General's own channels and the moves he was making to fulfil his peace agenda. Gorbachev concluded that Pérez de Cuéllar was an authoritative figure enjoying universal trust, who had to be encouraged in his missions of mediation, conciliation and good offices. Pérez de Cuéllar knew sooner than most about New Thinking, *novoe politicheskoe myshlenie*, which amounted to a complete reform of Soviet foreign policy. A reformed and revitalised UN was at the heart of New Thinking. It was as revolutionary as *perestroika* and *glasnost*, but was less well known in the West; it was, after all, harder to pronounce. By the time Gorbachev came to power, such attitudes about foreign policy were common among the Soviet political elite: its appearance was not sudden.

The UN celebrated its fortieth birthday in 1985 and achieved limo-lock on First Avenue, with hundreds of sleek black cars inching towards the General Assembly building, a nightmare for protocol; each King, President, Prime Minster and Head of State was to have the appropriate amount of diplomatic courtesy and appear on time at the podium. There was panic when the President of Finland, impatient from sitting in his car, quite simply walked. The New York police requested a ten-car limit to each motorcade, exempting only President Reagan.

Reagan addressed the General Assembly on UN day, October 24, which commemorates the day in 1945 when sufficient member states had ratified the Charter to allow the UN to become operational. At the fortieth they celebrated with a lunch for 350 for which a special table was built. There were hundreds of parties and, as it got dark, a giant neon on the side of the Secretariat building facing Manhattan was lit. "UN 40", it said. Like everything else, the wording of the neon was a compromise, words mulled and argued over by diplomats in endless committees. Another anniversary committee had less success; its diplomats failed to draft an Anniversary Declaration.

Further evidence of a retrenchment from the American post-war commitment to internationalism had come just a few weeks before Reagan's speech to the General Assembly, when Washington officially notified the UN that it would no longer accept the jurisdiction of the International Court of Justice. The impetus for this decision was the case brought to the court by Nicaragua against the US for illegally supporting paramilitary attacks by rebels, and the mining of harbours. The US argued the court lacked jurisdiction and would no longer take part in the case. The announcement ended a thirty-nine-year policy, declared by President Harry Truman, under which the US would abide by court decisions automatically. There were fears that the fragile edifice of international co-operation was collapsing.

When the fortieth celebrations were over and the Secretariat went quiet and all the delegates went home, Washington announced it would hold back yet more of its dues to the UN. Just as Pérez de Cuéllar and his beleaguered officials thought it could not get much worse it did. The truth about Kurt Waldheim's wartime career broke upon the world giving final proof, if any were needed, of the UN's "moral bankruptcy".

The disclosure of Waldheim's past had been threatening him for years. In 1980, while he was Secretary General and desperate for Western support for a third term, the most indefatigable UN critic, Shirley Hazzard, wrote an article in January, 1980 for the *New Republic* which reported that Waldheim had "dutifully followed the normal path by . . . serving in Hitler's Army in various campaigns including the Eastern front." At the same time the *Washington Post* ran a long interview with Waldheim and asked about the recent accusation; Waldheim said that his family was persecuted by the Nazis and that he was released from active service in 1941. Another story was published in September, 1980 which repeated a rumour that Waldheim had been active in the Nazi Youth movement.

Stephen J. Solarz, a Democratic Congressman from Brooklyn, was so concerned at these stories that he wrote to Waldheim. The Secretary General wrote back to deny membership of the Nazi Youth movement and to point out that he had left the German military after 1941. Solarz remained suspicious and he wrote another letter – this time to the CIA. Solarz received an answer from Frederick P. Hitz, legislative counsel to the Director, Stansfield Turner. Hitz told Solarz that Waldheim had not been a member of the Nazi Youth. Hitz denied the CIA had any "intelligence reporting in detail on Waldheim's military service" but that from open sources the agency gleaned that Waldheim served as a "staff intelligence officer with rank of lieutenant assigned to the 45th Infantry Division". This was Waldheim's story too. Waldheim saw action in the Polish campaign in September, 1939 and the assault on France in May 1940. In June 1941 he was sent to the Eastern Front to take part in the invasion of the USSR. There was not a word in the letter about Waldheim's subsequent service in the Balkans where the Wehrmacht was fighting not a regular army but guerillas. The CIA letter maintained the lie that Waldheim was discharged from the German army following his recovery from a leg wound in 1941.

By the time the matter was raised in public again, Waldheim had just left the UN. In 1982, a Polish born Orthodox Jewish historian, Hillel Seidman, published a book, *United Nations – Perfidy and Perversion*. The book contained a chapter about how Waldheim was schooled in the Nazi Youth and the German army. Seidman accused Waldheim of censoring his own biography about the war years, although Seidman was still ignorant of the full details of Waldheim's army record.

Seidman argued that whatever should emerge, Waldheim was culpable because as his book proved, there was mass murder of Jews by regular army units of the Werhmacht. Any officer in the German army at the Soviet front would have been aware of massacres; Waldheim could not have been unaware of what was happening at the time to Jews in Occupied Europe. And yet there was not one word from this man, not a scintilla of remorse or compassion for the suffering of the tortured and killed. Seidman believed Waldheim was "the most visible symbol of the poisonous hate and anti-Semitic incitement in the UN". The UN was turned into a "Goebbels-like machine for the inflammation of base, destructive instincts directed primarily against Jews". Four years after Seidman published his book Waldheim's Balkan service was finally exposed.

The responsibity for the appointment of a war criminal as Secretary General rested with the permanent members of the Security Council. At the time, December 21, 1971, three of the veto powers – America, Britain and France – had possessed the UN War Crimes Commission lists of suspects since 1947, which contained Kurt Waldheim's name. Immediately after the war Waldheim became well known in Austria as an assistant to the Minister of Foreign Affairs in Vienna, then under Allied control.

Waldheim was nominated Secretary General twice by the five, once in 1971 and again in 1976. Even before the first nomination, gossip in the Secretariat hinted that Waldheim, then the Austrian ambassador, was a former SS officer. Arrogant and high-handed in management matters, Waldheim had enemies. One morning, while Waldheim's remorseless campaign for office was in full flight, little flags were found floating on corks in the pool by the fountain on the Secretariat's forecourt. The flags bore swastikas.

There was not a suggestion in the newspapers of Waldheim's past. One British paper greeted his election by naming him the least controversial candidate but his own government certainly had doubts and it ordered its Army Intelligence Service look through the records but, by the time researchers found the secret of Waldheim's service in the Balkans, about which he lied by omission for years, he was comfortably installed on the thirty-eighth floor and had become Austria's most prominent citizen. Later the Austrian Chancellor, Bruno Kreisky, claimed he did not actually read the army intelligence file on Waldheim. Had he done so he would have found that Waldheim served as an intelligence officer with the Wehrmacht's Army Group E which, in order to protect the Belgrade-Zagreb railway lines from 2,000 partisans, had rounded up men, women and children for certain death at the Jasenovac concentration camp. The concentration camp was twenty miles from where Waldheim served. Waldheim must have known of the Kozara campaign when 66,000 men women and children were killed or sent to camps. Waldheim's unit collated statistics regarding the number of prisoners to be sent to camps, deciding how many trucks and railway cars were needed. On July 22, 1942 Waldheim was awared the Silver Medal of the Crown King of Zvonimir with Oak Leaves by the Croatian Fascist leader Ante Pavelic for courage in West Bosnia.

A year after his appointment the Americans, for reasons which are obscure, looked at Waldheim's records. The CIA undertook research into his case. In 1979, French military authorities in Berlin consulted the Waldheim file held in German Army archives. The file contained proof needed that contrary to Waldheim's assertions about medical discharge from the Germany army in 1941, he had in fact served until 1944. In 1979 the government of Israel's Prime Minister, Menachem Begin, asked Simon Wiesenthal, the Vienna based Nazi-hunter, to find out if there were anything compromising about the UN's Secretary General. Wiesenthal made contact with someone who agreed to research the French-controlled archive of German Army documents in Berlin. The researcher told Wiesenthal that no record of SS or Nazi party membership for Waldheim existed and, as far as Wiesenthal was concerned, the matter was closed. Waldheim knew about war crimes but was not personally involved in them.

On the day of the election, on December 21, 1971 a throng of journalists surrounded the Austrian mission; among them a young Israeli television reporter named Haim Yavin. For a time Yavin sat quietly alone until a member of the Austrian delegation approached him. The person whispered that perhaps he ought to ask the newly elected Secretary General about his Nazi past. Yavin thanked the nervous informer. He followed up on the tip. As Waldheim's on-camera interview was concluding, Yavin asked him: "Did you have any links with the Nazi Party?" Waldheim smiled and shook his head. He said that he had no links of any sort. On the contrary his family had endured a lot of problems; his father was a resolute anti-Nazi. It was true, up until the Anschluss in 1938.

Yavin sent back a four-minute interview and afterwards in Tel Aviv, he was chastised for asking Waldheim such a "nasty question". The *Jerusalem Post* said he was too aggressive. At the time, good Israeli relations with Austria were vital. An influx of Soviet Jews was expected who would pass through Vienna.

The truth was that Waldheim had become Secretary General in 1971 because all that mattered to the permanent five was to find someone quickly. At the time, George Bush was America's UN ambassador and the State Department would later claim that it was ignorant of the lie. The Secretary of State William Rogers said that Waldheim was acceptable because he was a former Foreign Minister from a neutral country friendly to the United States and he assumed a background check was carried out by the UN. This assumption was repeated in London at the Foreign and Commonwealth Office where the British claimed to have been unaware. Such carelessness is a gross dereliction of duty; they were fooled by the wartime censorship of Waldheim's record. The decision to obliterate Waldheim's past was taken in 1945.

Waldheim was no one's choice but Austria's and Austria provided him every facility for his fervent campaign. Austria seems to have been the only country to have checked the relevant German Army archives prior to his appointment as Secretary General.

The government of Prime Minister Edward Heath claimed to have known nothing and when Waldheim's war background was finally exposed in 1986 and a public uproar ensued, the Ministry of Defence reopened a government review into the murders of British undercover agents, last seen alive by members of Waldheim's army group. Eventually, the government review absolved Waldheim of complicity in the loss of these men. The only documents which might have connected Waldheim to these murders were destroyed by the Foreign Office in 1978 – apparently without the knowledge of the then Foreign Secretary David Owen.

As for the British vote in the Security Council when Waldheim was selected, it remains a mystery. In a Parliamentary answer in February 1988 Prime Minister Margaret Thatcher told the House of Commons: "It has been the practice of successive Governments not to reveal how they voted in secret ballots in the UN, or why they voted as they did". No one was accountable. A much more extraordinary reply came in a letter from Thatcher to B'nai B'rith in June 1986 when the Prime Minister wrote: "The circumstances of his election to that position (Secretary General) were not within the control of the British Government", a misleading phraseology.

There is black irony in the notion of a UN Secretary General accused of war crimes, for the promise during the war was that wartime atrocities would be punished. "The Allied powers will pursue these wicked men", Chruchill said, "to the uttermost ends of the earth . . . "

A War Crimes Commission was set up, the first attempt at institutionalising war-time allied co-operation and it owed its existence to an inter-allied conference that met in London in January, 1942. It was constituted on November 7, 1943 in the Foreign Office in London and was called the UN War Crimes Commission, the first organisation to have UN in its title. It was quite apart from the UN itself which was not created until 1945. One of the Commission's primary tasks was to collect, investigate and record evidence of war crimes and to report to the governments concerned those instances where material available appeared to disclose a *prima-facie* case. It was up to governments to pursue prosecution for crimes committed on their territory or against their nationals.

After the Second World War the International Military Tribunals at Nuremberg and Tokyo used evidence collected by the Commission and these trials, although symbolically important in their establishment of international moral principles, still left thousands and thousands of people unpunished. The details of their alleged crimes were carefully recorded by Commission and stored in files.

Seventeen member governments formed the Commission, who eventually decided that, as the Cold War hampered their efforts to bring justice, they might as well disband. Thus three years after the end of the war, on March 31, 1948, the UN War Crimes Commission ceased to function. Commission records including some 40,000 files on those charged with crimes remained. These files contained all available evidence together with witness statements. Approximately 24,500 people on the list were assigned an "A" rating, signifying that enough evidence existed for bringing a prosecution. When the UN War Crimes Commission disbanded, all these files were given to the UN for safe-keeping, among them the file on Kurt Waldheim in the "A" category which determined that he should stand trial for murder.

The rules about about who would have access to these files were drawn up jointly in 1949 between the Commission and the UN, the Commission's Legal Adviser, Dr. J. J. Litawski, a consultant to the UN's Human Rights Division, together with the Australian Chairman of the Commission, Lord Wright, and lawyers from the UN's Department of Legal Affairs. They decided that the list of war criminals was to be open to historians only, apart from the sensitive files containing the charges which were to be restricted because they contained unsubstantiated reports and allegations which had never been tested in a court of law; none of the charges in the files had ever been subject to independent enquiry as the Commission's Investigation Committee relied solely on information supplied by Commission offices in each Allied capital. Access would only be given to the Commission's seventeen member governments on a case-by-case basis on the understanding that material obtained was confidential.

Government requests for access to the files were quite numerous. Over the years and at various times requests for information on certain people came from, among others, Australia, Canada and the US. All requests were granted. In some cases a massive amount of material was obtained – much material on Joseph Mengele was supplied from these archives. Israel had been granted access, the only non-member of the War Crimes Commission, for material on Adolf Eichmann. But the rules prevented individuals searching the records for fear that information could be used for blackmail, though the files were used extensively by America's own Office of Special Investigations. In fact, such was the level of co-operation between the Americans and the UN archivists that on April 28, 1980 the then Attorney General, Benjamin Civiletti, wrote to Secretary General Kurt Waldheim to confirm an arrangement with the UN's archivist that the information obtained would be treated with the utmost confidentiality: "I am confident that the co-operation which the UN is extending will assist the office in its duties". The arrangement lasted until 1986 when the Americans wanted to do a general trawl through the records rather than submit requests on a name-by-name basis and the UN's legal department had to point out that, like all other member governments on the Commission, the US was already in possession of a copy of the complete list of names of war criminals anyway. A copy of the list was provided to every member state when the Commission ceased its activities. The complete list of the 37,000 names was readily available to anyone who should ask, on an open archive shelf in libraries in both Washington and London.

Some weeks after a journalist finally broke the story about Waldheim's lie, Waldheim's own file was discovered in the UN War Crimes Commission file. It charged him with being a war criminal. There were howls of outrage and press claims about a cover-up by the UN. Pérez de Cuéllar announced simply that he regretted the international tensions the discovery caused.

Confronted by such an onslaught of criticism the UN's Department of Public Information was helpless. The UN, already perceived as anti-Israel, run by Communists, in league with Third World terrorists and despots, now had to admit it had once been run by a Nazi collaborator. The Security Council, attracting little blame for voting him into office kept a very understandable silence.

Now the diplomatic community annouced to anyone who would listen that Waldheim had always been detested. His peers painted a picture of a Secretary General totally without qualities. Waldheim, it turned out, had pocketed the official presents he had received while in office. He accepted diamonds from the Shah. He tried to persuade the Metropolitan Museum in New York to hang a few Gainsboroughs and Corots on his walls. The criticism gushed. Waldheim never read a book and was completely without culture. Waldheim was arrogant and contemptuous of UN staff, helping his daughter to a plum job with a good salary in Geneva. A disgraced Waldheim was almost more useful than when he was in office. Officials could blame him for the UN's decline.

There were rumours that Waldheim had been blackmailed but Secretariat staff laughed at such ideas; everyone knew that with Waldheim there was no need for anything so crude. He caved into pressure every day anyway, giving UN jobs and other perks to countries of all ideologies. Waldheim's desire to please accounted for a twenty-five per cent increase in senior appointments at the UN. His interference in personnel matters caused much resentment and he had a total disregard for the rights of employees. U Thant, Waldheim's predecessor, told anyone lobbying for a job that he did not deal with such matters. Waldheim on the other hand used UN jobs as a way of ingratiating himself with governments. The Soviet ambassador used to tell him bluntly that unless Soviets were favoured, Waldheim would not be re-elected.

That the story broke at all was owing to the diligence of a persistent journalist on an independent Viennese news magazine *Profil*. The story was published in March 1986 while the ambitious Waldheim was still campaigning, this time to be President of Austria. The journalist, Hubertus Czernin, taking rumours about Waldheim seriously, started an investigation. He discovered that Waldheim had served in the Balkans and his story went world-wide. The former Secretary General had been a Germany army intelligence officer serving in Yugoslavia in 1942 and in Greece in 1943, and would have been all too well aware of the persecution of Yugoslavs, Greeks, Italians and Jews. After the initial disclosure, there followed a period of feverish research to try to prove that Waldheim ordered or incited atrocities. The World Jewish Congress was the most persistent believing that were Waldheim ever elected President of Austria, it would be tantamount to condoning the Holocaust. The Congress, founded in 1936 to warn the world about Nazism, now hired a consultant, a professor from the University of South Carolina, Robert Herzstein. Herzstein was a specialist on the history of the Third Reich and eventually his skill and knowledge produced the body of evidence against Waldheim. Herzstein found that Waldheim had a role in the Kozara massacre when an estimated 68,000 Yugoslavs were brutally killed, thousands of women and children deported to death camps, a German army "clean sweep".

October 1943 found Waldheim in the intelligence section of Army Group E with the German 12th Army in Greece where he enjoyed a good relationship with the group Commander, Alexander Lohr, the Austrian-born Commander-in-Chief of Army Group E. Lohr was convicted of war crimes by a Yugoslav tribunal and shot in Belgrade in 1947. In August 1944 Waldheim married Nazi Party member Elizabeth "Cissy" Ritschel but was soon back in Greece stationed only a few miles from Salonika from where more than 60,000 Jews were deported. Most died in Auschwitz.

Waldheim said he knew nothing about deportations, claimed he was in Vienna when such things took place and seemed not have noted that entire sections of Salonika were suddenly empty. Waldheim was described as one of the best informed officers in the Balkans. This was why he received special treatment and why, shortly after being demobilised, he was interned by the Americans at their camp at Bad Tolz in Upper Bavaria, an interrogation centre specialising in prisoners of interest to US military intelligence. Waldheim stayed in Bad Tolz from the end of May to the beginning of August 1945, from where he returned to Vienna. From that moment he pretended that his service had ended on the Russian front. He maintained the falsehood for forty years, some believe with the help of the American intelligence community. Perhaps Waldheim, like so many others, bought his new record by giving the Americans first-hand knowledge of Tito's partisan army.

Waldheim was always eager to please and perhaps he particularly pleased American intelligence. While researching his book, Herzstein discovered that the CIA was in possession of a document about Waldheim, dated 26 April, 1947, which identified Waldheim as a German army intelligence officer. The CIA refused to declassify it: the reason being that Waldheim was of operational interest. Herzstein concluded that Waldheim therefore had the protection of the American government.

After the war, Waldheim was recruited to the Austrian foreign ministry by Karl Gruber, the Foreign Minister and former resistance hero. At the time, Gruber's senior aide was Fritz Peter Molden, also a veteran of the resistance who had worked for the American OSS. Molden married the daughter of Allen Dulles, who ran a spy network in Switzerland between 1942 and 1945 and who headed the CIA between 1952 and 1961. Gruber, before employing Waldheim, had asked Molden to check his credentials. Molden reported that nothing detrimental was found.

Years later Molden explained that unless a man had been a Nazi Party member or had taken direct part in atrocities it was not important. "The bottom line," Molden said, "is that Kurt Waldheim was not a Nazi."

Waldheim had a few close shaves. The Yugoslavs had taken a particular interest in the atrocities of German Army Group E, whose Commander was fellow Austrian Alexander Lohr. Yugoslavia's first Communist President, Josip Tito, would let no one forget the role of the Austrians in Nazi war crimes. In September 1947, Waldheim's name was discovered on a staff list and a link was made to a man working in the Foreign Ministry. It was quite a discovery. Waldheim was an aide to the Foreign Minister of Austria; at the time both Austria and Yugoslavia were in dispute over territory, the Slovene areas of Carinthia, the subject of fanatical Austrian nationalism. The West supported Austria; the Soviets supported Yugoslavia.

Extradition of war criminals from Austria was far from easy and the Soviets were accusing the Austrian government of protecting war criminals. Thousands of Nazi and Utashia collaborators had fled to Austria and Germany. The Americans were stalling, demanding proof before handing anyone over to Communist Yugoslavia. But extraditing Waldheim from Austria to stand trial was not the intention anyway. The Yugoslavs would use Waldheim to embarrass Gruber, to expose the Foreign Minister of Austria as a man who harboured a murderer. The Yugoslavs hastily assembled a file on Waldheim and submitted it to the UN War Crimes Commission in London. Oberleutnant Waldheim was charged with murder and the putting to death of hostages.

Waldheim's case was heard in London on February 26, 1948 at the UN War Crimes Commission offices in Berkeley Square. There was no investigation, no questioning of witnesses. Like thousands of others the case was given a few minutes' scrutiny after which, along with 148 others considered that day, Waldheim's name was put on a list of war criminals wanted for murder. Waldheim's name would go forward to the Anglo-American Central Registry of War Criminals and Security Suspects known as CROWCASS which worked out of Berlin.

In spite of it all, the Yugoslavs failed to discredit Gruber. Gruber packed Waldheim off to Paris to another posting before the crucial negotiations to put him out of harm's way. Soon it was no longer in Yugoslavia's interest to embarrass the Austrians. Tito broke with Moscow and needed to reopen trade with the West. The Waldheim case was filed away and never came to court. The files of the UN War Crimes Commission were shipped to New York to the safe keeping of the UN archives. Waldheim was on his way. Waldheim quickly climbed through the ranks of the Austrian Foreign Service and, by June 1955, he was appointed Austrian observer at the UN and joined in the rarified circles of international diplomacy. A routine notification of the appointment from the British Embassy in Vienna reports to the British UN mission in New York that Waldheim and his wife were a "charming addition to any dinner-table". Waldheim was honest and hard-working. He had been helpful to the British beyond the bounds of diplomatic politeness. Along with this letter was a copy of Waldheim's biography in which there was no mention at all of his war years.

As for the Soviets, they waited until Waldheim was President of Austria before springing to his defence. In June 1986, the Soviet news agency Tass issued a statement accusing the US administration and Zionist circles of launching a personal and hostile attack. This "unseemly undertaking" was part of the psychological warfare launched by the Zionist forces and the US government to try to discredit the UN. Tass pointed out that the accusations were levelled by America, a country which sheltered thousands of Nazi criminals and had organised a rat-run through which useful Nazis and members of the SS went to work for US secret services.

Waldheim's election slogan in his campaign to become President of Austria was "Vote for a man whom the world trusts". Once elected he was ignored and isolated, living in the Habsburg Palace, but he endured it all, showing himself every inch a diplomat. He could not understand why people would want to demonstrate against him – he was no more a war criminal than most of his fellow citizens. By then, the Austrian Government had commissioned an international panel

of six historians and military specialists who concluded that although
not a war criminal, Waldheim was a congenital liar.

The elderly Karl Gruber, Austria's post-war Foreign Minister, the
man who originally hired Waldheim to the diplomatic service, was
quoted as saying the commission was led by a Socialist and "the rest
were Jews".

In Washington there was a strong lobby to get Waldheim's name
on the watch list, a move that would ban him from entering the US.
An integral part of the Department of Justice, the Office of Special
Investigations was established by Congress in 1979 to direct
America's Nazi-hunting efforts. Officials prepared a 200-page report
on Waldheim, giving it to the Attorney General, Edwin Meese, to
persuade him to comply with a 1978 Amendment to America's
immigration laws. This prevented anyone who was involved in Nazi
persecution between 1933 and 1945 from entering the US.

No Head of State had ever been barred and the more cynical
members of Washington's establishment assumed that the efforts to
have Waldheim blacklisted had more to do with a request to
Congress that the budget for the Office of Special Investigations be
increased. The report which was given to Meese stated that
Waldheim's unit was responsible for the deaths of 1,200 Greek Jews
loaded on barges that the Germans scuttled in the Mediterranean.
Waldheim belonged to German army units responsible for killing
civilians, executing prisoners and shipping prisoners to slave labour
camps. Nothing in the file proved that Waldheim had personally
killed or tortured anyone but he provided the intelligence
information that enabled others to do so and may have ordered
some prisoners shot.

In Spring 1987, a year after receiving the initial request, Meese
added Waldheim's name to the watch list which barred him ever
again from entering the US.

In May 1986, a few weeks after the initial revelations, Benjamin
Netanyahu, Israel's UN Ambassador in a well-publicised campaign,
demanded access to the UN War Crimes Commission files together
with all the charge lists. The result was a fury of headlines that the
"UN" was refusing to allow access, that there was a "UN war crime
cover-up". The *New York Times* reported it as a vast secret archive which
"officials of the UN have kept hidden from historians, journalists and
other interested members of the public for nearly forty years".

"If you hide the past," Netanyahu chided, "you will bury the future." He said it was imperative the archives be opened for study. They contained the single greatest source of information about the holocaust. There were details about the death camps, staff lists of Gestapo personnel and the records of entire Jewish communities who had disappeared without trace. Netanyahu told how the files were securely protected in "the bowels of the UN" and subsequent newspaper headlines accepted his argument. No one looked at the rules, at the extensive use made of the files by member goverments. Netanyahu continued his high-profile and emotional campaign, accusing the "UN" of preventing disclosure of Nazi atrocities. In the end, in October 1986, Pérez de Cuéllar reassembled War Crimes Commission, called the ambassadors of its seventeen members together to review the rules of access and perhaps allow non-governmental researchers to consult them. But it emerged that most of the member governments wanted to retain restriction, to permit access to government-only requests on individuals to be brought to trial.

By the time of the informal get-together, Israel already possessed the complete charge lists and was by now requesting information from the archives on a name-by-name basis in their thousands. But the campaign for complete and open access for everyone continued.

At another meeting between the seventeen governments France and Poland continue to hold out for continuing the restrictions until finally, in November 1987, the access was liberalised. Netanyahu appeared on NBC's *Today* show to announce that a principle of justice was established; there were thousands of untried war criminals, "So opening the files will now bring them to justice", he said.

The UN became a focus for hatred. The Zionism is racism Resolution, a war criminal as Secretary General and now the UN involved in a "war crimes cover-up" all turned the perception of the organisation into an enemy with malevolent intent. In February 1987, a twelve-hour soap opera entitled *Amerika* was produced by ABC Television. A hugely expensive mini-series it told a story of UN troops occupying the US on behalf of the Soviet Union. These UN soldiers, wearing UN insignia and blue helmets, were executioners of a brute force doing the Soviets' dirty work. The film's warning was about "One Worldism" and what would happen if the US ignored warnings of Soviet encroachment. In the series, the UN Special Service Units, UNSSU, blow up the Capitol and slaughter Congress. In one scene a US resistance heroine, raped by UN soldiers, describes her attackers as a "very international group" – an Angolan, two South Americans and a Vietnamese.

"But", she says, "it is so hard to tell them apart." Sometime during the filming a script found its way to the Secretary General and he wrote to the Chair of ABC to object. *Amerika* made a travesty of one of the UN's finest accomplishments – peacekeeping. It would do harm to the memory of the many UN soldiers over the years who had died in the cause of peace.

Even in defending itself against libel, the UN could not prevail. A *Washington Post* editorial stated: "What an odd expense of anger . . . for an institution that has had so much trouble addressing the travesties and conflicts that have a true claim on its moral attention . . . "

10. A HARD SELL

While the world's great unresolved crises continued to preoccupy the thirty-eighth floor, in other parts of the Secretariat there were different concerns. Certain staff members believed that the UN's problems stemmed from its lack of "image" and there were attempts to promote the UN and give it a hard sell. Media consultants believed that the UN would have to adopt a higher profile were it to survive the media-age and the "sound bite". In order to adopt a higher profile communications experts were hired to teach Under Secretaries General how to look good on US television and, during one strategy meeting in the Secretary General's office in January 1988, Pérez de Cuéllar was told bluntly that he was part of the problem. He should give more television interviews and appear on chat shows. He should invite influential members of the press to his residence, write letters to people of influence in the media and invite them to UN headquarters. Communications experts advised that the news media was incapable of identifying with an institution, it needed a personality. The UN should adopt a "pro-active media strategy" otherwise it would continue its decline, becoming a lifeless, bureaucratic machine.

Thérèse Paquet-Sévigny, at the time the most senior woman in the UN, the first to be appointed Under Secretary General and the first female director of the UN's Department of Public Information, was keen on this approach. She was courageous if not foolhardy in her determination to restore the UN's good name. She was also an advocate of corporate sponsorship of the UN to help solve the increasingly severe financial crisis. At this particular meeting in

January Pérez de Cuéllar quietly said: "Madam, I think you should be promoting the car, and not the driver".

The UN's founders believed that enlightened public opinion would be key. The UN could not possibly work without public support; the better informed the people were about its aims, activities and the realities with which it had to cope, the more likely the UN was to succeed. To that end in 1946 the General Assembly established an Office of Public Information to "promote to the greatest extent possible an informed understanding of the work and purposes of the UN among the peoples of the world". The Office of Public Information would be grandiose with its own UN radio, TV station and newspaper. World news about political unrest, the direct cause of international tension, would be broadcast by objective journalists working from the Secretariat. These plans were quickly shelved when delegates realised the cost involved and the 1946 General Assembly, while giving the Office of Public Information its grand mandate, also made savage cuts in budget. The Office became an abject failure and Secretary General Trygve Lie soon lamented how little the UN had touched world opinion. The public failed to understand its limitations and was ignorant of its undramatic but fundamental development work.

The Office of Public Information lacked an overall strategy. Member states could not agree about what it should be doing and it became a clear reflection of the growing ideological rift among them. There were frequent disagreements about the UN's promotional material. In November, 1949 the Americans judged "utterly unacceptable" a UN film, *The Death of a Child* which graphically portrayed the poverty and misery of Latin America and attacked the "colonial economic system", charging foreign companies with exploiting natural resources. The State Department was appalled because the film had made no mention of the US's ten-year technical aid programme to the region. "If the film were shown in other parts of the world, it would be a rather damming comment on our often mentioned neighbourly attitude towards Latin America." A Directive was issued that the Secretary General be made "informally" aware of US objections. The film was shelved. For years similar arguments appeared. In 1986, there were complaints involving a UN film about homelessness with footage shot in Brazil, Sri Lanka and in New York City. The US mission grumbled to the Secretariat and the New York footage was removed. In answer to criticisms of caving in, Japanese official Yasushi Akashi, then Under Secretary General for Public Information, commented; "We have to take into cognisance the kind of atmosphere in this country. It is an important country and our largest contributor."

The Office of Public Information changed is name to The Department of Public Information (DPI) and by the early sixties, when rapid decolonisation changed the Assembly's voting majority, there were different ideas for UN promotion. DPI was mandated to concentrate on providing the press with information about the UN's role in decolonisation, in development, the struggle against apartheid and the rights of the Palestinians. The West considered that the DPI's work had been hijacked and the arguments between delegates over what DPI should be doing continued. The debate broadened and eventually centred on the Third World proposal for a New World Information Order. The West's reaction to this particular New World Order was to accuse the Third World of wanting government control of the press.

In 1978, the General Assembly created the Committee on Information, comprising seventy member states, which was to review DPI's role. The Committee was to examine how DPI could best promote the new world orders, promoted by the Third World for a more equitable division of the world's wealth. DPI was to promote the establishment of a new, more just and more effective share of the world's information to strengthen peace and international understanding.

Over the years the mandates this committee gave to DPI became more specific and detailed: in 1980 it was directed to promote human rights, the struggle against racial discrimination, the integration of women in the struggle for peace. The staff who worked in DPI walked a tightrope: on the one hand they were asked to inform the world of the work of the UN, on the other to present areas of UN involvement which did not enjoy the support of all member states.

In 1986 the Americans launched an enquiry which focused on DPI. Ambassador Jeane Kirkpatrick had testified to Congress that DPI was Soviet dominated with agents writing Communist propaganda. She told Congress that the new world orders submitted by the Third World were prepared under Soviet influence. The Americans made an analysis, paragraph by paragraph, of information contained in UN press releases, articles, radio transcripts and weekly briefing materials concerning apartheid, disarmament, new world orders and the question of Palestine and, in April 1986, concluded that much of the material was opposed to US interests, or took positions contrary to US policy. Only one of the press releases was favourable. This damning evidence prompted action on the Hill in the form of an amendment by Representative Patrick Swindall, a Republican from Georgia, proposing a reduction of the 1986 US contribution to the UN regular budget of $7.57 million.

By this time the Directorship of the Department had been given to Akashi and he talked to the American General Accounting Office, which had conducted the investigation, to tell them that he received even more complaints from the Soviets about bias in UN material. The most recent concerned a booklet on decolonisation which had not given sufficient credit to the role of Lenin.

Within the DPI, the staff found it hard to function without offending one of the great powers. Their solution was an institutional fudge; workers went through the motions of implementing controversial mandates but did not strive to succeed. It was an unfortunate set of circumstances as DPI was the UN's first line of defence.

There was more than the UN's image on Pérez de Cuéllar's mind that year. In July 1988, he took a plane to Washington. It was his first official invitation from President Reagan to lunch at the White House, and it came after seven years into the Reagan administration.

Javier Pérez de Cuéllar had managed a brief meeting with the President a few years earlier when Reagan listened politely to gentle complaints about the increasing US debts to the organisation. Reagan had remained lighthearted and charming. He laughed about how the UN was like an actor he once knew who wanted to buy an expensive house but could not afford to do so. For Reagan never held more than a vague notion about the UN, even though he made use of it as a world stage and he set the record for having made more speeches there than any other American President. Reagan, ironically, was now crucial to the the UN's survival. It was the President's duty to see to it that the Charter, like other treaties and statutes signed by the US government was faithfully executed. The Charter was a treaty, part of the supreme law of the US. It was

241

the US policy towards the UN, a part of foreign policy set by the President working with the Secretary of State, which Pérez de Cuéllar came to discuss.

When Pérez de Cuéllar arrived in Washington he went straight to the State Department to meet Deputy Secretary John Whitehead. Whitehead wanted to make sure that the Secretary General was not going to be embarrassing at the lunch and talk to the President the following day about unpaid dues. Pérez de Cuéllar played along, understanding all too well. He made a friend of Whitehead, a former Wall Street investment banker and avid fundraiser for Reagan. The friendship proved to be a lifeline.

That night in an almost empty State Department, sitting alone in the Protocol Office, was John Washburn, the Director of the Secretary General's Executive Office, who helped the Secretary General interpret the increasingly confusing signals emanating from Washington. Washburn, one of Pérez de Cuéllar's two senior American advisers, knew the State Department, having worked there before the Reagan administration drove him out. Washburn was new to the UN and had recently take on some of the tasks performed by the legendary Jim Sutterlin who had guided the Secretary General through the worst days of American antagonism. Sutterlin was the architect of the UN's much criticised low-key strategy in the face of increasing hostility from the right and had delayed his retirement to help. "Dear Jim", as Pérez de Cuéllar called him, was thoughtful, patient and seemed shy but held fierce convictions, and was deeply ashamed of American policies towards the UN. Sutterlin was never in any doubt about the severity of what they faced – the Secretary General had recently been advised to start letting the UN go, to wind down its operations.

Two other UN officials who had come to Washington with Pérez de Cuéllar waited for him to return. Fred Eckhard, from the Department of Public Information and Martti Ahtisaari. Ahtisaari was responsible for implementing the UN reform programme in 1986 and knew how deeply the cuts could affect the system. These two were sunk deep in armchairs in the luxury of the Hay Adams lobby, the Washington hotel grand enough for Heads of State and senior UN bureaucrats. They tipped the doorman to let them know the minute the Secretary General stepped out of his limousine, for they suspected Whitehead of plotting, of making an offer which would not amount to enough. They imagined Whitehead sweet-talking the Secretary

General into not upsetting Reagan. They worried that Whitehead would ruin the hours spent preparing for this big moment and that Pérez de Cuéllar would not be forceful as it was not his style to take charge of conversation and become the centre of attention. Worse, the Secretary General had not once criticised American behaviour. While the UN disintegrated, Pérez de Cuéllar remained the coolest of all. When he at last walked into the lobby, he went straight to his suite. Washburn told the others the little he knew: on the way back in the car Pérez de Cuéllar had given a one-line reaction. "Better," he had said, "but not good enough."

Finance was Pérez de Cuéllar's least favorite subject: his family joked about how he could not read his own bank statements and here he was, in charge of the world's international civil service and trying to stave off bankruptcy. He lacked enthusiasm for his role as Chief Executive. He was old-fashioned, a classical diplomat, and diplomacy was his vocation. His great gift was his psychological equilibrium. Unemotional and unflappable, his successes would be obtained through constancy. He never once uttered the words "breakthrough" or "breakdown". for sound diplomacy is based on realism and Pérez de Cuéllar was a "stone cold" realist. He had no illusions about peoples and nations and second guessed the problems diplomats faced as well as the needs and requirements forced upon them by their own ethnic backgrounds or pressures from their governments.

To most of his staff he was unknown. They saw him fleetingly, escorted to his shiny limousine which took him to and from the grand mansion on the East River, the Secretary General's New York residence. He was blamed for lack of leadership and the UN's loss of direction; it was a time of further insecurity. Pay cheques were threatened and, as the Secretariat tottered on the brink, the UN's staff felt adrift in a world where internationalism was a dirty word. The risks were real.

The trouble had started at the end of 1985, at a bitterly inappropriate time. The fortieth Anniversary General Assembly had been the largest gathering of world leaders in history, when every President, Prime Minister and Head of State had declared un-wavering faith in and commitment to the UN. Two days into the clearing up Ambassador Joseph Reed from the US mission to the UN asked for an urgent meeting with senior UN officials. Bounding across First Avenue from the US mission to the UN Secretariat building, Reed told a hastily gathered group that he was sorry but because of legislation enacted in Congress to try to reduce America's increasing budget deficit, the last installment of US dues would not be paid. There would be no cheque – the one always used to pay the end-of-year salary bill.

Everyone knew the arithmetic: a $20 million shortfall with the UN's salary cheques due. The immediate problem was the December payroll. The UN spent more than sixty per cent of its budget on staff – the interpreters, typists, precis writers and translators needed to service the UN's endless conferences and meetings. If UN salaries were not met, more than 11,000 people, the majority foreign nationals, would be stranded in America with no money – and no legal right to work elsewhere. The UN was already owed $242 million by its debt-laden member states. The Controller's reserves were already used to cover existing deficits.

In the end the UN had to borrow from three reserves: the fund set aside to pay for sudden peacekeeping requests, for emergency disaster relief from Geneva and money in Vienna which was for a drug abuse control programme. Anyone who kept half an eye on Washington knew it would worsen. Throughout the mid-eighties a number of witnesses had testified to Congress about UN deficiencies and by now most legislators were convinced that the UN was inefficient, wasteful and corrupt. Congress had decided that as US paid a proportionately large share of the UN budget, the US should have increased control over the UN budget. This was an impossible demand. Enshrined in the Charter was the principle of one nation one vote which applied to UN expenditure.

In Washington, Congress quickly caught on to UN-bashing. The UN was an easy target. Who would ever deny effectively that American dollars were not paying for the salaries of Soviet spies, that the champagne and the caviar in the East River dining rooms of the UN headquarters were not subsidised by America tax dollars? Didn't the UN help terrorists? Had it not allowed the terrorist PLO to open an Observer Mission in New York?

The UN's Department of Public Information was helpless. The UN's budget was already a time-bomb, a point of contention between the Third and First Worlds. The Third World never tired of reminding the industrialised states of their Charter commitment – to promote economic and social advance, to alleviate poverty and disease. The industrialised states, who paid the majority of the bills, argued increasingly that the international community would have to learn to live with shrinking resources. For the Reaganites, the UN was reduced to a forum where hostile dictators from the Third World could moralise at the Democratic West, and the Secretariat was a job-creation scheme for diplomats. Increasingly Congress withheld funds from the UN.

In April 1986, when the UN deficit reached one-third the total budget, Pérez de Cuéllar, in an unprecedented move, reconvened the General Assembly. The US was not the only delinquent: out of the 159 member states, only 25 had paid their contributions in full. The Secretary General reminded them of the recent fortieth anniversary. "There was not then, any serious suggestion that the goals of the Charter should be disregarded simply because they are difficult to attain", he said. The Assembly agreed immediate economies. Directives were sent to all UN departments that there should be a reduction in first-class travel, a ban on overtime, the cancellation of maintenance and cleaning of the Secretariat building. There were memoranda pleading for a limit to the number and duration of UN meetings, recruitment was frozen and promotions suspended. But more economies were needed and there was a determination to stop the biggest project: the UN's Economic Commission in Africa, the planned conference centre costing millions in Ethiopia, a country bled by endless civil war and famine. When the conference centre idea was voted through the Assembly, in December, 1984, an American delegate called it a "perversion . . . a cruel rebuff to the poor, the hungry and the downtrodden who have invested their hopes and dreams in the promise of international co-operation." They were trying to cope with one of the worst famines in modern times; what would people contributing to the relief efforts in Ethiopia think of UN priorities. The money proposed could feed 125,000 Ethiopian families by providing cash grants for one year. "In the light of the human suffering in Africa, surely we can establish more humane priorities for this organisation?"

The $73.5 million dollar conference centre was valuable ammunition for UN critics, particularly those in the Heritage Foundation in Washington. The building was deferred. But nothing could prevent bankruptcy. So bad was the financial crisis that, in the guarded and secret enclave on the thirty-eighth floor of the UN Secretariat, worst-case scenarios were discussed. The Secretariat could close, but who would pay the the cost of redundancy? In any case, member states would never agree. They would take to the podium to denounce American financial blackmail and hope that the traditional supporters, the Nordics and Canadians, would eventually bale them out.

The Controller knew that could not happen. The sums were too great. A month after he raided the peacekeeping fund, he was told that a further estimated $100 million was to be withheld from the American assessment of $210 million. They appealed to the President for help. Jim Sutterlin wrote the letter leaving Reagan in no doubt as to the gravity of what they faced. It warned that planned Congressional cuts in American funding would lead to the "disintegration of the organisation as a constructive force in world affairs". The letter reminded Reagan that the UN Charter "reflected the greatness of American ideas on the nature of justice, on the human aspirations for freedom and on the objective of peace". Without sustained American support the UN could not have made the

> very considerable accomplishments . . . over the past forty years . . . I often think of the great vision with which Franklin D. Roosevelt formulated the concept of the United Nations, of the determination with which President Truman went forward with its realisation, of the reliance of President Eisenhower on the organisation for the most sensitive measures in the interest of international security.

The letter further reminded Reagan that he himself had come four times to the Assembly. "The objectives of the UN remain, as we all know, far from realised. As a result, confidence in the organisation . . . has eroded." Without the US, the UN could not function and yet under legislation millions of dollars were to be withheld from American dues. The cuts would be devastating to the orderly managment of the UN. "I am equally disturbed by the potential political effect. The withholding of assessed contributuions amounts to a derogation of Article 17 of the UN Charter." Were there any doubt that the UN needed strong American participation, "one need look back to the experience of the League of Nations which most not be repeated". Although the amount the US owed was small for the US, to the UN it would literally determine whether the costs of daily operations in the coming months could be met. Reagan was told of the plans to curtail the General Assembly and to phase out many of the programmes. The pleas fell on deaf ears.

While scores of officials spent time in the Secretariat trying to juggle the funds, it was common for furious Third World ambassadors in meetings with the Secretaray General to complain about American behaviour. Whatever game they were playing with the UN, the Americans were moving the goal posts. Hadn't the Assembly met Congressional demands and cleaned up the Secretariat? After all, in 1986 the General Assembly had voted overwhelmingly to approve the Group 18 reforms; it had mandated the Secretariat undergo the most serious managerial, administrative and fiscal reforms ever attempted. Reagan ought to be able to certify to Congress that these were genuine changes and ask Congress to restore the US payments.

In Pérez de Cuéllar's office, optimism was in short supply. Congress was not about to abandon an easy target. Anyway Washington was in chaos as Congress and the adminstration tried to shape the US budget. Relations between the White House and the Hill were strained to the limit after the Balanced Budget and Emergency Deficit Control Act of 1985, the "Gramm Rudman Hollings" measure, which demanded spending cuts across the board to reduce the federal deficit. The issue in Washington was not about money for international organisations, but the hefty tab for the State Department. It was tough to argue that America must fund the UN when the Secretary of State, George Shultz, was claiming he was a staggering $7.8 billion short and was closing missions abroad.

The Secretary General was right to be nervous and Congress shrugged off the new budget process which had been part of the Group 18 reforms and increased its demands. The Americans would pay only if the new budget procedure was working, a fifteen per cent staff reduction was implemented equitably by nationality and the UN stopped the practice of employing staff who were seconded from civil services to which they expected to return. The last demand would be impossible to meet. Secondment was an old custom, dating from the League of Nations, which allowed governments to give employees leave of absence to serve the UN for a limited time. It suited the developing countries who could not afford to let their best trained people stay away indefinitely. But systematic secondment, as practised for years by the Soviet bloc and China, was a way for governments to exercise control over UN employees. Secondment had become an abuse of Charter principle. Congress was told that secondment allowed Communists to shuffle agents in and out of New York and that the Soviet employees were Soviet agents who worked to Moscow orders. Those UN employees from the Soviet bloc handed in a portion of their dollar salaries to their governments.

Pérez de Cuéllar had no choice but to send another pleading letter to Reagan. By early 1987, the US owed $212 million plus a further $147 million in back dues for 1986 and was behind to the tune of $61 million for peacekeeping in the Middle East. Worried that the President might not see the letter, Pérez de Cuéllar sent it with the US Ambassador to the UN, Vernon Walters.

Reagan did not reply. Eventually, the Secretary General received a letter from John Whitehead at the State Department to tell him that a $90 million payment would be forthcoming. It would be just enough to get them through another few months. "I must tell you in all candour that reform has not proceeded as fully and rapidly as we had hoped," Whitehead wrote. Congress and the Reagan administration were watching the situation carefully.

Pérez de Cuéllar sent telegrammes to world leaders pleading for money. He asked for permission to borrow commercially and, in so doing, infuriated the Americans who told him they would refuse to pay their share of the interest incurred. No one knew what else to do. The one crisis the organisation could not resolve was its own. A personal appeal to Ronald Regan was dismissed. With his acute sense of protocol, Pérez de Cuéllar would never bring himself to ask. They were at a loss and then help came from an unexpected quarter. Reed, the US Ambassador who first brought them the news about the withholdings, had been appointed to the Secretariat by Reagan. Reed had connections. He had been a banker, a Vice-President at Chase Manhattan, a special assistant to David Rockefeller, when he was suddenly appointed an ambassador by Reagan in 1982. Reed's appointment to Morocco was a settlement of a favour for the White House: Rockefeller had backed the Reagan-Bush ticket. By July 1985 Reed's diplomatic career continued with an appointment as one of four ambassadors assigned to the UN and in April, 1987 he was nominated by Reagan to the Secretariat to become America's most senior employee there, Under-Secretary General for Political and General Assembly Affairs. At first Reed did not quite understand the international civil service; he upset colleagues when he presented himself for his official UN photograph wearing a tie woven throughout with the word "Reagan". In his office he kept a huge American flag and was bemused when asked to take it down; eventually his colleagues compromised and brought in a UN flag of equal size to stand beside it. Soon Reed was enamoured of the UN, though not of his official role, which entailed setting the General Assembly schedule and co-ordinating its discussion. He saw himself as the Secretary General's "roving ambassador and trouble-shooter". The UN became the "organisation I love".

Reed had arrived at the UN Secretariat in the middle of the financial crisis and believed that it was partly the fault of George Shultz, the Secretary of State, for keeping Reagan in the dark about the consequences to the UN of the US withholding money. Shultz disliked Reed and refused even to take his outstretched hand. Reed had warned Shultz that so bad was the anti-American feeling in New York about the non-payment of dues, if Reagan wanted to make an historic farewell address to the General Assembly in September 1988, there could well be a walk-out. He told Shultz that if Reagan wanted a last ovation from the General Assembly, he had better certify to Congress that the UN was reformed to obtain enough money to keep the doors open.

In the early summer of 1988, Reed picked up the phone, dialled the California White House and told his friend Colin Powell of the National Security Council that an outgoing President really ought to extend an official invitation to the White House to the Secretary General of the UN. Without Reed's connections there would never have been a White House lunch at all.

By the time Pérez de Cuéllar arrived in Washington to have lunch with President Reagan in July 1988, the Americans owed $467 million – more than half the UN's yearly budget. Pérez de Cuéllar was told that the best he could try to achieve would be the promise of enough money to avoid insolvency. He should use the lunch to encourage Reagan to push for an immediate release of $44 million, the amount the US owed for the previous year, already agreed but withheld because Reagan had failed to send the letter to certify progress on UN reform. If the Secretary General were successful, they could muddle through until October when the Soviet payment was due.

A month before the lunch, Pérez de Cuéllar held a secret and informal meeting in his office with twenty-one handpicked ambassadors. He told them that as all UN reserves were exhausted, the UN was unlikely to meet the October payroll. With uncharacteristic force, Pérez de Cuéllar said that he was fed up with trying to deal with the finances: the crisis was of their own making. He described the staggering human costs which would follow UN closure. From now on he wanted the UN member states to take responsibility. Plans were being drawn to cancel the next General Assembly and to keep the Secretariat going with a skeleton staff. The Security Council would be kept alive for as long as possible. He would meet them again after the White House lunch.

At the White House the "pre-brief" was tense. As they filed into the Oval Office, John Whitehead, who had dined with the Secretary General the previous evening, thought a slanging match inevitable. At issue were statements by America's Ambassador to the UN, Vernon Walters, who was saying that America should abide by its Charter obligation and pay.

Walters had enormous clout. Reagan trusted him with the most delicate tasks and his reputation was such that he was not easily contradicted. Walters was a Zelig-like figure, the one who turned up everywhere. He had served Presidents Roosevelt and Truman, he helped to implement the Marshall Plan and was General Eisenhower's aide at NATO. He served in Vietnam, worked for Nixon, had been a defence attaché in the Paris Embassy and Deputy Director of the CIA. Before his UN appointment he was Ambassador-at-Large – a job which suited his talents and was an apt description of his physique. As for the UN, Walters had his own views.

The pre-brief opened with an Assistant Secretary from the State Department named Richard S. Williamson, who explained the policy of pressure to the President. Only by withholding money was there hope of effective UN reform and fiscal restraint. In 1987 the Africans, objecting that the US had not kept its part of the bargain and paid up, had refused to agree a budget ceiling. Williamson said that because the recent UN budget was far too big, the State Department could not advise the President to write to Congress to release any of the money the UN was requesting.

Walters was silent. He was angry that his reduction in the number of anti-American Resolutions passed by the General Assembly cut no ice with the State Department. There was sniping. The National Security Council Adviser, General Colin Powell, had his own agenda for the UN. He thought the State Department lacked a "game plan". Powell was preparing to direct future UN policy; he had recently given Reagan a classified background paper on the progress of UN reform whose aim, he remembered, was to allow the US to meet her obligations as a great power. Powell knew the dangers: every cent of the US's contribution had to be voted by Congress and the vociferous and well-fuelled anti-UN campaign continued unabated while Heritage claimed slush funds and questionable expenditure.

At the meeting that day in the White House, Powell was uncertain about UN reforms, unsure America could get sufficient influence over the budget, unsure consensus would work. Powell, briefed by a National Security Council staffer who had made a study of the UN's arcane bureaucracy, was told that the key committee, the Committee on Programme and Co-ordination, (CPC) had failed to agree two important items – the budget ceiling and the amount put aside for emergencies, a contingency fund. Furthermore, membership of this strategic committee was recently increased. Powell wanted pressure maintained until the committee's next meeting a month later. No change in strategy should take place until then.

There were more important issues than UN committees on Powell's mind that morning. In July, 1988 the less hostile relationship between Moscow and Washington was turning the UN into an important instrument in international security policy and the orgnisation was being asked to undertake new missions and increasing responsibilities. Recently, the UN had gained much needed prestige as broker, mediator and catalyst in the Soviet decision to withdraw troops from Afghanistan. The withdrawal was the first instance of the world's two great powers becoming co-guarantors of an agreement negotiated under the auspices of the Secretary General. There was cautious optimism for the Western Sahara; Vietnam had withdrawn some forces from Kampuchea where the UN had outlined proposals to restore peace; the PLO seemed to be developing pragmatism and an adviser of Yasser Arafat had affirmed acceptance of the key UN Resolutions 242 and 338. The leaders of the Greek and Turkish parts of Cyprus were soon to meet in New York to continue UN sponsored efforts at settling their differences. Namibia seemed on the road to independence and Angola on the way to peace. Unprecedented unanimity in the Security Council had resulted in informal meetings of the five permanent members at ministerial level.

Powell knew the UN's crowded and lengthening agenda would mean additional and hefty peacekeeping bills; the cost could rise from between a few hundred million to two billion a year, of which the US would be liable for thirty per cent. The existing peacekeeping forces were labouring under massive debt and those countries who were providing troops were less and less willing to absorb the costs. Recently a delegation of ambassadors from UN member states whose countries were owed money for peacekeeping costs had petitioned Whitehead directly for payment.

But Powell's thinking had another major influence too – Moscow's rediscovery of the UN. Mikhail Gorbachev was promoting his New Thinking and asking for a comprehensive system of international security with the UN at its heart. The policy left America on the defensive and her own attitude towards the UN was confused and aimless. The US seemed ambivalent and was abdicating leadership.

"At stake", Powell said later, "was the reputation of the United States."

The new Soviet foreign policy, or New Thinking, contained revolutionary ideas for the UN. The Soviets wanted a revitalised Security Council with meetings at ministerial level to discuss nuclear disarmament. They wanted direct communication between the Security Council in New York, the five permanent members, and the chairs of the non-aligned members. The UN could be used in arms control and could monitor compliance with its own satellite-based verification capability. There could be a new international organisation to co-ordinate peaceful uses of outer space. The Soviets put forward the idea of a UN navy – an international force to protect shipping in the Persian Gulf where tension was mounting in the final days of the Iran–Iraq war. The Soviets wanted a broader UN role in the Middle East, Angola, Ethiopia, Nicaragua and Cambodia.

There seemed to be no end to Soviet support for the UN. After decades of penny-pinching, the Soviets began to honour their UN debts for the first time. A cheque arrived to begin repayment of the $197 million, part of their share of peacekeeping costs in the Middle East, which they had long opposed. The Soviets pledged $28 million for the regular budget and donated $10 million to the emergency fund. They even called the congressional bluff on secondment, declaring they were going to modify their approach to the international civil service and in future would allow a reasonable combination of permanent and short-term contracts for their nationals who worked for the UN.

The US was isolated. Even her closest allies had lost patience. As one, the EEC urged Reagan to certify progress on UN reforms so that Congress would release some money for the UN. The US was accused of bad faith, and failing to deliver a bargain. In a joint statement, the Europeans reminded America that the payment of UN contributions was a legal obligation. "At the basis of international law is the adherence by states to obligations they have freely entered into . . . " The Americans were warned that the withholding of UN dues was eroding international order and there would be serious consequences. They were not prepared to make up the short-fall. Ambassador Walters was sympathetic, telling the German ambassador to the United Nations, Alexander Count York Von Wartenburg, that if one owed money one ought to pay it. Walters put great store by Pérez de Cuéllar. He considered him a world statesman. When in 1986, the Secretary General had undergone by-pass heart surgery and there were rumours he would retire, Walters was one of the first at the bedside. "Don't let him leave the UN," he said to Pérez de Cuéllar's daughter Christina.

White House tradition dictates that before lunch with a head of state a private meeting is held with the President in the Oval Office. The honour was accorded to the Secretary General, who took Reed, his most senior American employee, with him. Reed remembers Pérez de Cuéllar to have been unhesitating. He had opened the conversation with the crisis, saying that were they owed money he would consider it quite improper if terms were dictated about repayment.

"At the close of business last night, the United States owed the UN $467 million." Reed was suprised at his frankness.

"I'll see what I can do", the President had smiled.

The lunch was held in a large room on the first floor of the White House, dominated by a crystal chandelier and heavy ochre drapes at the windows. There were huge gilt mirrors and a silver-laden sideboard. In the Reagan years it was called the family dining-room and protocol decreed it was not a place where grand speeches were made; the President was adept at relaxing his guests. This time he told some of his Soviet jokes: he had returned from the May summit meeting in Moscow with quite a repertoire.

"We'd heard them all before", Whitehead recalled.

Whitehead, present in the absence of George Shultz, who was

visiting China, sat next to Claude Pepper, the octogenarian Miami Democrat. Pepper kept nudging his neighbour to find out what was being said. Whitehead was baffled as to why Pepper had been invited and someone heard a whisper that the President wanted to have someone at the table older than himself. In fact Pepper had recently taken part in the UN's Year for the Aged.

Another elderly Democrat, Claiborne Pell, Rhode Island, sat one removed from the President. As Chairman of the Senate Committee for Foreign Relations, Pell was quick to remind them that he was the only person sitting round the table to have been present at the signing of the Charter in 1945. But he was frail. "If Pell's our only friend on the Hill," someone from the thirty-eighth floor once said of the aging senator, "then God help us."

On the Secretary General's right sat his Chef de Cabinet, an Indian national, Virendra Dayal, and on his other side, the UN lawyer, Carl-August Fleischhauer, former legal adviser to the Federal Republic of Germany's Foreign Office and living proof of his country's UN commitment. Fleischhauer rarely displayed what was deep shock at the collapsing UN and the debts owed by the US. He felt let down. The legal department increasingly spent time and resources not on peace plans, treaties and international law, but on defending the organisation. Fleischhauer had recently fought a long legal battle to retain the international status of the PLO's Observer Mission to the UN. Congress wanted the PLO mission shut down but Fleischhauer won a favorable opinion from the International Court of Justice and his final vindication came when an American Federal Court ruled that the PLO mission could not legally be forced to close. On American debts, Fleischhauer argued that not once had the Charter principle of paying dues been challenged. The International Court of Justice had ruled in 1962 that an international treaty obligation could not be avoided by arguing that subsequent domestic law made it impossible to meet. The state's responsibility was to bring its own domestic legislation into line. There was no justification whatsoever for unilateral withholding, particularly if such a policy were designed to coerce member states to amend the Charter.

Pérez de Cuéllar waited for a lull and his words at first seeemd predictable. It was quite natural, he said, for the Americans to want more power over the budget and yes, the organisation had needed streamlining. As a result there was now a keener awareness of the need to economise. The last UN budget had been approved. All but four countries had supported it – a dramatic departure from the twenty votes registered against the previous year.

"You have to trust that this will work," he said of the reform package. "The UN is in a state of emergency . . . we can only keep going for a few more weeks." There was a touch of irritation. "My work is hampered", he said. Day after day he was interrupting peace negotiation to cope with financial questions. Only yesterday, when he left New York, there was a crucial Security Council debate after Iran suddenly ended her eight years of exile from the UN. Here was the first opportunity to stop the bloody Iran–Iraq war – the longest between independent states since the UN was founded. It had already cost one million lives. Chemical weapons were used. Some of the conscripts in the armies were of school age, sheltering in dug-out trenches, untrained to fight. It was a war which symbolised the UN's tragic weakness. In 1980, no one in the Security Council moved a muscle, yet everyone had known war was imminent.

In the weeks ahead the UN could seize an opportunity to redeem itself. The five permanent Security Council members were now in rare and unexpected unanimity. They had managed to agree on a resolution which mandated a ceasefire between Iran and Iraq. The UN was transforming. Its new and tremendous potential was invaluable. "I don't need another problem," Pérez de Cuéllar said. "We have enough." He begged the President to send the letter to Congress certifying that the UN had undergone reform. All he wanted was $44 million, money which had already been authorised; it was less than ten per cent of America's total debt, but it would determine whether or not the UN doors stayed open.

There was silence. Pérez de Cuéllar had spoken with intensity, as though mortally offended. He had thrown off his diffidence and unease. Throughout, Reagan listened in silence, as though hearing it for the first time.

Some claim to have heard Reagan say: "I have heard enough . . . Let's give the UN the full funding it needs." It caused a start among some government officials because at no time had any briefing even mentioned "full funding". The words were not on the cue cards which Reagan held in his lap. Powell turned quickly to the NSC staff member taking notes and then to Whitehead. Both of them heard the President, he could tell by their faces. No one else seemed to have heard. The UN officials were too busy giving their own views.

"They blew it," the notetaker remembered. "They should have thanked the President there and then and got up from the table."

Instead Ambassador Reed, at the other end of the table, had tapped his glass for silence.

"Mr President," he said "as the highest ranking American official in the UN it is incumbent upon me, Sir, to present to you how I see the situation vis-à-vis the US contribution to the UN. We are nearly $500 million in arrears and with due respect, Franklin Roosevelt's legacy was to have created the organisation and it may well be that in your last hundred days you will go down in history as having closed the house of peace."

The UN officials took away a slither of hope. Apparently, as Reagan walked down the White House steps to say goodbye to his guest, he looked towards Pérez de Cuéllar, just a step in front. Turning to Ambassador Walters the President said: "I'm with him". A UN official heard him say it.

Ambassador Walters organised an Air Force jet to take the Secretary General back to New York. During the short flight Reed kept going over the notes he had made, and he called the Secretary General a "superstar". The Secretary General would believe the lunch had made a difference only when he saw a cheque.

The President, walking up the White House steps, turned to one of the National Security Council staff and said: "Why is he so mad at me? I like the guy."

Nearly two months later in September, 1988, only weeks before President Reagan was to make his last address to the UN General Assembly, the Americans gave Pérez de Cuéllar a cheque for $15.2 million, all Congress would approve of the $44 million owed. It was too small a payment to get them out of trouble. A furious Joseph Verner Reed exploded: "What's next? Reforming the cafeteria?" Attached to the announcement of the payment was an added insult, – the promise of only another $144 million before the end of the year. It was a quarter of the total. There was righteous fury on the thirty-eighth floor and none of it was helped when Pérez de Cuéllar told waiting reporters that he retained his faith in "my American friends". A White House statement accompanied the cheque which implied that the US would henceforth be paying all its UN debts but, in fact, all Reagan had done was to issue a Presidential Order to the State Department instructing them to come up with a three-to-five year plan to pay the money. The way was clear for Reagan's last address to the General Assembly. He paid for the privilege with the next President's money.

All the while, two enormous problems were dumped by the Security Council into the UN's lap; two small and vital UN missions were created. One of them was the UN Good Offices Mission in Afghanistan, two inspection teams whose mandate was to oversee a peace agreement during what was bound to be a rocky and violent transition period. And after years of doing little about the Iran–Iraq war the Security Council had thrown itself behind the emerging peace process and a 300-strong mission, called the UN Iran–Iraq Military Observer Group, was created to verify a ceasefire along the blood-soaked border. Both missions were short of equipment and money.

11. CADILLAC STYLE

When Pérez de Cuéllar returned to New York from the White House lunch the more experienced warned against too much optimism. Others on the thirty-eighth floor looked for a way to signal success. The forecourt where the single-jet fountain had long been turned off in the first round of desperate economy measures became a symbol: they wanted the fountain to run again.

There was more to their hopefulness than Ronald Reagan's chance remarks. On the Sunday of his return to New York, Javier Pérez de Cuéllar received a midnight visit from the Iranian ambassador to the UN, Mohammad Ja'afar Mahalatti, who wanted him to be the first to know – before anyone else – that Iran wanted an end to war with Iraq. She would accept Security Council Resolution 598 which mandated peace.

It was an extraordinary *volte-face* and most diplomats were stunned when they heard; Tehran had consistently dismissed the UN's right to intervene in the Gulf, determinedly turning her back in disgust on the international organisation which, from the start of the war, had failed to condemn Iraq as the aggressor. So unlikely was this sudden change that some speculated that Ayatollah Khomeini must be dead.

The decision was less of a surprise to Pérez de Cuéllar who long enjoyed the secret confidence of Iran; it was his dogged efforts which had kept Resolution 598 alive. He had already sensed a shift in Iran's position and said as much in a private meeting with George Bush. He confided in the Vice President that Tehran was profoundly shocked at the recent destruction of one of her civilian airliners by American missiles fired from the cruiser *Vincennes* in the

258

Gulf; the Iranians believed that the shoot-down was deliberate. Bush blamed reckless Iran for the tragedy and told the Security Council that the Iranians had allowed the aircraft to proceed over the path of a warship engaged in battle. It was an unprecedented intervention in the Security Council by a Vice-President but Bush and his staff welcomed the debate over the airliner to put Bush back in the spotlight: Bush was the Republican standard-bearer in the November presidential election. Pérez de Cuéllar explained to Bush that the accident could prove a rare chance to end the war; it would allow Iran to claim the moral high ground and to come before the UN as victim. Tehran described the attack as a barbaric crime and, contrary to the American version, claimed that the pilot received no warnings. Pérez de Cuéllar knew that Tehran was looking for a way out: the war was lost and the Iranians were running out of weapons and men. Willing martyrdom was over; Iran was war weary and disillusioned. A decisive blow was Iraq's use of poison gas – nerve gas. Because of arms embargoes, Iran was incapable of equipping itself with adequate supplies of protective clothing. On the battle-field they used poorly armed schoolchildren against tanks and artillery. Security Council Resolution 598 was the only escape and Pérez de Cuéllar knew it. That Resolution would remain one of Pérez de Cuéllar's proudest accomplishments. It was an historic first in more than one respect: it mandated peace, and for the first time ever, the five permanent members had worked together to settle a war. In 1987, a year before, during unprecedented meetings over tea and sandwiches in one of the UN's more luxurious lounges, ambassadors from the Big Five agreed a way of working together in the future. The more cynical believed that the result, Resolution 598, was owing to the fact that Washington was eager to undo the political damage from covert arms sales to Iran. If the five veto powers really wanted peace, all they had to do was impose an effective arms embargo, and put an end to the secret arms sale bonanza created by the war. The Security Council could be proud of little. When the war was imminent in 1980 everyone looked away: America was obsessed with hostages in the embassy in Tehran, and the Soviet Union had invaded Afghanistan only months before. Seven years later Resolution 598 pointed to the reality of an emerging new relationship between the superpowers.

Once he had heard from the Iranian Ambassador, Pérez de Cuéllar began the demanding job of turning a paper Resolution into an effective ceasefire and the process tested even his legendary patience; Iraq stalled and evaded, putting up every possible barrier of substance and procedure. At one point the Iraqi Foreign Minister, Tariq Aziz, insultingly refused to take a document from Pérez de Cuéllar's outstretched hand. In August 1988, when a date was finally set for an end to hostilities, the Iraqi delegation packed its bags and announced it might return to New York for talks "perhaps in a week or so". Pérez de Cuéllar called their bluff: he told them he would announce a ceasefire without them, testing if they dare face down the unified might of the Security Council. He only tempered the threat by telling them he trusted to the wisdom of Saddam Hussein. The Iraqis unpacked.

This delicate diplomacy made it impossible for the Security Council to denounce either side, made it impossible to provoke either with criticism. Under that cover, while diplomatic brinkmanship took place in New York and Geneva, Saddam Hussein quickly made the most of the opportunity to try to settle once and for all the Kurdish separatist problem. With a cease-fire in the war with Iran he was able to divert more troops and equipment and a new offensive began. With bombs and poison gas he massacred thousands of villagers in the hills and valleys which the Peshmerga had made their own. Thousands fled to Turkey. Iraq was not condemned in the Security Council and continued to deny the use of chemical weapons despite the US announcing in September it possessed compelling evidence to the contrary. Muted responses always emboldened Saddam Hussein.

The guns fell silent along the 740-mile Iraq–Iran border at the end of August, 1988 and a thin unarmed blue line of 350 UN observers arrived for what was one of the most awful UN missions to date. This small group was to supervise and verify the withdrawal of troops and to establish areas of separation along an inhospitable and blood-soaked frontier which had changed hands more times than either Iraqis or Iranians could remember. This little group went by the name of the UN Iran–Iraq Military Observer Group (UNIIMOG) and their safety depended on world opinion – and a communications unit donated by Canada.

The Secretary General was cautious. A ceasefire was not peace. This was no more than an uneasy truce and direct meetings had not yet taken place between Iran and Iraq. A final settlement could take years. But the world saw it differently and it turned into a huge UN triumph of which, by then, there were several. The UN was part and parcel of the Soviet pull-out from Afghanistan, an early gift from Mikhail Gorbachev. There was a new-found sense of relevance and usefulness. More and more countries were beginning to look for UN solutions to intractable conflicts – Western Sahara, Cyprus and Cambodia.

The UN was centre stage. When the Nobel Committee gave the 1988 Peace Prize to the peacekeepers, the 500,000 who served over the years and the more than 700 hundred who died, it did so to "congratulate and encourage the UN family".

Pérez de Cuéllar smiled wryly and said the UN was "back in fashion". Others talked of the possibility of a Grand Settlement, a world summit, to be as important as the nineteenth century Congresses of Vienna and Berlin. Pérez de Cuéllar, who believed the recent achievements neither sudden nor fortuitous but the hard-won results of persistance and dedication, warned in his annual report of "points of strain and danger, visible or lurking". The success had done nothing to stave off bankruptcy.

At the General Assembly that year Reagan, who was making his final appearance in the world theatre, found himself up-staged. Mikhail Gorbachev came to New York.

The last time a Soviet Head of State appeared before the General Assembly was twenty-eight years earlier when Nikita Khrushchev had angrily denounced Dag Hammarskjöld, had said the Secretary General was a servant of Western colonialists in the Congo, and demanded he be sent packing and replaced with a troika. In other respects, Khrushchev's visit to the UN was discreet to a fault; he arrived quietly on the Russian passenger liner, *The Baltica* and New Yorkers glimpsed him only occasionally from a limousine.

In contrast, Gorbachev was treated like a movie star. The Hammer and Sickle flashed in Times Square while crowds screamed "Gorby, Gorby". Raisa Gorbachev lunched with Marcela Pérez de Cuéllar who was by all accounts one of New York's "beautiful people" and a proficient social butterfly: they took vintage champagne and poached eggs on crepe, served by discreet, uniformed staff in the Secretary General's luxurious residence. Afterwards, Raisa joined her husband for a forty-two-car motorcade down Broadway.

When Gorbachev went to UN headquarters he was welcomed by former President Richard Nixon, former US Secretary of State

Henry Kissinger, Armand Hammer, and David Rockefeller. He afterwards shook hands with 500 Manhattan grandees. And throughout the gathering was one topic, Gorbachev's startling speech that day to the General Assembly. Even Ed Koch, the New York Mayor who once called the UN a "cesspool" said the speech would surely become the UN's Isaiah Chapter Two – swords were turning into ploughshares.

The part of the speech which everyone loved was when Gorbachev announced a drastic, dramatic and unilateral cut in Soviet conventional forces deployed in Eastern Europe. There was less about the real emphasis of Gorbachev's speech, which amounted to an outline of a revolutionary vision for international relations, the blue print of the "New Thinking".

Gorbachev began: "We have come here to show our respect for the UN which increasingly has been manifesting its ability to act as a unique international centre . . . come here to show our respect for the dignity of this organisation capable of accumulating the collective wisdom and will of mankind." Gorbachev's proposal was to transfer the responsibility for maintaining world order back to the UN – in accordance with the UN Charter. It was an urgent task; the world was facing conflicts of a new and different kind. The planet's survival depended on a balance of interests between states. "We feel that states must, to some extent, review their attitude to the UN, this unique instrument without which world politics would be inconceivable today."

Gorbachev spoke of a threatened environment, of the dangers caused by the North–South divide and later some accused him of having managed to present a shrewd list of issues around which the world could rally. Even so, in the history of the ending of the Cold War, the speech was regarded a milestone.

Its immediate effect was on UN staff, never a happy group at the best of times. But at the end of 1988 it was different. The energy inspired by the Nobel Prize for peacekeepers, by Gorbachev and the world's spotlight shining on them, lasted from the autumn General Assembly well into 1989. For the staff a new sense of purpose took hold. The UN was to undertake its biggest ever operation. It was going to help Africa's last colony to independence and staff applied in droves to be part of it. Here was a rare opportunity to implement a Security Council Resolution, to put right years of failure.

For the UN Namibia represented the enormous gulf which existed between theory and practice – between promise and reality.

For the people of Namibia, the organisation was always the last resort, their suffering the oldest problem on the UN agenda. Namibia was a duty inherited from the League of Nations. It was occupied by the most brutal of regimes: first the Germans who in 1905 had massacred the Hereros in reprisal for a revolt, reducing them from a population of 80,000 to some 15,000 starving refugees, a genocide. The South Africans took over early in the First World War. In 1920, South-West Africa as it was known, became a League of Nations mandate which allowed South Africa to administer the country. When the League ceased to exist and the UN was created in 1945, the General Assembly voted to have Namibia under UN trusteeship. South Africa disagreed. Pretoria argued that no nation had any obligation to the League, it no longer existed, and she claimed the right to annex the territory. The General Assembly turned to the International Court of Justice for an opinion on the matter which, in 1950, found that under the terms of the Charter South Africa could not unilaterally alter the status of South-West Africa; Pretoria was obliged to accept international supervision and control. South Africa refused to recognise the validity of the Court's opinion and stayed in the territory,

Ten years passed before the international community was stirred to action and that came only when Ethiopia and Liberia charged South Africa with violating the human rights of the Namibian population – racial registration and segregation, forced removals of black communities to dirt-poor areas, inferior education and lack of health care, and preventing self-government. The International Court took six years deliberating, and in July 1966 handed down a judgment which shocked and amazed African states: the Court found that only the League of Nations had the right to enforce the mandate and, as the League no longer existed, legal enforcement was impossible. The ruling was made even more unpalatable by the fact that the justices were tied 7-7 with an Australian, Sir Percy Spender, using his prerogative as President to cast his vote.

In despair, the people of South-West Africa began an armed struggle; South-West Africa People's Organisation (SWAPO) was created and, within the General Assembly, those members disappointed at international inaction reacted in their own prompt and drastic way. South-West Africa became a priority item on the 1966 Assembly agenda and the vote was to terminate the mandate. The General Assembly created an eleven-member Council to protect and provide material assistance for Namibians in exile and to represent its people in the international community. A UN Commissioner was appointed and three years later the Security Council added its weight by trying to force the issue by setting a deadline for the withdrawal of South African troops. The Council was ignored and there was no likelihood of enforcement; France, the UK and the US opposed full mandatory sanctions. There was yet another approach to the International Court, this time by the Security Council and in 1971 the Court, in another landmark decision, declared the continued occupation of Namibia by South Africa illegal, reversing the earlier ruling. The puzzle remained: how to make the declarations practical.

A new initiative had to wait for a new American President, Jimmy Carter and in 1977 the US, together with Britain, France, West Germany and Canada, formed a group to try to solve the problem. The result was Security Council Resolution 435, which outlined a comprehevisve settlement plan. It provided that during a transition period, the South African administration would remain largely in control. Under the Resolution, elections would be supervised by a UN Special Representative with UN civilian and military staffs to ensure they were free and fair. The UN representative would work with a South African Administrator General. It was a Resolution full of ambiguity. In any event, resolution 435 was destined for a filing cabinet, along with all other unimplemented Security Council resolutions. There was no way the South Africans were going to allow an election in Namibia with Marxist SWAPO guerillas taking part.

South Africa played for time and gave the appearance of co-operation while actually blocking progress. She would not agree to a ceasefire, one of the conditions for transition to start. She stalled interminably over the establishment of a demilitarised zone and by 1982, there was another hurdle: the South Africans wanted linkage – in exchange for elections in Namibia, they wanted the withdrawal of Cuban troops from Angola and this seemed to be the biggest hurdle of all. No UN body would countenance linkage on the grounds that Cuban troops had been invited to Angola following the involvement of South African troops in 1975.

Linkage, however, was vital. It was part of Reagan's foreign policy for the region. Its architect was Chester A. Croker, Assistant Secretary of State for African Affairs, the longest serving Assistant Secretary in the State Department. Croker, after years of patient diplomacy, finally brokered negotiations between South Africa, Cuba and Angola, using Resolution 435 as a cornerstone; his target date for final agreement coincided with the tenth anniversary of the passage of the Resolution through the council.

A methodical and reticent professor from Georgetown University's Centre for Strategic and International Studies, Croker spent seven years shuttling between one country and another making offers he believed no one would in the end refuse. To South Africa he offered guerilla-free borders and greater international legitimacy, to Angola and Mozambique, relief from South African destabilisation, to the Cubans, an opportunity to pull-out and claim success. But Croker had his critics. Many wanted punitive action against the evils of apartheid, believing Croker to be duped by South Africa's rulers into promoting quiet diplomacy, tacit collusion and that South Africa used linkage purely to stall. Croker was accused of blocking the imposition of economic sanctions. Conservatives criticised him too: in Congress senators wanted his dismissal for opposing and then delaying administration efforts to arm anti-Communist guerilla forces in Angola.

That his linkage should ultimately succeed, Croker put down to "the right alignment of local, regional and international events like planets lining up for some rare astrological happening". Actually, it took a new realism in Moscow where the government was looking for ways to reduce regional competition and the cost to a collapsing economy of funding third parties in regional conflicts. There was a new co-operation between the US and the Soviets. Also attitudes were changing in Pretoria where the government knew that it was unlikely to get a better deal; Angola and Namibia were becoming increasingly costly and there were significant white casualties. South Africa was increasingly forced to reconsider her pariah status and its effect on the economy plus the war in Namibia against SWAPO was costing $1 million a day. As for Angola, it was an economic shambles unable to repay its debt to the USSR and no longer able to pay Cuba its soldier fee. Even Fidel Castro was demoralised by what had become a war of attrition. Croker was in touch with everyone to whom he presented a get-out: in Namibia, the UN would provide the logistics and oversee the elections. It would deploy a 7,500-member force, plus 350 UN policemen and 2,000 civilians. They called it the UN Transitional Assistance Group – UNTAG for short.

Shortly after the White House lunch, the National Security Adviser, Colin Powell, again turned his attention to the UN and this time brought the full weight of his military experience to bear. Powell had commanded a battalion in South Korea and served two tours in Vietnam. He was a three-star Lieutenant-General. He was concerned about the cost of Namibia for the UN. His worst fears about waste and inefficiency were confirmed, for the UN plan encompassed too many troops and expensive air transport, instead of the less costly sea transport, for both equipment and men. The UN's plans would have to be seen by the Joint Chiefs of Staff, and a colonel would be detached from the Pentagon to give the UN military advice. Powell's dictum that UN troops were not going to travel "Cadillac style" had taken hold in the National Security Council.

The US was liable for a third of the mission's budget. The total cost for Namibia stood at $640 million and no one was in any mood in Congress to vote money to the UN. The Senate had already rejected an administration request for $150 million to pay the US share of the Iran–Iraq border patrols, the monitoring of the Soviet pull-out in Afghanistan and the start-up funds for the Namibian operation. Croker was also worried about costs. "We had bureaucratic sceptism", he recalled of the Washington attitude. The UN operation was considered "a bit of a cadillac".

Any change in the budget for Namibia would have to go through a majority vote in the Security Council and an American diplomatic offensive began with the result that the US quickly won the support of the permanent members. Warning that Namibia was going to set a precedent for all future UN operations, the Americans said that extravagance and inefficiency could be repeated in the future. As a group, the permanent five were liable for fifty-seven per cent of UN peacekeeping costs – costs which were predicted to reach some $2 billion a year. But the American view did not wash with everyone. Opposition came from some of the non-permanent members of the Council – at the time Zambia, Algeria, Senegal, Nepal, Yugoslavia, Argentina, Brazil, the Federal Republic of Germany, Italy and Japan. The African front-line states believed it would be folly to cut costs for the Namibia mission now, and warned that South Africa, administering the territory during the transition period, was bound to interfere. The situation in Namibia was more delicate than when the original plan was devised ten years earlier. If anything, the situation called for a larger force: the South African military presence was much greater and settled into place.

Croker was clever, though. The agreements which tied South Africa, Angola and Cuba to his timetable had the permanent five of the Security Council as guarantors – a startling precedent. Here was a benefit of the recent shift in world affairs and the five were beginning to steer the UN. The five would not budge and for three weeks there were arguments about the costings for Namibia. This time the Council divided North versus South. There were many who said that this was not about money but about power politics; the Third World felt excluded from a newly united Security Council which was taking all the decisions. In the end, because they could not agree, they turned a tine-honoured solution and gave the problem to the Secretary General.

Pérez de Cuéllar warned time was running out. If they were to adhere to the Croker deal, the independence process for Namibia was due to start in fewer than four months and yet there was no money to start work. Quickly, he came up with a compromise suggesting that the total bill could be reduced from $620 to $416 million: the troop numbers could be cut from 7,500 to 4,650 with the rest on stand-by in their respective countries, on seven days' notice, for emergencies. To compensate for the reduction, the UN-proposed police force could be increased from 350 to 500. There would be no reductions in the administrative staff whose main job was overseeing the elections. This was obviously far from satisfactory to everyone. Indeed, he did not find it wholly satisfactory himself but it was this "best available prospect for independence" or nothing at all.

There was a storm of protest. African diplomats argued that the odds were stacked against the mission. The UN would be monitoring an area twice the size of California. It was a near-impossible task. The military component would be responsible for the cessation of hostilities by all parties at the same time as monitoring the maintenance of law and order, hitherto the job of the South-West Africa Police force, known as SWAPOL. Within the ranks of SWAPOL was a notorious counter-insurgency unit, Koevoet, Afrikaans for Crowbar, created in South Africa and transferred to Namibia to fight SWAPO. Koevoet was not a conventional force but one indoctrinated to exterminate guerillas. Its reputation rested on search-and-destroy raids of such brutality that they were the subject of human rights campaigns for years. The UN's job was to ensure that this force was dismantled and neutralised. At the same time, UN troops would have to ensure the restriction of the South African defence forces. While Pretoria admitted to 25,000 troops, others believed it more like 100,000. Of particular concern was the recent and sudden conscription by the South African army of 3,000 Namibian recruits to serve in SWATF – South-West African Territorial Force. South Africa, if she were to comply with Resolution 435, would have to withdraw all but 1,500 SWAFT troops – under UN supervision.

This was hardly peacekeeping. The UN would be implementing a settlement which demanded on-going negotiation, at the same time as rolling back centuries of repression and racism.

The Security Council argued and argued. Yet another row ensued when it turned out that the UN's Namibian mission would buy equipment and supplies, from fuel to mine-resistant vehicles, in South Africa. Pérez de Cuéllar's lower budget was based in part on the assumption that the UN would purchase goods and services in South Africa. This would cut across the non-binding but long-standing call by the General Assembly for a trade embargo against South Africa. Only when African member states received assurances that as little as possible would be purchased from South Africa was final approval likely.

As time ran out, the Security Council and the General Assembly voted through the much-trimmed Namibia budget; there were barely four weeks left to start the mission and it was so ill-equipped and inexperienced and in such a disorganised state that some predicted it was doomed from the beginning and Bernt Carlsson, the much admired Swedish diplomat, the UN's Commissioner for Namibia, had died in the Pan Am flight over Lockerbie on his way to New York to sign the Accords which set the independence process in motion.

If there were ever two men guaranteed to conflict it was Martti Ahtisaari and Louis Pienaar. Pretoria made a clever appointment for Pienaar, the South African appointed Administrator General for Namibia, was a mellifluous, white-haired ex-Ambassador to Paris. An elegant executive and shrewd advocate, he was, by all accounts, a man of cunning with no visible emotion. Pienaar had nothing but mistrust for internationalism and he hated the UN. An organisation capable of recognising SWAPO as the sole representative of the Namibian people and which spent lavishly on her exiles had no right to pretend to be an honest broker. Pienaar feared a secret agenda to install a Marxist government in the capital Windhoek.

Ahtisaari, the UN's Special Representative for Namibia by contrast was a rumpled and overweight UN bureaucrat. Like most UN appointments, Ahtisaari's was partly owing to nationality: he was a Finn and therefore acceptable to both superpowers. He had devised the guidelines for the United Nations Transition Assistance Group in Namibia and understood the huge task the UN faced. He had private fears that the organisation would not be able to cope, for he had seen at first hand the damaging effect of the emergency economies. In the current UN, efficient administration and advance planning were almost impossible because of the lack of ready cash. Ahtisaari wanted Namibian independence, a chance to make UN history. He knew Namibia was vital as it gave the UN a rare chance actually to implement one of the policies which the Security Council so easily voted into existence. Ahtisaari was a member of the Finnish Evangelical Lutheran Church which had been the principal missionary presence in northern Namibia for more than a hundred years, a Church accused by South Africans of undermining its authority – SWAPO drew most of its support from the predominantly Lutheran Ovambo people. When Ahtisaari was a student he headed an organisation which looked after Namibians who came to Finland in search of education.

These two men whose relationship could never have been anything other than confrontational, were set to guide Namibia through a rocky transition to independence.

It began on April Fools' Day, a Saturday, at 04:00 hours Greenwich Mean Time with a formal cessation of hostilities. At that hour the UN mandate was established and the organisation assumed joint responsibility along with South Africa. The peace lasted three hours – then fighting broke out in the north between SWAPO and police forces. Journalists who left the crowded capital Windhoek to witness the celebrations of peace were confronted with airbursts, gunfire, explosions and flashes. A rumour spread in the northern town of Oshakati that a SWAPO army was crossing the border, heading south into the white farming area, intending to march on Windhoek.

269

Pienaar broke the news of the fighting to Ahtisaari who had just arrived in Windhoek. Just unpacked, he was taking a first look at his new home and had difficulty believing what he was hearing. It appeared that 150 heavily armed SWAPO guerillas had crossed from Angola within the previous ten days and 700 more were on the border and poised to cross it.

Later on the same day, Pienaar contacted Ahtisaari again. Fifty more had crossed the border and intense fighting was continuing; throughout the morning Pienaar's news worsened. Ahtisaari, with no means of independent confirmation of what was happening 300 hundred miles north, was in the worst possible position. There were no UN communications in the northern border area. Only a small advanced group of the British Royal Corps of Signals had arrived, relying on the most basic equipment. Their expensive satellite communications system was still sitting on the dock of Walvis Bay. By lunchtime Ahtisaari was increasingly concerned; Pienaar persuaded him of the wisdom of a request that South African Defence Force Helicopters fly over the area. An hour later Pienaar said that the helicopters were fired upon and that he had authorised their personnel to take defensive action.

Ahtisaari left Windhoek for the five-minute drive to Pienaar's official residence. There he was to meet the British Prime Minister. Margaret Thatcher had flown to Namibia, an unscheduled stop on her way home from a week-long tour of five African states, a significant political gesture of support for the negotiated Accords. She had spent the day meeting members of the British signals contingent and visiting the British-owned Rossing Uranium Mine at Swakopmund. Her presence at this time of crisis, Pienaar thought, a "happy coincidence".

At a late-afternoon briefing with Pienaar, Thatcher was told about what he had begun to call a "major incursion" on the border with Angola. Pienaar told her that the South-West African Police Force could not cope and that although he was ready to fulfil his responsibility to maintain law and order, the international community also had a duty. Ahtisaari found himself in the unfortunate position of telling them that UNTAG was not yet fully deployed: barely 1,000 of the UN force was in place. Even if troops were quickly airlifted, there was no communications, food or accommodation. Thatcher left to talk to South Africa's Foreign Minister, "Pik" Botha, in a hurriedly arranged meeting at Windhoek airport.

At the airport, Botha, not the calmest of people in the best of circumstances, was furious. He told Thatcher what he had earlier told the Secretary General in a telephone call to New York. He wanted an immediate withdrawal of the UN, the mission expelled from the territory. He wanted the release of South Africa Defence Forces from barracks to repel the "incursion". SWAPO guerillas had wrecked the ceasefire, bringing in mortars and anti-tank and anti-aircraft weaponry and they were continuing to cross the border in groups of between 30 and 100 at dozens of places. There would soon be 1,000 armed guerillas in the north and the casualties were mounting. If the UN could not control SWAPO then Ahtisaari might just as well pack his bags, climb aboard his Lear Jet and get out of the country and leave South Africa to bring SWAPO to its senses. South Africa had kept her word, had scrupulously adhered to the ceasefire arrangements and had started to dismantle her force.

Pérez de Cuéllar's response had been to ask Botha to wait and not to make any decisions until Ahtisaari had heard from UN officials sent north from Windhoek to find out what was happening on the border. Botha said he knew what was happening and he would not wait.

By all accounts it was Mrs Thatcher who calmed him. She told him it was imperative he avoid unilateral action, that he should do nothing without the international community. Without the UN the independence plan would fail and the consequences would be enormous. Cuban troops would remain in Angola and South Africa would be responsible for destroying eight years of tortuous diplomacy. Why not claim the moral high ground?

From the airport Botha telephoned Pienaar and asked to find a formula whereby, within the framework of Resolution 435, South African troops could be released from base. Two hours later, as Thatcher's plane finally left the runway, a calmer Botha announced to waiting journalists that the South African defence forces, with the UN Secretary General's agreement, were to be released to counter the SWAPO invasion in the north.

What happened exactly will be the subject of debate for a long time. In Pérez de Cuéllar's secret account to the Security Council he claimed that both Ahtisaari and the Commander of the UNTAG forces, the Indian Lt-General Prem Chand, both urged him to allow some South African troops out of barracks. Ahtisaari recalls the

Secretary General, faced with such a critical decision, wanting to convene the Security Council. But it was the weekend and the end of the month; the presidency of the Council had just changed. Few ambassadors had stayed in New York for the weekend and so Pérez de Cuéllar kept pleading for time. Ahtisaari, with indecision in New York about whether or not to approve the troops' release and bullying from the South Africans, had burst into tears of frustration and anger. At one point he was telephoning New York every ten minutes. "I want, I need an answer", he would say. Senior officials in the Secretary General's entourage let it be known he had not wanted to approve the release of the South African troops – but in the end he did.

Elsewhere in Namibia that first day of transition, both main parties in the forthcoming election celebrated the start of the election campaign. There was an exuberant cacophony of motor horns and singing at a rally organised by the Democratic Turnhalle Alliance, the inter-racial association of political parties which had the benefit of South African finance. A rival SWAPO rally was held in a corner of the rundown Katatura township and when at dusk word of the clashes on the northern border filtered among the crowd it seemed that once more the prize was gone. Worse was to come; in the next few days they heard that their best fighters had been massacred by South Africans, fighting under a UN flag.

South African soldiers at Walvis Bay, the largest port on the East African coast, waiting for sea transport home, were at first jubilant, their tour of duty at an end. Then they were told to turn back to a war they thought was over. In northern areas, journalists watched the release from barracks of the remaining soldiers. Scores of armoured troop carriers soon filled the roads, ferrying police and troops. The 101 (Ovambo) Battalion, of the South-West Africa Territorial force, mostly black with white commanders, was quickly reorganised in the border town of Ondangwa, with their legendary Bushmen trackers normally used to hunt down guerillas. Even the most cautious diplomats said that what happened next was a Turkey Shoot, a desperately unequal battle, with ten SWAPO men dead for every one of their South African opponents.

The UN was powerless. Although Ahtisaari insisted on UN monitoring of the South African troops it was virtually non-existent. At the Ondangwa military airport someone spotted two brand new

UN helicopters sitting in a hangar – the only visible presence of UN blue. At the massive army base at Oshakati there was one Bangladeshi captain sporting a white cravat and a UN helmet: when not reading his novel in the shade of a tree, he watched armoured conveys thundering past showering him with dust. He used a clipboard to note down the number plates. A British journalist remembers seeing two Polish officers in Ovamboland lurching along in a new minibus; they could not get the vehicle out of first gear because they did not know how to drive.

When SWAPO fighters began to cross the border from Angola on March 31 there were only 280 UN soldiers in the region. There were only 921 in all of Namibia, groups from twenty-one countries, speaking eighteen different languages, mainly officers preparing for troop arrival, establishing communications and in the words of one UN spokesman "looking into whether it would be possible to get bread, water and the laundry done". The remaining 3,000 UN troops were nowhere to be seen; as for equipment, some was on its way by sea and some had not yet been purchased because of a lack of funds.

Forty-eight hours after fighting began in the north, Ahtisaari, by now totally exhausted, faced another dilemma. Back in New York, the Secretary General was hurriedly preparing a report for a crisis Security Council meeting and Pérez de Cuéllar asked Ahtisaari for a first version of what had occurred but when he read what Ahtisaari had written, he would not accept it. He claimed Ahtisaari was not sufficiently impartial. Ahtisaari had included in his account the testimony of two SWAPO prisoners, interviewed by UN officials, who reported to Ahtisaari that they were instructed by their regional SWAPO commanders to enter Namibia, but not to engage the security forces because a ceasefire was in effect. They were told there was no more fighting. They were instructed to take all their weapons, even rockets and anti-aircraft devices, and to go to Namibia where the UN would look after them. Each of these prisoners repeated several times they were told the war was about to be over and they were to establish bases under UN supervision.

The implications of the interviews were enormous, for the responsibility for the bloodshed was attributable to the side which first broke the ceasefire, and here was evidence that Pretoria's forces opened fire first. By now Ahtisaari was desperate for the security forces to show restraint.

Chester Croker, meanwhile, was sure the incursion by SWAPO had been a deliberate act by a guerilla movement trying to "pull a fast one". He said that the Americans were reading SWAPO internal communications and SWAPO knew that their guerillas were supposed to stay north. The Cubans told them as much but SWAPO leaders felt they would be in a stronger position if they were in control of Namibian territory. SWAPO guerillas, living in camps in Angola, talked for years about going home and opening bases in Namibia and had for years been told they could not. According to Croker, after the incursion, Fidel Castro in Cuba "went ballistic" and accused SWAPO of putting the Cuban army at risk. As far as Croker was concerned SWAPO was always the world's least successful liberation movement.

The eventual report to the Security Council reads: "UNTAG . . . feels that this infiltration [by SWAPO] may not have offensive intent". As for the brutality of the South African defence forces, there should be "maximum restraint" as a matter of the greatest "humanitarian urgency". Pérez de Cuéllar told the Council that he had been left with no other choice but to approve the release of the South African troops. It was SWAPO, he said, who violated the ceasefire. Like a headmaster admonishing pupils, Pérez de Cuéllar reminded the Council how they themselves had severely hampered the operation from the very beginning because of their disputes about money. He had warned many times in the last few months that the absolute minimum period necessary to enable UNTAG to be ready was six to eight weeks. In the Secretariat all they had was four weeks. As a consequence UNTAG was in no position to supervise anything – not until the end of April. Even if all UN troops were urgently airlifted, there would be no accommodation for them.

The South Africans accused the Secretary General of being pusillanimous: they were in possession of intercepted intelligence reports which proved that SWAPO came across the border with hostile intent. The responsibility for maintaining the ceasefire rested with the UN and the Secretary General. Prime Minister Margaret Thatcher told the House of Commons that the incursion into Namibia by the guerillas was a most serious challenge to the UN's authority.

Elsewhere the UN's reputation was tainted. The Organisation of African Unity immediately announced the Namibian people had been betrayed. There should be an immediate return to base of

South African troops and all UN reserve forces should be immediately airlifted.

The fighting reached a fifth day and Botha announced the collapse of the peace process. Ahtisaari flew to the border to see for himself. The UN spokesperson in Windhoek, Cedric Thornberry, Director of Ahtisaari's office, was widely quoted describing Namibia a "twilight zone". Journalists pointed to the incompetence of the international community because it emerged that no one knew what SWAPO was meant to have done when transition started. There was no agreement about their role. There was no SWAPO signature on the main treaty between Angola, Cuba and South Africa, known as the Brazzaville Accord, signed with fanfare in New York in December, 1988. No other agreement was signed by SWAPO and SWAPO was not party to any of the negotiations. Croker argued that linkage was a regional strategy not concerned with internal conflicts and that SWAPO had been well informed about its role through its links with the UN in New York.

The only official document which bore the signature of Sam Nujoma, the President of SWAPO who lived in exile in the provisional headquarters of the freedom movement in Dar es Salaam, was a letter, written six months previously to the Secretary General, which stated SWAPO would comply with the ceasefire "in accordance with the Geneva Protocol". The Protocol, signed in August 1988, was the first step to the final settlement, the first piece of paper which was signed, the first indication of intent by all parties. The only mention of SWAPO in this document was the urging of its fighters to cease hostilities prior to the ceasefire and it urged Angola and Cuba to use their good offices to ensure that SWAPO forces complied, remaining in Angola well north of the Namibian border.

Whether Cuba, banned from southern Angola under the Accord, or Angola, with little sway over SWAPO, would be able to ensure SWAPO remained north, never seems to have been properly queried and yet the problem of what happened to SWAPO during transition had existed for years. The South Africans had ceaselessly objected to a UN idea that SWAPO fighters be confined to bases inside Namibia itself. SWAPO believed that once the process began, exiles would be allowed to return home and make contact with UN officials in UN camps. SWAPO believed UN Resolution 435 could not be superseded by any agreements or protocol. South Africa and the Western world disagreed. SWAPO stood condemned, having crossed the border, of breaching the little-known Geneva Protocol.

At first, the UN team in charge in Windhoek had no idea which agreements bound SWAPO. Thornberry said he could not talk about the Geneva Protocol because he had not read it. It was secret. As it turned out, it was published quite openly as a Security Council document. Thornberry was confused. He was quite adamant that the Protocol provided for SWAPO to remain well north in Angola, although he admitted: "We have no official knowledge of that treaty . . . ". The failure was spectacular. SWAPO's absence from the negotiating process, its treatment as a mere accessory, the problem of what to do with its forces, had been swept under the carpet and no one seemed to know which provisions of the international agreements the UN was meant to be monitoring. That fact added chaos to disorder. In the days leading to transition, Nujoma gave every indication that he feared being led into a fiendish Western plot. He warned that if South African and Western "mischief" did not stop, SWAPO would "fire and fight to the end". In the run-up to transition, Nujoma was uneasy. SWAPO's former allies, the Soviets, were walking away and would not be funding SWAPO during the forthcoming election. It was significant that SWAPO did not attend any of the ceremonies in Luanda to mark the beginning of the Cuban withdrawal from Angola. The day before transition the *New York Times* published an article by Nujoma in which he claimed that South Africa was turning its former military bases into police stations, that the security forces were decreasing in numbers while the police force was increasing. The dreaded Koevoet had been secretly integrated into civilian police units. "These are the very people responsible for law and order during the transition period." Nujoma said the security situation in the north was dangerous and atrocities and intimidation continued.

Pretoria too issued warnings. The South African government claimed to have known that SWAPO was heading south. Between the signing of the Brazzaville Accord in December, 1988 and the beginning of transition in April the following year, South African officials claimed to have protested no fewer than twenty-seven times to the Angolans and Cubans that SWAPO insurgents were nearing the border. A week before transition, South African intelligence reports were given to the Joint Military Monitoring Commission, set up to oversee the delicate Accord, that more than 3,000 guerillas were south of the 16th parallel.

South African diplomats said the guerillas had the intention of crossing into the territory and setting up bases.

The fighting was the bloodiest of the twenty-three-year war. Among the corpses dug from mass graves and laid out in the sun to await SWAPO burial services was a young man who seemed to have been filleted from the waist up, his head an eyeless mask of skin. An estimated 316 died by the time the South African forces finally withdrew to barracks. There was a widespread belief that some SWAPO guerillas were executed after capture: exhumed bodies had faces blown away by small-arms fire. Some were said to have been civilians and some bodies in Oshivat were of men taken from prison to the border and shot. The UN reported none of this; no one from UNTAG oversaw the exhumations although Pienaar had agreed that all known casualties should be exhumed from the mass graves in the bush. SWAPO said that two letters to the UN for assistance went unanswered.

"It was either a colossal bungle or one of the most callous orders ever issued in guerrilla warfare . . .", a member of the UN team in Windhoek mourned. The South-West African police, in breach of Resolution 435 which limited it to small arms, was equipped with heavy machine guns mounted on armoured personnel-carriers. The paramilitary unit, Koevoet, was still a presence. Koevoet's founder, Major General Hans Dreyer, was Regional Commissioner of Police for the northern border area.

The talks to end the crisis were held under the auspices of the Brazzaville Accord, those Croker-mediated agreements to which the UN was not a party. Ahtisaari waited in the wings. The signatories to the peace settlement, Cuba, South Africa and Angola, sent ministers to a game lodge at Mount Etjo 120 miles north of Windhoek to meet Chet Crocker and Anatoly Adamishin, the Soviet Deputy Foreign Minister. Namibia was one chip in a larger gamble. Botha told them he wanted more of the defence force released from barracks: the six battalions doing battle were not enough to contain it. Botha was under domestic pressure. It was election year. The prospect of Namibian independence was greeted by South African whites as an omen of change closer to home. What raised the stakes for Botha were the deaths during the fighting of sixteen white soldiers, young South Africans who had been conscripted into the South African Army, and who thought the South African war against the SWAPO guerillas was over.

The agreement which came out of the Mount Etjo hunting lodge established that SWAPO guerillas should lay down their arms. When told of this decision, Ahtisaari drew a breath and described it as precarious; there was no official ceasefire in place. Nevertheless, he began to prepare a welcome for SWAPO fighters in Namibia and would find the tallest flagpoles in town upon which would be hoisted the UN's blue and white flags. They would indicate assembly points in the battle zone. Each would be staffed by ten UN soldiers and five observers. Somehow these 1,000 guerillas, scattered in small groups over nearly 4,000 square miles of bush, were to be told the news. Radio broadcasts from Angola and Namibia would transmit the locations of course, but only the most sophisticated of maps would have them marked and the fleeing guerillas were not likely to be carrying radios.

The UN's greatest weakness was that it was dependent on the South African forces for food for its troops. In most assembly points, camped alongside the UN troops, were highly visible South African army mechanised infantry units. Pienaar announced that guerillas would be questioned on arrival about where they had hidden their arms before being escorted north by the UN: Ahtisaari said Pienaar had no authority to issue such a statement. The assembly points remained empty.

The weeks wore on and reports of brutality continued. The UN monitors out in the field, Church relief workers, lawyers from human rights organisations and journalists all reported intimidation. Members of the security forces, out of uniform, were openly campaigning for the Democratic Turnhalle Alliance (DTA). Koevoet members were roving around the north at night, going from village to village and terrorising inhabitants. In May, foreign correspondents described a heavy armoured vehicle driving at a boy herding goats, maiming the animals and causing the boy to collapse with fear and exhaustion. It was, they said, a new sport. There were reports of people forced to dig their own graves, the armoured cars driven into political rallies and over fields to ruin crops.

The UN mission had no chance to monitor the reports. A major constraint was a fear of mines. The UN force could not operate in a large part of the north because it had no mine-proof vehicles. The South-West African police had more than 200 of these vehicles and eventually Ahtisaari persuaded Pienaar to lend him ten, but when they were delivered they turned out to have machine faults. At one point the South Africans offered UN monitors a chance to ride along with them, a plan which was rejected. The situation was hopeless. Even when UN monitors heard of intimidation and violence, all they could do was file a report through Ahtisaari's office. The reports were then be handed to SWAPOL – the police were charged with investigating charges against themselves.

May to September was the voter-registration period. Exiles began to return. The United Nations High Commission for Refugees managed the largest airlift in history – 42,000 Namibian refugees home from Angola and Zambia. Not all of them were jubliant at returning and jammed the reception centre near Windhoek airport, refusing to leave because they feared violence. In the north they heard that armoured personnel-carriers full of South African soldiers were going from village to village seeking out the returnees to terrorise and kill them.

SWAPO threatened to take no part in the election. Ahtisaari, who under the mandate had to satisfy himself at each stage as to the fairness of the election, wrote to Pienaar in the strongest possible language, a letter which was leaked to the press. In it Ahtisaari said the violence was "unacceptable". Pienaar replied that there would be a progressive removal of the previous Koevoet members from SWAPOL. But, by the end of June, the violence was increasing and Pérez de Cuéllar brought the matter to the Security Council, telling members that an atmosphere of fear and intimidation existed. Later, in July, Pérez de Cuéllar went to Namibia and had a two-hour meeting with Pienaar himself, after which the two men announced SWAPOL was to be scaled down in future. Minimal use would be made of the armoured personnel-carriers.

Nothing much changed. In August a gang of whites armed with hand grenades and automatic weapons attacked a UN office killing a black Namibian security guard. And in early September Anton Lubowski, a South African trained barrister, the first white ever to join SWAPO, was shot dead in front of his house. It was just two days before Sam Nujoma was due home from his thirty-year exile in Dar es Salaam.

Ahtisaari flew to Pretoria for crisis talks and, like nothing else, the Lubowski murder exposed the reality of what an upsurge in violence would mean: it would lead to the collapse of transition. It seemed as though the country were slipping out of control; death threats were common. The Editor of the newspaper *The Namibian*,

Gwen Lister, fled Windhoek in fear for her life. The Lubowski killing was a watershed and after it was a transformation.

By now, there were rifts in SWAPO. Revelations about its lack of democracy, refugees unaccounted for, and stories about how SWAPO tortured and killed its own dissidents in detention camps in Angola. Allegations were consolidated by the Supreme Court in September that SWAPO was illegally detaining Namibian citizens abroad. Amnesty International later recommended an inquiry into violations of human rights by SWAPO prior to the country's independence: at least 350 people imprisoned by SWAPO were missing.

The framework for peace was faulty and there were flaws in Resolution 435 – it was, after all, a compromise. As for the delays in deployment, thirty years earlier, Dag Hammarskjöld had sent troops to the Congo on three days notice and 5,000 troops were in place within a week. Brian Urquhart, closely involved with that operation, was amazed at the mistakes made by the Council over Namibia and the lengthy squabbles over money. Urquhart had visited Windhoek's African township, Katatura, and saw its abject misery. He was never in any doubt of the urgency for change and thought it unpardonable to argue about costs. He was shocked too at the the total disregard for the basic principle of peacekeeping – that trouble always occurs in the first two weeks – when everyone tries to gain advantage.

Others looked at the lessons of the past. Nine years earlier Rhodesia had become Zimbabwe and the fighting factions of Robert Mugabe's ZANU-PF and Joshua Nkomo's ZAPU were dealt with under the Lancaster House Accords. During that transition, troops gathered at sixteen assembly points with their weapons where they remained under the supervision of a Commonwealth monitoring force of 1,200. The Rhodesian Security Forces were treated in much the same way. Although the elections leading to the creation of Zimbabwe were hardly free from intimidation, there was none of the chaos of Namibia – not the least because all members of the Commonwealth monitoring force were in place when the ceasefire came into effect. The UN was not involved.

The UN's mission to Namibia troubled the organisation for if it could not get this mission right, in which other would it succeed? No other UN plan had been so long in preparation. For years Namibia had been studied, more than any nation on earth; for eight years bureaucrats in the New York Secretariat worked hard to produce long reports on how freedom would be achieved.

And yet, when the time came, the mission was not prepared to manage elections adequately. To the astonishment of most independent observers, it accepted the Administrator General Pienaar's own plans for the voting whereby registration entailed fingerprinting every voter and then checking the fingerprints before the ballots were counted. It was so complicated a system that Scotland Yard, asked its opinion by the Commonwealth Secretariat in London, said it would take at least six months before the results of the election would be known. A month before the elections took place a confidential report written by a group of lawyers and diplomats who had spent two weeks in the territory was given to all Commonwealth Heads of Government. It was damning of the UN mission's activities. They did not follow even the most basic procedure, failing even to test how long it took the average Namibian to vote. Without this knowledge, it was impossible to determine the number of polling booths needed. In Namibia there was seventy per cent illiteracy. The population was adjusting to an uneasy and incomplete peace after a long period of war and many voters would be frightened. Yet the voting time allowed by the UN officials was less than that in other African countries where there were higher rates of literacy and voters used to voting.

Commonwealth observers found a loophole in the Voters' Registration Proclamation, which the UN approved, allowing for South Africans who had lived in Namibia as civil servants, soldiers and police to cross the border and vote. Buses, car pools and trains were being organised to bring thousands of South Africans to the border. The Commonwealth Observers found instances of South African registration officers issuing registration cards, unsigned with wrong spellings, and incomplete – they were therefore invalid. At one point the Commonwealth Secretary General, Shridath Ramphal, was in almost daily contact with New York, stressing to Pérez de Cuéllar that unless changes were made to the election laws the ballot would be far from free and fair.

It was not all criticism. The civilian component of the UN mission worked far from the relative comforts of Windhoek, out in the field in difficult and dangerous and uncomfortable conditions. Of the calibre and dedication of this multi-racial staff, observers noted, there was no doubt. Their efforts to defend the integrity of the process resulted largely in its success.

In November the five-day vote was the most closely supervised in history. The election was monitored by the UN and by Church groups and by observers from all over the world. After it was over and after Ahtisaari had endorsed the process as free and fair, he announced that the whole world had been given a lesson in democracy. No one contested his judgment.

SWAPO's own victory was qualified: it failed to win the two-thirds majority needed to write the Constitution and would clearly have to work with the Democratic Turnhalle Alliance in forming a government. Nujoma pledged a mixed economy and reconciliation and kept his word. At the stroke of midnight on Tuesday, March 20, 1990, Namibia became an independent nation. The blue, red and green flag of Namibia was raised and Pérez de Cuéllar swore in Nujoma as President.

Namibia was now, for a short time, the youngest member of the United Nations.

Ahtisaari claimed to have run the most successful mission in UN history – and in the light of subsequent UN operations he was right. They would look back at Namibia as an operation which broke new ground and which emboldened UN efforts in other long-running conflicts. Even with all the problems, it was a rare UN success.

As for the Namibians, no promised land was ushered in. In terms of a ladder of justice for its people, the election was but the first rung. The South Africans left a foreign debt of nearly $250 million, an estimated 65 per cent of land in white ownership, the mining industry controlled by European and South Africans and Walvis Bay, the largest harbour on the south-west African coast, and a vital transport link, remained in South Africa's hands. Namibia would need ties to South Africa to keep its economy working.

Pérez de Cuéllar warned that the Namibian government would have a tremendous job just to stand on its feet and to free itself from economic dependence. "Otherwise, you know, the whole exercise would be.. an exercise in futility," he said.

12. NEW THINKING

The extraordinary changes in Soviet foreign policy known as New Thinking were dismissed at first as another in a long line of Soviet peace initiatives. The idea of revamping the UN was considered a business-as-usual initiative to attract the support of the Third World; a clever way to rally the General Assembly. When the Soviets introduced a Resolution in 1986 calling for a redefinition of the UN's system of international peace and security, it was greeted as incomprehensible by the West. The following year the idea was better defined. On the eve of the General Assembly, on 17 September, 1987, Gorbachev published "Realities and Guarantees for a Secure World" in both *Pravda* and *Izvestia* and it called for a comprehensive rethink of international co-operation.

A few days later on September 23, the Soviet Foreign Minister, Eduard Shevardnadze, made a speech to the Assembly calling for a strengthening of universal security. Reversing more than forty years of Soviet disdain for peacekeeping, he promoted it instead. Shevardnadze suggested the UN manage and contain conflict. He thought they could create a UN enforcement mission at sea: a UN naval force to police the Persian Gulf. At the time, the war between Iran and Iraq was threatening the free transit of oil shipments through the waters of the Gulf and Shevardnadze suggested the safety of navigation ought to be ensured by the world community. In Washington the Reagan administration quickly decided it was a Soviet ploy to ensure the withdrawal of the US fleet from the area.

All the talk of a common destiny was greeted with considerable scepticism. The Soviets were behaving as though international co-operation were first devised in the Kremlin. The Americans thought the Soviets were buying goodwill at a relatively small price, keen to insure their superpower status. Only when the Soviets started to pay their thirty-year-old UN debts, including money owed for the Congo operation in 1960, did diplomats begin to think that New Thinking might be more than a Soviet trick.

By October, 1988, the Soviets were calling for a UN army to enable the Security Council to stave off emerging conflict and to maintain observer posts in explosive areas. The Soviets wanted to to repair the UN's powers of enforcement, to reactivate the Military Staff Committee, dormant since 1947. Under the Charter, the Committee had a vital function. The Committee was to advise the five permanent members about enforcement and was to be responsible for organising the Security Council's military requirements, to help to clarify the roles and divisions of labour between the Security Council and the Secretary General. The Military Staff Committee was to consist of the Chiefs of Staff of the permanent members. In 1945 the Committee's first task was to decide the strength and degree of readiness of troops and national air forces which were to be put at the disposal of the Security Council by member states. The Committee, an American idea in 1945, was based on the military co-operation between America and Britain during the Second World War but because the drafters of the Charter could not decide who would have the actual command of these forces, they left this crucial problem to the Committee to sort out once the UN was created.

The Military Staff Committee was among the least successful UN endeavours. For three years, from 1945 to 1948 it negotiated and then, unable to agree where the UN should base its troops, it formally advised the Security Council on August 6, 1948 that it had reached deadlock. Throughout the Cold War the Soviets had taken the view that in the absence of the Military Staff Committee, the UN could not engage in the use of force at all.

But the Committee's story did not end with Cold War deadlock; in a bizarre UN ritual the Military Staff Committe continued to meet, senior military representatives of the big five, wearing full-dress uniform, parading into a meeting-room in the basement of the Secretariat in New York twice a month. For all these years the Committee has met only to adjourn immediately in a charade which never produced anything, although these military personnel were known for their sumptuous parties. The tradition developed that in

UN peacekeeping, governments gave operational control of UN troops to the Secretary General.

By 1988, the Soviets wanted the Committee to be reactivated. It could give valuable help at a time when the UN was needed as never before. It could advise the Council on the military implications of providing forces, and on the rules of engagement.

New Thinking, which was devised by Soviet specialists on international relations, increasingly confronted Reagan with an embarrassing problem. America's own attitude to the UN and the continuing American debts were causing untold damage to the running of the Secretariat where there was no money for present committment, let alone new responsibilities. After hectoring the Soviets for years to meet their obligations, the US was now, as the *New York Times* described, "the biggest deadbeat".

New Thinking became increasingly ambitious. Gorbachev compared the UN member nations to a pack of mountaineers, tied together by a climbing rope. They could climb on, or fall together into an abyss. Others used dramatic images: Vladimir Petrovsky, deputy Foreign Minister and former Ambassador to Canada, saw the world as a spaceship. He wanted the International Atomic Energy Authority to prevent an arms race in space. Later the Soviets suggested a world laboratory of scientists and special units of UN servicemen to give aid to the Third World. The Soviets were taking internationalism into realms never previously contemplated while claiming that New Thinking was the result of an objective and scientific analysis of the dangers facing the planet. A strong UN was the only alternative for the sick and ailing world and New Thinking was an historic opportunity for survival.

At first, hollow laughter greeted New Thinking in the Secretariat but that was soon silenced when in 1987 the Kremlin allowed large numbers of Soviet nationals who worked for the UN to live outside the central Soviet diplomatic compound. In May the following year, Petrovsky announced that most Soviet nationals could henceforth serve the UN on permanent contracts – free at last of government control.

The ending of the Cold War substantially improved the Secretary General's diplomatic successes; there were prospects for peace in Angola, Cambodia and the Iran–Iraq war and more than ever before he received requests for help. Iraq wanted the UN to clear the Shatt al-Arab waterway, clogged by sunken ships. A few Palestinians were talking of turning the Occupied Territories over to a temporary UN administration. Ministers from five Central American countries agreed in principle that the UN should verify compliance with a peace plan to ensure that no state harboured rebels fighting neighbouring governments. The pull-out of 100,000 Soviet forces from Afghanistan would have been inconceivable if the UN had not played a role in shaping the conditions for withdrawal and providing a team of observers following negotiations. An exercise of unimaginable difficulty, as the Americans had proven in Vietnam, in contrast the Soviet withdrawal from Afghanistan excited a new mania: "leave it to the UN" and there were many who believe that it helped the Soviets to understand the UN's many possiblities. But New Thinking was not solely the result of the lessons of Afghanistan. That the way of the world was towards inter-dependence was demonstrated in 1986 with the nuclear disaster at Chernobyl. The Soviet Union turned to the International Atomic Energy Authority in Vienna for help in recouping some of the early damage caused by delay in reporting the meltdown. And, similarly, the destruction of the airliner of KAL 007 in September 1983, helped the Soviets to appreciate the usefulness of the International Civil Aviation Organisation when American and Japanese experts helped them to try to strengthen worldwide communications in the air. Since the UN could help them out of costly and strategic nightmares, the Soviets co-operated fully in the plans for Namibia and helped to strike the deal for the withdrawal of Cuban troops from Angola.

The peace dividend extended. But in the Secretary General's office pessimism continued. There were fires all over the horizon – torture and violence in Central America, great suffering in the Lebanon, Sudan, Ethiopia, Indonesia, Cambodia, Somalia and endless refugees.

"Everyone praised the UN peacekeepers" said Pérez de Cuéllar, "but when I present the bill there is no response." It was the year he had appealed to the White House for money to keep the UN's doors open.

In the New Year in 1989, and with a new President, the UN hoped for better times. As George Bush was a former UN ambassador, it looked promising. Within days of his inauguration, Bush invited Pérez de Cuéllar to dinner at the White House. But the

US debts remained unpaid and, while the workload increased in New York, the planning of the UN's increasing agenda became more and more difficult and one senior official described peace-keeping as being run from a grocery store. No wonder the Namibia operation was shaky. Similar weaknesses elsewhere obviously would lead to tragic consequences. A creaking UN bureaucracy did not concern the permanent five who were full of self-congratulation and sent their Foreign Ministers to a meeting of the Security Council. This was the year that the Iron Curtain was lifted in Europe and the ministers met with the Secretary General to issue a statement to announce that this was a time of change and that the UN had an important role in the future. A first General Assembly Resolution, sponsored jointly by the Soviet Union and the United States, called on all members to co-operate more closely in the spirit of the Charter. It was triumphant. Pérez de Cuéllar advised caution. An expansion of the UN's role, he said "has taxed the capabilities of this organisation to conceive, plan, direct and execute and administer peacekeeping operations". The cost cutting and staff reductions imposed in the 1986 reform package were having disastrous effects.

In the razzmatazz of 1989, the Secretary General's report on the financial crisis went almost unnoticed. By now the US owed $430 million. Soon such troubles were forgotten as a crisis came to overwhelm them.

On August 2, 1990 after massing on the border, 100,000 Iraqi troops invaded the small Emirate of Kuwait. There was little resistance from Kuwait's 20,000 strong army. Under the Old World Order there would not have been much for the Security Council to do. Saddam Hussein, in the light of previous experience and armed by some of the permanent five, might have expected a meeting of Arab Heads of State to censure him, while he retained the oil fields and the islands he wanted, but he would not expect any opposition. He probably thought the UN an irrelevancy. When he started the war with Iran in 1980 the Security Council was silent; Britain and the US welcomed the prospect of putting down the Ayatollah Khomeni who had deposed their ally, the Shah, and all efforts were directed towards ensuring that Iraq could not be defeated. At the height of the war between Iran and Iraq, Prime Minister Thatcher dismissed the idea of the UN as the arbitrator in the dispute. Saddam Hussein remained in his dominant position while the world's wealthy states enjoyed an arms bonanza. Iraq spent one-third of its gross domestic product on arms; millions of dollars were spent on missiles: biological, chemical and the development of nuclear weapons. Saddam Hussein's foreign debt amounted to $800 billion. An invasion of Kuwait gave him the chance for some extra capital, offering him a new source of oil production and a deep water port on the Gulf. He counted on the Soviets not to abandon a treaty ally and to give him tacit support; he counted on the Arab world to protect him from outside intervention. Under the Old World Order the Soviet Union would probably have vetoed any possibility of Security Council action.

The invasion of Kuwait should have come as no surprise because Saddam Hussein had given every indication of his intentions. Only months before, in May 1990 at an Arab summit, he had demanded some $27 billion from the Kuwaitis for oil which he claimed had been pumped from an Iraqi section of an oil field. In July, on the eve of an OPEC meeting in Geneva, Iraq moved troops to the Kuwaiti border. Direct negotiations with Kuwait took place at the end of July, but talks broke down.

Saddam Hussein badly misjudged the timing of his invasion because America suddenly embraced universal order. The result became the most extensive use ever of the Security Council's powers.

Within hours of Iraqi troops overruning the Emirate, the Council adopted a Resolution condemning the invasion and demanding total withdrawal. When Iraq did not comply, the Council acted again. Four days later the most comprehensive trade embargo was imposed to stop the sale of oil. Ninety per cent of Iraq's earnings came from oil and support for the action from UN members was overwhelming. The Council's actions, impelled by great power unity, were portrayed as the first test of a New World Order. President Bush later spoke of a vision of a "new partnership of nations . . . based on consultation, co-operation and collective action". This partnership would be based on the rule of international law and not the law of the jungle. The rule of law would be based on the UN, which was "poised to fulfil the historic vision of its founders" and its promise of a world parliament of peace. Bush quoted Winston Churchill, defining the New World Order as one in which "the principles of justice and fair play protect

the weak against the strong". The New World Order was: "a big idea
. . . where diverse nations are drawn together in common cause, to
achieve the universal aspirations of mankind: peace and security,
freedom and the rule of law". With the invasion of Kuwait, sixty per
cent of the world's oil reserves fell into the hands of a dictator.

Saddam Hussein's only support came from the Palestinians. His
natural ally, King Fahd of Saudi Arabia, shown American satellite
pictures of Iraqi troops on his own borders, feared his country was
next. An emergency Arab summit endorsed a Saudi decision to call
in American or "multi-national troop support" and at the summit
only Iraq and Libya voted against – Algeria, Sudan, Yemen, Jordan,
Mauritania and the PLO abstained. Without recourse to the Security
Council, six days after the invasion, Washington announced it was
sending land, air and naval forces to prevent a possible Iraqi attack
against Saudia Arabia, in response to a request from King Fahd.
Later this force would expand to a twenty-eight-nation military
coalition including Syria, Egypt and Morocco. The British, French
and Canadians joined and when the time came to retake Kuwait by
force, fifty-four nations were providing military or financial help.

The trade embargo was almost universally supported. On August
6, when the Security Council approved the Resolution which
imposed the embargo, only two non-permanent Council members
abstained: Cuba and Yemen argued that the intention of the
resolution was to starve the Iraq people, since Iraq imported 75 per
cent of its food requirements. But the determination of both the US
and Britain was evident. When, soon after the Resolution was
approved, five Iraqi tankers were heading towards Gulf ports, both
these permanent members announced their intention of
intercepting vessels suspected of breaking the UN sanctions. The
Americans, arguing that Saddam Hussein should be aware of a
united Security Council, presented another Resolution to sanction
searching Iraqi ships. Lest Saddam Hussein be in any doubt of the
resolve, the US and Britain announced they were preparing to
enforce the embargo themselves under the mandate for action
already provided in Resolution 661 of August 6, which had imposed
mandatory trade sanctions.

Within eight days of the invasion, the Security Council acted three
times to make it unmistakably clear that the world rejected Iraq's
latest act of barbarity. Not one vote had been cast against. But the
Council was not quite as united as it seemed. China objected to the

word "force" in any Resolution and wanted the milder "such measures commensurate to the specific circumstances". At the time, the French were not keen to become "co-belligerent" with the US. Security Council Resolutions needed the support of nine of the fifteen-member Council, including the concurring votes of the five permanent members. The Americans were having to give careful consideration to the views of Malaysia, Yemen, Cuba and Columbia – or the Gang of Four as they became known. The governments of these four states were concerned that enforcement of the trade embargo was nothing less than a blockade which, under international law, was an operation undertaken only in time of war.

In the private meetings held between the five, France and the Soviet Union both argued that only the UN could mount a blockade. What was the point in UN consensus if all major action were taken outside? America ignored the arguments. On August 12, Bush ordered the US military forces to enforce the UN trade sanctions and choke Iraq's oil exports. On Thursday, August 16, rules of engagement were sent to US warships to stop, board and search Iraqi vessels. At this point Moscow raised once more the revival of the Military Staff Committee, the moribund military arm of the Security Council. If a blockade were to be undertaken through the UN in accordance with the Charter, the Military Staff Committee should be reactivated. The Soviets indicated that if this were done, they would allow their own navy to participate. The US ambassador, Tom Pickering, argued that the Committee would be unwieldy and impractical; the US was resolved to keep control of its own forces.

The five Iraqi tankers were heading for Gulf ports. President Bush could wait for UN sanction – and may not get it at all. If that happened, his leadership of the coalition would be in doubt. America believed that the Iraqis were using Moscow to split the Security Council.

The vote took place on a Saturday morning, August 25 and the Resolution gave the Americans – and anyone else who chose to be involved – the right to disable ships which refused to stop and have their cargoes inspected. The Chinese and the Soviets insisted that the Resolution clearly spell out the UN authority. The measures taken had to be "commensurate to the specific circumstances . . . to inspect and verify their cargoes and destinations . . . " The Resolution required states to co-ordinate their action "using as appropriate mechanisms of the Military Staff Committee". It was the first Security Council Resolution to authorise the use of miltary means since 1966 when Britain was encouraged to use naval force if necessary to stop oil shipments to Southern Rhodesia. These were the latent enforcement powers of Chapter 7, the only part of the Charter under which the Security Council had the authority to take enforcement decisions which the members were legally bound to obey. Power of compulsion was the backbone of the UN's security system. The Security Council had never employed these powers against a state which had invaded its neighbour; in 1950 the Council responded to the North Korean invasion of the South, recommending the use of force, but it did not compel.

The Resolution of August 25, elicited naval co-operation from a surprising number of countries although not everyone was keen on this startling development. After the Resolution was approved, the Chinese assured Third World allies that the Americans had promised to work within agreed UN guidelines. The Soviets showed reluctance to resort to military means to enforce the embargo and did not participate in bringing pressure against Iraq; it wanted military action to be co-ordinated by the Military Staff Committee, to reactivate the carefully drawn enforcement structure of Chapter 7 of the Charter, but the Resolution's only mention of the committee was that it should be used "as appropriate". In the weeks ahead the committee met several times but all that transpired was that the three NATO permanent members briefed the others in a general way on military preparations in the Gulf. The senior military officers who met did not even wear uniforms, at the request of China. Whatever the new-found co-operation in the Council, it did not extend to the five sitting down to discuss military strategy. Those countries providing troops did not wish for the involvement of the Security Council or its Committee.

The hostage issue took precedence. There were 200,000 Indian nationals trapped in Kuwait and their treatment gave every indication that Saddam Hussein was attempting to drive a wedge through Council unanimity. He used the North–South divide. Whereas the hostages from the West were comparatively comfortable, those from the Third World were denied ration cards and left to manage alone, dependent on the support of neighbours and friends. When the Indian government in Delhi announced that a ship with medicine and food was being sent to try to ease the suffering, this caused a bitter row in the Security Council's Sanctions Committee. The US argued strongly that humanitarian assistance should be given only under clear guidelines because Saddam Hussein's priority was food for his army. Here was a basic dilemma: Saddam Hussein was obviously uncaring about the sufferings of his people, and in the Council, the Yemen, Cuba and Colombia steadfastly argued that the Iraqi people were paying the price for his aggression. China also had misgivings. Never before had an embargo been so complete and the world so determined. The Security Council turned to a time-honoured solution of handing the problem over to the Secretariat. The Secretariat would conduct a study to see if there were "persons who might be specially suffering, such as small children" because of the embargo. Saddam Hussein was claiming baby food to be in short supply.

In late September, the CIA went public and announced that the sanctions, neither in the short or medium term, would have the desired effect and get Saddam Hussein out of Kuwait. The British Joint Intelligence Committee was said to concur. Stories were coming from Kuwait about Iraqi violence, pillage and rape.

The military build-up by the allied coalition in Saudi Arabia continued. Designed to deter an attack from Iraqi troops, logistics and equipment were pouring into Saudi Arabia. There was no international management of this force. Some countries had sent troops under bilateral arrangements with Saudi Arabia and at the beginning there was ambiguity about who decided which forces might be employed. There was no formal arrangement for command or co-ordination among the air, land and sea forces. The coalition of countries which sent troops was constructed with bilateral diplomacy and it was unclear who established rules of engagement. The Soviet Union refused to send troops unless they were placed under a UN command.

Baghdad, watching the build-up, threatened the coalition with the "mother of all battles". Saddam Hussein would not contemplate a pull-out in the face of increasing and massive force. He considered himself to be the champion of the Arab masses. His only offer was to trade the ending of the occupation of Palestine in exchange for his withdrawal from Kuwait.

By October, 1990, President George Bush was in political trouble at home. He had reneged on his read-my-lips election pledge not to raise taxes and his policy on the Gulf seemed uncertain. It was three months since the invasion. Towards the end of October there was a meeting in the White House between the President, Colin Powell, Chairman of the Joint Chiefs of Staff, Secretary of Defence Dick Cheney, Secretary of State James Baker, and the National Security Adviser, Brent Scowcroft. It was at this meeting that there was apparently a major policy switch – from defensive to offensive – and a doubling of US forces. By now there were some 360,000 Iraqi troops in or near Kuwait.

Powell wanted enough men and hardware. He wanted "enough to make sure" of a decisive win. NATO's central front would be denuded of troops in order to do it. "First we are going to cut (the Iraqi Army) in Kuwait off, then we are going to kill it", he later explained. On November 8, Bush announced an increase in troops; he wanted to ensure that the coalition had an offensive military option. Pentagon planning was well advanced. Months prior to the Kuwait invasion, Colin Powell had ordered an immediate overhaul of the Pentagon's military planning for the Middle East crisis. He had wanted a contingency to protect the Saudi oilfields from attack. In April 1990, Powell became familiar with a recent speech by Saddam Hussein in which the dictator warned: "Whoever threatens us with the atomic bomb, we will annihilate him". The speech came shortly after a debate on Israeli television about whether or not Israel should bomb Iraq's rapidly expanding chemical warfare capability.

Why not repeat the Israel's June 1981 bombing of the Iraqi Osirak nuclear reactor? Preparations were in hand to move to the offensive.

The announcement, on November 8, of a redoubling of US forces in the Gulf, including heavy tank divisions from Europe, saw a swift reaction on Capitol Hill where a Democratic Congress feared a sudden lurch to war. The influential Georgian Democrat, the conservative Senator Sam Nunn, Chair of the Armed Services Committee, was unhappy that he was not consulted and planned a series of hearings intended to call into question government policy and to force issues of cost into the open. His was not the only challenge to the administration. Senator Daniel Patrick Moynihan feared the President's coalition would wreck any chance of a collective security system. Some Republicans wanted a special session of Congress to debate the Gulf. Public support too seemed to be waning.

In New York, at the US mission to the UN, they dusted down the files on Korea. The two cases were not dissimilar. The troops who fought in Korea were authorised to fly the UN flag but the force was under US command. In the Korean case, the Security Council voted a Resolution which asked member states to "render every assistance" to the UN whilst President Harry Truman ordered air and sea forces to South Korea before the Resolution was passed. A later Resolution had ordered member states to furnish such assistance as necessary, under a unified US command to repel armed attack and restore international peace and security. In 1950, only Yugoslavia, a non-permanent council member, had abstained. As for reaction in the General Assembly, other states, particularly the Arab ones, argued double standards, and pointed to UN inaction on previous aggression – particularly against the Palestinians.

There was debate on similar issues in the months to come. Those who objected to the US's, sudden show of concern about aggression against the weak cited Israel's occupation of Arab territories, the Chinese destruction of the people and culture of Tibet, Syria's involvement in the Lebanon, the killing fields of Cambodia, the Indonesian rape of East Timor and the UN's miserable failure to act against Iraq's attack on Iran in 1980. The Charter was breached daily. This time, all that happened over Kuwait was that the US, out of self-interest, was reduced to providing mercenaries for feudal rulers to protect their riches.

President Bush preferred the analogy of the failure of appeasement in the 1930s. He warned: "Our jobs, our way of life, our own freedom, would all suffer if control of the world's great oil reserves fell into the hands of one man . . . " What the US needed now was the Security Council to be persuaded to authorise the multi-national force to use all necessary means to liberate Kuwait.

In November 1990 it was the US's turn to hold the Security Council Presidency. In December, in accordance with monthly alphabetical rotation, the Yemen would take over. As a consequence, November saw feverish activity by the Americans to draft a Council Resolution with acceptable wording. It was far from easy. Gorbachev suddenly announced that the word force could not be used and any resolution which contained it would be vetoed. On November 20, ten days from the end-of-the-month deadline, Gorbachev refused to commit the Soviet Union to a Resolution which would implicitly authorise the use of force against Iraq. He wanted more consultations. Baker would have to make concessions. Moscow and Peking wanted to give Iraq time, a period of goodwill, a deadline. The Americans were loathe to tie the coalition's hands and risk the appearance of vacillation. Ambassador Tom Pickering had little room to manoeuvre and told the President that only a Resolution stipulating a deadline would stand a chance of getting through the Council. They settled on January 15, 1991. If Saddam Hussein had not pulled out by then, all necessary means would be used to uphold and implement previous Resolutions and to restore international peace and security. A few days before the vote was taken, the exiled government of Kuwait, aided by a New York public relations company, presented Security Council members with a two-day display of atrocities in Kuwait City as the Iraqis plundered and dismantled the country. Witnesses gave the council examples of torture, rape and execution.

President Bush visited US troops at Dhahran military airport in Saudi Arabia. He told them that Saddam Hussein had never possesed a weapon he had not used: "Every day that passes brings Saddam Hussein one day closer to realising his goal of a nuclear weapons arsenal . . . another reason why . . . our mission is marked by a real sense of urgency."

In New York two Council members held out: Yemen and Cuba were determined to vote against the Resolution authorising the use of force if Iraq did not meet the deadline. The Republic of Yemen was the poorest, the most populous and the youngest Arab state, formed only six months previously with the amalgamation after years of violence between of the Yemen Arab Republic and the People's Democratic Republic of Yemen. Now proud of being a united country, the Yemen turned down every American offer for her Security Council vote. It was not for sale. Her President, Ali Abdallah, told them that he believed the great powers were making cynical use of the UN. Yemen's Foreign Minister, Ambassador Abdalla Saleh Al-Ashtal, warned them that the they were putting the credibility of the Security Council at risk. Far from laying the framework for a New World Order, the Resolution gave blanket approval for the use of force without adequate oversight and control. As for the trade embargo imposed on Iraq, it had no parallel in history and would soon be causing great suffering.

Yemen paid dear. Afterwards Secretary of State James Baker sent a message to the Foreign Minister telling him he had just lost his country $70 million in aid. Yemeni loans were blocked by the World Bank and the IMF and 800,000 Yemeni workers were thrown out of Saudi Arabia.

The other speech against the Resolution 678 was from the Cuban Foreign Minister, Isidoro Malmierca, who said that if the UN used force to retake Kuwait it would prove only that the Council was incapable of finding a peaceful political solution. This would be the worst possible expression of the UN's new role in the future. The Resolution gave no definition of "all necessary means", and member states seemed free to interpret it as they chose. In any event, a desire to protect one's friends did not constitute collective security. The UN was being used as a convenience.

James Baker made the speech for the US with appeasement the theme. Baker took for his opening a section of the 1936 Haile Selassi address to the League of Nations after Ethiopia had been overrun by fascists.

> There is no precedent for a people being the victim of such injustice . . . there has never before been an example of any Government proceeding with the systematic extermination of a nation . . . .in violation of the most solemn promises made to all the nations of the earth that there should be no resort to a war of conquest . . . there should not be used against innocent human beings terrible poison and harmful gases.

Baker explained how Selassi's plea had fallen on deaf ears: the League failed to act and world war was the result. Baker said they were now given a second chance and this was the most important decision the Council had ever taken. Together, member nations of the UN could build the world which had been envisioned by the founders and turn the Security Council into a true instrument for peace and justice across the globe. The UN's future was at stake.

Afterwards, Baker said that it had been imperative to dispel Saddam Hussein's belief the coalition would not go to war. Saddam Hussein did not believe the coalition forces deployed to defend Iraq's neighbours would remain united. But the dissenters were not persuaded by the Baker speech; it looked to them as though the Soviet Union were little more than a junior partner in America's own world order.

The Americans celebrated a triumph. There was particular pride at having prevented the Chinese veto, as China had abstained. After the vote Baker had seen to it that in return China was relieved of her pariah status, forgiven for the massacre of protestors during student-led pro-decmocracy demonstrations in Tiananmen Square in June, 1989. The World Bank helped by depositing $114 million in Peking. Other votes were assured with similar sweetners. Ethiopia was given an investment deal, Zaire was promised military aid. In the weeks before the Council meeting, Baker held more than 200 meetings with Foreign Ministers and Heads of State to get support.

The American triumph was short-lived. The morning after Resolution 678, President Bush, mindful of public opinion, reversed the US policy and offered high-level talks with Saddam Hussein. Seizing the initiative, Saddam Hussein released his Western hostages and it looked to outsiders as though there had been a secret deal. Bush reassured the allies but there was increased talk of a diplomatic solution. Foreign Minister Eduard Shevardnadze called for an international conference on the Middle East. This last proposal was the linkage with Palestine which Saddam Hussein so desperately wanted in order to drive home his point about double standards.

Shevardnadze, an avowed internationalist, was under pressure from all quarters. In November the USSR Supreme Soviet held an emergency debate on the state of the nation while there was increasing tension between the central government and the governments of the individual republics. Gorbachev leadership was at issue. The Soviet Union seemed to be disintegrating. There was pressure from the powerful Soviet military watching a massive army massing 800 miles south of the Russian border. Shevardnadze told Baker that the Soviet Union intended to submit a draft Resolution calling for a conference on Palestine. Baker said he would veto it because such a move would embolden Saddam Hussein and infuriate Israel. The danger passed. Bush approved US credit guarantees for Soviet purchases of medical supplies and technical assistance in food distribution.

In a side room of the Security Council one evening, Giandomenico Picco, an Assistant Secretary General, noticed that in not one Security Council Resolution on Iraq's invasion of Kuwait was there one word about the Secretary General. Pérez de Cuéllar almost laughed. "Don't be naive," he had said. "Can't you understand reality? This is the New World, and there is no role for us." Recently, he had received a request from the Americans for the coalition forces to fly the UN flag, but he turned them down. This was not a UN force: it was a coalition of forces created by the US, authorised by the Security Council. He considered that the past weeks of sparring between Iraq and the US had been a wasted opportunity for diplomacy. He had deep distaste for the political manoeuvring deadline and there was no role for him until the last minute. As the deadline neared, one of the last attempts to find a diplomatic solution took place in Geneva when Baker met Iraq's Foreign Minister, Tariq Aziz. The talks failed and it was agreed that Pérez de Cuéllar could go to Baghdad for a final plea. On January 12, 1991, following a three-day debate, Congress sanctioned the use of American force in the Gulf. Aziz warned an attack on Iraq would result in an Iraqi attack on Israel and, as the last American diplomats flew out of Baghdad, Pérez de Cuéllar flew in. There were demonstrations for peace in the US, including a vigil outside the Secretariat in New York. All hope now rested with the Secretary General. He was the world's last resort, a man with one chance of averting a war of chemical and possibly nuclear horror.

It did nothing for his reputation that when he was in Baghdad, Pérez de Cuéllar was seen to resent every minute of it. He showed his irritation in front of the world's press during a long and humiliating wait. When he was finally ushered in to see the Iraqi leader, Saddam Hussein proceeded to berate him for American Resolutions passed by the Security Council. Pérez de Cuéllar pleaded with him not to give the warmongers a chance but nothing came of their meeting. Hussein lectured him on the Israeli occupation and annexation of territory and yet Israel was never subject to sanctions or military intervention: "These are American Resolutions . . . it is the era of America", Hussein said.

Although he was given an unprecedented two hours, Pérez de Cuéllar had hurried away, appearing desperate to leave Iraq because war was about to begin. The deadline was twenty-four hours away. Back in New York he found the mood sombre, and the staff frightened and depressed. He was ill-advised by his retinue of spokespeople, and stopped to answer questions to a gang of press in the lobby. Of Hussein he said: "You need two for tango. [sic] I wanted to dance but I did not find any nice lady for dancing with. Saddam did not express any desire to withdraw."

It was a rotten performance for someone who possessed a retinue of press advisers. It did nothing for either Pérez de Cuéllar's reputation nor for that of the UN. In the Secretariat they speculated that it cost him a third term as Secretary General, and that to have displayed such evident despair in such an inarticulate way was unbecoming. From then on Pérez de Cuéllar was generally ignored by the media and his attitudes to the war received scant attention.

On January 23, a week after the war started and after the devastation of Iraq from the air, with 8,000 bombing missions and incalculable civilian casualties, Pérez de Cuéllar was interviewed for BBC radio and seemed better prepared. He told the correspondent that the war over Kuwait was not justified. Although action in the Gulf was underpinned by a Council Resolution, this did not mean it was a UN war conducted in accordance with the Charter. For it to be a UN war, command and control of the forces would be with the Security Council, with the active involvement of the Military Staff Committee whose chief would have supervised it. In the Gulf, the only involvement of the Council was to have given the American coalition a "very large mandate". A New World Order would need full implementation of the Charter. Pérez de Cuéllar called for restraint.

The war began on January 17, the second day after the deadline set by the Security Council. Bush appeared on television to say allied planes had struck at Iraq's nuclear bomb potential, chemical weapons, artillery and tanks. Bush declared that the war would lead to a New World Order based on the rule of law. The twenty-eight-nation force had 690,000 troops in the region. The US weapons included Stealth fighters and ship-launched Tomahawk cruise missiles. In the first wave of bombing, Baghdad was pounded with missiles and bombs and in the weeks to come Iraq was all but flattened. The Gulf was a testing site for the most advanced military technology, battlefield justification for the billions of dollars spent on stealth and smart-bomb technology. A massive military might had found justification for existence.

One of the only Iraqi retaliations came on the second day of the war, on Friday January 18, when five Iraqi ballistic missiles landed in Tel Aviv. Yet the war was contained, making it easier for the Americans to retain Arab support. The Syrians went out of their way to castigate and ridicule Hussein's strategy.

From the beginning, the American commanders knew that a

weakness in Operation Desert Storm was the high number of civilian casualties. By the time the allied bombing campaign entered its fifth week, the growing clamour for a Security Council meeting reached a crescendo. Gorbachev warned that bombing exceeded the mandate given to the allies, though it had stipulated "all necessary means". The Chinese wanted to distance themselves. Cuba was drumming up support for a ceasefire Resolution. On February 13, when the Council did finally meet, two laser-guided bombs hit a ventilation shaft in an air-raid shelter in Baghdad, killing hundreds of women and children. The allied commanders claimed that Hussein was protecting his command and control units on top of schools, and protecting his MiG aircraft by parking them in front of ancient shrines. He put a military headquarters in a hospital.

On Saturday, February 23, Bush threatened Hussein with the biggest land offensive since the Second World War, unless the last Iraqi soldier left Kuwait within seven days. At dawn the following day the offensive, with 200,000 allied troops, began and two days later Iraqi troops began to pull out of Kuwait. The month-long pounding from the air weakened the capacity and the resolve to resist. The estimates of Iraqi soldiers killed was 100,000 and the allies took up to 175,100 prisoners. There were untold civilian deaths in Iraq and immense suffering among the people left alive.

Even before the Iraqi pull-out began, the coalition determined to destroy the Iraqi army and fleeing Iraqi soldiers were bombed as they tried to retreat along the Basra road which became a scene of carnage. Piles of bodies were bulldozed into the sand. On February 28 the American Marines took Kuwait's international airport and then stood aside to let the Kuwaitis retake their city. Bush declared victory and announced the suspension of military operations.

The Resolution which dictated the terms for peace was presented to the other four permanent members of the Security Council by American Ambassador Tom Pickering. It demanded an unconditional surrender and a formal ceasefire. It made clear that Iraq would not be accepted back into the community of nations without paying a heavy price. The sanctions would continue. Pérez de Cuéllar spoke against it: "As Secretary General I cannot agree with measures that are aimed at overthrowing the government of a country which is a member of the UN", he said. A joint mission of the World Health Organisation and UNICEF reported malnutrition and a cholera epidemic in Iraq. In March, Pérez de Cuéllar spoke in support of a Security Council Resolution proposed by Yemen, Cuba, Ecuador, India and Zimbabwe which called for the end to sanctions for humanitarian needs. The allied coalition sent food and relief supplies to Iraq, on the promise that the Resolution be abandoned. On March 20, UN Special Representative, Martti Ahtisaari, reported from Baghdad that Iraq was bombed into the pre-industrial age. Conditions were apocalyptic. The irrigation and draining systems had failed with the collapse of water treatment facilities. The sewage system was clogged, rats proliferated. There was disease, starvation and a sharp rise in infant mortality. Baker was as good as his word. He had reportedly told Aziz at their last meeting in Geneva that Iraq would be bombed "back to the pre-industrial age". With the continuation of sanctions and other draconian measures, the Security Council ensured that the Iraqi people would be paying the price for years to come.

The diplomats joked and called it the mother of all Resolutions. Resolution 687 was voted on April 3, 1991, the longest in UN history. Pickering said that the Resolution was intended to "rebuild the peace". It dealt with the demarcation of the Iraq-Kuwait border and created a demilitarised zone. Under its terms Iraq was liable for all environmental damage and all injury to nationals and corporations. Sanctions would be maintained apart from medicine and health supplies. Iraq could sell none of her oil without UN permission. The Resolution created a UN observer force to manage the peace and the UN Iraq-Kuwait Observation Mission would monitor the demilitarised zone. It departed from peacekeeping practice in that it did not have the agreement of the host country. The particular terms on locating and eliminating Hussein's biological, chemical and nuclear weapons were formulated by the British and the Council was to co-ordinate action with the International Atomic Energy Agency to deal with Iraq's clandestine program to acquire nuclear weapons. Iraq had to agree not to acquire or develop these weapons and was to allow on-site inspection.

Iraq was crippled and in chaos, yet Saddam Hussein unleashed more terror. After a rebellion in the south Hussein sent Iraq's elite Republican Guard, still largely intact, to set upon the Shias, in the holy cities of Najaf and Karbal. The Guard arrested and shot thousands of civilians. People were tied to tanks and used as shields, men women and children were massacred. There were public beheadings.

By mid-March Hussein turned his attention to the Kurds who, in the belief that the West would back them, were making a dash for freedom, believing in an imminent collapse of Baghdad. The Kurds expected an American response and believed Hussein had no more right to Kurdistan than to Kuwait. Kurdish leaders called for UN-brokered autonomy, demilitarisation and a substantial UN presence to protect them. Iraqi helicopters, allowed to fly in accordance with ceasefire agreements, bombed Kurdish villages. No help came. A White House spokesman said: "We don't intend to get involved in Iraq's internal affairs."

When the Iran–Iraq war ended in 1988, Iraq had diverted military resources to brutalise the Kurds in the north, stepping up a scorched earth policy with genocidal attacks using chemical weapons. Hussein wanted a final solution to the problem of the Kurdish separatist movement. Now, in 1991, after the war to retake Kuwait, and at a time of growing domestic unrest, the Kurds were unable to resist an Iraqi onslaught and they fled across the northern mountains trying to get to Turkey and Iran. By early April 1991, a tragedy of epic proportions had developed. An exodus of people trudged over barren mountains, through ice and snow. Some were refused entry to Turkey; weakened refugees were beaten back by soldiers with rifles, and thousands were dying, trapped and starving. The few relief trucks available were stuck in mud on the access roads. Help could not reach the dying. "We are waiting for the UN", they told the television cameras. On the eastern border with Iran there was a different nightmare. Iran already had more refugees than any other country and now a million Kurdish people were on the move, joining the 600,000 already there, plus the two million Afghans who fled the 1979 Soviet invasion. In Jordan there were one million refugees from Iraq before the bombing started and the Jordanian authorities were overwhelmed.

Every television screen in the West broadcast the tragedy and there was a clamour for culpability. Almost everyone blamed the UN for it seemed that those same nations capable of flying thousands of bombing missions a day found it hard to deliver aid to the destitute and dying.

The reason is all too familiar. Before Operation Desert Storm, the Geneva-based UN Disaster Relief Organisation estimated there would be a refugee problem amounting to half a million people. As the war approached in January 1991, the organisation made desperate appeals to governments for money so that preparations could be made. The relief organisation was dependent on voluntary funds from governments and an appeal was launched for $175 million. By the time the tide of humanity started to move, only $38 million had been received and the organisation made another more desperate appeal to governments for money. The crisis exposed another serious faultline, the lack of co-ordination among the UN agencies. There was further condemnation of the UN for its failure: Pérez de Cuéllar told the Security Council that the UN system could move no faster. It had no resources and, by now, to appease public opinion, individual governments were by-passing the UN and giving funds bilaterally, causing chaos in the field.

The Security Council met behind closed doors to discuss the plight of the Kurds, for this was far too delicate for public consumption. The French were pressing for action and had long supported moves to intervene in Iraq on humanitarian grounds. President François Mitterrand had already announced that the Kurdish tragedy put the political and moral authority of the Council at risk. But other permanent members urged caution and took cover behind the Charter which prevented interference by the UN in the domestic affairs of states. They feared a precedent which could be used elsewhere to disadvantage, to help other minorities wanting independence. But the French argued that the rights of states should give way when the rights of humankind were at risk and that this great tragedy should force them all to re-examine the protection in the Charter. Following the Cold War the persecution of minorities was a new priority; France warned that Europe itself might one day be called upon to answer similar pleas from ethnic minorities closer to home.

The result was a landmark Resolution, the first to intervene effectively in an internal state matter, to stop the persecution of a people by its own government and against the wishes of the state authorities. To avoid setting a precedent Resolution 688 justified intervention in Iraq because the consequences of what was happening to the Kurds was threatening international peace and security in the region. Voted through on April 5, 1991, it condemned the slaughter in north and south Iraq. Its detractors said it was illegal because it clearly breached the principle of non-intervention in the affairs of member states enshrined in Article 2, paragraph 7; others pointed to the fact there were already deep breaches in Iraqi sovereignty caused by the fierce sanctions imposed by the Council after the end of the war.

The real reason for the Resolution was to appease public opinion, outraged at what it was seeing. There had never been a refugee situation which had developed so quickly and in such full horror on television. In those early days the aid which did get through was dropped from the air by the allies, and it sometimes killed refugees where it fell.

Britain sponsored the idea of safe-havens for the Kurds within northern Iraq; Hussein was told by the allied coalition that violation of the sanctuary of these havens would be responded to with international retaliation. In April, 1991, while an estimated 1,000 died on the mountains, an understanding was reached between the UN and Iraq for the establishment of camps which the US and allied troops would protect until a full UN protection force was ready.

Although Resolution 688 insisted that Iraq allow immediate access for humanitarian organisations, Pérez de Cuéllar believed that for UN protected areas a degree of co-operation was essential and on the thirty-eighth floor the priority was agreement for a UN humanitarian presence. Negotiations led, on April 18, 1991, to the first Memorandum of Understanding between Iraq's Foreign Minister and the Secretary General's Executive Delegate, Prince Sadruddin Aga Khan which secured Iraq's assent to the operation. Pérez de Cuéllar later felt harried into organising a force of UN guards to police these safe-havens temporarily. He was angered at complaints from member government that the UN had been negligent: the UN was accused by Britain's Overseas Development Minister Lynda Chalker of being ineffective in its response to the tragedy. Pérez de Cuéllar said that mounting a rescue was beyond the UN's means; there was no money available and in the Secretariat they were fed up handing out begging bowls. Indeed, the diplomatic community was much more interested in the forthcoming election for his successor as his second five-year term was up in six months. Jockeying for position had been going on for at least two years and several newspapers had already written articles saying that the UN needed someone stronger, someone of international stature, who could deal with emergencies. There was a need for someone adventurous who would commit the UN to much needed reform. "For once", commented the BBC's diplomatic editor, John Simpson, "it really matters who gets the job." These were historic times. In September, 1991, in an address to the General Assembly, Bush said "On the ruins of conflict, these brave men and women built an era of peace and understanding. They inaugurated a New World Order, an order worth perserving for the ages." The UN was presented with a chance to fulfil the Charter, to fulfil the Premable promise to save succeeding generations from the scourge of war. Bush told member states, "Take this challenge seriously. Inspire future generations to praise and venerate you",

The question of how to cope with the harsh winter for the Kurdish refugees was serious. The possibilities of another human catastrophe were real. There was a reluctance to make a long-term commitment to the Kurds: James Baker explained that the US did not want to be sucked into a civil war.

With the origins of the Second World War firmly in their minds, the founders of the UN believed that in order to have a stable World Order the Security Council should have the means to forestall conflict. This was the lesson of the thirties when Hitler's aggression against neighbouring states was met with impotence by the League of Nations. To avoid such a repetition, the Charter laid down a continuum of steps to deal with threats to world peace. Rather than picking up the pieces after war, the Security Council was intended to be an instrument of mediation: Article 34 of the Charter allowed it to investigate any dispute or situation between states which could potentially lead to international friction. Article 36 required that legal disputes between states should be referred by the parties to the International Court of Justice, established at the same time as the UN and which was to reconcile legitimate claims and interests. The first responsibility lay with the belligerents themselves who would use the international community as a guarantor. Threats of political and economic sanction by UN members would be used to focus minds on settlement. Should the parties fail, regional organisations should try to mediate, under the auspices of the Security Council.

When it came to keeping the peace, the UN's founders intended that the International Court of Justice should be central to the rule of international law.

Pérez de Cuéllar ardently promoted preventive diplomacy and he returned to its possibilities in 1991 in his last annual report. "The Charter does not contemplate that the UN should wait for fighting to erupt, for aggression to take place, for violations of human rights to attain massive proportions before it moved to rectify the situation." But the UN lacked an effective global watch and it was not possible to comply with this part of the Charter. Unlike industrialised nations, in the Secretariat there was no early warning or intelligence capability. The great powers kept their own counsel and did not share what they knew. The Secretary General had no means of monitoring incipient conflicts or detecting preparations for military conflict, for the little information which was available was inadequate and primitive.

By the time Pérez de Cuéllar left office in 1991, his faith in preventive diplomacy was born out by the bloodshed in Yugoslavia.

In 1989 Amnesty International first warned about what was happening to the Federal Republic of Yugoslavia, held together during the Cold War by Communism. A year later it was the CIA, warning in November that there would be civil war and the collapse of the country within eighteen months.

For more than forty years the unity among six republics and two autonomous provinces was guaranteed by the Yugoslav League of Communists and the Yugoslav People's Army. The Serbs, Croats, Slovenes, Bosnian Muslims, Macedonians and Albanians had lived together in peace. But by the late eighties human rights abuses were beginning to signal disaster. The Serbs were beginning to oppress ethnic Albanians in Kosovo, an autonomous province in the south. The trouble in Kosovo, the Serb birthplace, was that it was once populated by Serbs but was now eighty-five per cent ethnic Albanian. The Serbs forced through the adoption of Serbo-Croatian as the official language and dismissed 6,000 ethnic Albanian secondary-school teachers. Land was confiscated and turned over to Serbs. By 1990, when the CIA reported, the Yugoslavs themselves were talking openly about the growing danger of civil war.

Yugoslavia had held a special place for the West. Tito, who had run the country since the end of the war, was the only East European leader not to be a Soviet puppet and the West had courted him, ignoring his tyranny and cynical manipulation of ethnic identity. A bulwark against Soviet expansion, Tito broke with Stalin and the Cominform in 1948 and was rewarded with a place at the heart of international diplomacy. Yugoslavia was truly a country which punched above her weight. She was a bridge which spanned East and West and North and South. Yugoslavia was the first host of the non-aligned group, created in Belgrade in 1961. It consisted of twenty-five states who refused to adhere to the main East–West military and political blocs. It prompted the establishment of a New Economic Order, wanted better terms for those countries producing raw materials. It promoted co-operation between developing countries. President Tito would travel all over the world in an effort to preach the power and rights of the Third World. The non-aligned movement's last ever meeting in Belgrade was in 1989 when millions were spent renovating hotels and guest houses for the occasion. The conference ended with an appeal that member states pay greater attention to minorities and human rights.

Yugoslavia's special status ensured that for an unprecedented four times she was elected a non-permanent Security Council member. But the end of the Cold War spelled the end of Yugoslavia's international status and of her strategic interest. After the Cold War the Balkans were considered less vital and, when Yugoslavia was breaking up, the great powers were preoccupied with momentous events elsewhere. In August 1989 Gorbachev resigned as head of the Communist Party and its central committee was dissolved. There were new alliances to consider and, looking back, the European leaders would later claim that their diplomatic resources were stretched to the limit. At first they were unconvinced that Western interests were at stake. Whatever the excuse, little attention was given to Slobodan Milošević, who had come to power in mid-December 1987 and who spoke of restoring the Serbs to their "rightful place", beginning to harness nationalism to his own purposes. In the next few years, in Serbia and Croatia, there would be unrelenting diets of hysterical warmongering propaganda. In Belgrade, Milošević controlled Serbian state television, the main source of information for the country. The Serbs were encouraged to see themselves as victims of a history about to be avenged. By mid-1990, Milošević's people were preparing for war in Croatia, arming the Serbs there and reviving memories of the slaughter of Serbs by the Croat Nazis during the Second World War.

Yugoslavia, comprising the Republics of Serbia, Croatia, Macedonia, Montenegro, Slovenia and Bosnia-Hercegovina as well as the autonomous provices of Kosovo and Vojvodina, had been united. The Serbs made up one-third of the Yugoslav Republic's population but of all the nations that formed Yugoslavia when it was created in 1918, the Serbs formed the only group which had liberated itself from foreign rule and set up an independent state. When Communism began to fall apart in 1989 about 600,000 Serbs lived in Croatia; the Croats began to sack Serbs from their jobs and replaced them with Croats. Problems re-emerged which some thought gone for ever. During the Second World War, the Nazis had dismembered the country, making Croatia a Nazi puppet state where the butchery more than matched the horror elsewhere. The Nazis and their Croatian militia the Ustasha, inflicted appalling atrocities on Serbs and Jews. Tito, a Communist, organised a partisan army against the Fascists; in one anti-partisan campaign alone 66,000 people were deported or executed. In another operation the Ustasha separated 23,000 children from their parents, murdering 11,000 of them. Hundreds more of the children died of starvation or from typhoid in cattle wagons. Others were given to Croats and their mothers were deported to German labour camps. Neither were the Croats allowed to forget the revenge meted out by Tito's resistance army on their prisoners at the end of the war. The propaganda machines drew heavily on history. During the First and Second World Wars the Serbs had fought on the side of the Western powers. In the west of Yugoslavia the Slovenes and the Croats argued that history had placed them in the civilised camp of Europe with Catholicism and Latin. They had nothing to do with Orthodox Serbia in the East with its Cyrillic script.

In the 1980s the Serbs built the largest orthodox cathedral in the world. They set up regular militia, built up a network in towns and villages and Milošević removed the autonomous status of Vojvodina in October, 1988, of Montenegro in January 1989 and of Kosovo in Febuary 1989. Milošević knew how to transport crowds to adoration and was a master of propaganda. While Croatia wanted independence, Milošević played on the fears of the Serbian minority there and invoked genocidal images. By February 1991 it was possible to predict that a Serb – Croat war was only weeks away.

On 25 June, 1991. Slovenia and Croatia proclaimed their independence and the very next day Yugolsav army tanks attacked

Slovenia provoking fierce fighting. The Yugoslav National Army withdrew on July 7, and opened hostilities in Croatia; there were almost no Serbs in Slovenia but in Croatia a substantial Serb minority had already clashed with Croatian forces. There was a breakdown of law and order in war zones with reports of atrocities against civilians. The word "cleansing", found in documents written by the Ustasha, referring to giving away of farms and small holdings which belonged to Serbs or Muslim victims, had returned to haunt them.

By the end of the year the Serbs had driven native Croats out of more than thirty per cent of Croatian territory. The historic cities of Osijek, Zadar, Dubrovnik and Vinkovci were under siege. Croatia declared it would keep fighting until it retrieved its lost territory. The Serb-dominated Yugoslav army and air force ensured a consolidation of Serb-territory by driving out the Croats and looting everything they owned.

There was a reluctance to intervene. "We're not the world's policeman", said President Bush on June 11, 1991. Bush did not want to pursue the possibility, not with a worsening economic crisis at home and a Presidential election the following year, in 1992. Secretary of Defence Dick Cheney said that the situation did not merit a Desert Storm-like military intervention. In Washington people believed that there would be little public support for the use of force to stop the fighting in Yugoslavia. The New World Order was being tested in the Middle East where new alliances in the post-Gulf war world were providing new opportunities. Balkan self-determination was way down the agenda. On June 21, 1991 the Secretary of State James Baker went to Belgrade and said that Europe and the US believed that Yugoslavia should remain a single state. This visit came five days before the war started and it is possible that the Serbs in Belgrade thought that if they were to hold the state together by force no one would bother very much.

At this stage the UN was not involved. This was a regional problem and the Europeans were keen to find a diplomatic solution themselves, to prove a co-ordinated foreign policy; 1991 was to have been an historic year for European union. "This is Europe's hour", Jacques Poos the Luxembourg Foreign Minister said when Europe's mediation effort for Yugoslavia was launched in August 1991. Endless ceasefires followed, all signed and broken and, in the end, European diplomatic activity seemed no more than hopeless haggling while the Serbs achieved their objectives.

Finally and belatedly, the Security Council became involved. Everyone seemed relieved and said that only the Council possessed the necessary clout and confidence. The first Resolution on the crisis was passed on September 25, 1991 and it imposed a complete embargo on all deliveries of weapons and military equipment to the whole of the Yugoslav territory. The impetus for action came from Canada and Austria. Both states argued that the civil war was a threat to international peace but Resolution 713 was confirmation of a European view of what was happening, that this was a civil war and there should be an impartial attitude to both sides. The embargo would have little effect on the Yugolsav army which had massive stockpiles but it weakened the Croatian forces, desperately trying to hold on to the city of Vukovar under a savage seige by the Yugoslav national army. In Vukovar people were living in cellars and there was a relentless bombardment of the Dalmatian coast of Croatia including the port of Dubrovnik, a medieval town, one of Europe's architectural jewels which had for centuries survived warring empires. In early Nov-ember, Dubrovnik crumbled into rubble. Vukovar was destroyed: the centre of the town was flattened and deserted, desolate and uninhabitable. The Serbs had destroyed the past, burning books, archives, registers and smashing monuments and churches. Pitiful trails of refugees took what they could carry. Europe had gone backwards, to another age.

On November 27, 1991, the Security Council met again and approved Resolution 721 which appeared to give the go-ahead for a UN peacekeeping force for the Balkans. Its wording betrayed a lack of resolve. Resolution 721 approved "efforts towards the possible establishment of a peacekeeping operation", which was conditional upon the latest shaky ceasefire between Serbs and Croats, the fourteenth since the war began, although it had the distinction of being the first brokered by the UN. In neighbouring Bosnia-Hercegovina, the republic's foreign minister wanted a force within weeks to stop the war spreading but the Council did not yet have a plan, even if troops could be found. Some were talking about the blue helmets patrolling borders and others favoured the inkspot approach which entailed putting peacekeepers in flashpoint areas.

The British were reluctant and had shown their displeasure earlier, at the end of September 1991 when European foreign policy was being decided in The Hague. Britian's Foreign Secretary Douglas Hurd refused a French proposal to send in 30,000 troops, expressing fears of being sucked into a Balkan equivalent of Northern Ireland. "We have experience of fighting from village to village", he said. The French and Germans had wanted a European buffer force which would have the approval of the Security Council but military experts warned that a peace mission in the Balkans could turn into the most expensive UN operation yet. There was reluctance in the Security Council; both China and the Soviet Union were opposed to UN intervention fearing precedents for their own internal conflicts. All the while, Yugoslavia, a founder member of the UN and, in the past, one of the most important troop contributors to UN peacekeeping, was receding into darkness.

Yugoslavia finally collapsed in mid-December when Germany decided that two former republics were equivalent to nation-states and gave international recognition to Croatia and Slovenia. There was no provision for the rest of the country. As a result others were persuaded to pursue political objectives and refused to compromise. Germany was sympathetic to Croatia and Slovenia, they were natural allies, linked for centuries. Germany wanted to play a greater role in European affairs, to carve out a sphere of influence. The decision caused a serious split in European ranks for other countries favoured a political solution to the break up of Yugoslavia. The British, supported by Washington, did not agree with recognition because a minority of Serbs, more than 600,000 in Croatia, would become an unwilling minority. The last time Croatia had been a separate country, from 1941 to 1945, it was Nazi-supported. In 1991 Croatia's Franjo Tudjman had reintroduced the chequered flag of the old Fascist state.

Pérez de Cuéllar cautioned Hans-Dietrich Genscher, Germany's Minister for Foreign Affairs, to reconsider and warned that recognition could provoke the most terrible war. Pérez de Cuéllar wanted to keep Yugoslavia together and he wrote to the European Community advising it not to follow Germany's lead. It would hamper efforts to find a negotiated settlement. Genscher ignored the Secretary General and the European Council of Ministers who had entrusted the problem to a special commission. Just prior to German recognition for Croatia and Slovenia, this European commission reported that whereas Slovenia could be said to constitute a state, this was not true of Croatia. First, the government of Croatia was not in control of all its territory and second, Croatia had not provided sufficient guarantees for the safety of its ethnic groups, particularly the Serbs. Germany, however, would succeed in persuading the members of the European Community to follow suit and grant recognition. Britain was opposed to recognition but the Maastricht Treaty was being negotiated at the time and the fate of Yugoslavia was part of a trade-off. The EC was bound by a commitment to a single foreign policy. When Pérez de Cuéllar left office in December 1991, the German decision to recognise Croatia and Slovenia was one more folly which ensured that the war would spread. The Balkan crisis demonstrated the need for preventive diplomacy for what happened there was preventable and it was an early warning, unheeded, of what post-Cold War conflict would entail.

On Thursday, December 13, 1991, Pérez de Cuéllar went once more to Washington, to the White House for President Bush's special, pre-Christmas, family occasion to listen to Christmas carols, in the presence of the five American hostages freed from the Lebanon. It was here that Pérez de Cuéllar was awarded the Medal of Freedom, the highest civilian honour the US can bestow. On the steps leading to the rose garden, Bush said that Pérez de Cuéllar was an architect of peace. He treasured his friendship and he thanked him for his tireless work to sustain the coalition during the war. "His tenure marked literally the rebirth of the UN." Pérez de Cuéllar kept his doubts to himself.

Pérez de Cuéllar left office on the last day of 1991 at the stroke of the New Year, just minutes after completing a last diplomatic success with a minute-to-midnight signing of a preliminary agreement to end the decade-long civil war in El Salvador. This first tentative step to peace had taken an arduous three days of negotiation but was the culmination of more than a year's work. He worked with his Special Representative for Central America, Alvaro de Soto. The Cold War battle in El Salvador between government and guerilla armies had caused 75,000 people to be slaughtered and a million uprooted in a decade of terror. The war was perceived as the Vietnam of Central America. El Salvador absorbed $4 billion of economic and military aid from the US, desperate to prop up the regime, while the opposition drew strength from Cuba and the Soviet Union. Reagan regarded the guerilla FMLN army (Frente Farabando Martí para la Liberación Nacional) wanting to destabilise the region in order to bring chaos to the American border.

The agreement for El Salvador was a fitting conclusion for Pérez de Cuéllar. The press called it the crowning of a ten-year reign and in those last months there were very public milestones. In August, 1991 Pérez de Cuéllar met John McCarthy, the British journalist who had spent five and half years in appalling conditions as a prisoner in the Lebanon. When Pérez de Cuéllar left office at the end of 1991, all but two of the Western hostages were released. When, in front of the world's cameras on the tarmac at RAF Lyneham on August 11, McCarthy had handed him a letter from Islamic Jihad, it was the culmination of years of diplomacy. Granted, Pérez de Cuéllar's success was largely thanks to the seismic changes in world affairs and in the end the kidnap groups had become a liability to their sponsors. But, for a long time, Pérez de Cuéllar was Iran's only link. It was through the Iran's State President, Ali Akbar Rafsanjani and Pérez de Cuéllar's secret go-between, Assistant Secretary General, Giandomenico Picco, that many deals were effected. What Iran wanted was international recognition that it was Iraq's attack on Iranian territory on September 22, 1980 which started the eight-year war with Iran. Iran wanted compensation for the civilian Iranian airbus shot down over the Gulf in 1988 by US missiles and she wanted the return of four of her citizens who had disappeared without trace from the Iranian embassy in Beirut in June, 1982 when Israel invaded the Lebanon. Rafsanjani trusted Pérez de Cuéllar and Picco. Picco met the families of the four missing men in Tehran and made pleas on their behalf but he was not successful. Picco concluded the missing Iranians were probably killed by Christian militiamen. When Iran returned to the international community, it was Pérez de Cuéllar who welcomed her back. In the end, it suited everyone to use him, particularly Britain, who could deny breaking a vow not to deal with hostage takers, and Israel who could deny dealing with enemies. Through Iran's UN Ambassador Kamal Kharrazi, Pérez de Cuéllar traded the freeing of all Western hostages in the Lebanon. The deal also included ninety-one Lebanese returned home and the remains of fifteen more. There were grim exchanges. Just days before Pérez de Cuéllar retired, the decomposing body of the blue helmet, US Marine Lieutenant Colonel William Higgins, abducted in February, 1988, from his command of the UN Truce Supervisory Force, was found dumped in a Beirut street. Returned too were skeletal remains of William Buckley, who seven years previously, had been in charge of the CIA operation in Beirut when he was kidnapped by the pro-Iranian Islamic Jihad.

Others did not come back. There remained forty-four members of the UN and related agencies missing in the region. There was little concern from the member governments for staff killed, injured or kidnapped whilst on UN service. Picco tried to find them, but he was not successful.

From the chancelleries of Peru to the summit in New York, Pérez de Cuéllar was a model diplomat who hears, speaks and sees no evil. He won the confidence of the world's powers and pariahs and, at midnight on December 31, 1991, he became the only Secretary General in history to leave office in some triumph. This betrayed the legacy left to his successor.

13. THE MOGADISHU LINE

When Boutros Boutros-Ghali made his inaugural speech as the sixth Secretary General of the UN, it was the culmination of his two-year campaign for office. Boutros-Ghali, a former Egyptian deputy prime minister, was a man of the Third World, an African-Arab, and a Coptic Christian married to an Egyptian Jew – and who spoke French. The Security Council thought him a perfect neutral. Among the five permanent members this gave him a built-in, natural majority. At sixty-eight, Boutros-Ghali's age was against him but doubts were dismissed after President Bush's White House doctor gave him a medical.

Boutros-Ghali, the first African to hold the office of Secretary General, made ambitious promises. He said he would adapt the UN to the new, post-Cold War world, strive for Third World development, streamline UN operations and strengthen UN peacekeeping. He said that by the UN's fiftieth anniversary in 1995, there had to have been a fundamental renewal. He believed that there was a "fervent desire to raise the banner of peace" and that the course decided now would determine the UN's future for the next generation. An immense opportunity presented itself; not since the end of the Second World War had the expectations of the world's people depended so much upon the capacity of the UN. "A better world is within our reach. It is time to move forward . . . towards the realisation of the vast potential of this organisation and to bring new life to the world of the Charter", he wrote.

Such certainties were echoed in the Security Council. At the end of January 1992 the Council held its first meeting at summit level, a meeting billed as "an unprecedented recommitment . . . to the purposes and principles of the Charter". The UN was entering a new chapter. The summit was inspired by Britain whose diplomats maintained that a chance should be given to the world's influential leaders to establish a role for the UN in the New World Order. "Now that the Cold War is over", the Foreign Secretary Douglas Hurd wrote in the *Guardian* newspaper, "the UN, and particularly the Security Council, is working as the founding fathers intended." Britain held the Presidency of the Council that January and Prime Minister John Major, facing a general election at home, spoke grandly of a reaffirmation of the principles of collective security and the need for preventive diplomacy. "The aim must be to equip the UN to lead in crisis prevention", he said.

But practical proposals were avoided. President Mitterand could interest no one in his idea to revitalise the Council's Military Staff Committee, in spite of his promise that France would provide the Council with a rapid reaction force of 1,000 troops available at forty-eight hours' notice. American attitudes were unchanged: a committee was ill-suited to military planning and command. Their only concrete suggestion was a request to the new Secretary General to formulate some ideas to expand the peacekeeping, peace enforcing and preventive diplomacy.

The five permanent members planned another Security Council summit for January 1995, the start of the UN's fiftieth anniversary year, which would be a grand restatement of everything the UN stood for and the proper role of the great powers within it. The summit never took place.

There was no doubt that in January 1992 the triumphant Security Council meeting marked a turning point. The first meeting at the level of heads of states and government, after it was over, the UN enjoyed an enhanced international reputation and there was a remarkable expansion of UN activity. In the Secretariat, it was in the Department of Peacekeeping Operations that the greatest challenges were felt. Shortly after the world leaders returned to their capitals, the Council voted to create the UN's biggest mission for Cambodia. That same month saw the expansion of the UN Angola Verification Mission II where more than 500 UN observers went to implement the Peace Accords. UN personnel were in El Salvador to verify a peace agreement, on the Iraq-Kuwait border a UN commission was drawing a boundary line, and the Council, together with the International Atomic Energy Authority, was to eliminate

Iraq's mass destruction capability. UN personnel were supervising a compensation fund for Kuwait. These missions broke new ground and in addition to military personnel a substantial number of experts in human rights, health, finance, engineering and administration were required. The Secretariat was overburdened and soon the strains began to show. Boutros-Ghali was quickly discovering the gulf between the tasks imposed and the means to carry them out.

In the summer of 1992 the UN hit a discordant note. In August, a public, humiliating and embarrassing row over resources ensued between Boutros-Ghali and the British. Boutros-Ghali refused to endorse a plan for UN troops to supervise heavy weapons around the besieged city of Sarajevo in Bosnia-Hercegovina. Weapons' supervision was written into a peace agreement concluded in London. Boutros-Ghali complained that it was most unusual for the UN to be asked to help implement an agreement in which it played no part. He accused Lord Carrington, the European Community's negotiator, of assigning tasks to UN troops without consulting him and told Carrington that the peacekeepers in Sarajevo were already stretched to breaking point and the troops did not even know where the heavy weapons were to be found. If the UN troops tried to collect the weapons the UN would be drawn into "a new Vietnam". The heavy weapons' supervision would drain UN resources much needed elsewhere. Boutros-Ghali pointed out that regional organisations had greater resources than the UN, resources which could be harnessed at a time of crisis. He wanted the Europeans and NATO to take over the UN's mission in former Yugoslavia and to provide their own troops. At the time, only field ambulance and other related services were provided by European nations for the UN's mission to former Yugoslavia. Many UN members were critical that the Europeans negotiated ceasefires which did not hold and expected other UN members to provide soldiers on the ground. Boutros-Ghali told Council members that in agonising over former Yugoslavia they were concentrating on a "war of the rich". There were thirty armed conflicts around the world and most did not flicker across Western television screens. He believed that the real problems of the next ten years were going to be mainly in the countries of the Third World and they would not only be military confrontations but the problems of refugees, hunger, drought. For Boutros-Ghali, Somalia wa the first test of his mandate.

Three months after the triumphant 1992 summit, the Council found one tragedy eclipsing the other. In Somalia hundreds of people were dying every day from starvation. In disease-ridden camps pneumonia, tuberculosis and measles were rife. Child beggars filled the streets. "People are dying like flies", a Médecins sans Frontières doctor said. The entire country was reliant on food aid. Rival clans were vying for control of food distribution. The famine in Somalia in 1992 was worse than that of Ethiopia in 1985. The newspapers called it the world's worst horror story.

In former Yugoslavia the savagery was enormous: concentration camps had returned to Europe and the Security Council created a large UN mission with 14,000 civilian staff and peacekeepers. In Somalia, where more than half the six million population was on the verge of starvation, there was no UN presence at all. Was the compassion of the West racially based? African ambassadors said that Somalia was a silent genocide, caused by the neglect of the great powers to clean up their Cold War mess. The northern port of Berbera once suited great power strategic interests and was used by the Soviet Navy and then the US Navy. Somalia was now an orphan and her people had suffered a three-year civil war. Gunmen roved across the country's fertile land and throughout Southern Somalia, stripping huge areas of livestock and food and displacing hundreds of thousands of people. Families were travelling from place to place in desperate searches for food. Somalia was awash with weapons from the disbanded armies of the former Ethiopian dictator Mengistu Haile Mariam and his Somali counterpart, Siad Barre, whose brutal, corrupt and inefficient rule lasted twenty-two years. The Somali army, first equipped by the Soviets and then the US, was one of the most powerful military machines in Africa. It was now dispersed among warlords. Somalia had descended into hell.

The Somali capital, Mogadishu, once a beautiful city with white stucco villas, tree-lined boulevards and Italian-style pavement cafés, was destroyed. In early 1992, 11,000 people were killed there in battles between rival gangs. The streets were full of wild marauding thugs, youths with machine guns who drove about in "technicals", jeeps and trucks armed with anti-aircraft guns and rocket launchers. In the markets the sale of grenades and ammunition was prevalent. The young fighters looted the food aid and voluntary workers were having to recruit armed guards for protection; some organisations were paying $100,000 per month for the privilege. It was the only time the International Committee of the Red Cross had allowed such payment. As for the UN agencies, most pulled out in 1991, leaving the International Committee of the Red Cross and a small number of non-governmental organisations including Médecins sans Frontières and Save the Children who were attempting to draw attention to the deteriorating situation. There was no overall UN strategy for the country, a lack of co-ordination between the UN agencies and no concerted attempt to try to prevent the country's total collapse. The UN agencies were despised by many voluntary workers and many of them held officials criminally negligent for not acting to prevent the Somali tragedy. Alex de Waal, Associate Director of the human rights group Africa Watch said the tragedy was not caused by a lack of funds but by institutional inertia. De Waal said: "The scale of incompetence, callousness, greed and sloth in the specialised agencies of the UN that deal with famine relief is horrifying." Parts of Somalia looked like a post-nuclear wasteland. One million people had sought refuge in neighbouring states and were living in overcrowded and disease-ridden camps. There were fears the Horn of Africa would destabilise.

This massive tragedy could not leave the Security Council unmoved and a deployment of blue helmets in Somalia was approved in April 1992. It was minimal. It was a small mission with only 500 troops and fifty unarmed observers who were to oversee a fragile ceasefire between two warlords fighting for control in Mogadishu, the "Interim President", Ali Mohammed and the Chair of the United Somali Congress, General Farah Aideed. The ceasefire was negotiated by the Organisation of African Unity in Addis Ababa, the League of Arab States and the UN. The Americans objected to the mission at first. Congress would never approve payment for yet another UN operation, but the objections were later undercut by public horror and total UN humiliation at the scale of the catastrophe.

The diplomats tried to build fast on the ceasefire; the Organisation of African Unity promised a national reconciliation conference. The Security Council promised that if the ceasefire held, there would be an expansion of UN relief. Though there was an impetus for a settlement, when the commitment of the Security Council was put to the test, the UN force, the vital external support to enable the ceasefire to hold, failed to arrive. Although the UN's Office of Planning and Support and the Department of Peacekeeping

Operations found a country willing to contribute soldiers, no country was willing to provide transport to Somalia. It was not until July that the UN observers turned up in Mogadishu and the troops from Pakistan, airlifted eventually in September, were unable to leave the confines of the airport first, because there were no barracks available and, second, the gangs on technicals were not going to allow troops to deprive them of their authority and their access to food, now Somalia's main currency. One of the warlords, Mohammed Farrah Aideed, insisted that the blue helmets be unarmed. At the time, an average of forty Somali civilians a day were admitted to Mogadishu's Digfer Hospital with bullet wounds. The situation was so anarchic that Somali fighters managed to strip a UN relief ship of all its fuel oil together with 200 tons of food. Fears that the Pakistani UN troops would be massacred led to the Security Council authorising a further 3,000 troops to Mogadishu.

On November 10, the director of the American government Office of Foreign Disaster Assistance, James Kunder, said that Somalia was the single worst humanitarian crisis in the world. Boutros-Ghali told the Council that the tragedy was a threat to international peace and stability and that the Council had a moral duty to respond. To the outside world the Security Council looked like a callous debating society and it might well have continued to do nothing but talk had the US not made a dramatic gesture in offering to send in the marines. In a broadcast to the nation, the outgoing President, George Bush, mindful of his role and recently beaten in the election by Bill Clinton, announced a force of American troops to rescue Somalia. It would be called Operation Restore Hope. "Only the United States", said Bush, "has the global reach to place a large security force on the ground in such a distant place quickly and efficiently and, thus, save thousands of innocents from death." They were words that were to haunt his successor.

On December 3, the Security Council invoked Chapter Seven and created a military intervention for humanitarian purposes, an historic precedent and the first time that all necessary means were given to establish a secure environment for the delivery of aid to the starving.

With the storming of Somali beaches by American troops in the glare of television lights on December 9, Boutros-Ghali was ecstatic.

There were to be 28,000 Americans along with a further 17,000 from twenty other countries and Boutros-Ghali believed the situation would stabilise quickly. In Somalia itself there was less enthusiasm. Although this was the largest humanitarian mission ever, it was considered to be media-driven and one agency, Médecins sans Frontières, said that what the UN really needed was a coherent long-term strategy. Such arguments were lost. Bush announced that the troops were going to do God's work and the American press was enthusiastic. The *Los Angeles Times* headlined a story: "Bush sending troops to save millions from starvation". The *Washington Post* commented: "The weaponry of Somalia's armed factions appears to be no match for a well-trained division of American ground troops with night vision capability, protected in armoured personnel-carriers and amphibious landing vehicles and operating with air support for helicopter gunships." All of this was in accordance with the Colin Powell doctrine. Chairman of the Joint Chiefs of Staff and an architect of Operation Desert Storm, Powell believed in intervention by US troops only with overwhelming force, clear policy guidelines and a clear exit strategy. Powell's military men called it the principle of "doability".

Only the US ambassador to Kenya broke ranks. In a strongly worded warning to Washington, Smith Hempstone told the Under Secretary of State for International Security Affairs Frank G. Wisner that the Somali clans were tougher and meaner than Washington thought and that they would harass US troops. Hempstone said help was as compelling in the Sudan where a cycle of civil war and famine was causing great suffering. But such thoughts were brushed aside and in the new year Bush flew to Somalia to announce that Operation Restore Hope was a reality. He lifted a Somali orphan in his arms. "It's a beautiful, wonderful mission", he said.

Boutros-Ghali hoped the US-led mission in Somalia would set a precedent in the post-Cold War era. It was not to be. From the very beginning there were problems with Washington. According to John Bolton, Assistant Secretary of State for International Organisations, on the day that the American troops landed on the beaches, Boutros-Ghali started to talk about an American obligation to disarm the warlords. American officials were surprised and denied that disarmament was part of their mandate. A rift developed. The US maintained their only mission was to deliver food to stop the famine. Their troops would use force only to remove obstructions to a relief effort. What bothered Boutros-Ghali was that if the Mogadishu warlords were to be allowed to keep their weapons, the UN would never be able to resume control when the time came for the US troops to leave and hand the mission back to the UN. He believed that disarmament was at the heart of the problem; without it, Somalia stood little chance.

When the time came for the US troops to leave, the US was accused of exaggerating the success of Operation Restore Hope. There was an indecent haste to get the troops out of Somalia. But the US did improve conditions. The port of Mogadishu reopened, most of the looting ended. The "technicals" stayed off the streets. The number of people daily receiving treatment for gunshot wounds reduced. Key ports and hundreds of miles of roads were repaired and food and medical supplies moved deep into the country. The death rates were down. The price of a fifty-pound sack of wheat fell from $100 to about $10 although the price of an AK-47 had risen from $50 to $1000. Some of the heavier weapons were in storage sites. But as the time neared for the UN to take over there was unrest. Shootouts and skirmishes between the US troops and Somali gunmen occurred frequently. Without the backbone of the US force the UN would be vulnerable. "Anybody who thinks the UN won't be tested", said a State Department official, "doesn't know Somalia." What worried officials in the Secretariat was that of the 28,000 troops mandated for the take-over mission, only 16,000 of them had arrived.

The hand-over went ahead anyway. On May 4, 1993 US troops lowered the Stars and Stripes over the Mogadishu headquarters and command transferred to the UN. Somalia was now in the hands of Boutros-Ghali's recently appointed Special Representative for Somalia, retired US Navy Admiral Jonathan Howe, a former Commander in Chief, Allied Forces, Southern Europe.

Howe was in charge of an unprecedented UN enterprise, larger even than the mission for Camobodia. When the US-led Operation Restore Hope was originally conceived, it was envisaged that the mission would return to peacekeeping once the Americans had left. But now peacekeeping was abandoned. Under Resolution 814 of March 26, 1993, the Council decided that what Somalia needed was an enforcement operation to restore law and order. US Ambassador Madeleine Albright was enthusiastic. She said the UN was to "embark on an unprecedented enterprise aimed at nothing less than the restoration of an entire country as a proud, functioning and viable member of the community of nations". The UN was to re-establish the Somali police force, repatriate thousands of refugees, remove thousands of landmines, monitor an arms embargo, facilitate disarmament and provide aid.

Built into a peace agreement between fifteen chiefs of Somalia's warring clans the Resolution provided for a three-tiered federal-style administration. A National Council was the key element, allowing negotiators to satisfy the fears of smaller groups and clans. More importantly, the agreement committed the Somali factions to complete simultaneous disarmament throughout the country within ninety days and although they signed the agreement, warlords in Mogadishu read Resolution 814 as the first direct challenge to their power. Clan leaders who sat back in the face of US firepower were not intending the same for the UN. The warlords watched the UN force slowly assemble: a patchwork of troops from Italy, Morocco, France, Pakistan, Nigeria, Egypt and Turkey.

The Council had mandated 28,000 troops and civilian staff. The troops were to be equipped with armoured personnel-carriers, tanks and attack helicopters. Member states were urged to contribute on an emergency basis to enable the UN to deter attack effectively. The reality was somewhat different. Howe was shocked. The operation was desperately understaffed and ill-equipped and Howe had to plead for troops and equipment. He persuaded the US to leave some troops behind. "The US turned over some troops because I begged them", he remembered. The US left behind its 1,200 strong Quick Reaction Force which would include an army battalion and a helicopter squadron. The US would also leave 2,700 troops for logistics. Machinery was in desperately short supply; the UN wanted the US to leave behind its air control equipment.

The Secretary General appointed Lieutenant General Cevik Bir from Turkey as UN force commander and his deputy, an American, Major General Thomas Montgomery. Montgomery would keep control of the Quick Reaction Force. With Admiral Howe as Special Representative, there were suspicions that this mission to Somalia was going to be dominated by the US.

The tragedy begins on the morning of June 5, when Pakistani commanders, in accordance with orders from mission headquarters, directed soldiers to inspect several weapons dumps in Mogadishu, in accordance with the terms of the Council mandate. Under an existing agreement with the warlords in Mogadishu, the weapons' sites remained under their control with UN troops permitted inspection. One of the warlords, Aideed, was told about the inspection, but this was as far as peacekeeping practice went. Further requirements were ignored. It is peacekeeping policy to reach agreement between the parties about how inspections are to proceed, otherwise there could be trouble. On this occasion, for want of expert advice, this did not happen. One of Aideed's lieutenants threatened all out war if the inspection went ahead as planned. The Pakistanis were not told about the threat.

On the morning of the search a hostile crowd gathered outside one of the weapons dumps which also housed the tramsmitting equipment for Radio Mogadishu, owned by Aideed, which spewed forth anti-UN propaganda. The crowd was angry and accused the troops of wanting to destroy the radio station. A Somali was shot, probably killed trying to snatch a Pakistani rifle and the Pakistanis, trying to get back to their base, were ambushed. In another part of town three Pakistanis were already dead. Armed only with rifles strung over their shoulders they were distributing sacks of wheat when a mob hacked them to death. Howe later described how the whole town erupted as if on cue: it was like the Wild West with AK-47s. Every Pakistani soldier was vulnerable; they had no tanks or armoured personnel-carriers for protection and no contingency plan for such an occurrence. The ambushed Pakistanis who had conducted the weapons search were in urgent need of help; only the Italian contingent had tanks and it took five hours for them to arrive. In the meantime Italian soldiers, hovering overhead in helicopters and unable to locate the precise position of Somali gunmen, had opened fire with machine-guns, injuring three Pakistani soldiers. By the end of the day, twenty-three Pakistani soldiers had been murdered and fifty-seven injured, many with appalling wounds. It was the highest peacekeeping casualty figure since the Congo.

The next day in New York, in Resolution 837, and under the enforcement powers of the Charter the Council mandated all necessary measures to arrest Aideed. He and his lieutenants were held responsible for public incitement and the murders of the UN troops. The Resolution emphasised the crucial importance of disarming the warlords and neutralising the radio broadcasting system which was spreading anti-UN propaganda. In Mogadishu, at UN mission headquarters, the Resolution was interpreted allowing for the destruction of Aideed's power base. Resolution 837 was a point of no return and a new term entered peacekeeping vocabulary. The Mogadishu line would henceforth be the name for the dividing line between keeping the peace and the dangerous task of using military means to enforce it.

The line was crossed six days later in a hail of missile fire and cannon bursts overhead. There were arms searches, aerial bombardments of weapons sites by airborne AC-130 gun ships and the destruction by bombing of Radio Mogadishu. "If UN peacekeepers are to be effective agents for peace and stability in Somalia and elsewhere," Clinton announced in Washington, "they must be capable of using force when necessary to defend themselves and accomplish their goals." In New York, Boutros-Ghali reminded everyone how he had urged the US to disarm the factions; "Everybody would have been much better off had it been done sooner," he said.

From now and throughout the summer of 1993 an untold number of Somali civilians were killed in raid after raid by US forces, under US command. "It became", a UN lawyer said in New York, "a rogue operation." The American Quick Reaction Force swept through Aideed's strongholds while Somali casualties littered the hospitals. The high civilian casualty was partly blamed on the Somali fighters' use of women and children as active participants, a strategy which became increasingly more common. At one point the US shelled the hospital accusing Aideed's militia of using it as a vantage point to fire on troops. In September, an American helicopter opened fire on women and children "posing an imminent threat against our soldiers". One US operation alone killed more than fifty Somalis and wounded more than 170, including key religious and clan elders. Although these American operations were outside the command and control of the UN, to the Somali people and most aid workers it was the UN, the organisation set up to ensure the observance of human rights, which was flouting them with impunity.

Boutros-Ghali distanced himself. He said the raids in Somalia were conducted by the US under US command and that the UN had been obliged to agree to this as a condition of maintaining a US military presence in May. He denied any personal involvement in the extraordinary decision to put up wanted posters offering a $25,000 reward for the fugitive Aideed. Boutros-Ghali blamed Howe for the posters although Howe maintained this was not so and said that at every important juncture, decisions went through the Secretary General. Aideed taunted the UN forces by appearing on an American television news programme saying that the UN was making war on the Somali people.

In the UN force there was insurrection. Other troop contingents accused the US-led Quick Reaction Force of wrapping themselves in UN blue to carry out Rambo-like raids and of not even telling the UN they were about to take place. Italy threatened to pull out her 800 soldiers. "A peace mission is transforming itself into an operation of war and that's no longer acceptable", said Carlo Azeglio Ciampi, Italy's Chief of Staff. Every contingent had a different approach which led to antagonism. The Italian and Nigerian troops nearly came to blows. Nigerian soldiers had fired at a roadblock while Italians, on the other side, were conducting negotiations. The Nigerians alleged that the Italians had failed to come to their help when asked to do so. At one point, Boutros-Ghali had demanded the removal of the Italian Commander, General Bruno Loi, but later retracted. The mission was a mess.

When President Bill Clinton assumed office in January 1993 he brought to Washington a renewed commitment to the UN. Clinton was committed to reversing previous American policy and early on a new post of Assistant Secretary General for Peacekeeping and Democracy was created in the Pentagon. There were new offices for peacekeeping in the State Department. Ambassador Madeleine Albright pledged that the US would ensure that the UN would be equipped with a capacity to plan, organise, lead and service peacekeeping. But after a few months in New York Albright was describing the Secretariat as "programmed amateurism and a near-total absence of contingency planning, lack of centralised command and control". The military and civilian components of peacekeeping were "hastily recruited, ill-equipped and often unprepared". Clinton lost enthusiasm, certainly by the time of his maiden speech to the General Assembly on September 28, 1993. "The UN simply cannot become engaged in every one of the world's conflicts," he said. "If the American people are to say yes to UN peacekeeping, the

UN must know when to say no." Since America had been enthusiastic about the creation of the new UN missions in the Security Council, and was one of the few nations with the power to have vetoed them, there were quite a few ambassadors sitting in the Assembly who were unimpressed with this first speech.

During his visit to the UN that day Clinton warned Boutros-Ghali that Congressional opposition to American troops in Somalia was becoming so strong that without progress towards reconciliation, the US troops would pull out. Aideed was still on the loose and the Pentagon wanted a review of the Somalia policy. Boutros-Ghali was horrified at talk of exit plans for US troops. He later wrote a pleading letter to Clinton: "Actual withdrawal of the force would in my judgment lead to the rapid decomposition of the whole . . . operation". Withdrawal would condemn the people of Somalia to a resumption of civil war and all the horrors that would result to say nothing of what it would mean for the UN. It would be tantamount to "a humbling of the UN and of the efforts of the US and other countries to restore peace and human decency to Somalia".

In Mogadishu only half the required civilian staff had arrived. In the confusion of hastily setting up the mission the sum of some $4 million went missing. There were no banks in Mogadishu and the money which arrived in leather pouches, needed to pay Somali staff, was kept in a locked filing cabinet. The theft was thought to have been an inside job although the culprit was never found. The missing money became a popular story and would be quoted as symbolic of UN mismanagement, appalling inefficiency and waste. Howe, meanwhile, was trying to obtain equipment for the UN troops; he needed tanks and personnel-carriers as most of the Third World contingents had no protection. He prepared a list of his needs for Boutros-Ghali to take to Western capitals. Though his list was specific, in the end all he received were some 1950s tanks from the US which were in storage in Turkey.

Howe eventually came round to the conclusion that only special forces would be able to arrest Aideed. The British SAS turned it down and after that the idea went on hold. But after the deaths in August of four US military policemen, blown up in a remote-controlled detonated bomb, attention focused again on the possibility of special operatives. Later that month Clinton authorised the despatch to Mogadishu of the best soldiers the Pentagon could offer.

The US special forces arrived in Mogadishu in late August, 1993. There were 400 Army Rangers and a number of Delta Force commandos; Delta specialised in counter-terrorism, in hostage rescue and its presence was classified information. The Army Rangers, an elite paratroop unit was, like Delta, part of the Pentagon's special operations. No fanfare greeted their arrival in Somalia but even as they were bunkering down at the airport, they were fired at with mortars. In their early missions they failed to impress; they arrested an Aideed lookalike by mistake and raided a house which belonged to the UN Development Programme. In another operation the Rangers arrested a staunch Aideed opponent and former head of Somali national Security, General Ahmed Jili'ow.

It was their last mission which would be most remembered and, the day it started, Howe was returning from Ethiopia and his aeroplane was unable to land. He had no idea what was happening. All he knew was that Mogadishu was paralysed by fighting. The UN was blamed for what happened that day and the tragedy would be called a UN fiasco. It was not. When the secret operation began, the UN knew nothing about it.

That day, October 3, the Rangers had received intelligence from a few of the twenty or so CIA operatives in the town that Aideed's senior loyalists were meeting in a building about one mile east of the central Bakara market. The plan was to arrest the principle lieutenants in order to force Aideed to be more visible. The raid was to take just fifteen minutes and was to be a Rambo-like snatch; the Rangers would slide down ropes from helicopters and arrest the lieutenants who would be taken to a twelve-vehicle convoy nearby. The operation was to be carried out by the Third Battalion 75th Rangers whose infantry unit in Mogadishu was commanded by Major General William Garrison, commander of the Joint Special Operations Command. General Garrison's presence in Mogadishu was classified. He consulted with General Wayne A. Downing, overall commander of US Special Operations and General Joseph P. Hoar, head of the US Central Command in Tampa, Florida.

At first, the operation went as planned. The Delta commandos got their men. But Rangers in helicopters were hit by a barrage of weapon fire and a Black Hawk helicopter was shot down by a rocket-propelled grenade and its crew were killed. A second helicopter was shot down and the pilot was captured. Approximately 100 Rangers stormed to the rescue. They came under intense fire and found they could not get out from the densely packed tin shacks and houses. By nightfall the US elite force was trapped. Helicopter rescue would be useless. Only soldiers in tanks could get them out.

The UN came to the rescue. In a truly international effort, the battle to free the US soliders lasted most of the night. Troops from the US Quick Reaction Force grouped together with four Pakistani tanks and twenty-eight Malaysian armoured personnel-carriers took two hours to travel a short distance to the trapped Americans. The convoy came under constant attack. Two Malaysian armoured vehicles were destroyed by rocked-propelled grenades and a Malaysian driver was killed, the Americans with him injured. The Pakistani tanks were old (the 1950s models from Turkey) and at one point they ran out of fuel; the Malaysian commander had nightvision equipment but had been called to duty so suddenly he forgot it. The Rangers and Delta force commandos were scattered and many had to be rescued one by one. It was an exhausting and humiliating retreat but by early morning all American wounded were evacuated. There remained on everyone's television screen the body of a American servicemen being dragged through the streets to a jeering and jubilant crowd. There was a feeling of deep grief among the Americans, a Pakistani commander recalled. "There were heavy hearts, they were in a state of shock." These were images akin to those from Vietnam.

Aideed's men, portrayed as a bunch of rag-tag militia, were in fact well commanded by former officers of the national armed forces, some Soviet-trained. They were operating in their own familiar urban maze where they knew every twist and turn. They had hundreds of rocket-propelled grenades stockpiled in weapons caches and, after the battle, Aideed's local prestige could not have been higher. The world's "globo-cop" had failed to find him.

A total of eighteen Americans and one Malaysian were killed, eighty-four Americans and seven Malaysians wounded, casualties unlike any seen in the US army since Vietnam. A patchy video of some of the fighting, taken from an American helicopter, showed such horrible mutilation that the film was immediately classified. As many as 1,000 Somalis were believed killed and the Somalis took to calling the war-shattered neighbourhood where the fighting occurred, Bosnia.

President Clinton visited the Walter Reed Army Medical Centre to meet the American wounded. One soldier had lost his right hand, his right leg, sight and hearing. "Clinton was visibly moved", a doctor said. "He did not know what to say."

The battle in Mogadishu robbed the US of any further appetite for UN peackeeping. The Clinton administration distanced itself quickly, and maintained correctly that the doomed mission had been "under the authority of the UN". Within months a Presidential Directive was issued which set limits on future American involvement with the UN. The reaction from Congress was swift. Funding for peacekeeping was cut and, when the Republicans swept into Congress in 1994, a further retreat was inevitable. Many Republicans were prepared to write the UN off. Soon a National Security Revitalisation Act was proposed to cut $1 billion from the US peacekeeping contribution. This could effectively cripple all UN efforts and destroy any chance of an international security system. Congress prepared a Peace Powers Act to make it impossible for the President to commit troops to UN operations. In future no American would be asked to sacrifice his or her life for a purpose not related to the defence or in the interests of the United States. "We must stop placing the agenda of the UN before the interests of the US," said the Senate Republican leader, Bob Dole.

As for the Security Council, it ordered an enquiry and concluded that ex-gratia payments should be made to Somali civilians who suffered injury and recommended that the UN refrain from further enforcement actions. "We were a bunch of diplomatic amateurs," the New Zealand Ambassador Colin Keating recalled. If ever there was a case for the involvement of a Military Staff Committee this would have been it. "The UN has had forty-five years of stunted growth and it is not yet ready to deal with all this." The ambassador for Pakistan, Jamsheed Marker believed that a lack of resources was the biggest impediment.

The "Mogadishu line" would be used in future to delineate the difference between peacekeeping and peace enforcement. The line became something to dread. Sir Michael Rose, one-time Commander of UN forces in the former Yugoslavia, used it often and warned politicians to beware of it. "Once you start acting like that," Rose said, "you are crossing the River Styx." It meant loss of control. "Once on the other side," a British Army peacekeeping document details, "there is very little chance of getting back and the only way out is likely to be by leaving . . . " The British Defence Secretary, Malcolm Rifkind, believed that crossing the line meant becoming partisans in a war.

The effort by the world community to rescue and rebuild Somalia ended in March, 1995 when the UN pulled out completely. The world was unlikely to see a similar resort to military force. The Security Council had tried to apply traditional peacekeeping to a civil war and the result had been the loss of UN prestige, credibility and US leadership. Launched in the afterglow of the Gulf War, Somalia was to be a new type of operation. "The international community will be very careful in future," said a peacekeeping official. "We've learned . . . that (troop contributing) states don't want to take casualties . . . you can't do coercive disarmament." The UN had neither the expertise, structure nor resources to control forces in combat.

While the world watched Somalia, the UN had some achievements. Few countries were as devastated by war as Cambodia and its tragedy bridged both eras, from the heady days of the triumphant Security Council in 1992, to those when violence and tragedy filled the post-Cold War vacuum. For years the UN had stood idly by, even when the Cambodian people were victim to the most genocidal regime since the fall of Nazi Germay in 1945. The Khmer Rouge was one of the most heinous forces in history and yet, because of the overriding national interests of states, it had a seat in the General Assembly.

The post-Cold War world brought change and, in 1990, an Australian peace initiative was approved by a united Security Council. The peace effort led to a plan for a rescue of Cambodia by the UN: peacekeepers would oversee a transition to democracy. They called it the UN Transitional Authority in Cambodia, UNTAC, and it was to assume executive power and take control of foreign affairs, defence, press and finance. At the time it was the UN's most ambitious mission with 22,000 people including troops, police monitors, election officials and civilian administrators.

Most commentators predicted failure. Even while the Security Council was finalising a plan, the Khmer Rouge refused to honour its commitments and continued its terror, refusing to take part in the elections. The problems the mission faced were huge. There were an estimated seven million landmines laid in Cambodia which had rendered large parts of arable land unusable. In some areas 700 people a month lost their lives or limbs through landmines; many victims were children tending cattle. Cambodians literally risked life and limb scavenging for food and Cambodia had the highest proportion of amputees in the world.

Sir Anthony Parsons, a former British Ambassador to the UN, asked the one important question about the UN mission, a question most asked: why were so much time, trouble, manpower and expense committed there and so little elsewhere? Parsons thought that perhaps it was guilt. Cambodia had been massively bombed by US during the Vietnam war. By 1971 the US succeeded in bringing the war to the whole country, paving the way for the establishment of the Khmer Rouge regime. The Khmer Rouge changed its name to Democratic Kampuchea and restructured society. They murdered professional people killing hundreds of doctors, engineers, professors and lawyers. Their new "work sites" were part of a society without cities, with no property, money or families. Those who objected were eliminated in the most brutal ways, to save on bullets. There were no reliable statistics for the dead but some said that fatalaties amounted to two million people. Only an invasion in 1979 by the Vietnamese stopped the killing fields. A pro-Vietnamese government was formed which continued to be harrassed by the Khmer Rouge. In New York the murderous Democratic Kampuchea retained UN membership which suited both the US and Britain: Vietnam's war against the Khmer Rouge's secure Western bases was resupplied by the Soviets. In time Cambodia became a burden on Vietnam and Vietnam's decision in January 1989 that it would withdraw from Cambodia led to fears that the Khmer Rouge would return to power and that the genocide would begin again. A comprehensive UN settlement would reduce the prospect of a renewed Vietnamese involvement and would give Vietnam an opportunity to end its international isolation.

When the UN mission got underway in March 1992 in Phnom-Penh it seemed that every other car was a brand new Toyota with UN markings, and the city was smothered in UN blue. The cost of all this amounted to $2 billion and the mission was constantly criticised for its expense. Ill-discipline led to some UN contingents committing rape and robbery and there was little chance for the victims to obtain redress. There were extortion rackets and some soldiers stole UN equipment. The civilian staff too were criticised for extravagance.

The UN force was called a paper tiger. The Khmer Rouge refused to open its territory or disarm its forces and attacked Cambodian civilians, UN peacekeepers and slaughtered whole villages. Yet the

Security Council kept the way open to Khmer Rouge participation in the elections and never excluded it from Cambodia's sovereign council during transition. The twenty-nine countries contributing troops had no intention of trying to dislodge the Khmer Rouge. Vietnam once sent a 180,000-strong army to try to defeat the guerillas and failed. At one point, Yasushi Akashi, the Special Representative for Cambodia, was humiliated, forbidden to enter a Khmer Rouge area, a bamboo pole placed across his path. But by January 1993 the UN mission ensured that more than 4 million Cambodians, ninety-five per cent of the electorate, had registered to vote and an estimated 360,000 refugees had returned and thousands of political prisoners freed. Although the election was inconclusive, and there were allegations of fraud, an interim administration was established. There was a sharp drop in infant mortality, hundreds of roads were demined and reopened. The UN mission wound down and had left by November, 1993, staff staying just long enough to help the new Assembly draft the constitution. Peace was within reach, but not yet assured.

Cambodia lacked the institutions necessary for a mature democracy. The government, an uneasy alliance of former Communist rulers and one-time royalist guerillas, was corrupt. The notion of human rights brought in by the UN barely survived; all sides in the election committed gross human rights abuses which were left unpunished and the justice system was a shambles. The prisons were severly overcrowded and unsanitary, leading to malnutrition and disease. The government urgently needed international advice on a viable justice system. The Khmer Rouge remained a real threat and still had sufficient power to hamper the rebuilding of the country.

Elections do not produce justice or development and Cambodia remained one of the poorest countries in the world, its grinding poverty undermining society: malnutrition was endemic, less than twenty per cent of the population had access to clean water. There were not enough doctors, family planning was unavailable, two to four million landmines remained uncleared. Yet the mission in Cambodia was a crucial development in peacekeeping. In Namibia and Cambodia success was owing to the presence of a political settlement, to an exhaustion with war and a willingness for peace. What these missions taught was that even for limited success, large-scale field operations need advanced planning, clear mandates, trained peackeepers, assured financing, an effective and integrated UN command, logistical support and they have to be sustained by a united and purposeful Security Council. Without any of these prerequisites peacekeeping missions were doomed to failure.

If some believed that the New World Order was in trouble in Somalia, none could have imagined how catastrophic its end in former Yugoslavia would be. Boutros-Ghali was always reluctant about peacekeepers going to the Balkans and said later that the savagery of the war drained the attention, resources and emotion of the Security Council. Before the mission began, he warned that the UN's reputation would be tarnished and he feared the loss of peacekeepers' lives. Lord Carrington, who had led the European Community's peace effort for former Yugoslavia was more optimistic. "I am inclined to doubt", he said, "unless things go very wrong, that the Serbs will fire on blue helmets."

The mission to former Yugoslavia was the first to be created in the wake of the 1992 Security Council summit. Like the UN mission for Somalia, created two months later, the operation for former Yugoslavia was intended to be traditional peacekeeping. The decision to go to the Balkans was taken after a ceasefire agreed in February, 1992, negotiated between the Croats and the Serbs by Cyrus R. Vance, the UN's Special envoy. It was the fourteenth ceasefire in six months and by then the Yugoslav Army (JNA) and Serb forces had already overrun all ethnic Serb areas in Croatia. With the consent of the parties, UN personnel were needed to police four areas, Northern and Southern Krajina and Eastern and Western Slovenia. The troops would carry light weapons only but would give appearances of a strong force and be supplied with armoured personnel-carriers and helicopters. The mission would include 500 unarmed police monitors responsible for law enforce-ment and, under the agreement, the Yugoslav Army would withdraw under UN supervision and the Serb militia would surrender weapons to the UN. The Council's aim was to "create the conditions of peace and security required for the negotiation of an overall settlement". But the deployment of the troops was delayed while the great powers bickered about how much money the operation would cost. The funding of UN peacekeeping was by assessed contributions but the Big Five paid a larger share because of their special responsibility in the establishment of the operations.

Russia's finances were so perilous that it could not be expected to meet its share. There were doubts about a Congressional willingness to appropriate the necessary funding and the Council rejected Boutros-Ghali's initial estimate of $600 million for one year.

Although the Yugoslav Army withdrew, the ethnic Serb forces refused to disarm and only some heavy artillery was under UN control. The delay in deployment gave the militants a breathing space to plan for UN arrival and to hide large quantities of weapons. In New York the Department of Peacekeeping Operations struggled to find soldiers for the mission while Third World countries argued that this was a European problem. In spite of fine words at the Security Council summit, the British declined to provide troops, arguing commitment elsewhere, in Cyprus. States which did eventually provide soliders were Belgium, Luxembourg, Denmark and France but troops from the Third World were in a majority. The commander was an Indian Lt-General, Satish Nambiar.

The fears that a delay in deployment might cause the ceasefire to collapse were justified and when the fifteenth ceasefire had ended, Marrack Goulding, then Under Secretary General responsible for peacekeeping, recommended to Boutros-Ghali that the troops should not be sent. But deployment went ahead as planned and four UN-protected areas were created. There remained a lack of equipment and adequate transport. In Croatia, in the face of this lack of commitment by UN member governments, Cedric Thornberry, the UN's Director of Civil Affairs, told the press: "I am sorry to say we are not fast enough on the ground".

The headquarters for the UN's mission to Croatia were established in a former post office building in cosmopolitan Sarajevo, the capital of neighbouring Bosnia-Hercegovina. Sarajevo was an elegant city, known for its sophisticated cuisine and its religious tolerance but the war, frozen in Croatia, had moved further south and UN officers had bets on when full-scale war would begin in Bosnia-Hercegovina. The UN headquarters were shelled five times, caught up in the siege which started on April 4, 1992. The UN eventually evacuated on May 18, in an eighty-vehicle convoy. Only a few blue helmets were left behind. The evacuation convoy ran the gauntlet of Serbian roadblocks. At one of them militiamen fired over their heads. Negotiating the same ninety roadblocks the other way between Zagreb and Sarajevo was a convoy belonging to the UN High Commissioner for Refugees carrying medicines and food for Sarajevo's desperate population. Roadblocks along the way were staffed by ill-disciplined and drunken Bosnian Serb soliders under no authority. An International Red Cross convoy tried to get through but was hit by mortar bombs, killing its Swiss leader, and the food and medicines went up in flames.

The Serbs pounded Sarajevo with tanks, heavy artillery, mortars and rockets. The shelling was intermittent and left gaping holes in the streets and showered concrete blocks across the roads. The weaker Bosnian-Hercegovina government forces counter-attacked Serb strongholds in the city, including the suburb of Ilidza but the Serb stranglehold tightened. Some people tried to escape. One day several thousand women and children waited in a mile-long queue in the rain on the airport road but were eventually turned back as night fell by Serb militia with Kalashinikovs. On August 1, 1992 Serb snipers fired on a coach taking orphans out of the city. The snipers had high-powered rifles with telescopic sights and, after a first volley at the tyres they fired through the windows at the screaming children killing a fourteen-month-old boy and a mentally handi-capped girl aged three. Then the snipers ran down from the hills and divided the children by ethnic group and nine were forbidden to travel further because they were identified as Serbs.

The European community wanted the peacekeeping effort in Croatia extended to Bosnia-Hercegovina but Boutros-Ghali rejected the idea. There was no peace to keep. In May 1992 two officials from the Secretariat's Department of Peacekeeping Operations had gone to Sarajevo to try to discover whether the mission in Croatia should be extended for the neighbouring country. When they returned to New York they reported that Bosnia-Hercegovina was tragic, dangerous, violent and confused and not susceptible to peacekeeping. A peacekeeping operation would require the parties to respect the UN and one of the more distressing features in former Yugoslavia was that none of the parties did. The blue helmets in Croatia were abused, detained and disarmed by militiamen. UN property, uniforms and flags had been stolen.

"The worst prescription for any sort of action," said one of those experts, "is 'something must be done'." But Sarajevo was the focus of attention. Its crisis was too powerful to ignore. The conflict was tearing European credibility to shreds, the Security Council could not agree. Forceful intervention was already ruled out. Damage limitation became the only solution with peacekeeping the option. Boutros-Ghali was persuaded by the promises of adequate resources for the mission and, on June 8, the Security Council mandated 1,000 blue helmets to "facilitate" the opening of Sarajevo airport to ensure the unimpeded delivery of aid to the civilian population. The deployment would take place only if there were a ceasefire.

The Serbs willingly sucked the UN in and easily agreed that military observers could supervise the withdrawal of their anti-aircraft weapons systems from the range of airport runways and that the shelling around the airport would cease. The Council despatched a reconnaissance team with experts from other, long-established, peacekeeping missions from the Middle East. On June 19, in accordance with long-standing, peacekeeping procedures, secure locations for weaponry were agreed with the Serbs. The developments were encouraging and, in a much publicised valediction of policy, President François Mitterrand flew to Sarajevo for a six-hour visit on Sunday, June 28. On June 29, confident of this victory, the Security Council authorised more troops stationed at the airport. The following day the UN flag was raised and a French relief plane landed. It was a small victory, but seemed huge at the time.

The airlift of aid into Sarajevo airport, organised by the Office of the UN High Commissioner for Refugees, became the longest such airlift in aviation history but there was little peace to keep and the principal threat to the airport was the frequent firings at aircraft, mainly by the Bosnian Serbs with mortars and heavy machine-guns which were easily concealed and quickly moved. Shortly after the blue helmets arrived the Serbs resumed their brutal bombardment of Dobrinje, a suburb of Sarajevo close to the airport, built to house athletes in the 1984 Winter Olympics. From within Sarajevo the forces of Bosnia-Hercegovina government were fighting back. In July Boutros-Ghali told the Council: "the Sarajevo airport operation is based upon foundations of the utmost fragility". As for keeping the airport permanently open, military experts believed that to do it the UN would have to secure the surrounding hills and this would take in the region of 100,000 combat troops. Even then one soldier with a howitzer could close it again.

Alija Izetbegović, the President of Bosnia-Herzegovina, believed that the initial deployment of Canadian peacekeepers at Sarajevo's airport was a stunt aimed at assuaging Western guilt. The opening of the airport would solve only two per cent of the problem. He asked the UN for 15,000 peacekeepers to open other supply routes to beleaguered Muslim communities, cut off by the war. But he was told that peace was a pre-condition for deployment. As for peace enforcement, Izetbegović was told that many tens of thousands of troops would be required, many more than the Council would approve. Izetbegović asked for 77,000 infantry to unblock roads and to protect Sarajevo airport, but it was no use. The decision was made not to intervene militarily. "To send hundreds of thousands of people into a civil war", explained the British Secretary of Defence, Malcolm Rifkind, some time later, "and tell them to sort it out would be grossly improper, grossly irresponsible and would not work."

Soon, Bosnia-Hercegovina was destroyed. The Serbs helped themselves to two-thirds of it in order to create ethnically pure regions and the Croats helped themselves to bits that the Serbs did not want. Bosnia-Hercegovina was the shortest-lived country in Europe, brought to catastrophe by the war in Croatia between Serb and Croats and doomed the moment Croatia and Slovenia were recognised as independent states. Recognition left Bosnia-Hercegovina with three choices: to stay in Yugoslavia and be ruled by Serbia, to divide Bosnia between Serbs and Croats, or to become an independent state. The European Community urged Izetbegović to hold a referendum to decide the issue and Izetbegović believed that a referendum would fulfil one of the conditions required by the EC for recognition. He kept saying that the danger of war was past, but he was wrong. His government was shaky, the democracy fragile with an Assembly divided between Muslims with eighty-six seats, the Serbians seventy-two and the Croats forty-four. There was a seven-member collective Presidency and Izetbegović, a Muslim, was elected to head it. Although he maintained he had pluralist intentions a government based on national groups was hopeless. The Croatian Democratic Union (HDZ) and the Serbian Socialist Party (SPS) had increasingly nationalistic agendas.

The referendum was held in Bosnia-Hercegovina on March 1, 1992 and the Muslim and Croat populations voted for secession from Yugoslavia, and so did some of the Serbs. The rest of the Serbs, making up more than one-third of the country, declared the referendum to be illegal under the principle of the three constituent nations, Bosnia-Hercegovina's central mechanism of constitutional parity. In holding a referendum, Izetbegović had set in motion a fundamental constitutional change. The Serbs wanted their own parliament with a guaranteed constitutional connection to the others. Later on there were negotiations to divide Bosnia-Hercegovina into ethnic cantons but no plan secured the agreement of all three parties. The Security Council tried everything to find a solution: diplomatic isolation, high-level conferences, expulsion from the international family, arms and economic embargoes, naval blockades, no-fly zones, weapons monitoring. The priority was to prevent the conflict spreading. But once the Council had refused to undertake a combat role to push back the Serb forces, there was nothing left but a humanitarian mission for the victims.

In the Pentagon they call it "mission creep" when an operation's aims and policies are enlarged halfway through. This happened to the UN in Bosnia-Hercegovina. The mission grew. So desperate was the plight of Muslims cut off in Serb-conquered territory in towns and villages in Eastern Bosnia, around Srebrenica and Gorazde, that in 1992 with winter approaching the UN operation was stepped up to encompass humanitarian intervention. The Council mandated 4,000 troops to escort aid convoys for six winter routes. The troops would follow normal peacekeeping rules of engagement and could use force only when prevented from carrying out their mandate or in self-defence. There was considerable hesitation within the Department of Peacekeeping Operations about the Resolution and no one quite understood how the escorts would work in practice; the troops were to travel through on the basis of "negotiated passage" and there was a risk that they would be taken hostage by heavily armed Serbs. Military experts told Department officials that armed assistance for aid convoys would require combat troops; the dangers would not come from roadblocks but from fire by mortars and artillery located and hidden some distance from the road. The Secretary General warned, "for some of the parties the infliction of hardship on civilians is actually a war aim as it leads to the desired movement of people". In Bosnia-Hercegovina there was a "pre-disposition to use force to obstruct relief supplies". Unless there was respect on the ground for the freedom of movement for blue helmets they would not be able to fulfil their tasks. Boutros-Ghali again thought that this difficult operation must be taken over by European nations with their well-equipped armies and that the UN had neither the money nor troops for this sort of exercise. Britain promised soliders and in October the first British troops landed at Split.

By the end of 1992 Sarajevo was destroyed, her centuries old monuments, her precious libraries and her art reduced to rubble. Her shops and restaurants had been looted and every building of any consequence was damaged. Thousands of people were struggling for survival. In a highly unusual statement, Egyptian Brigadier-General Hussein Abdul al Razek, commanding a contingent of his UN troops at Sarajevo airport, felt that the mission was no longer worth it. "All our efforts here to save lives and restore utilities have completely failed," he said. The key peacekeeping ingredient of consent was lacking and the conditions for peacekeeping were inappropriate. The Council should send the Serbs an ultimatum and then intervene by force to save the population. The assessment was echoed when Lt-General Nambiar said that because the credibility of the troops was gone there were increasing blue helmet casualties. Boutros-Ghali despaired, told the Council that the performance by all sides at honouring agreements was "lamentable". There was less respect for a UN presence in former Yugoslavia than anywhere else in the world. Agreements were violated as routinely as they were signed. The UN troops at Sarajevo airport were powerless, their safety precarious. The no-fly zone which had been imposed by the Council on October 9, 1992 which was intended to prevent air attacks by Serbs against Croats and Muslims was breached. Every impediment placed in the way of blue helmets led to an increasing loss of authority. Blue helmet commanders asked for permission to proceed, allowed Serbs militia to inspect UN vehicles and complied when Serbs demanded to know the identity of all personnel, in breach of all peacekeeping rules. Aid was plundered. The lack of will of the great powers was obvious every day. An aircraft carrying UN commander, General Philippe Morillon of France, was fired at; a Danish blue helmet was briefly kidnapped. It was a taste of what was to come.

The people of Sarajevo gave up all hope that the UN would rescue them; the organisation capable of authorising Operation Desert Storm was not going to save their city. The UN, an organisation which Yugoslavs as a nation had ardently supported, would not even provide for them. Sarajevo hospital had no more blood, no antibiotics and only local anaesthetic. The aid convoys brought flour but there was no water to cook it with. The elderly and the sick were dying. "You have not come to save us", a doctor said to some blue helmets, "but to preside over our death."

Sarajevo was the symbol and its siege exposed those nations whose armies were part of mighty NATO. Conceived in 1949 at the height of the Cold War, NATO had been an alliance held together by political goals. It was a security umbrella. The most powerful military alliance in the world was not prepared to fight for a New World Order in its own backyard in Europe.

The recognition that former Yugoslavia had fallen into an abyss of human rights abuses owed much to memories of the Holocaust and the determination that systematic killing should never happen again. In 1945 genocide was a newly coined term to describe the destruction of human groups either racial, religious or political, the deliberate destruction of culture, history and the memory of a people. The crime of genocide was the subject of the first session of the General Assembly in 1946 and one of the Assembly's first Resolutions was for co-operation to prevent and punish it. Two years later the Convention of the Prevention and Punishment of the Crime of Genocide was ready to be signed and henceforth member governments were pledged to prevent it. From then, the Convention was forgotten. Offending governments were protected because of state interests; China's allies maintained that Tibet was an integral part of China and domestic jurisdiction forbade involvement. The genocide of the East Timorese after the invasion by the Indonesians in 1975 was ignored because Indonesia was a large Islamic state, an important producer of oil, a major area for US investment. Most genocides faded into international oblivion.

The recognition of what was happening in Yugoslavia also owed much to the world's underfunded human rights organisations. As early as March 1992, Amnesty International exposed the return of camps to Europe run by Serbian paramilitaries in Croatia. Particularly appalling evidence emerged in May of a strategy to cleanse Muslim areas with house burnings, deportations, summary executions, shootings on the Bosnia-Croatia border. There was a report that 200 people had been taken out of a stadium where they had gathered for safety and shot. In August, the International Committee of the Red Cross reported that serious violation of humanitarian laws were being committed by all parties. So overwhelming was the evidence that, in August 1992, the UN Commission for Human Rights, which usually met three times a year, was forced to hold its first-ever emergency session but even so, international diplomacy worked slowly. The first step was the appointment of a Special Rapporteur for former Yugoslavia and a former Polish Prime Minster, Tadeusz Mazowiecki, agreed to serve. Mazowiecki was appalled at what he learned and by September he pleaded for military intervention to stop the killings and torture. He wanted the peacekeepers to have a stronger mandate and reported to the Security Council there were "massive and systematic" violations of human rights. He said that all groups were guilty, but warned that the risk to the Muslims was "extermination". Mazowiecki wanted an investigative commission to find out what happened to thousands of people who had disappeared.

The leader of the Bosnian Serbs, Radovan Karadžić, was a great believer in population transfers. He had outlined this policy earlier in 1991 when he had said that with the help of state agencies the transfers of the population in Bosnia could be completed in five years. In May, 1992, in Banja Luka, the Office for Population Resettlement and Property Exchange had opened and those who wanted to leave their homes would be allowed to register their property available for a Serbian family. In practice this meant that anyone who did not want to go was robbed, tortured and killed. Karadžić wanted the Serbian Republic of Bosnia-Hercegovina to be sixty-five per cent of Bosnia-Hercegovina. He told his soldiers that they were in a valiant struggle to prevent a giant conspiracy whereby the Muslims intended to create their own state which would spread from Sarajevo to Tehran. They were to fight for a Europe without "foreign religion". Those who joined the Serbian militia called themselves crusaders against Islam.

In Belgrade, Karadžić's supporter and ally, the Serb President Slobodan Milošević also had a population persuaded by propaganda. His Radio Television Belgrade, with its xenophobia and war-mongering, fed a doctrine of racial superiority. Those who did not agree were "traitors to be cleansed". Those who did not support national extremism were silenced.

Few can tell when the plans were laid. Throughout 1991, convoys of lorries with guns and munitions entered the eastern part of Bosnia-Hercegovina. Bosnian-based units of the Yugoslav army were gearing up for action. Yugoslavia had a massive defence capability designed for the Cold War. An arms producing country, Yugoslavia held more than sixty per cent of its military industries in Bosnia-Hercegovina; the Serbs held the stockpiles of the former federal army. In spite of the fact that Yugoslavia was one of the largest exporters of arms to the underdeveloped world, in 1991 the Yugoslav army had purchased 14,000 tons of weaponry from the Middle East, just before the Security Council imposed an arms embargo on the entire region. The embargo favoured the well-stocked Serbs and ensured that the Muslims could not adeaquately defend their territory.

Mazowiecki's suggestion for a Commission of Experts was taken up by the Security Council and, in October 1992, the Council established a five-member Commission to prepare evidence for possible Nuremberg-style trials. The Commission was modelled on the Allied War Crimes Commission of 1943 which after the Second World War provided the evidence used in trials of Nazis. The Commission for former Yugoslavia was discredited at first and its creation was believed to be a way for President Bush to court public opinion in an election year.

There was no shortage of atrocity evidence. A captured Serbian militia in Sarajevo told of how men were shot and thrown in a furnace at a steel plant in Illijas and told of a prison for Muslim women outside Vogosca on the main road north from Sarajevo to Zagreb. In early 1993 a team of European Community investigators concluded that an estimated 20,000 Muslim and Croat women had been raped by Serbs. In August 1992, British journalists revealed the realities of ethnic cleansing and the investigation centres created close to the towns overrun by Serbs. There were coils of barbed-wire behind which there were skeletal men, some with shaven heads with staring, helpless eyes. "In my room I had dead men at my feet and on my legs. The beatings were constant . . . they used knives and axes", was one story from a camp. In another in Trnopolje, Western Bosnia, there were 3,000 men, women and children in an old school, nearly all Muslims. At night they were beaten and the women raped.

The decision of the Security Council in February 1993 to found the International Criminal Tribunal for the former Yugoslavia was the first time since the Nuremberg and Tokyo trials that a Tribunal was created to try individuals for violations of international law. "The lesson that we are all accountable to international law may have finally taken hold in our collective memory", Madeleine Albright told the Council when the vote was taken. The Tribunal would implement the Convention on the Prevention and

Punishment of the Crime of Genocide and, mandated under the enforcement powers of the Charter, all UN member states were obliged to comply with its requirements.

Council determination was not matched in the General Assembly where the creation of the Tribunal was greeted with resentment over valuable UN resources going to Europe. Assembly committees blocked funds to pay for the Tribunal and for a year the International Criminal Tribunal for the former Yugoslavia was unable even to rent office space. It took a year for diplomats to argue about who should be appointed Prosecutor. And even with a Prosecutor, a South African, Richard Goldstone, some of those on the wanted list, Slobodan Milošević and Radovan Karadžić, were taking part in peace negotiations. When the court opened its doors in November 1994 there had been two more years of cleansing, massacres and rape and some believed that the Tribunal was created only because the Council could think of little else to do. But others were more optimistic and considered the Tribunal a tentative step towards the long-term goal of a permanent international war crimes tribunal. Human rights groups could at least hope for a historic record of events and the Tribunal would individualise what was too often seen as collective guilt. An arrest warrant would turn the individual into a pariah who could be immediately detained if he or she ever stepped outside the boundaries of his isolated state. Others maintained that there was little use proclaiming minimum international standards of human conduct when nothing was done to enforce them.

Srebrenica was a spa resort in Eastern Bosnia-Hercegovina, one of many towns and villages cut off since the beginning of the war. Serb forces were trying to "cleanse" areas by surrounding and starving into submission Muslim communities. The siege of Sarajevo was one of several; Srebrenica was also a prison. By February 1993 there were an estimated 500,000 Muslims in packed communities under Serbian attack and control; people had flocked for shelter around the villages and towns. The Americans carried out an air-drop of food and medicine parcels. There were desperate pleas for help from ham radio operators who gave gruesome news. José Maria Mendiluce, of the UNHCR, Special Envoy for the former Yugoslavia, was prevented from getting medicines and food through to starving people and lost his temper at Serb stonewalling."You just don't know how tired I am of listening to lies." In Srebrenica an estimated 70,000 were trapped and of those 40,000 were refugees. There were more Muslims in Srebrenica than anywhere else. The water was cut off to the town, there was no electricity and refugees were sleeping in the streets. More than half the town had been destroyed by shelling. Some people were wandering into Serbian fire or fields full of landmines to find food. Within the town thirty to forty people were dying every day from starvation, the cold or lack of medical treatment. Surgeons in the hospital were operating without anesthesia or antibiotics.

It was from Srebrenica that the Muslims launched attacks in December and January, 1992 with armaments smuggled in by shepherds using donkeys to cross the mountains. The Muslims began to move through Serbian villages slaughtering a large number of civilians but the Serbs drove them back to Srebrenica.

On March 12, 1993, the French UN Commander General Philippe Morillon managed to get into Srebrenica with fifteen soldiers carrying side-arms only, one armoured personnel-carrier and four soft-top vehicles. The roads were under deep snow and the tortuous route through the mountains was mined. Morillon said Serb soldiers did not think he would succeed.

Nothing could have prepared Morillon and his team for what awaited them. "I saw this crowded city, thousands of women and children and babies just living in the streets with no protection and they were starving." Morillon negotiated with the Serbs for an evacutation of the most urgent cases of sick women and children by helicopter and then a gradual evacuation by road of the most vulnerable. Morillon was told that he would be co-operating with ethnic cleansing. The idea was doomed anyway. The moment the first rescue helicopters landed, the Serbs shelled the landing pad. And when the UN trucks arrived to take the wounded women and children, thousands of people turned up wanting places. Children were crushed in stampedes to get on UN trucks and two people were killed. Only two journalists were there to witness it. One of them described: "Women fought to get on, and in the end, in desperation, weeping uncontrollably handed their babies and young children to those already on board". Six people died in the crush on the trucks; four more died from falling off. On April 1, shelling killed seventy-seven people, including fifteen children.

"Srebrenica", a State Department official said in Washington, "was a wake up call for a lot of people."

The Security Council wanted its own impartial report on Srebrencia and a group of six diplomats from France, Hungary, New Zealand, Pakistan, Russia and Venezuela arrived in Bosnia-Hercegovina and among the UN troops there was a feeling this was more public relations than anything else. The team reported on April 30, 1993 telling the Council in some detail what they had found. Srebrenica was an "open jail" in which its inhabitants and thousands of refugees were "controlled and terrorised" by Serbs. The Serb stranglehold was total. There was no way in or out without Serb permission and officials of the UNHCR who brought tents to Srebrenica were prevented from entering and the tents were confiscated by Serb soldiers. The Serbs were not allowing surgeons to enter. The only surgeon in the town was not authorised to stay. There were hundreds of wounded needing medical aid. The diplomats saw the mutilated and "scattered" remains of fifteen children killed on a school playing field, blasted by mortar fire while playing soccer. They said that what the Serbs were doing was a "a slow-motion process of genocide".

The public horror at the nightly news increased and so did pressure for something to be done. Five of the Security Council's non-aligned Third World states, Pakistan, Djibouti, Morocco, Venezuela and Cape Verde wanted the Muslim enclaves to be liberated by force and warned that if the Council tried to protect them and created havens, these places would turn into camps in perpetuity. But the Security Council was paralysed. There was no agreement among the Big Five. In Washington there was a widespread determination not to put US troops into the Balkan quagmire but Congress wanted air strikes against the Bosnian Serbs and the removal of the UN arms embargo to allow the Bosnian government to buy arms and to protect its people and country. The UN accepted Bosnia-Hercegovina as a member state, yet prevented it receiving weapons in its own defence. These were Clinton's first months in office and he inherited a State Department in revolt. In a highly unusual petition, twelve specialists urged that the US had to act militarily to save the Muslims from genocide. The US was hoisted by Gulf War rhetoric about a new world order: Operation Desert Storm taught that vital interests could be defended in a video-game

346

war. There were rumblings from Moscow at the suggestion of tougher action. "Do not do anything unilaterally", Andrei Kozyrev the Russian Foreign Minister warned, "if you want to avoid a Balkan War." The Russians did not want airpower used and Moscow was reluctant to see military pressure. Europe, with its policy of UN peacekeeping and accused by a Republican Congress of appeasing the Serbs, resented the US refusal to provide ground troops and told Warren Christopher, US Secretary of State, that air strikes would put peacekeepers at risk. The Europeans feared that were the arms embargo lifted, the Balkans would be set alight, the war would spread and Russia would be tempted to come to the aid of a traditional ally, Serbia.

The edifice of international co-operation cracked. At a meeting of NATO on April 27 it was clear that Western governments were reluctant to intervene with force and that the Balkans had become a serious threat to the NATO alliance. NATO lacked political consensus. Out of this weakness, dithering and confusion came a compromise.

The procedures for the creation of "safe zones" for the safety of civilians in war are outlined in detail in the Geneva Conventions of 1949. They are areas where safety is dependent on demilitarisation. Without demilitarisation they are not safe. At the time of Morillon's arrival in Srebrenica the Commander of the UN Protection Force in former Yugoslavia was Lt-General General Lars-Eric Wahlgren, Swedish peacekeeping expert, five years Commander of the UN Interim Force in Lebanon. He ordered Morillon to negotiate demilitarisation for Srebrencia and an inspection team was set up with both Muslim and Serb representatives. It worked. Wahlgren believed that the same could be achieved in other Muslim pockets in Serbian-conquered territory as long as the well-established procedures of peacekeeping were adhered to and the thin blue line was respected.

At first it was straightforward. On May 6, 1993 the Security Council passed Resolution 824 which demanded that enclaves under siege, Tuzla, Žepa, Goražde, and Sarajevo should be "treated as safe areas by all the parties concerned". Bihac in the Krajina region was also included. Srebrenica was designated the first "safe area" on April 16 in Resolution 819. But both Resolutions used confusing language, wide open to different interpretation. In

Resolutions 819 and 824 the Council demanded that these areas should be "treated as safe", requested that all parties co-operate with the UN troops and demanded the unimpeded delivery of humanitarian aid. Resolution 824 specified that if the Serbs failed to comply, additional measures would be taken, including air strikes. The votes on the "safe areas" Resolutions were unanimous and intended to coincide with peace negotiations conducted by the UN and the European community, part of a carrot-and-stick procedure, an attempt to get agreement to turn Bosnia-Hercegovina into ten autonomous provinces.

Boutros-Ghali was unconvinced about the wisdom of the "safe areas" and told the Council that there already were thirty-five Resolutions dealing with former Yugoslavia. "I have no more money and no more troops," he said. Officials from the Department of Peacekeeping were concerned enough to go to the Council to try to prevent "safe areas" being created.

But it was the Council itself, in a further Resolution on June 4, which demolished its own "safe area" policy. When Wahlgren heard what was proposed he was shocked for the Resolution contained a sentence which made a nonsense of whole idea. Resolution 836 determined that demilitarisation would apply only to Serb forces and that the Bosnia-Hercegovina government troops, exercising a right to self-defence, could remain. Wahlgren sent a cable to the Council to ask that the Resolution not go through. The Geneva Conventions required that "safe areas" could be created only after demilitarisation and this should apply to both armies. There was a precise procedure; there had to be agreement, a timetable for withdrawal and an inspection mechanism. What the Council was trying to do was to manage the mission through unworkable resolutions, not based on fact in the field.

The Wahlgren cable was ignored. "After that," he said, "there was no more demilitarisation. Keeping peacekeepers in areas where there are two fighting forces is impossible." Resolution 836 also gave the peacekeepers a Chapter Seven enforcement mandate, allowing them the use of force in reply to bombardments against the safe areas. Wahlgren saw little point to this. A Chapter Seven mandate was useless unless the UN soliders were adequately equipped. Furthermore, the Council, although mandating an increase in troops, had no idea where they were to come from. Wahlgren told the Council that a "safe area" policy, with the necessary agreements on the ground, would take an extra 34,000 soldiers. Eventually a further 7,600 soliders were found but it took three months for the first to arrive and for the rest, one year. Protecting the "safe areas" was never a viable option.

"The safe areas", said another UN military commander in Bosnia-Hercegovina, "were unilaterally declared in New York and the whole idea was a farce . . . it was folly." Of the five "safe areas", four had been under unremitting siege for more than a year. Žepa, the smallest, in fact no more than a village, was the scene of fighting between Serbs and Muslims. The military believed that, at present strength, once in Eastern Bosnia the blue helmets would find it hard to keep lifelines open for their own needs, let alone protect the people under siege.

Resolution 836 was approved by the Council before troop numbers, the rules of engagement or the precise role of NATO and close air support were agreed. The "safe areas" themselves were ill-defined and no one knew their perimeters. The troops were mandated to deter rather than to defend and were to take necessary measures, including the use of force, but acting only in self-defence. There was little enthusiasm among the UN troop commanders for linking the creation of the "safe areas" to the threat of NATO air-power because Serb retaliation would see blue helmets taken hostage. In early May, 1993 a group of American Senators visited the UN troops in Bosnia-Hercegoniva and were shocked at the truth of it. "These forces need to be beefed up," said Senator Sam Nunn, Chair of the Senate Armed Services Committee, a Democrat from Georgia. "They are so lightly armed now they are, in effect, hostages." The Pentagon agreed. The UN troops were woefully understaffed to accomplish any of the mandates, be it the safe passage of convoys, monitoring heavy weapons sites, trying to maintain security and few of them were trained for peacekeeping.

From the moment the "safe areas" were created, there was confusion. The Western Press described these towns and villages as "UN-guaranteed havens", "UN-protected territory". The consequences of the policy were inevitable. Without being demilitarised or defended they were vulnerable. There were bets among UN officials as to when these enclaves would fall – because there was no doubting that they would. In June, 1995, when the Serbs trampled over security zones, resumed shelling and stopped aid deliveries, a UN spokesman in Zagreb, Christopher Gunness spoke desperately of a mission crying out for direction and resources from the Security Council.

Srebrenica exposed the gulf between reality and rhetoric. "Tears were in our eyes when seeing the desperate displaced persons . . . and seeking help we cannot give them", one Dutch UN Military Observer wrote in a report after Srebrencia fell in a Serbian onslaught in July. There were 400 Dutch peacekeepers in the town and one by one their observation posts were taken over, thirty soldiers were captured and taken away to the north of the town by the Serbs. The UN headquarters ordered the rest to block the road into the town against the Bosnian Serb army advance which they did, with seven armoured personnel-carriers, but the next day they were attacked by Bosnian government troops with small arms and anti-tank missile fire. The Dutch were trapped in a firefight between the enemies. A Dutch soldier was killed by a grenade. The peacekeepers were running out of ammunition, for weeks it had been impossible to get supplies to them. They were completely overwhelmed. Their commander called for close air support and there was one NATO air strike, one Serbian tank destroyed and in retaliation the Serbs threatened to kill the Dutch soldiers they captured. There were 1,500 Serbs with rocket launchers and tanks moving on the town. "The good guys bottle out", wrote Patrick Bishop, a British journalist about these peacekeepers. "Instead it is the drunken, unshaven agressors who carry the day." Humiliation for the UN, he wrote, was a way of life. The Dutch peacekeepers had been "shamed". The UN mission's every action was criticised, every failure a dereliction of duty.

Srebrenica was overrrun in an operation under the direct command of the Bosnian Serb military leader, Ratko Mladić. Most of its 40,000 refugees were expelled in terror, the men separated from the women and children. It was barbaric. People were summarily executed. Women were raped during the forced evacuation, thousands more went missing. Thousands of Bosnian government soldiers were taken away and there were increasing reports of massacre. Ten days after the fall of Srebrenica, the Dutch blue helmets were released. Some weeks later, Tadeusz Mazowiecki, the human rights Special Rapporteur who was completing his report on what happened after the fall of Srebrenica, resigned in despair.

The commanders of the blue helmets wondered how diplomats, who clearly did not understand the basic rules of peacekeeping, were qualified to produce this haystack of orders in the Council, leading to danger and death on the ground. The UN mission to former Yugoslavia, the largest and most expensive in UN history, was plagued by ambiguities, for although the Council made frequent references to the enforcement powers in the Charter, the mission was not a peace-enforcement operation. By mid-1995, there were seventy-three Security Council Resolutions on the war and more than sixty Security Council Presidential Statements – a record number and an end in themselves. The Council decisions were bewildering with phrases such as "strategic consent" and "protection through deterrance". To the outside world the Security Council had deployed an army of peacekeepers on the polite assumption, unlike other armies, that this one could not take risks delivering the most basic humanitarian assistance – medicines, food, blankets for winter – this humane notion could only rarely be put into practice, because of fears for the safety of the peacekeepers. And yet the peacekeepers were constantly at risk. They called the mission the UN Protection Force, UNPROFOR, but it was a force barely capable of its own protection, marooned in the midst of war. The blue helmets in Bosnia-Hercegovina came to believe that the Security Council never intended them to fulfil the mandates, and that the whole exercise was a charade. One blue helmet described his job as a "human debris Hoovering system". They were blamed for failing to do things for which they were never mandated, staffed, financed, equipped or deployed to do. Never before had the UN appeared so humiliatingly helpless.

"As a child I felt so proud and so important among the kids when my father travelled to Sinai on a UN military mission", a journalist from Sarajevo, Zlatko Dizdarević, wrote. " . . . the day I entered the hall in which the General Assembly was in session was the most important day of my life . . . those were still good days . . . when it seemed that you were not alone . . . " After the experience of indecision and ineffectiveness he says: "Today, all that we in any way feel about the UN has been reduced to rubble . . . we feel a little contempt . . . for them so small and so miserable, and yet still convinced that they can impress or even frighten somebody." Not one single Sarajevan would want to visit the UN building on the East River.

We shall never know the exact figures but by mid-1995 the war in former Yugoslavia had killed an estimated 250,000 people and made more than three million people refugees. More than 40,000 children do not know if their parents are dead or alive. Villages and towns have disappeared from the map. In four years there has been the largest forced population movement since the Second World War. Ethnic cleansing has been successful. But while the blue helmets did not stop this war, they did along with the UN High Commissioner for Refugees feed more than two and a half million destitute civilians; that is no small achievement in a fragile world.

In the UN's fiftieth anniversary year more blue helmets were in Europe than in anywhere else in the world. The UN was spending more money on peacekeeping in Europe than on all the other continents put together and after four years of war in May, 1995, Boutros-Ghali took several ambassadors from the non-permanent members of the Security Council to one side for a quiet and confidential chat. Sarajevo had no airlift of aid for weeks, tons of food bound for the safe areas had been seized by Serb soldiers, UN-brokered ceasefires were flouted and the blue helmets increasingly at risk; 162 blue helmets were killed and 1,420 wounded. The troops were continually abused and insulted. The time for short-term solutions was gone. The loss of UN credibility was too great and it would eventually effect all UN work elsewhere, its endeavours for development, for the environment and for human rights. The UN's role in Bosnia-Hercegovina would effect the standing of the UN for years to come.

Boutros-Ghali reached the conclusion that if more forceful action were advocated by the Council then the Council should replace the blue helmets with a multinational force under the command of one or more of the countries contributing troops to it. If the Council decided to undertake peace enforcement, there would have to be substantial reinforcement. The UN did not have the capacity or the expertise to manage a combat operation, nor did it have the finance; as it was, the mission to the former Yugoslavia peacekeeping account was owed $898 million by member states.

The withdrawal of the UN troops in the Balkans was a last resort, although one which the troop contributors believed to be increasingly likely. Evacuation would be tantamout to abandonment of the people of Bosnia-Hercegovina and an admission of inability to help to resolve a war in which, to the world's horror, one group used force of arms to try to change the ethnic map of a member state. NATO would need to execute withdrawal and US troops would have to escort the blue helmets to safety. It would be treacherous. There were more than two million landmines littering the country and partisans on both sides would try to prevent the troops leaving, would blow up bridges and block tunnels and seize UN equipment. Much of the terrain was mountainous and some blue helmet units were isolated and vulnerable. There would be the highest risk they would be massacred. There was a constant threat of hostage-taking. Some soliders would have to fight their way through desperate people abandoned to slaughter. There would be a humanitarian disaster which the world had not yet seen. The war would expand and the repercussions would go far beyond Bosnia's borders. Another UN failure so soon after Somalia and Rwanda would be a humiliation from which the UN was unlikely to recover.

After the Cold War there was an unprecedented chance for UN renaissance. It seemed that the moment had come when during the triumphant Security Council summit in 1992 world leaders declared that the UN was guaranteed a central place in the international system. They affirmed their reliance on it: a united Security Council would ensure that the organisation was central to a New World Order. But the grandiose talk was premature. The discrepancy between promise and performance was huge. By 1995 the Council had ensured that the future course for the UN was framed by three tragedies shaming the world – Somalia, Bosnia-Hercegovina and Rwanda. These three missions exposed a Council whose intrigues and manoeuvrings made a decisive difference between life and death for millions of people. The tragedies were avoidable, they were preventable. The UN operations in these three UN member states were ill-conceived, short-sighted and proved the organisation not yet mature enough for such responsibiities. The Council, with a patchwork command structure as unstable as it was dangerous, was unable to be an effective instrument for collective security. It did not have the resources, financial or military nor the political will to move quickly and decisively and the Council brought peacekeeping to chaos and the day came when the blue helmet ceased to be a guarantee of safety in a war zone. In these three missions and at crucial points the Council without the use of a Military Staff Committee lost effective political and military control and the world edged closer to international anarchy.

For more than forty years the blue helmets had been a pragmatic response to the Cold War. Peacekeeping, appropriately used, was an enormously useful device. Peacekeepers helped to save thousands of lives. Their worth was recognised in 1988 when they were awarded the Nobel Peace Prize. The citation described them representing "the manifest will of the community of nations to achieve peace". Peacekeeping depended not on war-fighting soliders but on troops trained in mediation and conciliation. A single blue helmet at a check point flying a UN flag was a symbol. The blue helmet's weapon was not the rifle slung over the shoulder but his credibility; the blue helmet represented a world community of states and the Security Council's will for peace.

We are far from the promise made at San Francisco and fear and bloodshed continue to be the hallmark of the twentieth century. In 1945, the Charter was devised as a treaty which bound member states to an international rule of law which would be enforced by the Security Council; diplomacy without teeth had already proved useless. Powers of enforcement were an essential element in a New World Order and the Charter remains the only multilateral treaty of its nature, binding on all states. "Now the world must use it," President Truman said on the day it was signed, "otherwise, we shall betray all those who have died in order that we might meet here in freedom and safety to create it."

If the UN story proves nothing else, it is that while professing a public UN policy, governments maintain a secret agenda. They themselves corrupt the UN system. Within the Council, votes are bought for trade, there is blackmail, there is coercion, wrangling and bribing. There is hypocrisy. The frequent demands for reform of the UN system usually mask inadequate support for international co-operation. The UN is used as a last-ditch resort. To act only after a warmongerer has acquired massive weaponry is to lose influence over events. And while the five permanent members apparently struggle to bring peace and security to an anarchic world, the same five countries are responsible for eighty-five per cent of global arms exports. The US finds it difficult to contribute the equivalent of one-half of one per cent of its defence budget to pay for UN peacekeeping.

We are badly served by our chief executives. The Council is unheeding of the dreadful realities we face, unable to differentiate between short-term advantage and progress, between expedience and the creation of a more peaceful world. While we anguish at the world's agony, we tolerate a Council which casually mandates the impossible, refuses adequate resources, blames the UN when things go wrong and walks away from problems when they entail risk and cost. The Council hesitates; it haggles over money. There is no consensus about complying with the Charter, or even limiting its objectives. The slightest change would mean that any part of the Charter could be challenged – including the veto power, and the permanent membership of the Council itself. In the fifty years since the Allies defined themselves as the new great powers, there have been huge changes in economic and political influence around the world, but the Council stays conveniently frozen. The United Nations is not to be allowed a chance of reforming itself.

It is in the Council, the heart of the UN system, where change must begin. We face problems other than military aggression. There are crises so serious – pollution, environmental decline, militarisation, population growth, hunger – which demand international solution. We tolerate a chasm of inequality; one in four of the world's people lives in a state of absolute want, unable to meet basic needs. More than fourteen million children – thirty-five thousand a day – die from lack of the meanest necessities. Every successive year there are increasingly desperate warnings which should lead to questions both fundamental and terrifying; is international order a hopeless ideal? And if the UN system cannot reform, can we ever save ourselves? The questions are never posed. We are presented instead with two choices. "It's the UN with all its warts", the British UN ambassador, David Hannay said, "or it's the law of the jungle." Is the UN, designed as spectacle for a war-weary world, a PR exercise?

The impetus for reform could have come at the end of the Cold War, or during the triumphant Security Council summit in 1992, or it could have been inspired on the occasion of the fiftieth anniversary. "Let's change it", the Australian ambassador, Richard Butler pleaded that year. "It's going to be very tough. Some people don't want these changes. Some people have a vested interest in the existing system."

Major General Romeo Dallaire, UN force Commander in Rwanda, realised this when he found himself abandoned in the middle of genocide. His conclusion was that the UN exists only as a camouflage for the schemes and interests of its most powerful members and that is true: the UN is used as a cover-up, one of the most spectacular of this century.

CHARTER OF THE UNITED NATIONS

WE THE PEOPLES OF
THE UNITED NATIONS
DETERMINED

to save succeeding generations from the scourge of war, which twice in our lifetime has brought untold sorrow to mankind, and

to reaffirm faith in fundamental human rights, in the dignity and worth of the human person, in the equal rights of men and women and of nations large and small, and

to establish conditions under which justice and respect for the obligations arising from treaties and other sources of international law can be maintained, and

to promote social progress and better standards of life in larger freedom,

AND FOR THESE ENDS

to practice tolerance and live together in peace with one another as good neighbours, and

to unite our strength to maintain international peace and security, and

to ensure, by the acceptance of principles and the institution of methods, that armed force shall not be used, save in the common interest, and

to employ international machinery for the promotion of the economic and social advancement of all peoples,

HAVE RESOLVED TO COMBINE OUR EFFORTS TO ACCOMPLISH
THESE AIMS

Accordingly, our respective Governments, through representatives assembled in the city of San Francisco, who have exhibited their full powers found to be in good and due form, have agreed to the present Charter of the United Nations and do hereby establish an international organization to be known as the United Nations.

CHAPTER I
PURPOSES AND PRINCIPLES

Article I

The Purposes of the United Nations are:

1. To maintain international peace and security, and to that end: to take effective collective measures for the prevention and removal of threats to the peace, and for the suppression of acts of aggression or other breaches of the peace, and to bring about by peaceful means, and in conformity with the principles of justice and international law, adjustment or settlement of international disputes or situations which might lead to a breach of the peace;

2. To develop friendly relations among nations based on respect for the principle of equal rights and self-determination of peoples, and to take other appropriate measures to strengthen universal peace;

3. To achieve international co-operation in solving international problems of an economic, social, cultural, or humanitarian character, and in promoting and encouraging respect for human rights and for fundamental freedoms for all without distinction as to race, sex, language, or religion; and

4. To be a centre for harmonizing the actions of nations in the attainment of these common ends.

Article 2

The Organization and its Members, in pursuit of the Purposes stated in Article 1, shall act in accordance with the following Principles.

1. The Organization is based on the principle of the sovereign equality of all its Members.

2. All Members, in order to ensure to all of them the rights and benefits resulting from membership, shall fulfil in good faith the obligations assumed by them in accordance with the present Charter.

3. All Members shall settle their international disputes by peaceful means in such a manner that international peace and security, and justice, are not endangered.

4. All Members shall refrain in their international relations from the threat or use of force against the territorial integrity or political independence of any state, or in any other manner inconsistent with the Purposes of the United Nations.

5. All Members shall give the United Nations every assistance in any action it takes in accordance with the present Charter, and shall refrain

from giving assistance to any state against which the United Nations is taking preventive or enforcement action.

6. The Organization shall ensure that states which are not Members of the United Nations act in accordance with these Principles so far as may be necessary for the maintenance of international peace and security.

7. Nothing contained in the present Charter shall authorize the United Nations to intervene in matters which are essentially within the domestic jurisdiction of any state or shall require the Members to submit such matters to settlement under the present Charter; but this principle shall not prejudice the application of enforcement measures under Chapter VII.

CHAPTER II
MEMBERSHIP

Article 3

The original Members of the United Nations shall be the states which, having participated in the United Nations Conference on International Organization at San Francisco, or having previously signed the Declaration by United Nations of 1 January 1942, sign the present Charter and ratify it in accordance with Article 110.

Article 4

1. Membership in the United Nations is open to all other peace-loving states which accept the obligations contained in the present Charter and, in the judgment of the Organization, are able and willing to carry out these obligations.
2. The admission of any such state to membership in the United Nations will be effected by a decision of the General Assembly upon the recommendation of the Security Council.

Article 5

A Member of the United Nations against which preventive or enforcement action has been taken by the Security Council may be suspended from the exercise of the rights and privileges of membership by the General Assembly upon the recommendation of the Security Council. The exercise of these rights and privileges may be restored by the Security Council.

Article 6

A Member of the United Nations which has persistently violated the Principles contained in the present Charter may be expelled from the Organization by the General Assembly upon the recommendation of the Security Council.

CHAPTER III
ORGANS

Article 7

1. There are established as the pricipal organs of the United Nations: a General Assembly, a Security Council, an Economic and Social Council, a Truesteeship Council, an International Court of Justice, and a Secretariat.

2. Such subsidiary organs as may be found necessary may be established in accordance with the present Charter.

Article 8

The United Nations shall place no restrictions on the eligibility of men and women to participate in any capacity and under conditions of equality in its principal and subsidiary organs.

CHAPTER IV
THE GENERAL ASSEMBLY

Composition

Article 9

1. The General Assembly shall consist of all the Members of the United Nations.

2. Each Member shall have not more than five representatives in the General Assembly.

Functions and Powers

Article 10

The General Assembly may discuss any questions or any matters within the scope of the present Charter or relating to the powers and functions of any organs provided for in the present Charter, and, except as provided in Article 12, may make recommendations to the Members of the United Nations or to the Security Council or to both on any such questions or matters.

Article 11

1. The General Assembly may consider the general principles of co-operation in the maintenance of international peace and security, including the principles governing disarmament and the regulation of armaments, and may make recommendations with regard to such principles to the Members or to the Security Council or to both.

2. The General Assembly may discuss any questions relating to the maintenance of international peace and security brought before it by any Member of the United Nations, or by the Security Council, or by a state which is not a Member of the United Nations in accordance with Article 35, paragraph 2, and except as provided in Article 12, may make recommendations with regard to any such questions to the state or states concerned or to the Security Council or to both. Any such question on which action is necessary shall be referred to the Security Council by the General Assembly either before or after discussion.

3. The General Assembly may call the attention of the Security Council to situations which are likely to endanger international peace and security.

4. The powers of the General Assembly set forth in this Article shall not limit the general scope of Article 10.

Article 12

1. While the Security Council is exercising in respect of any dispute or situation the functions assigned to it in the present Charter, the General Assembly shall not make any recommendation with regard to that dispute or situation unless the Security Council so requests.

2. The Secretary-General, with the consent of the Security Council, shall notify the General Assembly at each session of any matters relative to the maintenance of international peace and security which are being dealt with by the Security Council and shall similarly notify the General Assembly, or the Members of the United Nations if the General Assembly is not in session, immediately the Security Council ceases to deal with such matters.

Article 13

1. The General Assembly shall initiate studies and make recom-mendations for the purpose of:

a. promoting international co-operation in the political field and encouraging the progressive development of international law and its codification;

b. promoting international co-operation in the economic, social, cultural, educational, and health fields, and assisting in the realization of human rights and fundamental freedoms for all without distinction as to race, sex, language, or religion.

2. The further responsibilities, functions and powers of the General Assembly with respect to matters mentioned in paragraph 1(b) above are set forth in Chapters IX and X.

Article 14

Subject to the provisions of Article 12, the General Assembly may recommend measures for the peaceful adjustment of any situation, regardless of origin, which it deems likely to impair the general welfare or friendly relations among nations, including situations resulting from a violation of the provisions of the present Charter setting forth the Purposes and Principles of the United Nations.

Article 15

1. The General Assembly shall receive and consider annual and special reports from the Security Council; these reports shall include an account of the measures that the Security Council has decided upon or taken to maintain international peace and security.

2. The General Assembly shall receive and consider reports from the other organs of the United Nations.

Article 16

The General Assembly shall perform such functions with respect to the international trusteeship system as are assigned to it under Chapters XII and XIII, including the approval of the trusteeship agreements for areas not designated as strategic.

Article 17

1.The General Assembly shall consider and approve the budget of the Organization.

2. The expenses of the Organization shall be borne by the Members as apportioned by the General Assembly

3. The General assembly shall consider and approve any financial and

budgetary arrangements with specialized agencies referred to in Article 57 and shall examine the administrative budgets of such specialized agencies with a view to making recommendations to the agencies concerned.

Voting

Article 18

1. Each member of the General Assembly shall have one vote.

2. Decisions of the General Assembly on important questions shall be made by a two-thirds majority of the members present and voting. These questions shall include: recommendations with respect to the maintenance of international peace and security, the election of the non-permenant members of the Security Council, the election of the members of the Economic and Social Council, the election of members of the Trusteeship Council in accordance with paragraph 1(c) of Article 86, the admission of new Members to the United Nations, the suspension of the rights and privileges of membership, the expulsion of Members, questions relating to the operation of the trusteeship system, and bugetary questions.

3. Decisions on other questions, including the determination of additional categories of questions to be decided by a two-thirds majority, shall be made by a majority of the members present and voting.

Article 19

A Member of the United Nations which is in arrears in the payment of its financial contributions to the Organization shall have no vote in the General Assembly if the amount of its arrears equals or exceeds the amount of the contributions due from it for the preceding two full years. The General Assembly may, nevertheless, permit such a Member to vote if it is satisfied that the failure to pay is due to conditions beyond the control of the Member.

Procedure

Article 20

The General Assembly shall meet in regular annual sessions and in such special sessions as occasion may require. Special sessions shall be convoked by the Secretary-General at the request of the Security Council or of a majority of the Members of the United Nations.

Article 21

The General Assembly shall adopt its own rules of procedure. It shall elect its President for each session.

Article 22

The General Assembly may establish such subsidiary organs as it deems neccessary for the performance of its functions.

Chapter V
THE SECURITY COUNCIL

Composition

Article 23

1. The Security Council shall consist of fifteen Members of the United Nations. The Republic of China, France, the Union of Soviet Socialist Republics, the United Kingdom of Great Britain and Northern Ireland, and the United States of America shall be permanant members of the Security Council. The General Assembly shall elect ten other Members of the United Nations to be non-permanent mambers of the Security Council, due regard being specially paid, in the first instance to the contribution of Members of the United Nations to the maintenance of international peace and security and to the other purposes of the Organization, and also to equitable geographical distribution.

2. The non-permanent members of the Security Council shall be elected for a term of two years. In the first election of the non-permanent members after the increase of the membership of the Security Council from eleven to fifteen, two of the four additional members shall be chosen for a term of one year. A retiring member shall not be eligible for immediate re-election.

3. Each member of the Security Council shall have one representative.

Functions and Powers

Article 24

1. In order to ensure prompt and effective action by the United Nations, its Members confer on the Security Council primary responsibility for the maintenance of international peace and security, and agree that in carrying out its duties under this responsibility the Security Council acts on their behalf.

2. In discharging these duties the Security Council shall act in accordance with the Purposes and Principles of the United Nations. The specific powers granted to the Security Council for the discharge of these duties are laid down in Chapters VI, VIII, and XII.

3. The Security Council shall submit annual and, when necessary, special reports to the General Assembly for its consideration.

Article 25

The Members of the United Nations agree to accept and carry out the decisions of the Security Council in accordance with the present Charter.

Article 26

In order to promote the establishment and maintenance of international peace and security with the least diversion for armaments of the world's human and economic resources, the Security Council shall be responsible for formulating, with the assistance of the Military Staff Committee referred to in Article 47, plans to be submitted to the Members of the United Nations for the establishment of a system for the regulation of armaments.

Voting

Article 27

1. Each member of the Security Council shall have one vote.

2. Decisions of the Security Council on procedural matters shall be made by an affirmative vote of nine members.

3. Decisions of the Security Council on all other matters shall be made by an affirmative vote of nine members includingthe concurring votes of the permanent members; provided that, in decisions under Chapter VI, and under paragraph 3 of Article 52, a party to a dispute shall abstain from voting.

Procedure

Article 28

1. The Security Council shall be so organized as to be able to function continuously. Each member of the Security Council shall for this purpose be represented at all times at the seat of the Organization.

2. The Security Council shall hold periodic meetings at which each of its members may, if it so desires, be represented by a member of the government or by some other specially designated representative.

3. The Security Council may hold meetings at such places other than the seat of the Organization as in its judgment will best facilitate its work.

Article 29

The Security Council may establish such subsidiary organs as it deems necessary for the performance of its functions.

Article 30

The Security Council shall adopt its own rules of procedure, including the method of selecting its President.

Article 31

Any Member of the United Nations which is not a member of the Security Council may participate, without vote, in the discussion of any question brought before the Security Council whenever the latter considers that the interests of that Member are specially affected.

Article 32

Any Member of the United Nations which is not a member of the Security Council or any state which is not a Member of the United Nations, if it is a party to a dispute under consideration by the Security Council, shall be invited to participate, without vote, in the discussion relating to the dispute. The Security Council shall lay down such conditions as it deems just for the participation of a state which is not a Member of the United Nations.

CHAPTER VI
PACIFIC SETTLEMENT OF DISPUTES

Article 33

1. The parties to any dispute, the continuance of which is likely to endanger the maintenance of international peace and security, shall, first of all, seek a solution by negotiation, enquiry, mediation, conciliation, arbitration, judicial settlement, resort to regional agencies or arrangements, or other peaceful means of their own choice.
2. The Security Council shall, when it deems nesessary, call upon the parties to settle their dispute by such means.

Article 34

The Security Council may investigate any dispute, or any situation which might lead to international friction or give rise to a dispute, in order to determine whether the continuance of the dispute or situation is likely to endanger the maintenance of international peace and security.

Article 35

2. Any Member of the United Nations may bring any dispute, or any situation of the nature referred to in Article 34, to the attention of the Security Council or of the General Assembly.

2. A state which is not a Member of the United Nations may bring to the attention of the Security Council or of the General Assembly any dispute to which it is a party if it accepts in advance, for the purposes of the dispute, the obligations of pacific settlement provided in the present Charter.

3. The proceedings of the General Assembly in respect of matters brought to its attention under this Article will be subject to the provisions of Articles 11 and 12.

Article 36

1. The Security Council may, at any stage of a dispute of the nature referred to in Article 33 or of a situation of like nature, recommend appropriate procedures or methods of adjustment.

2. The Security Council should take into consideration any procedures for the settlement of the dispute which have already been adopted by the parties.

3. In making recommendations under this Article the Security Council should also take into consideration that legal disputes should as a general rule be referred by the parties to the International Court of Justice in accordance with the provisions of the Statute of the Court.

Article 37

1. Should the parties to a dispute of the nature referred to in Article 33 fail to settle it by the means indicated in that Article, they shall refer it to the Security Council.

2. If the Security Council deems that the continuance of the dispute is in fact likely to endanger the maintenance of international peace and security, it shall decide whether to take action under Article 36 or to recomend such terms of settlement as it may consider appropriate.

Article 38

Without prejudice to the provisions of Articles 33 to 37. the Security Council may, if all the parties to any dispute so request, make recommendations to the parties with a view to a pacific settlement of the dispute.

CHAPTER VII
ACTION WITH RESPECT TO THREATS TO THE PEACE, BREACHES OF THE PEACE, AND ACTS OF AGGRESSION

Article 39

The Security Council shall determine the existence of any threat to the peace, breach of the peace or act of aggression and shall make recommendations, or decide what measures shall be taken in accordance with Articles 41 and 42, to maintain or restore international peace and security.

Article 40

In order to prevent an aggravation of the situation, the Security Council may, before making the recommendations or deciding upon the measures provided for in Article 39, call upon the parties concerned to comply with such provisional measures as it deems necessary or desirable. Such provisional measures shall be without prejudice to the rights, claims, or position of the parties concerned. The Security Council shall duly take account of failure to comply with such provisional measures.

Article 41

The Security Council may decide what measures not involving the use of armed forces are to be employed to give effect to its decisions, and it may call upon the Members of the United Nations to apply such measures. These may include complete or partial interruption of economic relations and of rail, sea, air, postal, telegraphic, radio, and other means of communication, and the severance of diplomatic relations.

Article 42

Should the Security Council consider that measures provided for in Article 41 would be inadequate or have proved to be inadequate, it may take such action by air, sea, or land forces as may be necessary to maintain or restore international peace and security. Such action may include demonstrations, blockade, and other operations by air, sea, or land forces of Members of the United Nations.

Article 43

1. All Members of the United Nations, in order to contribute to the maintenance of international peace and security, undertake to make

available to the Security Council, on its call and in accordance with a special agreement or agreements, armed forces, assistance, and facilities, including rights of passage, necessary for the purpose of maintaining international peace and security.

2. Such agreement or agreements shall govern the numbers and types of forces, their degree of readiness and general locations, and the nature of the facilities and assistance to be provided.

3. The agreement or agreements shall be negotiated as soon as possible on the initiative of the Security Council. They shall be concluded between the Security Council and Members or between the Security Council and groups of Members and shall be subject to ratification by the signatory states in accordance with their respective constitutional processes.

Article 44

When the Security Council has decided to use force it shall, before calling upon a Member not represented on it to provide armed forces in fulfilment of the obligations assumed under Article 43, invite that Member, if the Member so desires, to participate in the decisions of the Security Council concerning the employment of contingents of that Member's armed forces.

Article 45

In order to enable the United Nations to take urgent military measures, Members shall hold immediately available national air-force contingents for combined international enforcement action. The strength and degreee of readiness of these contingents and plans for their combined action shall be determined within the limits laid down in the special agreement or agreements referred to in Article 43, by the Security Council with the assistance of the Military Staff Committee.

Article 46

Plans for the application of armed force shall be made by the Security Council with the assistance of the Military Staff Committee.

Article 47

1. There shall be established a Military Staff Committee to advise and assist the Security Council on all questions relating to the Security Council's military requirements for the mainenance of international peace and security, the employment and command of forces placed at its disposal, the regulations of armaments, and possible disarmament.

368

2. The Military Staff Committee shall consist of the Chiefs of Staff of the permanent members of the Security Council or their representatives. Any Member of the United Nations not permanently represented on the Committee shall be invited by the Committee to be associated with it when the efficient discharge of the Committee's responsibilities requires the participation of that Member in its work.

3. The Military Staff Committee shall be responsible under the Security Council for the strategic direction of any armed forces placed at the disposal of the Security Council. Questions relating to the command of such forces shall be worked out subsequently.

4. The Military Staff Committee, with the authorization of the Security Council and after consultation with appropriate regional agencies, may establish regional sub-committees.

Article 48

1. The action required to carry out the decisions of the Security Council for the maintenance of intenational peace and security shall be taken by all the Members of the United Nation or by some of them, as the Security Council may determine.

2. Such decisions shall be carried out by the Members of the United Nations directly and through their action in the appropriate international agencies of which they are members.

Article 49

The Members of the United Nations shall join in affording mutual assistance in carrying out the measures decided upon by the Security Council.

Article 50

If preventive or enforcement measures against any state are taken by the Security Council, any other state, whether a Member of the United Nations or not, which finds itself confronted with special econimic problems arising from the carrying out of those measures shall have the right to consult the Security Council with regard to a solution of those problems.

Article 51

Nothing in the present Charter shall impair the inherent right of individual or collective self-defence if an armed attack occurs against a Member of the United Nations, until the Security Council has taken measures necessary to maintain international peace and security. Measures taken by Members in the exercise of this right of self-defence shall be immediately reported to the Security Council and shall not in any way affect the authority and responsibility of the Security council under the present Charter to take at any time such action as it deems necessary in order to maintain or restore international peace and security.

CHAPTER VIII
REGIONAL ARRANGEMENTS

Article 52

1. Nothing in the present Charter precludes the existence of regional arrangements or agencies for dealing with such matters relating to the maintenance of international peace and security as are appropriate for regional agencies and their activities are consistent with the Purposes and Principles of the United Nations.

2. The Members of the United Nations entering into such arrangements or constituting such agencies shall make every effort to achieve pacific settlement of local disputes through such regional arrangements or by such regional agencies before referring them to the Security Council.

3. The Security Council shall encourage the development of pacific settlement of local disputes through such regional arrangements or by such regional agencies either on the initiative of the states concerned or by reference from the Security Council.

4. This Article in no way impairs the application of Articles 34 and 35.

Article 53

1. The Security Council shall, where appropriate, utilize such regional arrangements or agencies for enforcement action under its authority. But no enforcement action shall be taken under regional arrangements or by regional agencies without the authorization of the Security Council, with the exception of measures against any enemy state, as defined in paragraph 2 of this Article, provided for pursuant to Article 107 or in regional arrangements directed against renewal of aggressive policy on the part of any such state, until such time as the Organization may, on request of the Governments concerned, be charged with the responsibility for preventing further aggression by such a state.

2. The term enemy state as used in paragraph 1 of this Article applies to any state which during the Second World War has been an enemy of any signatory of the present Charter.

Article 54

The Security Council shall at all times be kept fully informed of activities undertaken or in contemplation under regional arrangements or by regional agencies for the maintenance of international peace and security.

CHAPTER IX
INTERNATIONAL ECONOMIC AND SOCIAL CO-OPERATION

Article 55

With a view to the creation of conditions of stability and well-being which are neccessary for peaceful and friendly relations among nations based on respect for the principle of equal rights and self-determination of peoples, the United Nations shall promote:

a. higher standards of living, full employment, and conditions of economic, and social progress and development;

b. solutions of international economic, social, health, and related problems; and international cultural and educational co-operation; and

c. universal respect for, and observance of, human rights and fundamental freedoms for all without distinction as to race, sex, language, or religion.

Article 56

All Members pledge themselves to take joint and separate action in co-operation with the Organization for the achievement of the purposes set forth in Article 55.

Article 57

1. The various specialized agencies, established by intergovernmental agreement and having wide international responsibilities, as defined in their basic instruments, in economic, social, cultural, educational, health, and related fields, shall be brought into relationship with the United Nations in accordance with the provisions of Article 63.

2. Such agencies thus brought into relationship with the United Nations are hereinafter referred to as specialized agencies.

Article 58

The Organization shall make recommendations for the co-ordination of the policies and activities of the specialized agencies.

Article 59

The Organization shall, where appropriate, initiate negotiations among the states concerned for the creation of any new specialized agencies required for the accomplishment of the purposes set forth in Article 55.

Article 60

Responsibility for the discharge of the functions of the Organization set forth in this Chapter shall be vested in the General Assembly and, under the authority of the General Assembly, in the Economic and Social Council, which shall have for this purpose the powers set forth in Chapter X.

CHAPTER X
THE ECONOMIC AND SOCIAL COUNCIL

Composition

Article 61

1. The Economic and Social Council shall consit of fifty-four Members of the United Nations elected by the General Assembly.

2. Subject to the provisions of paragraph 3, eighteen members of the Economic and Social Council shall be elected each year for a term of three years. A retiring member shall be eligible for immediate re-election.

3. At the first election after the increase in the membership of the Economic and Social Council from twenty-seven to fifty-four members, in addition to the members elected in place of the nine members whose term of office expires at the end of that year, twenty-seven additional members shall be elected. Of these twenty-seven additional members, the term of office of nine members so elected shall expire at the end of one year, and of nine other members at the end of two years, in accordance with arrangements made by the General Assembly.

4. Each member of the Economic and social Council shall have one representative.

Functions and Powers

Article 62

1. The Economic and Social Council may make or initiate studies and reports with respect to international economic, social, cultural, educational, health, and related matters and may make recommendations with respect

to any such matters to the General Assembly, to the Members of the United Nations, and to the specialized agencies concerned.

2. It may make recommendations for the purpose of promoting respect for, and observance of, human rights and fundamental freedoms for all.

3. It may prepare draft conventions for submission to the General Assembly, with respect to matters falling within its competence.

Article 63

1. The Economic and Social Council may enter into agreements with any of the agencies referred to in Article 57, defining the terms on which the agency concerned shall be brought into relationship with the United Nations. Such agreements shall be subject to approval by the General Assembly.

2. It may co-ordinate the activities of the specialized agencies through consultation with and recommendations to the General Assembly and to the Members of the United Nations.

Article 64

1. The Economic and Social Council may take appropriate steps to obtain regular reports from the specialized agencies. It may make arrangements with the Members of the United Nations and with the specialized agencies to obtain reports on the steps taken to give effect to its own recommendations and to recommendations on matters falling within its competence made by the General Assembly.

2. It may communicate its observations on these reports to the General Assembly.

Article 65

The Economic and Social Council may furnish information to the Security Council and shall assist the Security Council upon its request.

Article 66

1. The Economic and Social Council shall perform such functions as fall within its competence in connexion with the carrying out of the recommendations of the General Assembly.

2. It may, with the approval of the General Assembly, perform services at the request of Members of the United Nations and at the request of specialized agencies.

3. It shall perform such other functions as are specified elsewhere in the

present Charter or as may be assigned to it by the General Assembly.

Voting

Article 67

1. Each member of the Economic and Social Council shall have one vote.
2. Decisions of the Economic and Social Council shall be made by a majority of the members present and voting.

Procedure

Article 68

The Economic and Social Council shall set up commissions in economic and social fields and for the promotion of human rights, and such other commissions as may be required for the performance of its functions.

Article 69

The Economic and Social Council shall invite any Member of the United Nations to participate, without vote, in its deliberations on any matter of particular concern to that Member.

Article 70

The Economic and Social Council may make arrangements for representatives of the specialized agencies to participate, without vote, in its deliberations and in those of the commissions established by it, and for its represntatives to participate in the deliberations of the specialized agencies.

Article 71

The Economic and Social Council may make suitable arrangements for consultation with non-governmental organizations which are concerned with matters within its competence. Such arrangements may be made with international organizations and, where appropriate, with national organizations after consultation with the Member of the United Nations concerned.

Article 72

1, The Economic and Social Council shall adopt its own rules of procedure, including the method of selecting its President.

2. The Economic and Social Council shall meet as required in accordance with its rules, which shall include provision for the convening of meetings on the request of a majority of its members.

CHAPTER XI
DECLARATION REGARDING NON-SELF-GOVERNING TERRITORIES

Article 73

Members of the United Nations which have or assume responsibilities for the administration of territories whose peoples have not yet attained a full measure of self-government recognize the principle that the interests of the inhabitants of these territories are paramount, and accept as a sacred trust the obligation to promote to the utmost, within the system of international peace and security established by the present Charter, the well-being of the inhabitants of these territories, and, to this end:

a. to ensure, with due respect for the culture of the peoples concerned, their political, economic, social, and educational advancement, their just treatment, and their protection against abuses;

b. to develop self-government, to take due account of the political aspirations of the peoples, and to assist them in the progressive development of their free political institutions, according to the particular circumstances of each territory and its peoples and their varying stages of advancement;

c. to further international peace and security;

d. to promote constructive measures of development, to encourage research, and to co-operate with one another and, when and where appropriate, with specialized international bodies with a view to the practical achievement of the social, economic, and scientific purposes set forth in this Article; and

e. to transmit regularly to the Secretary-General for information purposes, subject to such limitation as security and constitutional considerations may require, statistical and other information of a technical nature relating to economic, social, and educational conditions in the territories for which they are respectively responsible other than those territories to which Chapter XII and XIII apply.

Article 74

Members of the United Nations also agree that their policy in respect of the territories to which this Chapter applies, no less than in respect of their metropolitan areas, must be based on the general principle of good-neighbourliness, due account being taken of the interests and well-being of the rest of the world, in social, economic, and commercial matters.

CHAPTER XII
INTERNATIONAL TRUSTEESHIP SYSTEM

Article 75

The United Nations shall establish under its authority an international trusteeship system for the administration and supervision of such territories as may be placed thereunder by subsequent individual agreements. These territories are hereinafter referred to as trust territories.

Article 76

The basic objectives of the trusteeship system, in accordance with the Purposes of the United Nations laid down in Article 1 of the present Charter, shall be:

a. to further international peace and security;

b.to promote the political, economic, social, and educational advancement of the inhabitants of the trust territories, and their progressive development towards self-government or independence as may be appropriate to the particular circumstances of each territory and its peoples and the freely expressed wishes of the peoples concerned, and as may be provided by the terms of each trusteeship agreement;

c. to encourage respect for human rights and for fundamental freedoms for all without distinction as to race, sex, language, or religion, and to encourage recognition of the interdependence of the peoples of the world; and

d. to ensure equal treatment in social, economic, and commercial matters for all Members of the United Nations and their nationals, and also equal treatment for the latter in the administration of justice, without prejudice to the attainment of the foregoing objectives and subject to the provisions of Article 80.

Article 77

1. The trusteeship system shall apply to such territories in the following categories as may be placed thereunder by means of trusteeship agreements:

a. territories now held under mandate;

b. territories which may be detached from enemy states as a result of the Second World War; and

c. territories voluntarily placed under the system by states responsible for their administration.

2. It will be a matter for subsequent agreement as to which territories in the foregoing categories will be brought under the trusteeship system and upon what terms.

Article 78

The trusteeship system shall not apply to territories which have become Members of the United Nations, relationship among which shall be based on respect for the principle of sovereign equality.

Article 79

The terms of trusteeship for each territory to be placed under the trusteeship system, including any alteration or amendment, shall be agreed upon by the states directly concerned, including the mandatory power in the case of territories held under mandate by a Member of the United Nations, and shall be approved as provided for in Articles 83 and 85.

Article 80

1. Except as may be agreed upon in individual trusteeship agreements, made under Articles 77, 79, and 81, placing each territory under the trusteeship system, and until such agreements have been concluded, nothing in this Chapter shall be construed in or of itself to alter in any manner the rights whatsoever of any states or any peoples or the terms of existing international instruments to which Members of the United Nations may respectively be parties.

2. Paragraph 1 of this Article shall not be interpreted as giving grounds for delay or postponement of the negotiation and conclusion of agreements for placing mandated and other territories under the trusteeship system as provided for in Article 77.

Article 81

The trusteeship agreement shall in each case include the terms under which the trust territory will be administered and designate the authority which will exercise the administration of the trust territory. Such authority, hereinafter called the administering authority, may be one or more states or the Organization itself.

Article 82

There may be designated, in any trusteeship agreement, a strategic area or areas which may include part or all of the trust territory to which the agreement applies, without prejudice to any special agreement or agreements made under Article 43.

Article 83

1. All functions of the United Nations relating to strategic areas, including the approval of the terms of the trusteeship agreements and of their alteration or amendment, shall be exercised by the Security Council.

2. The basic objectives set forth in Article 76 shall be applicable to the people of each strategic area.

3. The Security Council shall, subject to the provisions of the trusteeship agreements and without prejudice to security considerations, avail itself of the assistance of the Trusteeship Council to perform those functions of the United Nations under the trusteeship system relating to political, economic, social, and educational matters in the strategic areas.

Article 84

It shall be the duty of the administering authority to ensure that the trust territory shall play its part in the maintenance of international peace and security. To this end the administering authority may make use of volunteer forces, faculties, and assistance from the trust territory in carrying out the obligations towards the Security Council undertaken in this regard by the administering authority, as well as for local defence and the maintenance of law and order within the trust territory.

Article 85

1. The functions of the United Nations with regard to trusteeship agreements for all areas not designated as strategic, including the approval of the terms of the trusteeship agreements and of their alteration or amendment, shall be exercised by the General Assembly.

2. The Trusteeship Council, operating under the authority of the General Assembly, shall assist the General Assembly in carrying out these functions.

CHAPTER XIII
THE TRUSTEESHIP COUNCIL

Composition

Article 86

1. The Trusteeship Council shall consist of the following Members of the United Nations:

a. those Members administering trust territories;

b. such of those Members mentioned by name in Article 23 as are not administering trust territories; and

c. as many other Members elected for three-year terms by the General Assembly as may be necessary to ensure that the total number of members of the Trusteeship Council is equally divided between those Members of the United Nations which administer trust territories and those which do not.

2. Each member of the Trusteeship Council shall designate one specially qualified person to represent it therein.

Functions and Powers

Article 87

The General Assembly and, under its authority, the Trusteeship Council, in carrying out their functions, may:

a. consider reports submitted by the administering authority;

b. accept petitions and examine them in consultation with the administering authority;

c. provide for periodic visits to the respective trust territories at times agreed upon with the administering authority; and

d. take these and other actions in conformity with the terms of the trusteeship agreements.

Article 88

The Trusteeship Council shall formulate a questionnaire on the political, economic, social, and educational advancement of the inhabitants of each trust territory, and the administering authority for each trust territory within the competence of the General Assembly shall make an annual report to the General Assembly upon the basis of such questionnaire.

Voting

Article 89

1. Each member of the Trusteeship Council shall have one vote.

2. Decisions of the Trusteeship Council shall be made by a majority of the members present and voting.

Procedure

Article 90

1. The Trusteeship Council shall adopt its own rules of procedure, including the method of selecting its President.

2. The Trusteeship Council shall meet as required in accordance with its rules, which shall include provision for the convening of meetings on the request of a majority of its members.

Article 91

The Trusteeship Council shall, when appropriate, avail itself of the assistance of the Economic and Social Council and of the specialized agencies in regard to matters with which they are respectively concerned.

Chapter XIV
THE INTERNATIONAL COURT OF JUSTICE

Article 92

The International Court of Justice shall be the principal judicial organ of the United Nations. It shall function in accordance with the annexed Statute, which is based upon the Statute of the Permanent Court of International Justice and forms an integral part of the present Charter.

Article 93

1. All Members of the United Nations are *ipso facto* parties to the Statute of the International Court of Justice.

2. A state which is not a Member of the United Nations may become a party to the Statute of the International Court of Justice on conditions to be determined in each case by the General Assembly upon the recommendation of the Security Council.

Article 94

1. Each Member of the United Nations undertakes to comply with the decision of the International Court of Justice in any case to which it is a party.

2. If any party to a case fails to perform the obligations incumbent upon it under a judgment rendered by the Court, the other party may have recourse to the Security Council, which may, if it deems necessary, make recommendations or decide upon measures to be taken to give effect to the judgement.

Article 95

Nothing in the present Charter shall prevent Members of the United Nations from entrusting the solution of their differences to other tribunals by virtue of agreements already in existence or which may be concluded in the future.

Article 96

1. The General Assembly or the Security Council may request the International Court of Justice to give an advisory opinion on any legal question.

2. Other organs of the United Nations and specialized agencies, which may at any time be so authorized by the General Assembly, may also request advisory opinions of the Court on legal questions arising within the scope of their activities.

CHAPTER XV
THE SECRETARIAT

Article 97

The Secretariat shall comprise a Secretary-General and such staff as the Organization may require. The Secretary-General shall be appointed by the General Assembly upon the recommendation of the Security Council. He shall be the chief administrative officer of the Organization.

Article 98

The Secretary-General shall act in that capacity in all meetings of the General Assembly, of the Security Council, of the Economic and Social Council, and of the Trusteeship Council, and shall perform such other functions as are entrusted to him by these organs. The Secretary-General shall make an annual report to the General Assembly on the work of the Organization.

Article 99

The Secretary-General may bring to the attention of the Security Council any matter which in his opinion may threaten the maintenance of international peace and security.

Article 100

1. In the performance of their duties the Secretary-General and the staff shall not seek or receive instructions from any government or from any other authority external to the Organization. They shall refrain from any action which might reflect on their position as international officials responsible only to the Organization.

2. Each Member of the United Nations undertakes to respect the exclusively international character of the responsibilities of the Secretary-General and the staff and not to seek to influence them in the discharge of their responsibilities.

Article 101

1. The staff shall be appointed by the Secretary-General under regulations established by the General Assembly.

2. Appropriate staffs shall be permanently assigned to the Economic and Social Council, the Trusteeship Council, and, as required, to other organs of the United Nations. These staffs shall form a part of the Secretariat.

3. The paramount consideration in the employment of the staff and in the determination of the conditions of service shall be the necessity of securing the highest standards of efficiency, competence, and integrity. Due regard shall be paid to the importance of recruiting the staff on as wide a geographical basis as possible.

Chapter XVI
MISCELLANEOUS PROVISIONS

Article 102

1. Every treaty and every international agreement entered into by any Member of the United Nations after the present Charter comes into force shall as soon as possible be registered with the Secretariat and published by it.

2. No party to any such treaty or international agreement which has not been registered in accordance with the provisions of paragraph 1 of this Article may invoke that treaty or agreement before any organ of the United

Nations.

Article 103

In the event of a conflict between the obligations of the Members of the United Nations under the present Charter and their obligations under any other international agreement, their obligations under the present Charter shall prevail.

Article 104

The Organization shall enjoy in the territory of each of its Members such legal capacity as may be necessary for the exercise of its functions and the fulfilment of its purposes.

Article105

1. The Organization shall enjoy in the territory of each of its Members such privileges and immunities as are necessary for the fulfilment of its purposes.

2. Representatives of the Members of the United Nations and officials of the Organization shall similarly enjoy such privileges and immunities as are necessary for the independent exercise of their functions in connexion with the Organization.

3. The General Assembly may make recommendations with a view to determining the details of the application of paragraphs 1 and 2 of this Article or may propose conventions to the Members of the United Nations for this purpose.

CHAPTER XVII
TRANSITIONAL SECURITY ARRANGEMENTS

Article 106

Pending the coming into force of such special agreements referred to in Article 43 as in the opinion of the Security Council enable it to begin the exercise of its responsibilities under Article 42, the parties to the Four-Nation Declaration, signed at Moscow, 30 October 1943, and France, shall, in accordance with the provisions of paragraph 5 of that Declaration, consult with one another and as occasion requires with other Members of the United Nations with a view to such joint action of behalf of the

Organization as may be necessary for the purpose of maintaining international peace and security.

Article 107

Nothing in the present Charter shall invalidate or preclude action, in relation to any state which during the Second World War has been an enemy of any signatory to the present Charter, taken or authorized as a result of that war by the Governments having responsibility for such action.

CHAPTER XVIII
AMENDMENTS

Article 108

Amendments to the present Charter shall come into force for all Members of the United Nations when they have been adopted by a vote of two thirds of the members of the General Assembly and ratified in accordance with their respective constitutional processes by two thirds of the Members of the United Nations, including all the permanent members of the Security Council.

Article 109

1. A General Conference of the Members of the United Nations for the purpose of reviewing the present Charter may be held at a date and place to be fixed by a two-thirds vote of the members of the General Assembly and by a vote of any nine members of the Security Council. Each Member of the United Nations shall have one vote in the conference.

2. Any alteration of the present Charter recommended by a two-thirds vote of the conference shall take effect when ratified in accordance with their respective constitutional processes by two thirds of the Members of the United Nations including all the permanent members of the Security Council.

3. If such a conference has not been held before the tenth annual session of the General Assembly following the coming into force of the present Charter, the proposal to call such a conference shall be placed on the agenda of that session of the General Assembly, and the conference shall be held if so decided by a majority vote of the members of the General Assembly and by a vote of any seven members of the Security Council.

CHAPTER XIX
RATIFICATION AND SIGNATURE

Article 110

1. The present Charter shall be ratified by the signatory states in accordance with their respective constitutional processes.

2. The ratifications shall be deposited with the Government of the United States of America, which shall notify all the signatory states of each deposit as well as the Secretary General of the Organization when he has been appointed.

3. The present Charter shall come into force upon the deposit of ratifications by the Republic of China, France, the Union of Soviet Socialist Republics, The United Kingdom of Great Britain and Northern Ireland and the United States of America, and by a majority of the other signatory states. A protocol of the ratifications deposited shall thereupon be drawn up by the Government of the United States of America which shall communicate copies thereof to all the signatory states.

4. The states signatory to the present Charter which ratify it after it has come into force will become original Members of the United Nations on the date of the deposit of their respective ratifications.

Article 111

The present Charter, of which the Chinese, French, Russian, English, and Spanish texts are equally authentic, shall remain deposited in the archives of the Government of the United States of America. Duly certified copies thereof shall be transmitted by that Government to the Governments of the other signatory states.

IN FAITH WHEREOF the representatives of the Governments of the United Nations have signed the present Charter.

DONE at the city of San Francisco the twenty-sixth day of June, one thousand nine hundred and forty-five.

NOTES

These notes single out the most important sources. The most useful archives for the early years is at the National Archives of the US, Washington D.C. Two main record groups were consulted: Record Group 84, the US mission to the UN and Record Group 59, State Department's Bureau of International Organisation Affairs.

A major source was *Foreign Relations of the United States*, United States Government Printing Office. These volumes constitute the official record of the foreign policy of the US. They have rightly been called a miracle of modern democracy. They contain declassified documents giving a comprehensive record of major foreign policy decisions within the range of the Department of State's responsibilities, together with appropriate material concerning the facts which contribute to the formulation of policies. In the notes which follow I have specified the relevant years together with volume numbers. The publication of similar source material should be required by law in the UK but the attitude of the sucessive British governments remains unchanged since 1957, when, on March 6, the Rt. Hon Selwyn Lloyd, then Secretary of State for Foreign Affairs told the House of Commons, "all instructions sent to UK permanent representatives are by their nature confidential". [FO 371/129902.]

The Federal Bureau of Investigation holds an enormous amount of material pertaining to the purges in the UN Secretariat in the late forties and early fifties. Following a Freedom of Information request in 1990, I was sent ninety pages of FBI material in which Trygve Lie, the UN's first Secretary General, who died in 1972, is mentioned. The release of this material made a nonsense of the Freedom of Information Act: everything but Xerox copies of news clippings was deleted. Only a costly and time-consuming lawsuit compelling the US government to comply with the Act would bring to light the material locked away on the UN by this agency. Release of such information is demonstrably and obviously in the public interest as it would lead to a better understanding of the foreign relations of the US.

The UN's own archive in New York contains a wealth of material but the archive suffers from lack of resources. The UN has a twenty-year access rule but it is severely restricted in that the Secretary General is allowed to keep classified records from his office which "could be expected to cause grave damage to confidence in the Secretary General's office or to the UN". Many files relating to the period of the purge remained classified. A further impediment to research is the disappearance of Trygve Lie's files. He took them with him when he retired and they are lost to history.

As is clear from my text, much material was made available from within the UN archive. In all cases where there is sensitive information from both the National Archives, from the Public Record Office, Kew, or from the UN Archives, photocopies are in possession of the author.

Resolutions of the Security Council, together with details of votes cast, are to be found in the annual publication, *Report of the Security Council*, which goes to the General Assembly each year. All current UN documents, including Resolutions, reports and speeches are UN Doc. throughout the notes. General Assembly and Security Council verbatim records, copies of Resolutions and Secretary General's reports should be available at UN Depository Libraries. These documents should also be available in the libraries of the UN's own network of Information Centres. In London the address is 18 Buckingham Gate, SW1E. 6LB. A periodical published by the UN is UN *Monthly Chronicle*, since May 1964. See also *UN Year Book*. Widely used: *United Nations Handbook*, a yearly publication of the Ministry of External Relations and Trade, Wellington, New Zealand.

Of immense value is the yearly *United States Participation in the UN*, *Report by the President to the Congress*, United States Department of State, Bureau of International Organisational Affairs. (Government Printing Office, Washington DC 20402.)

Besides my own reporting and research I have depended on several authoritative sources. On UN peacekeeping the definitive work is Rosalyn Higgins, *UN Peacekeeping*, four volumes, 1969, 1970, 1980, 1981, Oxford University Press. On UN history the work of Sydney Bailey and Evan Luard was invaluable. Similarly, without the books of Brian Urquhart, much UN material would now be unavailable.

In what follows, FRUS means *Foreign Relations of the United States*. The British Public Records Office, Kew is designated FO. The US National Archives are NA with the relevant record group and the UN Archive material is designated as UNA. United Nations documents are UN Doc.

Chapter One, pp. 1 – 22

GENOCIDE

The accounts of survivors are taken from an Africa Rights report, *Rwanda: Death Despair and Defiance*, published in September 1994. The witness interviews it contains were conducted by co-director of the organisation, Rakiya Omaar. The report is the only thorough account of the genocide. Further details come from copies of Oxfam news releases for April and May, 1994. The story of Mary Vainney Benoyeze was told to a British journalist, Jenny Crowther, who was in Kigali making a television programme. The detail of the aeroplane crash on April 6, 1994 comes from wire story dated April 7, 1994 by Andrew Katell, of the Associated Press, "Two African Presidents Killed in Plane Crash".

Further details of the genocide are to be found in "Rwanda, Mass Murder by Government Supporters and Troops in April and May, 1994", Amnesty International, May 23, 1994. On the immediate aftermath of the Presidential plane crash I relied on a telephone interview with Luc Arbegne in Brussels, Belgium, a doctor with Médecines Sans Frontières who was in Kigali the night it happened. Similar help came from Tony Bergener, International Committee of the Red Cross who was in touch with aid workers there.

The circumstances leading to the death of Rwanda's Prime Minister come from eye-witness accounts given in an internal memorandum dated April 20, 1994 from Yvon Le Moal, Acting Designated Official, Rwanda to Mr Benon Sevan, UN Security Coordinator and Mr G. Speth, the Administrator, the UN Development Programme. Unpublished. The details of the deaths of the Belgian commandos comes in part from the office of the magistrate in Brussels directed by the Belgian government to find out what happened. The UN's internal report on the deaths of Lotin and his men is unavailable. A valuable source was also *La Libre Belgique*, particularly Annick Hovine, "La Belgique a salué des para tués", April 15, 1994. Rwanda's immediate pre-genocide history is to be found in Human Rights Watch *World Report*, 1994, published by Human Rights Watch, New York. Similarly the report, Arming Rwanda, Vol. 6, issue 1, part of the Human Rights Watch Arms Project was informative and "Civilian Slaughter", Africa Confidential Vol 35 No. 9, May 1964 contained much needed political background.

Major General Romeo Dallaire was interviewed several times, including a lengthy interview in London on November 25, 1994. Security Council Resolutions written with scant attention to the realities on the ground, particularly true of former Yugoslavia: "UN Commander Wants More

Troops, Fewer Resolutions", *New York Times*, December 31, 1993. Copies of Dallaire's last reports from Kigali, unpublished. In the possession of the author.

The details of Security Council dithering come from lengthy interviews conducted over a period of weeks with Colin Keating, New Zealand's Ambassador to the UN and with the First Secretary at the New Zealand mission, Felicity Wong. I interviewed Ambassador Karel Kovanda, Ambassador of the Czech Republic in New York in June, 1994.

The attitude of the Clinton administration to the genocide is best described by the US Ambassador to the UN, Madeleine K. Albright in Douglas Jehl, "US is Showing a New Caution on UN Peacekeeping Missions", *New York Times*, May 18, 1994.

The letters from the Secretary General to the President of the Security Council are designated S/1994. Statements of the President of the Security Council are S/PRST/1994. The letter from the Secretary General to the President of the Security Council, Ambassador Colin Keating, April 13, 1994 is in the possession of the author.

The story of Rwanda's colonial past was helped by Jack Harris, a former Political Affairs Officer, Territorial Research and Analysis Section of the UN's Division of Trusteeship and by Alison des Forges, of Human Rights Watch/Africa. France's adventures in Rwanda were described in a thorough and revealing two-hour documentary on France 3, in the *Etas d'Urgence* series and broadcast on September 21, 1994. The film includes pictures of the index cards containing the names of the victims. The journalists involved found a pile of shredded documents left when the French Embassy was evacuated after the genocide started. An account of France's involvement is to be found in Patrick Marnham, "Speaking the Same Language in Rwanda", *Evening Standard*, June 24, 1994.

The change in the US policy on peacekeeping is described in Elaine Sciolino, "New U.S. Peacekeeping Policy De-emphasizes Role of the UN", *New York Times*, May 6, 1994. The unclassified text of the presidential decision directive has been released as "The Clinton Administration's Policy On Reforming Multilateral Peace Operation", The White House, Washington DC, May 1994. The refugee crisis was described in Guy Dinmore (Reuters) "Aid Efforts Overwhelmed by Rwanda's Dying", *Independent*, July 22, 1994. Also Lindsey Hilsum, "Silent Killer Follows the Massacres", *Observer*, July 1994. And Chris McGreal, "Beyond Despair", *Guardian*, July 27, 1994.

Chapter Two, pp. 23 – 47

THE GOLDEN GATE

The description of the UN's founding conference comes partly from interviews with: Oliver Lundquist, New York, April 1994 who was on loan to the Department of State from the Office of Strategic Services and who oversaw the design of the UN. His archive is with the Franklin D. Roosevelt Library, Hyde Park, New York.

Descriptions of the conference are to be found in I. F. Stone, *The Truman Era*, 1945-1952, Little, Brown, New York, 1972; Emery Kelen, *Peace in their Time*, Alfred A. Knopf, New York, 1963. FRUS, 1945. Vol 1. Also United Nations Information Organisation, *"We the Peoples..."*, *The Story of the Conference in San Francisco*, HMSO, London, 1946. James P. Connolly, "Simplicity Highlights Parly's Opening", *Evening Sun*, San Francisco, April 27, 1945. *Life*, Vol 19. No. 2, July 9, 1945. British attitude is in Robert Rhodes James, *Anthony Eden*, Weidenfeld and Nicolson, London, 1986. See also *Oral History Study of the United Nations*, DPI Communication and Project Management Services, New York, UN Secretariat: interviews with Alger Hiss, Harold Stassen, Lawrence Finkelstein.

The Soviet *Tass* report on Auschwitz is to be found in Martin Gilbert, *Auschwitz and the Allies*, Michael Joseph, London, 1981. Eden's attitude is in Rhodes-James.

The public relations campaign on behalf of the Dumbarton Oaks proposals and further descriptions of the proceedings at San Francisco are in Robert A. Divine, *Second Chance*, Atheneum, New York, 1967 and Thomas M. Franck, *Nation Against Nation*, Oxford University Press, Oxford, 1985.

Alger Hiss was interviewed in New York, March 1993 and April, 1994. The description of the Charter's journey from San Francisco to Washington see Divine. The meeting with Truman comes from an interview conducted with Hiss by a TV Producer, Michael Ryan, in July, 1994.

Detail of the Senate ratification is in Divine. The debate is to be found in Congressional Record, Vol 91, Part 6, 79th Cong., 1st Sess., July 2–September 10, 1945.

The details of Lie's election come from NA Record Group 59. Telegram from Stettinius to Secretary of State. Top Secret. January 28, 1946. Brian Urquhart, *A Life in Peace and War*, Weidenfeld and Nicolson, London, 1987. See also detailed account in James Barros, *Trygve Lie and the Cold War*, Northern Illinois University Press, DeKalb, Illinois, 1989.

Lie's reaction to his appointment in his memoirs, Trygve Lie, *In the Cause of Peace*, Macmillan, New York, 1954.

The British opinions of Lie and of the Secretariat are in FO 371/57060 (171543). Letter from V.G. Lawford, UK Delegation to J. G. Ward, UN Department, Foreign Office. Personal. Secret. May 10, 1946. See also CAB 134\435 Report on the Secretariat of the UN, Gladwyn Jebb, Chief Adviser to UK del. February 3, 1947. And FO 371/59757 171344. Telegram to UK DEL New York from Foreign Office. Secret Cypher. November 8, 1946.

Roosevelt's idea for the UN in Hawaii comes from *Oral History Study of the United Nations*. DPI. Interview Hiss.

The creation of the Secretariat is in FO/371/59757 Memorandum. "Memorandum on the State of the Secretariat and Suggestions for its Improvement". From Gladwyn Jebb to the Secretary of State for Air, October 28, 1946.

A verbatim record of the staff meeting in March, 1946 is in UNA. Perm Staff Committee file. Verbatim Record of the General Staff Meeting, March 11, 1947. See also FO/371/67485 (A) Summary Record of staff meeting, attached to letter from Cadogan to Attlee, April 11, 1946. Accounts are given in A. M. Rosenthal, "UN Staff Votes to Take Case to Governments", *New York Herald Tribune*, March 12, 1947. "Lie Denies he is a Tyrant", *New York Times*, March 12, 1947.

The Secretary General's attitude to staff and the fate of Rozan are in Brief of the Staff Association of the UN Secretariat on behalf of the Staff Association and Six Terminated Staff Members submitted to the UN Joint Appeals Board. Frank J. Donner, Counsel to the Staff Association of the UN, unpublished. Lie's pessimism is UNA, DAG 1, Binder 2. (Victor Hoo: SG Private meetings). Private meeting in Mr Lie's office at Lake Success on March 19, 1947.

Activities of the Staff Association are in UN Archives, Perm. Staff Committee File. Memorandum. To Hutson from Cordier. Subject: The Elimination of the Word Race from Personnel Forms. May 22, 1946. (Personnel General.) Memorandum. To the Secretary General from the Permanent Staff Committee. Subject: Morale of the Staff, August 27, 1946.

Working conditions are in Jebb: Memorandum on the State of the Secretariat and Suggestions for its Improvement.

Gromyko's opinion of Hiss is in Edward R. Stettinius, *The Diaries of Edward R. Stettinius, Jr. 1943-1946*, New Viewpoints, New York, 1975.

Early profiles of Hiss are to be found in "Alger Hiss of the US", *San Francisco Chronicle*, June 13, 1945; Postscript on Conference personality, San Francisco Chronicle, May 20, 1945. The James Reston comments are in *New York Times*, June 9, 1949. The Gouzenko detail is based on Philip Knightley, *The Second Oldest Profession*, André Deutsch, London, 1986. The most thorough analysis of the Hiss case is to be found in Allen Weinstein, *Perjury: The Hiss-Chambers Case*, Alfred Knopf, New York, 1978. Also Alan D. Harper, *The Politics of Loyalty: The White House and the Communist Issue 1946-1952*.

Greenwood, Connecticut, 1969. See also Alger Hiss, *In the Court of Public Opinion*, John Calder, London, 1957. Alger Hiss, *Recollections of a Life*, Arcade Publishing, New York, 1988. See also Alex Kershaw, "Framed, The Rehabilitation of Alger Hiss", *Guardian*, January 9, 1993; David Margolich, "After Forty Years, a Postscript on Hiss: Russian Official Calls Him Innocent", *New York Times*, October 29, 1992; Serge Schmemann, "Russian General Retreats on Hiss", 17 December, 1992; Victor Navasky, "Nixon and Hiss", *The Nation*, 4 January, 1993; Michael Wines, "Hiss Case's Bogeymen Still Not at Rest", *New York Times*, December 13, 1992.

The details of the Coplon–Gubitchev case come from the State Department file on the case, NA Record Group 59. My attempts in Moscow to find Gubitchev failed. The details of the case as textbook comes from interview with former KGB, Oleg Kalugin, Moscow, April, 1993, Immunity: only the Secretary General and his eight Assistant Secretaries General were granted the full immunity accorded to diplomatic envoys. Secretariat staff had immunity only when acting in an official capacity. On Coplon–Gubitchev case see also Charles Grutzner, "Gubitchev Draws 15 years; Goes Free if he Quits Country", *New York Times*, March 19, 1950. Charles Grutzner, "Gubitchev Sails for Russia with Wife and a Video Set", *New York Times*, March 20, 1950. Early FBI in New York is from Sanford J. Ungar, *FBI – An Uncensored look behind the Walls*, Little Brown, New York, 1975. Initial interest in Gubitchev from decryption: telephone interview with former FBI agent, Robert J. Lamphere, March 14, 1993. The detail about Novikov is from J. Edgar Hoover, *Masters of Deceit, The story of Communism and how to fight it*, Henry Holt and Co., New York, 1958.

On Price see Shirley Hazzard, *The Defeat of an Ideal; A Study of the Self-Destruction of the UN*, Little, Brown, New York, 1973. Thomas J. Hamilton. "Byron Price stays at UN as Lie Aide", *New York Times*, August 16, 1951. On the Price visit to Washington, NA. RG 84.IO: Program Coordination. Memorandum. To Ambassador Austin from Thomas F. Power. "Mr Price's Comments on his Visit to Washington", June 28, 1949. Secret.

The Cordier warning comes from NA. RG 84 IO: Secretariat Staff. Memorandum of Conversation. Case of Stephan Littauer, Polish National. Participants Mr A. Cordier, UN Executive Office. Mr Thomas F. Power, Jnr. USUN, March 30, 1948. Secret. Cordier's second warning comes from NA. RG 84.IO: Secretariat Staff, Office Memorandum to Mr Ross from Mr Power. "Political Reliability of Enrique Sanchez de Lozada", March 2, 1949, Attachment. Department of State, Division of Biographic Information. Sanchez de Lozada, Enrique a.k.a. de Lozada, Enrique. Secret, February 28, 1949. Also Memorandum of Conversation. "Enrique de Lozada". Mr Andrew Cordier, Secretariat. Mr T.F. Power, Jr., United States Mission, March 7, 1949. NA. RG 84. Non-Governmental Orgs. Confidential Memorandum SPA: Mr McClintock. OA Mr Sandifer, February 3, 1947.

Attachment: John A. F. Ennals, Secretary General of the World Federation of UN Associations, Non Governmental Assoc., World Federation. FBI memo detail is in Harry S. Truman Library, papers of Tom C. Clarke, Box 78. Letter from Attorney General to Hon. Robert A. Lovett, October 6, 1948. Vaughan's contact with the FBI see NA. RG 84. IO: Secretariat Staff. Memorandum of Conversation, Status of Mr P. Grigorovich-Barsky, Chief, Russian Translating Section, UN, March 24, 1948. Mission to the UN, Record of the Foreign Service Posts of the Department of State, NA. RG 84.IO: Secretariat Staff Memorandum of Conversation: "Investigations of US Nationals Employed by the Secretariat by the FBI". Mr David Vaughan, UN. Mr T. F. Power, USUN, January 20, 1949.

Mary Jane Keeney: NA. RG 84 IO: Secretariat Staff, Office Memorandum from Mr Power to Ambassador Austin, "Postponement of House Un-American Activities hearing for Mrs Mary Jane Keeney, (US) her Pending Discharge from UN." Secret. May 4, 1949. Testimony of Philip O. Keeney and Mary Jane Keeney and Statement regarding their background, Committee on Un-American Activities, House of Representatives, May 24, 25; June 9, 1949.

Press release: NA. RG 84. IO: Secretariat Staff. Release to Sunday Papers, July 24, 1949. "Testimony given by Witness no 8 – 6 in Executive Session before the United States Senate Subcommittee on Immigration and Naturalization on S. 1832 in Washington, D. C. See also Lie. Details about the Keeneys are in Cedric Belfrage, *The American Inquisition 1945-1960*, Thunder's Mouth Press, New York, 1973. Interviews with former UN employees, Marjorie Zap, Julia Older Bazer, Lukin Robinson, 1993/4. Also Ben Alper, January 1990 and lawyer Marshall Perlin, New York, 1994.

Details of the sackings of the Staff Association officials are in: "Brief of the Staff Association of the UN Secretariat on Behalf of the Staff Association and Six Terminated Staff Members", UN Joint Appeals Board, Frank J. Donner, Counsel to the Staff Association, Donner, Kinoy, New York. In possession of author. Telephone interviews with Ben Alper, Boston, January, 1990. Kehoe details in UNA. Perm Staff Committee file. "Biennial Report of the Staff Counselor", July 1948 – January 1951. Interview Arthur Kinoy, New York, July 1994..

Also UNA. Staff Association of the UN New York, SCC/121, August 8, 1951, Records of Staff Council, UN Administrative Tribunal. Opening Brief on behalf of the Applicants, Frank J. Donner, New York, unpublished. The result of the case is in UN Doc, press release ORG/201, Department of Public Information. Judgment of UN Administrative Tribunal, Administrative Tribunal, Second Ordinary Session, August 25, 1951.

Howrani's last letter to the staff is in possession of author. Leon Edel, "US Seizes Fired UN Aide, Holds Him for Deportation", *Daily Compass*, November 2, 1951. UNA, Staff Committee Archives: full details of

Howrani's last weeks in America are given in a long letter which he wrote to the Staff Council before he left the US, November 13, 1951. Also Leon Edel, "UN Friends Post Bail, Get Fired Syrian Off Ellis Island", *Daily Compass*,November 4, 1951.

The Robinson case see Administrative Tribunal, Judgement no. 15. Case no. 23, Against: The Secretary General of the UN. "UN Unit Reverses Lie Rule on Ouster", *New York Times*, August 11, 1952. Also UNA DAG 3\6, 2.0.5, the File of H. L. Robinson. See also letter from Suzanne Bastide to Mr Lie, September 5, 1952. Interview with Lukin Robinson, September, 1991 and July 1994.

UNA. DAG 3 (Office of Legal Affairs) letter to Lie from Feller. Geneva, July 24, 1952, file of Feller. Secretary General's Private Meetings August 15 and August 26, 1952.

Chapter Three, pp. 48 – 79

PAT McCARRAN

The most significant work on McCarran is Jerome E. Edwards, *Pat McCarran: Political Boss of Nevada*, University of Nevada Press, Reno, 1982. Further details are in Robert Laxalt, *Nevada, A History*, University of Nevada Press, Reno, 1977. The Patrick A. McCarran collection, which contains both documents and pictures and which is at the Nevada Historical Society, Reno, Nevada has interesting material although much was weeded from McCarran's Senate office files in Washington shortly after the Senator's death. See also, Eva Adams papers, Special Collections Department of the Library at the University of Nevada-Reno. A thorough exposé of the McCarran persecution of Dr Owen Lattimore is to be found in Robert P. Newman's address to the Carolina Speech Communication Association, 28 September, 1984, in possession of the author. A description of the Internal Security Act and other relevant details from the period is in Richard M. Fried, *Nightmare in Red*, Oxford University Press, New York, 1990. Truman's reaction to the Internal Security Act, 1950 is in Veto message, Internal Security (McCarran) Act of 1950. Congressional Record, 81st Cong., 2nd sess. (1950)

Testimony of Robert B Alexander, Assistant Chief, Visa Division, Department of State is in Testimony to Subcommittee on Immigration and Naturalization, July 1948. Senate Committee on the Judiciary. *Report to the Secretary of State by the Committee to Study the Question of Whether Persons have Entered the US in Connection with the Work of International Organisations whose*

Presence is Inconsistent with the National Security, Department of State, for the Press, September 1, 1948. In possession of author. On McCarran getting lists NA. RG 84.IO: Secretariat Staff. Memorandum for the files from Thomas F. Power, Jr., "McCarran Committee Request for Department Files". May 31, 1949. Secret.

Harris details come from interview with Jack Harris, London, July 1990 and Miami, 1994. The report is UN Doc T/218. Trusteeship Council, 1949. The House of Lords debate on the report was on May 11, 1949. On the attitudes to colonialism in the UN see FRUS Vol III, 1952-1954, Non-self governing territories. On Scott, hard copy version of story sent to the *News Chronicle*, London, November, 1949. In possession of author. Also interview 1993 with Scott biographer, Anne Yates. Also letter from Michael Scott to the Chairman of the Fourth Committee, October 13, 1954. David Soggot, *Namibia, The Violent Heritage*, Rex Collings, London, 1986. Profile, Michael Scott, *Observer*, December 4, 1949. *Namibia, A Direct UN Responsibility*, UN Institute for Namibia, Lusaka, 1987. Interview with Shridath Ramphal, July, 1992. Scott as agitator, FRUS Vol II 1951. Dulles attitude see FRUS Vol III 1952-1954.

The testimony of Harris and other witnesses is in "Hearings before the Subcommittee to Investigate the Administration of the Internal Security Act and other Internal Security Laws, Activities of US Citizens Employed by the UN", Senate Committee on the Judiciary, October, November, December, 1952.

Lie's response to questions on personnel comes from "Brief on Behalf of Nineteen Applicants", UN Administrative Tribunal, Frank Donner, Arthur Kinoy, Leonard Boudin and Morris Kaplan, New York. In possession of the author.

The Fifth Amendment is from Leonard Boudin, "Dark Days at the UN", *The Nation*, December 6, 1952. The loyalty order is in Sanford Ungar J., *FBI An Uncensored Look Behind the Walls*, Little Brown, New York, 1975. See also Alan D. Harper, *The Politics of Loyalty, The White House and the Communist Issue*, 1946-1952. Greenwood, Connecticut, 1969.

The Van Tassel conference is UN Document: "Proceedings of the UN Scientific Conference on the Conservation and Utilization of Resources". Published February, 1950, New York, UN Dag Hammarskjold Library, UN Secretariat, New York.

On the New Deal, William E. Leuchtenburg, *Franklin D. Roosevelt and the New Deal*, Harper & Row, New York, 1963. An important piece on the UN's early economic work is Susan Strange "The Economic Work of the UN", *Year Book of World Affairs*, 1954. Also interview with Sir Hans Singer, Institute of Development Studies. University of Sussex, Brighton, June, 1991. And Gerald M. Meier and Dudley Seers [Ed], *Pioneers in Development*, Oxford University Press, Oxford, 1984.

On Lattimore: Eric Pace, "Owen Lattimore, Far East Scholar accused by McCarthy, Dies at 88", New York Times, June 1, 1988. And Fried, Harper. Weintraub: Thomas J. Hamilton, "Weintraub Resigns UN Job under Fire", *New York Times*, January 5, 1953. Economic details: FRUS, Volume 1X. 1955-1957. The wailing wall quotation was made by Brazilian delegate Henrique de Souza Gomes, head of the Brazilian delegation and Permanent Representative to International Organisations at Geneva. UN Doc, Note to Correspondents, Note 585, January 6, 1953 contains both Weintraub's resignation letter and the Secretary General's reply.

On Feller: Russell Porter, "U.N. Counsel Dies in 12th-Floor Leap", *New York Times*, November 14, 1952. See also, "UN leaders pay tribute to Feller", *New York Times*, November 17, 1952. UNA DAG 3. Office of the Legal Counsel. Letter to Mr Rupert Emerson, October 30, 1952. (Subject files of A. H. Feller.)

Interview with Caroline Feller-Bauer, Miami Beach, July 1994. Interview with Bernice Bernstein, New York, July, 1994. Feller's FBI file, with deletions remaining: Federal Bureau of Investigation Files, US Department of Justice, Washington, D.C. Reference JPH:PMC. The file on Feller kept by the Senate Judiciary Committee is now in the National Archives. RG 316 UN General 1952, Box 317/282. It contains nothing more than xerox newspaper clips.

The Morris slip-up memo is November 19, 1953, To Eva from Bob, McCarranalia File, Patrick A. McCarran collection, Nevada Historical Society, Reno, Nevada. Further details on Morris and McCarran are in David Caute, *The Great Fear*, Simon and Schuster, New York, 1978.

The definite work on Cohn is Nicholas Von Hoffman, *Citizen Cohn*, Doubleday, New York, 1988. Cohn Presentment story in Von Hoffman and "Brief on Behalf of Nineteen Applicants", UN Administrative Tribunal prepared by Frank Donner, Arthur Kinoy. Leonard Boudin, and Morris Kaplan, New York, unpublished. See also Judith Crist, "US Jury Charges State Department Shield American Reds in UN And Tried to Sidetrack Report", *New York Times*, December 2, 1952. Freda Kirchway, "The War Against the UN", *The Nation*, November 22, 1952. Statements on Feller death: UN Department of Public Information, press release SG/268, 13 November, 1952; press release PM/2435. November 16, 1952.

Feller's book: A.H. Feller, *United Nations and World Community*, Little, Brown, Boston, 1952. The issue of Common Sense, Union, New Jersey, October 15, 1952.

The Executive Order: No. 10422. The White House, January 9, 1953. "Prescribing Procedures for Making Available to the Secretary General of the UN Certain Information Concerning US Citizens Employed or Being Considered for Employment on the Secretariat of the UN." On finger-printing: Shirley Hazzard, *Defeat of an Ideal, A study of the Self-Destruction of the UN*, Little, Brown, New York, 1973. See also A. M. Rosenthal, "UN Fingerprinting US Employees in Start of Loyalty Search on 1,600", January 29, 1953. For relevant documents and staff statistics, FRUS 1952-1953. Volume III. Lie quotation on finger printing is: UNA, DAG 1/1.1.3 – 2, Byron Price, "Memorandum for the Files", February 2, 1953. Assurances on FBI actions by Lie: Secretary General's Private Meeting, February 17, 1953. Memorandum to the Staff, December 11, 1952. Signed by Byron Price. In possession of author.

Threats to UN funding: A. M. Rosenthal, "Wiley Threatens Ban on UN Funds", *New York Times*, December 12, 1952. Staff ban from headquarters, Note to Correspondents, Note no. 490, October 23, 1952. The report by the three jurists is UN Doc A\2364, January 30, 1953, Annex III.

The attitude of the British: Letter from Gladwyn Jebb to Anthony Eden. December 14, 1952. FO\371\101310. And Memorandum from Gladwyn Jebb to Rt. Hon Sir Winston Churchill, Foreign Office, June 11, 1953, FO 371/107023. Foreign Office document: "The Jurists' Report to the Secretary General Regarding his Position in Relation to the Alleged Subversive Activities of Members of the UN Secretariat", G. G. Fitzmaurice, December 18, 1952, FO\371\107023.

Lie's tape of Crook: NA. RG 84 /315.3.11 153 (Declassified after appeal by author). Record of Conversation with copies of letters from Mani Stansen to Madame Paul Bastid, February 2, 1953 and letters from Suzanne Bastid to the Secretary General, February 6, 1953. See also Foreign Office document, Draft of a letter from Mr M. S. Williams from A. E. Drake, Minute A.A. Duff, November 20, 1953, FO 371/107046 172416. Lie's policy see UN Doc, Report of the Secretary General on Personnel Policy, January 30, 1953, A\2364.

British attitudes to Lie: Letter from Gladwyn Jebb to Paul Mason, Assistant Under-Secretary of State, Foreign Office, January 7, 1953, FO 371/107038. Jebb's thoughts: Foreign Office document. Letter from Sir Gladwyn Jebb to the Rt. Hon. Sir Winston Churchill, May 27, 1953, FO371/107050.

American attitude to Lie: Telegram from Henry Cabot Lodge, US Representative, New York to Secretary of State, Washington, February 18, 1953. NA. RG 59 (315.3\2-1853). The diplomatic operation for votes: Circular Airgram. From Matthews Acting. February 5, 1953. NA. RG 59.(315.3\2-553). On Dulles, Keith Kyle's definitive work, *Suez*, Weidenfeld and Nicolson, London, 1991. Dulles desperation: "UN Personnel", Telegram from Dulles to USUN, New York, February 12, 1953, NA. RG 59 (315.3\2-953).

Lie's report: UN Doc. "Report of the Secretary General on Personnel Policy", A/2364. March 10, 1953. As for the debate, the Hoppenot speech (in English) is to be found in General Assembly, Seventh Session, Official Records, 418th Plenary Meeting, March 30, 1953. UN Doc A\PV.418.

Lie's announcement about Hammarskjöld, UN Doc, press release SG/285. Statement by Secretary General Trygve Lie in the General Assembly, April 1, 1953. Paper in pocket: interview with Guri Lie-Zeckendorf, New York, November, 1989.

Hammarskjöld's fears: Foreign Office Document. Minute by C.L.S. Cope, FO 371/107044, June 11, 1953. And letter to Paul Mason from Sir Gladwyn Jebb, New York, April 24, 1953, FO 371\107042. Eda Galser case: Telegram from Lodge to Secretary of State, No. 634. Re: Meeting with SYG; UN Personnel, April 23, 1953, NA. RG 59 (315.3/4-2353). Also Foreign Office Minute. "Confidential", Selwyn Lloyd to UN (Pol) Dept, June 4, 1953, FO 371\107044.

Letter from Henry Cabot Lodge to John Foster Dulles, May 26, 1953, NA. RG 59 [315.3/5-2653], Hammarskjöld confiding: letter to Paul Mason, Foreign Office from R. B. Stevens, British Embassy, Stockholm, May 20, 1953, FO 371\107050.

Secret agreement: Testimony of John D. Hickerson, Assistant Secretary of State for UN Affairs, "Activities of US Citizens Employed by the UN", Subcommittee to Investigate the Administration of the Internal Security Act and other Internal Security Laws, Committee of the Judiciary, Wednesday, December 10, 1952. Also, "Brief on Behalf of Nineteen", as before. The result is in UN Administrative Tribunal, Judgments numbered 26 and 37 to 46 inclusive, Geneva, August 21, 1953. Ruth Crawford, "I Have a Thing to Tell You", *The Nation*, January 24, 1953.

The highest award of $40,000 went to Jack Sargent Harris. The tribunal had taken into account the limited possibility of his re-employment, his "outstanding professional competence" and the limited nature of his work as an African specialist. Harris never worked as an anthropologist again but he was one of the more fortunate victims. From a chance friendship with a delegate he was invited to live in Costa Rica where he emerged as one of Latin America's outstandingly successful entrepreneurs.

On reaction to the awards: FRUS 1952-1954, Vol III. Also, "UN Won't Rehire 4 Ousted US Aides", *New York Times*, September 3, 1953. C. P. Trussell, "M'Carthy Starting UN Loyalty Check", *New York Times*, September 11, 1953. Peter Khiss "Lodge Hopes to Upset Decision on 12 in UN", *New York Times*, September 25, 1953.

Hammarskjöld views on personnel: "UN Personnel Policy", Confidential Minute. P. E. Ramsbotham, New York to C.L.S. Cope, UN (Political) Dept., Foreign Office, London, September 19, 1953, FO 371\107044.

American threats to get vote: Telegram no. 1132, from New York to Foreign Office, Sir Gladwyn Jebb, November 18, 1953. Also UK Delegation Minute, to UN (POl.) Dept from A. A. Duff, November 10, 1953. Telegram no. 1132, From New York to Foreign Office, Sir Gladwyn Jebb, November 18, 1953, Foreign Office Minute, Telegram from Selwyn Lloyd to UN (Pol)

Dept. Telegram no. 1196, November 25, 1953. Telegram from Selwyn Lloyd to UN (Pol) Dept. Telegram no. 1196, November 25, 1953. Confidential telegram from Selwyn Lloyd, November 12, 1953, FO/371/107046.

American hysteria in Foreign Office Minute, FO/371.107047, J. E. Jackson, 26, November, 1953. Hammarskjöld absorbed: Minute by C.L.S. Cope, FO 371/107044. McCarthy in Secretariat: "Recent Decisions of the Administrative Tribunal", Memorandum of Conversation between Dag Hammarskjöld, Secretary General and Robert Murphy, Assistant Secretary for UN Affairs, September 11, 1953, NA, RG 59 [315.3\9-1153].

Hammarskjöld confides in the Americans: "Administrative Tribunal Decisions", Telegram from New York, Wadsworth to Secretary of State, September 21, 1953, NA. RG 59 [315.3\9-2153].

French problem: Telegram to American Embassy Paris from Dulles, October 29, 1953, Incoming telegram, "Personnel Policy Developments', from Lodge, New York to Secretary of State, October 29, 1953, NA. RG 59 [315.3\10-2153\2953]. Dulles insistence: Telegram to American Embassy, Paris from Dulles, "Personal for the Ambassador", November 4, 1953, NA.RG 59 [315.3\11-453]. Telegram from Dillon, Paris to Secretary of State, November 6, 1953, NA. RG 59 [315.311-653]. Telegram to American Embassy, Paris from Dulles, November 13, 1953, NA. RG 59 [315.3/11-653]. No one wants to help America: "French Views on the UN Administrative Tribunal Problem", Memorandum of Conversation, The Secretary and Ambassador Bonnet, November 19, 1953, NA. RG [313.2\11-1953].

Dulles threatens US to leave the UN: State Department Document, "Administrative Tribunal", Memorandum of Conversation, The Secretary, Ambassador Makins and Assistant Secretary Murphy, November 25, 1953, NA. RG 59 [320.15\11-2553]. Beautiful minds quote: Telegram, from Lodge, New York to Secretary of State. NO. DELGA 338, November 30, 1953, NA. RG 59 [315.3\11-3053].

Ending of the loyalty programme: Letter from Sol Kuttner, Adviser, Resources Management, US Mission to UN to Igor Radovic, Director of Recruitment, Office of Personnel Services, UN, June 3, 1986, unpublished.

Chapter Four, pp. 80 – 112

UNITING FOR PEACE

The British pull-out possibility is in "The United Nations: A Stocktaking", ITM Pink (Assistant Under Secretary of State) FO/371 129903. Pulling the levers is in Foreign Office minute, Annex A. "Future Utilization of the UN to Meet the Needs of the West", FO/371/129913.

Britain as pioneer: Emile de Groot, "Great Britain and the United Nations", *Year Book of World Affairs*, Stevens and Sons, Ltd. London, 1954. The jackal quote is from: Minute. I. T. M. Pink, March 30, 1957, FO 371 129903. Dixon's thoughts are in letter from Sir Pierson Dixon to the Rt. Hon. Selwyn Lloyd, June 4, 1957. Confidential. FO 371/129904. On uniting for peace, Foreign Office Document. Letter from Sir Pierson Dixon to the Rt. Hon. Selwyn Lloyd, June 4, 1957. Confidential. FO 371/129904.

On Suez and the UN there is no better account anywhere than Keith Kyle's, *Suez*, Weidenfeld and Nicolson, London,1991. Much valuable detail is also in Evan Luard, *A History of the United Nations, Volume 2: The Age of Decolonization, 1955-1965*, Macmillan, 1989. On Eden being a man of peace, Robert Rhodes James, *Anthony Eden*, Weidenfeld and Nicolson, London, 1986.

The best account of UNSCOP is in Brian Urquhart, *Ralph Bunche, An American Life*, Norton, New York, 1993. Another account is in Max Harrelson, *Fires All Around the Horizon*, Praeger, New York, 1989. Lie's thoughts on partition and international army are in Trygve Lie, *In the Cause of Peace*, Macmillan, New York, 1954. On UN army see: Arthur W. Rovine, *The First Fifty Years, The Secretary General in World Politics 1920-1970*, A. W. Sijthoff, Leyden, 1970.

Bernadotte's success is in the text of Bunche's acceptance speech for the Nobel Prize, December 1950. In Benjamin Rivlin, *Ralph Bunche, The Man and his Times*, Holmes and Meier, New York, 1990.

On UNTSO creation: William Durch [Ed], *The Evolution of Peacekeeping, Case Studies and Comparative Analysis*, Macmillan, 1994. Also UN Publication, *The Blue Helmets, A Review of UN Peacekeeping*, Department of Public Information, New York, 1985. The account and who is to blame for Bernadotte's assassination is in Urquhart on Bunche.

Pearson's suggestion is UN Doc. OR, GA, ES-1 562nd meeting, November 2, 1956. Hammarskjöld's reaction is in Kyle. The appeals from Hungary were Associated Press, November 3, 1956 quoted in Harrelson. On Guatemala see Robert Murphy, *Diplomat Among Warriors*, Praeger, New York, 1968.

On peacekeeping and Hammarskjöld: Evan Luard, *The United Nations*,

How it works and what it does, Macmillan, New York, 1979. Dixon's views: Letter from Pierson Dixon to the Rt. Hon. Selwyn Lloyd, June 4, 1957, FO/371 129904. On news department: Minute by I.T.M. Pink, February 27, 1957, FO 371/129902. Letter from Pierson Dixon to the Rt. Hon. Selwyn Lloyd, June 4, 1957. FO 371\129904. British policy for Bermuda summit, Foreign Office Document, Annex A. Future Utilization of the UN to meet the needs of the West, FO\371 129913.

America on China's UN membership, Foreign Office and Whitehall Distribution, No 66 INTEL, April 9, 1957. Confidential FO 371 129905. On British attitude UN Limitations, Sir Gladwyn Jebb, "The Peking Anomaly', *The Times* February 22, 1955. This story and following detail is in FRUS Vol. III p 642.

Eisenhower on Knowland see Stephen E. Ambrose, *Eisenhower Soldier and President*, Simon and Schuster, New York, 1990. The promises are in: FRUS Vol III, 1952-54. Eisenhower dilemma: FRUS Vol III, 1952-1954. The Cyprus detail is in FRUS: Vol III, 1952-1954, p 753. The linkage is in the same volume, pp 765–66.

Dreading the Tenth Anniversary: Letter Ramsbotham to Cope, January 12, 1955, FO/117504. Not so bad after all: Report from delegation San Francisco to Foreign Office, June 24, 1955, Sir Pierson Dixon's Report to Foreign Secretary, June 25, 1966, FO/ 370 117506.

The thaw in 1955 is in UK Delegation to the UN, *Annual Review for 1955*, March 2, 1956, FO 371\123744.

Dulles desperation is at FRUS Vol XI 1955-1957. Membership for Spain is in FRUS Vol XI, 1955-1957. Prevailing on Peru is in FRUS Vol III, 1952-1954.

Japan and the US signed a security treaty in April 1952 in which American occupation came formally to an end. A peace treaty was signed between Japan and 48 other states in 1951. Japan's position: FRUS Vol III. 1952-1954. British attitude: Foreign Office Document, Memorandum, "The Admission of New Members to the United Nations", UK Delegation, New York, May 13, 1955, FO371\117470

Lloyd's thoughts: FRUS Vol III 1952-1954. Non-member participation is in: FRUS Vol XI 1955-1957. Macmillan's attitude to membership is in Cabinet Document. Minutes meeting October 20, 1955, CAB 128/29.

French attitude to membership in: "Summary Record of Events Leading up to the Admission of Sixteen New Members to the United Nations on December 14, 1955 and January 7, 1956", FO 371/ 123736. Dulles thoughts on membership for Spain: FRUS, Vol. X1. 1955-1957.

In February 1945 at Yalta, Roosevelt made a secret deal with Stalin whereby Russia promised to enter the war against Japan within three months of the defeat of Germany in return for control over Outer Mongolia, transfer of the Kurile Islands from Japan. See Robert A. Divine,

Second Chance, Atheneum, New York, 1967. It is their Ireland: Eisenhower tried to persuade Dulles, damage limitation and Allen Dulles, Molotov/ Dulles meeting in FRUS Vol XI, 1955-1957.

Lodge's gloom: Letter from Pierson Dixon to the Rt Hon Selwyn Lloyd, January 6, 1956, FO 371\123736. Strategies for America: FRUS Vol. XI, 1955-1957. Americans lost grip see FO 371\123736. Eisenhower entreaties: never Outer Mongolia, FRUS XI 1955-57. Martin refuses: FO371\123736. See also D. F. Fleming, *The Cold War and its Origins*, Allen and Unwin, London, 1961.

On Japan and Moscow reactions FRUS Vol XI. 1955-1957. Dixon thoughts are in United Kingdom Delegation to the United Nations: Annual Review for 1955, March 2, 1956, FO 371\123744. America's UN evaluation: FRUS Vol XI, 1955-1957.

Security Council lunches: United Kingdom Delegation to the United Nations: *Annual Review* for 1955, Pierson Dixon, March 2, 1956, FO 371\123744. Hammarskjöld's view of his role in Arthur W. Rovine. *The First Fifty Years: The Secretary General in World Politics, 1920-1970*, A. W. Sijthoff, Leyden, 1970.

Hammarskjöld views on aid are in Brian Urquhart, *Hammarskjöld*, Harper and Row, New York, 1972. His more important speeches are published in *The Servant of Peace, A Selection of the Speeches and Statement of Dag Hammarskjöld*, edited by Wilder Foote, The Bodley Head, London, 1962.

Congo details: Linda M Fasulo, *Representing America, Experiences of US Diplomats at the UN*, Facts on File Publications, New York, 1984. Bunche request from Leopoldville and further detail on the UN's Congo mission is in Urquhart's book on Bunche. See also Brian Urquhart, *Hammarskjöld*, Harper and Row, New York, 1972. See also Emery Kelen, *Hammarskjöld*, G.Putnam and Sons, New York, 1966. Of special value on Congo operations is Indar Jit Rikhye, Military Adviser to the Secretary General, *UN Peacekeeping and the Congo Crisis*, Hurst and Company, London, 1993. See also Luard, Rovine.

The vote for the creation of ONUC: Security Council Official Records, July 14, July 22 and August 9, 1960. Macmillan thoughts: Harold Macmillan, *Pointing The Way, 1959-1961*, Macmillan, London, 1972.

The ONUC mission is also in Andrew Boyd, *United Nations, Piety Myth and Truth*, Penguin Books, London, 1962, p. 161. On shoe banging, a version is in Dwight D. Eisenhower, *Waging Peace, The White House Years, 1956-1961*, Heinemann, London, 1966.

Nash persuading the Indians re troika is in Andrew Cordier, Columbia University Oral History project, New York. The quiet in the Secretariat is Kelen. The crash: UN Doc A\AC.107\Hearing 27, Verbatim record of the 27th hearing of witnesses, Geneva, 27 February, 1963. "Commission to

Investigate Conditions and Circumstances Resulting in the Death of the Secretary-General and Members of his Party", unpublished. Also "Report of the Commission to Inquire into the Accident involving Aircraft SE-BDY", unpublished, in possession of author. George Ivan Smith and Conor Cruise O'Brien, Letters, *Guardian*, 11 and 30 September and 11 October, 1992. David Pallister, "Mercenaries Blamed for Death of UN Head in Air Crash in Northern Rhodesia", *Guardian*, 11 September, 1992. Also The Embassy of Sweden, Ministry of Foreign Affairs document, Bengt Rosio, *The Dag Hammarskjöld Report*, March 4, 1993, in possession of author. See also Cordier.

Chapter Five, pp 113 – 133

THE RED BOOK

The trip to Radio City Music Hall is to be found in Gladwyn Jebb, *The Memoirs of Lord Gladwyn*, Weidenfield and Nicholson, London, 1972. The most thorough account of proceedings at Dumbarton Oaks is in Ruth B. Russell, *A History of the United Nations Charter*, The Brookings Institution, Washington, D.C., 1958. Stalin's quotation about the spirit of unanimity comes from Hugh Thomas, *Armed Truce*, Hamish Hamilton, London, 1986. Roosevelt's announcement that the proposed organisation was the major objective of the war comes from Robert A. Divine, *Second Chance*, Atheneum, New York, 1967.

A good account of the disagreements over the membership of Argentina at the founding conference is to be found in John Lewis Gaddis's remarkable, *The United States and the Origins of the Cold War*, Columbia University Press, New York, 1972. I. F. Stone's account is to be found in I. F. Stone, "Anti-Russian Undertow", *The Nation*, May 12, 1945. I have drawn heavily on the Gaddis account of the fall-out over Poland. Stalin's letter in reply to Truman's threat about not going ahead with the UN is in Gaddis footnote, p. 205. The letter is dated April 24, 1945. See also FRUS: Volume V, 1945. Stalin's views on the UN are based on J. Frankel, "The Soviet Union and the United Nations", *The Year Book of World Affairs*, The London Institute of World Affairs. Stevens and Sons, London, 1954.

Molotov's decision not to attend San Francisco is taken from Graham Ross, Ed., *The Foreign Office and the Kremlin*, British Documents on Anglo-Soviet Relations 1941-1945, Cambridge University Press, Cambridge, 1984.

Moscow attempts to increase the power of the veto are from Frankel and from Herbert Feis, *Between War and Peace*, Princeton University Press, 1960.

The account of Hopkins meeting with Stalin is in Jebb. The anti-veto campaign is in Inis J. Claude, *Swords into Plowshares*, Random House, New York, 1959. Gromyko's attitude to the smaller states in Andrei Gromyko, *Memories, From Stalin to Gorbachev*, Hutchinson, 1989. The Stalingrad quotations come from Feis.

Further details about America and the use of the A-bomb is in Barton J. Bernstein, "The Atomic Bombings Reconsidered", *Foreign Affairs*, January 1995. Sharing the secret is from Charles Messenger, *World War Two, Chronological Atlas*, Bloomsbury, London, 1989. The tea-party analogy is from Divine. The American intentions on sharing the atomic bomb and the lack of control, come from Gaddis and Thomas. The Security Council's first dispute is in Gaddis, Thomas and in D. F. Fleming, *The Cold War and Its Origins*, Allen and Unwin, 1961. One of the most thorough accounts is in Evan Luard, *A History of the United Nations, The Years of Western Domination, 1945-1955*, Vol I, Macmillan, London, 1982.

The Fulton speech is in: Randolph S. Churchill, [Ed], *The Sinews of Peace, Post-War Speeches by Winston. S. Churchill*, Cassell and Co., London, 1948. The demonstration by pro-UN supporters against Churchill is described in Gaddis.

A detailed account of the American suspicions about Trygve Lie are to be found in the absorbing work by James Barros, *Trygve Lie and the Cold War, The UN Secretary General Pursues Peace, 1946-1953*, Northern Illinois University Press, Illinois, 1989.

Cadogan's view of Gromyko is in Memorandum, from A.R.K. MacKenzie, UK Del. to Rt Hon Ernest Bevin. Attached letter from Alexander Cadogan, September 23, 1946, FO 371/59718.

The conversation between Maxim Litvinov and Iverach Macdonald comes from Thomas. Further detail about Soviet purges and the Soviet attitude towards the UN comes from interviews in April 1993 in Moscow with Professor Gregori Tunkin, Russian journalist Felix Alexeyev. Dr Rein Mullerson, visiting Professor of International Law, London School of Economics. Also Grigory Tunkin, *Politics, Law and Force in the Interstate System*, Academy of International Law, Martinus Nijhoff, 1992. The early Soviet attitude to the UN is to be found in Adam B. Ulam, *The History of Soviet Foreign Policy, 1917-1967*.

Lack of Soviet personnel in the UN system is in the fascinating Alexander Dallin, *The Soviet Union and the United Nations*, Frederick Praeger, New York, 1962. The story of Zoya Mironova who led the Soviet campaign for jobs was unearthed in the UN archives. See DAG 1 22/1-2 which includes memoranda and letters. The details of geographic distribution of UN staff comes from Yves Beigbeder, *Threats to the International Civil Service*, Pinter Publishers, London, 1988. See also A. M. Rosenthal, "Soviet Widens Bid for key UN Jobs", *New York Times*, January 10, 1961 and Kathleen

Teltsch, "Soviet Produces few for UN jobs", *New York Times*, September 30, 1961. The Soviet pressing claims is in Theodor Meron, *The UN Secretariat*, Lexington Books, Lexington, Massachusetts, 1977.

The Soviet attitude on the UN Congo operation: interview in Moscow, April 1993, Richard S. Ovinnikov, Foreign Policy Association. Also Arkady N. Shevchenko, *Breaking with Moscow*, Alfred A. Knopf, New York, 1985.

The story about Potrubach and the code cables is in Brian Urquhart, *Ralph Bunche, An American Life*, Norton, New York, 1993.

Roosevelt's thoughts on the job of Secretary General come from Stephen M. Schwebel, *The Secretary General of the UN. His Political Powers and Practice*, Greenwood, New York, 1952.

The story about Hammarskjöld's meeting with Khrushchev in March, 1959 comes from Brian Urquhart, *Hammarskjöld*, Harper and Row, New York, 1972. The Soviet plan to move the UN to Vienna is in Dallin.

Chapter Six, pp. 134 – 158

BANKRUPTCY

On troika: "President Kennedy and the Russian Fable", *Saturday Review*, January 9, 1971. Also Sir William Hayter, "Where the Troika Might be Tried", *Observer*, July 16, 1961.

Thant on poverty (1966): Arthur W. Rovine, *The First Fifty Years: The Secretary General in World Politics 1920-1970*, A. W. Sijthoff, Leyden, 1970. U Thant coining Third World is in the invaluable Ramses Nassif, *U Thant in New York, 1961-1971*, C. Hurst and Co., London, 1988. See also Andrew Boyd, *United Nations, Piety Myth and Truth*, Penguin Books, London, 1962.

On Goa: John Bartlow Martin, *Adlai Stevenson and the World, the Life of Adlai E. Stevenson*, Doubleday, New York, 1977. Thomas M. Franck, *Nation Against Nation*, Oxford University Press, New York, 1985.

On Cuba missile crisis: Alan James, "U Thant and His critics", *Year Book of World Affairs*, 1972. U Thant, *View from the UN*, David and Charles, 1978. A superb account of the crisis is in Elie Abel, *The Missiles of October*, Mayflower-Dell, 1966. Also Bartlow Martin. The offer from Cuba is UN Doc, Address by Osvaldo Dorticos, President of the Republic of Cuba to the 1145th Plenary meeting of the General Assembly, OR., October 8, 1962.

On bankruptcy: H. G. Nicholas, *The United Nations as a Political Institution*, Oxford University Press, 1975 (Fifth ed.), *Secretary General's Annual Reports to the General Assembly* and *UN Year Book*, Budgetary Arrangements. On Article 19: Linda M. Fasulo, *Representing America, Experiences of US Diplomats at the UN*, Facts on File Publications, New York, 1984. Max Harrelson, *Fires All Around the Horizon*, Praeger, New York, 1989. Also interview with Robert Rosenstock, US Mission, New York, July 1989. Also Rovine. Cyprus peacekeeping force: Resolution 186 UN doc S/3375 March 4, 1964.

Congo: Interview with Indar Jit Rikhye, June 1994. Macmillan on troops: Harold Macmillan, *Pointing The Way, 1959-1961*, Macmillan, London, 1972. Evan Luard, *A History of the United Nations, Volume Two, The Age of Decolonisation, 1955-1965*, Macmillan, London, 1989. And Franck, Luard, Brian Urquhart, *Hammarskjöld*, Harper and Row, New York, 1972. Sydney D. Bailey, *The Procedure of the UN Security Council*, Clarendon Press, Oxford, 1988, (Second ed). Also Fasulo, U Thant, Rovine. The taking of Jadotville is in Indar Jit Rikhye, *Military Adviser to the Secretary General, UN Peacekeeping and the Congo Crisis*, Hurst and Company, London, 1993. On Struelens: Arthur M Schlesinger, Jr, *A Thousand Days, John F. Kennedy in the White House*, André Deutsch, London, 1965.

On Vietnam see U Thant. James A. Wechsler, "Citizen of the World", *New York Post*, November 26, 1974. Alden Whitman, "U Thant is dead of Cancer at 65", *New York Times*, November 25, 1974. Little yellow bastard quote: S. J. Taylor, "In the Best of Bad Taste", *Evening Standard*, December 30, 1993.

On UNEF withdrawal: Interview with Rikhye, June, 1994. James A. Wechsler, "The Ordeal of a Peacemaker", *The Progressive*, August 1967. UNA: Transcript of interview with Secretary General by Inter-nation Television Trust Ltd., November, 15 1969, unpublished. Andrew Boyd, *Fifteen Men on a Powder Keg*, Methuen, London, 1971. Also Urquhart, Nassif. Keith Kyle, *Suez*, Weidenfeld and Nicolson, London, 1991. C. V. Narasimhan, *The United Nations: An Inside View*, UNITAR, New York, 1988. Bunche's views are letter from Bunche to Eugene V. Rostow, Under Secretary for Political Affairs, US Department of State, UN Doc, Department of Public Information, Note to Correspondents, no 3426, February 14, 1968. Eban attack is UN Doc. GAOR, June 19, 1967. UN press release EMF/449, Notes on the Withdrawal of UNEF, June 3, 1967. Lord George Brown is in Max Harrelson, *Fires All Around the Horizon*, Praeger, New York, 1989. Thant's attackers are in Wechsler.

The September press conference: UN Doc. Department of Public Information. Speech by Secretary General, Luncheon of Memorial Scholarship Fund of the UN Correspondents Association, September 16, 1971. Press Release SG/SM/1531. See also U Thant's Farewell Address to Newsmen, *The Delegates World Bulletin*, November 1, 1971.

Chapter Seven, pp. 159 – 181

REFORM

China: see Linda M Fasulo, *Representing America, Experiences of US Diplomats at the UN*, Facts on File Publications, New York, 1984. Profile of Bush, "Has Bush at last come to Shove", *Independent*, August 13, 1988. Interviews with Michael Littlejohns, Robert Rosenstock, New York, January 1989.

On UN bankruptcy: UN Doc, Budget Estimates, GA/4395, August 16, 1971, press release. UN Doc, Statement by Chairman of the Advisory Committee on Administrative and Budgetary Questions at the 1427th meeting of the Fifth Committee, A/C5/1377 General Assembly, 26th Session. John G. Stoessinger, "It Takes Money to run a UN", *New York Times*, November 24, 1971. UNA, DAG 1.1.3. Letter from Ambassador Edvard Hambro, Norwegian Ambassador, to Secretary General, October 14, 1971.

Baroody report: UNA. DAG 1.60: 3. Report, no date. In Baroody file. Baroody personality and Bush unguided missile quotation is in William F. Buckley, Jr, *United Nations Journal*, Michael Joseph, London, 1975. Description in Arkady N. Shevchenko, *Breaking with Moscow*, Alfred A. Knopf, New York, 1985. Baroody speech about defence is in UN Doc. Fifth Committee, 1433 rd meeting, 19 October, 1971. Agenda item no. 76.

Waldheim first actions as Secretary General: Ramses Nassif, *U Thant in New York, 1961-1971*, C. Hurst and Co., London, 1988. Waldheim's cabinet meetings, UNA, Files of C.V. Narasimhan. Minutes of Secretary General's meetings with Under Secretaries General and Assistant Secretaries General, Secretary General's house and travel: UNA DAG 1.1.2.10-4. Memorandum from David B. Vaughan to C.V. Narasimhan, February 1, 1972. Memorandum from C. V. Narasimhan to Mr H.K. Matthews, Under Secretary General for Administration and Management, January 31, 1972. Inter-office memo from W. H. Ziehl to C. V. Narasimhan, Travel at UN expense of SG's Wife, February 16, 1972. Kittani's trip: letter from Kurt Waldheim to His Excellency Dr Adnan Pachachi, Minister of State for Foreign Affairs, Abu Dhabi, UAE, February 22, 1972.

Economic development: Report to the Senate Committee on Foreign Relations, US Senate, by Senator George McGovern, South Dakota and Senator Howard Baker, Tennessee, on their service as members of the US Delegation to the 31st General Assembly of the UN, July 1977. Charles William Maynes, "A UN Policy for the Next Administration", *Foreign Affairs*, July 1976 and Tom J. Farer, "The United States and the Third World: A Basis for Accommodation", *Foreign Affairs*, 1975. Moynihan's speech: Daniel Patrick Moynihan, *A Dangerous Place*, Little, Brown, New York, 1975.

UN reform: Antonio Donini, "Resilience and Reform: Some Thoughts on the Processes of Change in the UN", paper presented at Conference Fletcher School of Law and Diplomacy, Boston, November, 1987. And Interview with Donini, Geneva, December, 1988. There is no better than Yves Beigbeder, *Threats to the International Civil Service*, Pinter Publishers, London, 1988 and *Management Problems in UN Organisations*, Pinter Publishers, London, 1987. UN Docs. Report of the Joint Inspection Unit, Official Records of the General Assembly, June, 1969. One of the best explanations of the early failure of the UN's economic work is in Susan Strange, "The Economic Work of the UN" *Year Book of World Affairs*, 1954.

General Accounting Office: A summary of GAO work on the UN is to be found in Statement of Marion V. Creekmore, Deputy Assistant Secretary, Bureau of International Organisation Affairs, Department of State before Joint Meeting of the Subcommittee on International Organisations and the Subcommittee on International Operations, House Committee on Foreign Affairs, June 27, 1979. Statement of J. Kenneth Fasick, Director, International Division, US GAO, before a Joint Hearing of the Subcommittee on International Organisations and International Operations, House Committee on Foreign Affairs on Financial Management in the UN system, June 27, 1979. UN doc, Robert M Macy, "Report on Recurrent Publications of the UN", Report of the Joint Inspection Unit, August 20, 1971. On reform: Marie-Claude Smouts, "A Strategy of Avoidance", International Symposium on Sources of Innovation in Multilateralism, Lausanne, May 26, 1992.

The case of Wesolowska is in Seymour Maxwell Finger and Arnold A. Saltzman, *Bending with the Winds, Kurt Waldheim and the UN*, Praeger, New York, 1990.

The list of missing people: Ron Henson, Helen Hasselbalch and Lori Berliner, "States Continue to Outrage Human Rights of Staff", UN Report, November, 1988. Liviu Bota, "Canada Urges Freedom for UN Staff and Women's Equality", *Secretariat News*, November 30, 1987.

Spies: Interview with Oleg Kalugin, Moscow, April, 1993. Arkady N. Shevchenko, *Breaking with Moscow*, Alfred A. Knopf, New York, 1985. Shevchenko. Also: "Soviet Presence in the UN Secretariat", Report of the Senate Select Committee on Intelligence, May 1985. Meeting the Espionage Challenge: A Review of US Counterintelligence Security Programs, Report of the Select Committee on Intelligence, US Senate, October, 1986. Thomas M. Franck, "Unnecessary UN bashing should stop", *The American Journal of International Law*, Vol 80, 1986. Early travel restrictions: FRUS Vol III, 1952-54.

Maurice Bertrand personnel report: "Report on Personnel Problems in the UN", JIU, July, 1971. The 'UN Obituary': "Some Reflections on reform of the UN", JIU, Geneva, 1985. Maurice Bertrand, "Can the UN be Reformed?", a chapter in Adam Roberts and Benedict Kingsbury [Ed],

United Nations, Divided World, Clarendon Press, Oxford, 1988.

Group 18: The Members of Group 18 were UK, France, China, Sudan, Argentina, Yugoslavia, India, Singapore, Mexico, Zimbabwe, Cameroon, USSR, Japan, Nigeria, Brazil, US, Norway and Austria. Interviews, New York, July 1989: Fred Eckhard, Ambassador Tom Vraalsen, John Whitehead, James S. Sutterlin, also Ambassador Vernon Walters.

UN Doc, "Report of the High-Level Intergovernmental Group of Experts to Review the Efficiency of the Administrative and Financial Functioning of the UN, 1986". GA Official Records, 41st Session Supplement no 49. Interview with Ambassador Joseph Verner Reed, Washington DC, April 1989. Reagan speech: USUN Press Release 92-(86), dated September 22, 1986. Address by President Ronald Reagan to the 41st Session of the UN GA. Telephone call: Elaine Sciolino, "Reagan Plans to Ask Congress to Restore Contribution to UN", *New York Times*, January 1, 1987.

Walters is in: USUN press release 187-(86), December 31, 1986. Reagan speech to GA: The White House, Address by the President of the United States of America Ronald W. Reagan to the 41st Session of the UN General Assembly, press release September 22, 1986, USUN 92-(86). UN Doc, General Assembly Provisional Verbatim record, 19 December, 1986, A/41/PV. 102.

Chapter Eight, pp. 182 – 203

MISSION ACCOMPLISHED

Changes in 1981, Thomas Franck, *Nation Against Nation*, Oxford University Press, New York, 1985. The UN could not do everything: Summary Records of the Fifth Committee, 82nd Meeting, December 17, 1981. For Waldheim electioneering: Brian Urquhart, *A Life in Peace and War*, Weidenfeld and Nicolson, London, 1987. The Waldheim promise to the Chinese is in C. V. Narasimhan, *The United Nations. An Inside View*, UNITAR, New York, 1988. On the campaign turning nasty: Interview With Ambassador Ismat Kittani, February, 1989. Statement by the spokesman of the President of the General Assembly. October 1, 1981. Kirkpatrick: see interview in Linda M. Fasulo, *Representing America, Experiences of US Diplomats at the UN*, Facts on File Publications, New York, 1984.

An excellent account of the Pérez de Cuéllar election is in Michael Manley, "The Shoe Fits". *The Nation*, January 16, 1982. Waldheim's visit to China: Louis Halasz, "How a Byzantine Battle Produced a New UN Boss", *Baltimore Sun*, December 20, 1981. Interview with Olara Otunnu, Paris,

1988. Report to the Committee on Foreign Affairs by the Congressional members of the US Delegation to the 36th Session of the General Assembly, Congressional Delegates at the 1981 UN General Assembly, 1982.

The official version: "Diplomatic Pouch by Petronius", *Diplomatic World Bulletin*, December 14, 1981. This version also in: Paul Eddy, Magnus Linklater, Peter Gillman and the *Sunday Times* Insight Team, *The Falklands War*, André Deutsch, London, 1982. "Caution Takes Diplomat to the Top", *The Times*, December 13, 1981. James Reston, "New Man at the UN", March 31, 1982. Pérez de Cuéllar's view: Pérez de Cuéllar, Text of the Cyril Foster Lecture, Sheldonian Theatre, Oxford, May 13, 1986. Description of how he heard the news: Interview Alfredo Barnechea, Lima Politician, Lima 1989. Interview with Celso Pastor de la Torre, Lima, 1989.

Diplomatic postings: Interview with General Edgardo Mercado Jarrin, Lima, March, 1989 and with Fernando Belaunde Terry, Lima, March 1989.

Official Biographies: *Current Biography Yearbook*, the H. W. Wilson Company, 1982. *Encyclopedia Illustrada Del Peru*, Piesa Lima, Peru, 1987. Lewis Taylor has written extensively on the period: see particularly Dr Lewis Taylor, Peru's Alan Garcia: "Supplanting the Old Order?" *Third World Quarterly*, Vol 8. No. 1. For the junta's policies: David P. Werlich, *Peru, A Short History*, Southern Illinois University Press, Illinois, 1978. Pérez de Cuéllar offering his services: interview with Edgardo Mercado Jarrin, Lima, Peru, 1989.

On Peru foreign policy: Ronald G. Hellman and H. Jon Rosenbaum (eds), *Latin America: The Search for a New International Role*, Sage Publications, 1975. Heraldo Munoz and Joseph S. Tulchin, *Latin American Nations in World Politics*, Westview Press, Boulder, 1984. Ricardo V. Luna, Text of address to Liverpool University, Institute of Latin American Studies, Liverpool, March 30, 1987. On Pérez de Cuéllar and Velasco portrait: interview with Christina, daughter of Pérez de Cuéllar Lisbon, 1990.

Letters from Pérez de Cuéllar to Waldheim from Cyprus: January 6, 1976 and March 11, 1977. On resignation: Letter from Javier Pérez de Cuéllar, To His Excellency, Dr Kurt Waldheim, April 22, 1981. Letter from Kurt Waldheim to Javier Pérez de Cuéllar, Under Secretary for Special Political Affairs, April 29, 1981. On refusal to come to New York, Note for the Record by Diego Cordovez, November 13, 1981. UN Docs, unpublished.

Pérez de Cuéllar returns to Peru alone: "Nuevo Embajador Peruano en Brasil", *El Comercio*, June 17, 1981. Interview with Albert Brun, Lima, March, 1989. On election campaign: Interviews with Javier Arias Stella, Lima, March, 1989. "Pérez de Cuéllar Postulado a ONU", *La Prensa*, October 10, 1981. *Latin American Weekly Report*, 4 June, 1981. "Pérez de Cuéllar, No Sera Candidato a ONU", *La Prensa*, October 11, 1981. *Latin America Weekly Report*, July 31, 1981. Alvaro de Soto, "Notas de Una

Campana", *Caretas*, June 30, 1987. Celso Pastor de la Torre, *Como un Peruano Fue Elegido Secretario Genral de las Naciones Unidas*, Lima, Peru, 1987. Interview with Ricardo Luna, Lima, March 1989.

On American hopes for a Secretary General: Stevenson to Washington, Secretary of State, No. 618, 22 December, 1945, NA. RG 59, File 500.

Chapter Nine, pp. 204 – 237

A CESSPOOL

On world view of Pérez de Cuéllar, personality see the *Year Book of World Affairs, 1983. Report of the Secretary General on the work of the Organisation*, September 7, 1982. On Falklands see Brian Urquhart, *A Life in Peace and War*, Weidenfeld and Nicolson, London, 1987.

Koch: Steve Marcus and George Carpozi, "UN tells Koch: We'll Quit; Koch to UN: So Get Out". *New York Post*, February 11, 1982. Richard Johnson, "Koch Levels Blast at UN", *New York Post*, June 15, 1982. "Post Readers Tell the UN to Shove Off", *New York Post*, February 18, 1982. R. Emmett Tyrrell, "Where the UN Can Go", *New York Post*, February 15, 1982. Charles Carillo, "Angry Post Readers Veto UN's Welcome", *New York Post*, February 18, 1982. David Winder, "United Nations Tries to Put its House in Order", *Christian Science Monitor*, December 30, 1982. Assembly giving a mandate for terror is in: Harris O. Schoenberg, *A Mandate for Terror*, Shapolsky Publishers Inc., New York, 1989.

Kissinger's warning: Daniel Patrick Moynihan, *A Dangerous Place*, Little, Brown, New York, 1975. Bernard Lewis, "The Anti-Zionist Resolution", *Foreign Affairs*, October, 1976. The full debate on the Zionism is racism Resolution is in UN Doc, General Assembly, Official records, Agenda Item 69 A/PV.2400, November 10, 1975. "Arab League Envoy Defends UN Resolution on Zionism\Racism in Letter to US Governors", press release, The League of Arab States, New York, February 26, 1987. The Wyatt Earp quote is from Moynihan. Kirkpatrick: Elaine Sciolino, "Reagan Backs Efforts to Repeal UN Vote Attacking Zionism", *New York Times*, November 11, 1985.

Helms amendment: Susan W. Egan. "The Helms Amendment: A Congressional attempt through legislative tactics and incremental budgeting to force a change in the UN technical assistance policy", class presentation, Department of Health Care Administration, George Washington University, August 22, 1979. *The Problem of Meeting US Financial Obligations to UN Agencies*, Bureau of International Organisation Affairs,

Department of State, February, 1979. The Helms Amendment, Information Memorandum, United Nations Association of the United States of America. Not through voluntary payments: Statement of Marion V. Creekmore, Deputy Assistant Secretary, Bureau of International Organisation Affairs, Department of State, June 27, 1979.

Kirkpatrick and Marxist UN: Peter Samuel, "Jeane: Marxist UN Warns against US", *New York Post*, December 10, 1982. Bernard Nossiter, "Questioning the Value of the UN", *New York Times*, April 11, 1982. Woman in a world of bureaucrats: Bernard Weinraub, "Kirkpatrick Asserts Some in Washington Distorted her Views", *New York Times*, February 1, 1985. Linda M. Fasulo, *Representing America, Experiences of US Diplomats at the UN*, Facts on File Publications, New York, 1984.

Heritage: William Preston, Edward S. Herman and Herbert I Schiller, *Hope and Folly, The United States and UNESCO, 1945-1985*. University of Minnesota Press, Minneapolis, 1989. On anti-American lynch mob: Statement of Burton Yale Pines, "Should the US Acknowledge the Jurisdiction of the World Court", Subcommittee on Human Rights and International Organisations of the Committee on Foreign Affairs, House of Representatives. For a thorough examination of Heritage see Julian Behrstock, *The Eighth Case, Troubled Times at the United Nations*, University Press of America, New York, 1987. On UNESCO: Nicholas and Ernest van den Haag and John P. Conrad, *The UN: In or out*, Plenum Press, New York, 1987. Errors in Heritage see Pace. Kirkpatrick, friends in Heritage: Testimony Hon Jeane Kirkpatrick, Hearing before the Committee on Governmental Affairs, US Senate, "US Financial and Political Involvement in the UN", May 7, 1985. Heritage press releases: Making the UN a Winner, "How to Communicate the UN to People", Pace-UK International Affairs, London, 1987.

On New World Information Order see Behrstock. *Le Monde* exposure of M'Bow is in *Le Monde*, Paris, November 30 and December 1, 1984.

Trygve Lie and Cohen: UNA, Secretary General's private meeting, May 5, 1952. Confidential. DAG 1. Binder 2 [Victor Hoo SG Private Meetings].

Stephen Lewis defence and Whitlam in Haag and Conrad. See Appendix IV. Speech, Gough Whitlam to the General Council of the United Nations Association of Great Britain and Northern Ireland, 13 April, 1985. The Garrick Club dinner was on 19 October. Owen Harries (John M. Olin Fellow at the Heritage Foundation) was there with, among others, Lord Chalfont, Michael Charlton (BBC), Richard Hoggart, Roger Scruton, Sir Huw Weldon. At the Brook Club, October 22, Harries and Brian Beecham, Charles Douglas Home, Gerard Mansell and Roger Scruton. Whitlam also published an account in *Gough Whitlam, Whodunnit? The Assault on UNESCO*, Endpapers Twelve, Bertrand Russell Peace Foundation Ltd, Spring, 1986. Also Ralph Z. Hallow, "Attack on Heritage Foundation Ignites Furore",

Washington Times, May 8, 1985.

MacDonnell Douglas: "OK, Have it Your Way, There's No UN", *New York Times*, October 24, 1983.

Sunset quote: Richard Bernstein, "US Aide Suggests Members Take the UN Elsewhere is Dissatisfied", *New York Times*, September 20, 1983. Michael J. Berlin, "Rolling in to Kiss the UN Goodbye", *New York Post*, September 21, 1983. On Kal 007: R W Johnson, *The Verdict on KAL 007*, Chatto and Windus, London, 1986. Also Seymour M. Hersh, *The Target is Destroyed*, Random House, New York, 1986. Cesspool: "Koch Brands UN a Cesspool", *New York Post*, September 26, 1983. Veto five times as often: 1983 – USSR 3 vetoes, the US 15.

Thirty-eighth floor: Interview with Giandomenico Picco, July, 1994. And Gorbachev concluded: Richard C. Hottelet, "UN Growing Muscle in a Multipolar World", *Los Angeles Times*, March 12, 1989. Early New Thinking, see Margot Light, *The Soviet Theory of International Relations*, Wheatsheaf Books, London, 1988 and Peter Sherman, "New Political Thinking Reassessed", *Review of International Studies*, Vol 19, No 2, April 1993, Cambridge University Press.

Fortieth anniversary and Reagan speech: "US Participation in the UN, Report by the President to the Congress for the year 1985". US and world court: "US decision to withdraw from the International Court of Justice", Hearing before the Subcommittee on Human Rights and International Organisations of the Committee on Foreign Affairs, House of Representatives, October 30, 1985.

Waldheim: Shirley Hazzard, "The League of Frightened Men", *New Republic*, January 19, 1980. Shirley Hazzard, *Countenance of Truth, The United Nations and the Waldheim Case*, Viking Penguin, London, 1990. Myra MacPherson, "Waldheim: The UN's Muted Peacekeeper Amid the Passions", *Washington Post*, January 18, 1980. The most authoritative source is Robert Edwin Herzstein, *Waldheim, The Missing Years*, Grafton Books, London, 1988. The swastikas story was confirmed by two UN guards who decided not to make an official report, interviews New York, May, 1989. Least controversial: Stephen Fay, "The UN Men Most Likely to Succeed", *The Sunday Times*, December 12, 1971. Who looked at records: Paul Lewis, "Inspection of Waldheim Files in 1970s Reported", *New York Times*, June 5, 1986. John Tagliabue, "Soviet Was Reportedly told about Waldheim", *New York Times*, June 7, 1986. French discuss 1979 Report: David Horovitz, "Austrian Intelligence Lied to Kreisky about Waldheim's past", *Jerusalem Post*, March 30, 1988. On Haim Yavin see Joanna Yehiel, "TV's Haim Yavin: First to Question Waldheim on Nazi links in 1971 Interview", *Jerusalem Post*, May 5, 1986. Thatcher's answers are in Hansard, February 19, 1988, Vol. 127, No 98. And letter from Margaret Thatcher to Sylvia Lewin, July 7, 1986, unpublished. Luc Rosenzweig and Bernard Cohen, *Le Mystère*

Waldheim, Editions Gallimard, Paris, 1986. "Allegations Concerning Dr Kurt Waldheim", Hearing before the Sub-committee on Human Rights and International Organisations of the Committee on Foreign Affairs, House of Representatives, April 22, 1986. The Solarz letters are in Hillel Seidman, *United Nations, Perfidy and Perversion*, M.P. Press Inc., New York, 1982. Also press release, "Corruption and Downfall of UN Exposed", MP Press, Jersey City. Interview with Gerald Fleming, historian and with Michael May, World Jewish Congress, London, 1989. Sir Anthony Parsons, Radio Five Live, June 26, 1995. On election: Elaine Sciolino, "Austrian Says Waldheim Got Only Cursory Check", *New York Times*, April 26, 1986. Seymour Maxwell Finger and Arnold A. Saltzman, *Bending with the Winds: Kurt Waldheim and the UN*, Praeger, New York, 1990. Kurt Waldheim, *In the Eye of the Storm*, Weidenfeld and Nicolson, London, 1986. Waldheim as Secretary General, see Finger and Saltzman. Berlin Documents Centre: Michael Palumbo, *The Waldheim Files*, Faber and Faber, London, 1988. A defence of Waldheim: *Kurt Waldheim's Wartime Years, A Documentation*, Carl Gerold's Sohn, Vienna, 1987. Waldheim's role in the Kozara massacre: Richard Bassett, *Waldheim and Austria*, Viking, London, 1988. Addition to any dinner party: Letter to UK Del, New York, June 8, 1955, FO 371\117 452. On CIA links: A. M. Rosenthal, "The Waldheim File", *New York Times*, November 24, 1989. Herzstein would conclude: A. M. Rosenthal, "The Waldheim File", *New York Times*, 24 May, 1994. Tass: General and Western Affairs, June 10, 1986. Serge Schmemann, "Soviet Denounces Waldheim Critics", *New York Times*, June 9, 1986. The rest were Jews: "Waldheim Backer Cites Jews", *New York Times*, February 13, 1988. Report to Meese: Thomas W. Lippman, "US report Ties Waldheim to Atrocities", *Washington Post*, March 13, 1994.

Churchill on war crimes: William Scobie, "Revealed: Italy's Savage War Crimes", *Observer*, January 24, 1988. The seventeen member states of the UN War Crimes Commission: Australia, Belgium, Canada, China, Czechoslovakia, France, Greece, India, Luxembourg, Netherlands, New Zealand, Norway, Poland, Union of South Africa, UK, US, Yugoslavia. South Africa was only involved in the setting up of the commission and subsequently did not participate. Denmark joined the commission as a full member in July, 1945. The Soviet Union did not become a member. See particularly UNA, UN War Crimes Commission, 1943-1949. PAG-3/Rev. 1 1987. Civiletti letter unpublished.

Files kept closed: A. M. Rosenthal, "The Locked Files", *New York Times*, March 22, 1987. Richard Sisk, "Nazis? File 'em under UN-easy", *New York Post*, December 10, 1987. Benjamin Netanyahu, "Open up the UN Archives on Nazis", *New York Times*, October 11, 1987. Transcript, NBC *Today* show, Benjamin Netanyahu, Israeli Ambassador to the UN and Chuck Ashman, *Chicago Sun Times* interviewed by Jane Pauley, November 3, 1987. On meeting between governments: "Notes on Informal Meeting of the States

which were Formerly Members of the UN War Crimes Commission",
November 3, 1986, annex, views expressed by representatives,
unpublished. UK papers destroyed: Richard Norton Taylor, "Slamming the
Skeleton Cupboard Door", *Guardian*, June 6, 1989. Simon Wiesenthal,
"New Accusations about Waldheim Recycle Old Bitterness", letter to the
New York Times, 29 September, 1993.

Amerika film: *Mother Jones*, "The Soviets Take Over the US" January,
1987. David D. Newsom, "Blessed are the Peacekeepers", *Christian Science
Monitor*, February 11, 1987. "The UN vs. *Amerika*", *Washington Post*, January
31, 1987. "UN Bashing goes Prime-time", *Independent*, December–January,
1986–87. Jeff Gottlieb, "Discovering *Amerika*", *Village Voice*, June 24, 1986.
Letter from Carl-August Fleischhauer, Legal Council, UN to Alfred R.
Schneider, Vice President, Policy and Standards, American Broadcasting
Companies, Inc., New York, April 24, 1986, unpublished.

Chapter Ten, pp. 238 – 257

A HARD SELL

Secretary General and a better UN image: UN memorandum to François
Guiliani from Fred Eckhard, January 16, 1988 and attachment: The
Secretary General and UN–Media Relations in 1988. Meeting between the
Secretary General and Mme Sévigny, Executive Summary, interview with
Fred Eckhard, New York, January 1989. On DPI upheaval: B. P. Menon,
"Chaos in DPI as Reform Flounders", *UN Report*, October, 1988. Mandate
of DPI see Peter Fromuth (ed), *A Successor Vision, The UN of Tomorrow*, UN
Association of the US, University Press of America, New York, 1988. On
Death of a Child: UN script entitled *Death of a Child*, memorandum to PRS
from Howland H. Sargeant, November 16, 1949. And Memorandum to
John D. Hickerson, from Howland H. Sargeant, November 4, 1949. NA.
RG 59 Office of Assistant Secretary for Public Affairs, Department of State,
Box III. Akashi comment: "UN film of Homeless will omit US Scenes", *New
York Times*, December 29, 1986.

Soviets in DPI: Testimony of Hon Jeane J. Kirkpatrick, former US
Permanent Representative to the UN and senior fellow, American
Enterprise Institute, US Policy in the UN, Hearings before the Committee
on Foreign Affairs, Subcommittee on Human Rights and International
Organisations and the Subcommittee on International Operations, House
of Representatives, 29 October, 1985. GAO: Report to the Hon Arlen
Specter, US Senate GAO/NSIAD-86-98. "UN Analysis of Selected Media

Products shows Half Oppose Key US Interests", April, 1986. On Lenin: UN Doc, "Committee Continues Discussion of UN Information Activities", press release DPI\457 June 26, 1984.

On Charter as a treaty: Statement of Professor Robert F. Turner, "United Nations Peacekeeping: The Effectiveness of the Legal Framework", Hearing before the Legislation and National Security Subcommittee of the Committee on Government Operations House of Representatives, March 3, 1994.

On Pérez de Cuéllar and Reagan: Interview with James Sutterlin, Westchester, New York, June and July, 1989. Sutterlin is Fellow and Lecturer International Security Program, Yale University, Former Director, Executive Office of the UN Secretary General.

Whitehead: Interview with John Whitehead, New York, June, 1989. Also Michael Blumstein, "Diplomat from Wall Street", *New York Times*, April 19, 1985. Bernard Gwertzman, "Parting the fog at foggy bottom", *New York Times*, January 30, 1986.

Sutterlin: Interviews with James Sutterlin and Fred Eckhard, New York, June, July 1989. Pérez de Cuéllar finance: Interview with Christina, daughter of Pérez de Cuéllar, Lisbon, August, 1988. On Pérez de Cuéller's personality, interview with Sutterlin and other senior UN officials June, July, 1989.

UN 40th GA Review Period. "39 Chiefs of State, 47 Heads of Government, 103 Foreign Ministers", US Mission to the UN, Press Release, December 18, 1985. On Reed's announcement: Interviews with UN officials, New York, 1989. UN Doc. General Assembly, Current Financial Crisis of the UN, Report of the Secretary General, A/40/1102/Add, June 4, 1986. Also US Contributions to International Organisations, 35th *Annual Report*, US Department of State, Report to Congress for fiscal year 1986. Control over budget: Section 143 of Public Law 99-93 (Known as Kassebaum-Solomon Amendment), 1985. Emergency economies: UN Doc. Statement of the Secretary General to the Resumed Fortieth Session of the GA, April 28, 1986. Resumed Assembly: Press Release GA/7282 28 April, 1986. The US against conference centre in Ethiopia is in: Provisional verbatim record of the 105th meeting. Provisional. Statement by Mr Nygard, A/39/PV.105 January 7, 1985.

Letter from Pérez de Cuéllar, Secretary General of the UN to President Ronald Reagan, January, 10, 1986, unpublished.

On certifying reforms: Elaine Sciolino. "Reagan Plans to Ask Congress to Restore Contribution to UN", *New York Times*, January 1, 1987. On Shultz budget: Joanne Omang, "Shultz's Foreign Aid Plea Leads to Stiff Exchange", *Washington Post*, May 23, 1986.

The most useful account of the complexities of the financial crisis is in Margaret E. Galey, "Reforming the Regime for Financing the UN", *Howard*

Law Journal, Vol 31, no. 4, 1988. On increased demands see: Foreign Relations Authorization Act, Fiscal Years, 1988 and 1989 (Sec 702, PL 100-204). Reform not proceeding: Letter from John C. Whitehead to Javier Pérez de Cuéllar, Secretary General of the UN, December 3, 1987, unpublished.

On interest repayments: Interview with Ambassador Vernon Walters, Bonn, March, 1990. Reed: Interviews with Senior UN officials, April–June 1989. "Next UN Official from US: Political Flair" *New York Times*, May 1, 1987. Profile of Under Secretary General Joseph Verner Reed, USIA, "New Top US Envoy at UN: Style and Pens", *New York Times*, May 1, 1987. John Lichfield, "Well-born "Nitwit" Blocked as Protocol Chief", *Independent*, April 20, 1989 and "Next UN official from US: Political flair", May 1, 1987.

Shultz-Reed is in UN Memorandum, June 10, 1988 from Fred Eckhard to Joseph Verner Reed. Re: Talking points for Shultz, unpublished. Letter from Reed to Ambassador Vernon Walters, June 17, 1988, unpublished. Secret meeting with ambassadors: "Concluding Remarks of the Secretary General", attached to Financial Situation of the UN, June, 1988, unpublished.

Pre-brief: Telephone interview with Richard Williamson, March 27, 1990. Telephone interview with Colin Powell, Atlanta, June 26, 1989. Claims continue: Heritage back grounder no 593, October 1988. More on Powell's mind: Interview with former National Security Council staff member, Washington DC, July, 1989. Peacekeeping costs see: "Financing UN Peace Missions", August 18, 1988 by Fred Eckhard, unpublished.

Petition Whitehead: Elaine Sciolino. "Go Directly to Congress, Envoys told", *New York Times*, November 17, 1987. And Elaine Sciolino, "Allies in UN Protest on Budget", *New York Times*, March 18, 1987. Paul Lewis, "Europeans Urge US to Pay Past UN Dues". *New York Times*, June 15, 1988.

New thinking: Press Conference by Soviet Deputy Foreign Minister, prepared by DPI. Information UN Secretariat only, unpublished, October 15, 1987. Soviet briefing, "Press Conference by Mission of the Soviet Union", June 16, 1988. Edward C. Luck and Toby Trister Gati, "Gorbachev, the UN and US Policy", *Washington Quarterly*, Autumn 1988. Soviets paying debts: "USSR Mission to the UN", Press Release No 53, April 18, 1986. Paul Lewis. "Soviet Announces Shift in UN Staff Demanded by US", *New York Times*, June 4, 1988. On Secondment: Soviet briefing, "Press Conference by Soviet Deputy Foreign Minister", October 15, 1987. UN Doc. To Paul Szasz from Fred Eckhard. Re: Secondment and attached: Re: Kasten on Secondment, March 26, 1988, unpublished. On the European statement: Interview with Ambassador Joseph Reed, Washington, May, 1989.

The lunch: interview with Ambassador Joseph Verner Reed, Washington, April 1989. Interview with Deputy Secretary John Whitehead, New York, June 1989. Interviews with Ty Cobb, Washington, 1989, Colin

Powell, Walters and Senator Claiborne Pell, Washington, July, 1989.

Fleischhauer views are from: "Notes on the Obligation of Member States to Bear the Expenses of the UN". UN Doc, Legal Office. And Legal Character of General Assembly Assessments, unpublished.

Reed on reforming the cafeteria: Harry Anderson, Anne Underwood and Robert B. Cullen, "Getting Some Respect", *Newsweek*, August 8, 1988. My American friends: Remarks to the Press by the Secretary General upon leaving the Secretariat at 6.55p.m. From Department of Public Information, September 13, 1988, unpublished.

Plan to pay: Elaine Sciolino: "No Plan Known on How to Meet Debt to UN", *New York Times*, September 15, 1988.

Chapter Eleven, pp 258 – 282

CADILLAC STYLE

Iran–Iraq war: Interviews, New York, July 1989 regarding the private meeting between George Bush, Vice President and Secretary General Javier Pérez de Cuéllar on July 14, 1988. Ian Ball, "Reckless Iran is Blamed for Airbus Tragedy by Bush", *Daily Telegraph*, July 15, 1988 and "Outbreaks of Peace Put Spotlight on UN Chief", *Financial Times*, July 23, 1988. On the war and use of gas, see particularly John Bulloch and Harvey Morris, *The Gulf War*, Methuen, London 1989. Leonard Doyle "Pressure Mounts for Iraq to End Stalemate at UN", *Independent*, August 4, 1988. Interview with Giandomenico Picco, by Michael Lee, July 1989. Leonard Doyle, "UN Chief and Iraq Clash on Gulf Ceasefire", *Independent*, August 3, 1988. Chemical warfare. Security Council Resolution 620, August 26 1988, UN *Monthly Chronicle*, December 1988.

The deaths of peacekeepers: *Annual Register – A Record of World Events, 1988*. (By 1995 the figure was 1,000.) The Khrushchev speech is to be found in: GAOR (XV) 869th Plenary Mtg. 23 September, 1960. Raisa and Marcela: Georgia Dullea. "Raisa Gorbachev gets Place of Honor", *New York Times*, December 9, 1988. Koch: "Ed–UN Should Stay: we need a cesspool!", *New York Post*, September 27, 1983. On Gorbachev reception: DPI, UN Pool report. "UN reception for the Gorbachevs". Published in part.

Address by Mikhail Sergeyevich Gorbachev, General Secretary of the Central Committee of the Communist Party of the Soviet Union, Chairman of the Presidium of the Supreme Soviet of the Union of Soviet Socialist Republics, at the Plenary meeting of the 43rd Session of the UN General Assembly, Wednesday, December 7, 1988, GA OR.

"UN Arrangements set for Namibian voting", *The Diplomatic World Bulletin*, Vol 19, No.2, February 13-20, 1989. A thorough account of the International Court of Justice and Namibia: A. LeRoy Bennet, *International Organisations*, Prentice Hall, New Jersey, 1984.

Genocide of the Hereros: Leo Kuper, *The Prevention of Genocide*, Yale University Press, New Haven, 1985. An account of the UN and Namibia is in: Brian Urquhart, *A Life in Peace and War*, Weidenfeld and Nicolson, London, 1987. The most detailed account is in Mary Allsebrook, *Prototypes of Peacemaking, The First Forty Years of the UN*, Longman, London, 1986. Donald L. Sparks and December Green, *Namibia, The Nation After Independence*, West View Press, Boulder, Colorado, 1992. Faye Carroll, *South West Africa and the UN*, Greenwood, Connecticut, 1967. I. Goldblatt, *History of South-West Africa*, Jatu and Co., Cape Town, 1971. *Namibia, A Direct UN Responsibility*, UN Institute for Namibia, Lusaka, 1987. David Soggot, *Namibia, The Violent Heritage*, Rex Collings, London, 1986.

Linkage: Interview with Chester Croker, Georgetown, June, 1994. Croker's strategy: David B. Ottaway, "Cautious Optimism on Southern Africa", *Washington Post*, July 15, 1988. Robert S. Greenberger, "Diplomatic Success in Southern Africa Provides Lesson for US Policy Makers", *Wall Street Journal*, October 21, 1988. David B. Ottaway, "Africa Policy Experts Asking How Long Croker Can Last", *Washington Post*, March 14, 1986.

The Powell view UNTAG: Interview with Ambassador Vernon Walters, Bonn, March 1990. Interview with Ty Cobb, National Security Council, Washington, July 1989. Interview with Martti Ahtisaari, New York, March, 1993. "UN Approves Budget In first test of Reform", *Washington Post*, December 22, 1988. In the new year, 1989, five new members on Security Council: Malaysia, Canada, Columbia, Ethiopia and Finland replacing Japan, Zambia, Argentina, Germany, and Italy. Canada and Finland were opposed to cost-cutting in the Namibian operation.

The Secretary General: Security Council Resolution 629, January 16, 1989. This or nothing at all: "UN Arrangements set for Namibian Voting". *Diplomatic World Bulletin*, Vol.19, No. 2, 13-20 February, 1989.

Ahtisaari background: Paul Lewis, "UN's Finn in Namibia Finds Tied that Bind", *New York Times*, April 30, 1989. End of peace: Interview with BBC Correspondent Peter Godwin, London, November 1992. Interview with Jeremy Pope, lawyer, Commonwealth Secretariat, London, June 1992. UN presence in Namibia: Interview with Fred Eckhard, New York, May 1989. Kevin Clements and Robin Ward, *Building An International Community*, Allen and Unwin, Canberra, Australia, 1994. The fighting: Peter Stiff, *Nine Days of War*, Lemur Books, Alberton, South Africa, 1989. Reaction in New York: remarks by the Secretary General at informal consultations in the Security Council, Monday, April 3 1989, unpublished. Interviews with senior UN officials. New York, July 89. Interview with Martti Ahtisaari: New

York, March 1993. (South African backing for political parties was admitted by Botha in 1991. There was secret funding to seven parties opposed to Swapo in the election.)

The turkey shoot: *The Annual Register of World Events*, 1989. No UN presence: Anthony Robinson, "Swapo Pays a Heavy Price for Namibian Miscalculation", *Financial Times*, April 4, 1989. Stephen Robinson, "South Africa 'Poised' to Kill Hundreds of Guerillas", *Daily Telegraph*, April 4, 1989. Interview with BBC Correspondent Peter Godwin, London, November 1992. UN Doc., UNTAG Namibia. Status report on UNTAG Military Component, press release, April 3, 1989. DPI daily press briefing, April 4, 1989, unpublished. Christopher S. Wren, "Pretoria Warns UN about Namibia", *New York Times*, April 5, 1989. "Thatcher Blames SWAPO for Clashes", *Independent*, April 5, 1989. David Beresford, "UN Fails at First Fence", *Guardian*, April 5, 1989. The Geneva Protocol is UN Doc. S/20566 April 4, 1989.

Nujoma's fears: Richard Dowden "SWAPO Ill-Prepared for Electorial Combat after Decades of War", *Guardian*, March 31, 1989. Sam Nujoma, "In Namibia, Jubilation and Caution", *New York Times*, March 31, 1989. South Africans complain is in Stiff. Michael Holman, "UN Set to Back Pretoria Account of SWAPO raid", *Financial Times*, April 4, 1989. For the account of deaths see Sparks and Green. Victoria Brittain, "Injuries Show SWAPO Dead Must Have Been Executed", *Guardian*, May 25, 1989.

Paramilitary presence: UNTAG Press Briefing, UNTAG HQ Windhoek. May 24, 1989. John Macdonald, QC, "Police behaviour in Namibia", Letter to Guardian, June 24, 1989. Also Beresford. Richard Dowden "SWAPO Ill-Prepared for Electorial Combat after Decades of War", Guardian, March 31, 1989.

SWAPO reluctant: William Claiborne, "UN Force Waits in Vain for Swapo to Show up", *Washington Post*, April 12, 1989. Christopher S. Wren, "Namibian Transition Again Goes Awry", *New York Times*, April 12, 1989. On terrorising: UNTAG press briefing, UNTAG Headquarters, Windhoek, Namibia, Friday June 2, 1989. Gavin Bell, "UN is Told of Thuggery," *The Times*, May 18, 1989. Leasing mine-proof vehicles: UNTAG press briefing, UNTAG Headquarters, Wednesday, June 28, 1989, unpublished. Ahtisaari's letter: UNTAG Headquarters, Namibia, Letter from Ahtisaari, Special Representative of the Secretary General to Adv. L. A. Pienaar, Administrator General, Office of the Administrator General, Private Bag, Windhoek, June 9, 1989, unpublished.

Arguing over money: interview with Brian Urquhart, New York June 1989. Fingerprinting: interview with UN officials, New York, October 1989. Interview with Commonwealth Secretariat officials, London, June, 1990. Commonwealth: *Preparation for a Free Namibia: Elections, Transition and Independence*, Report of the Commonwealth Observer Group, Windhoek, Namibia, October 10, 1989. HGM (89) 23. Namibian economy: World

Development. November 1989, UNDP.

Exercise in futility: National Press Club Luncheon Speaker, Javier Pérez de Cuéllar, UN Secretary General, National Press Club Ballroom. Washington, D.C., Friday, February 17, 1989.

Chapter Twelve, pp. 283 – 314

NEW THINKING

New Thinking: Interviews with Oleg Bykov, Academy of Sciences, Deputy Director Institute of World Economy and International Relations, Sergey Lavrov, Deputy Minister of Foreign Affairs, Russian Federation, journalist Felix Alexeyev, Richard S. Ovinnikov, Foreign Policy Association, Georgy Shakhnazarov, Gorbachev Institute, Moscow, April 1993. Interview with Dr Rein Mullerson, London School of Economics, London, February, 1993. Steven Kull, *Burying Lenin, The Revolution in Soviet Ideology and Foreign Policy*, Westview Press, Boulder, 1992. Edward C. Luck and Toby Trister Gati, "Gorbachev, the UN and US Policy", *Washington Quarterly*, Autumn, 1988. Statement by V. F. Petrovski, "Soviet Concept of the Place and Role of the UN in Shaping a Comprehensive Security System", June 16, 1988, "New Political Thinking Reassessed", *Review of International Studies*, Vol 19, No. 2, April, 1993. David Armstrong and Erik Goldstein (ed), *The End of the Cold War*, Frank Cass, London, 1990. Also Mark Frankland, "Red Retreat", *Observer*, March 12, 1989. Gary Lee, "Soviets Alter View of UN", *Washington Post*, October 19, 1987. Eduard Shevardnadze, *The Future Belongs to Freedom*, Free Press, New York , 1991. Bruce D. Porter, "A Country Instead of a Cause: Russian Foreign Policy in the Post-Soviet Era", *Washington Quarterly*, Summer, 1992.

Five ministers from Latin America: "UN Verification Sought", *Washington Post*, 10 February, 1989. On Pérez de Cuéllar presenting the bill: Jane Rose, "Silencing the Guns of Aggression", *Guardian*, 14 April, 1989. The story of the UN in Angola is beyond the scope of this book.

The Joint statement and Resolution: Joint Statement of US Assistant Secretary John Bolton and Soviet Deputy Foreign Minister Valdimir Petrovsky, US mission to the UN, press release, USUN 133-(89), November 3, 1989. The American debt is in Financial Emergency of the UN, Report of the Secretary General, Fifth Committee, A/C.5/44/27 November 29, 1989.

The Military Staff Committee: Testimony of John Bolton, former Assistant Secretary, International Organisation Affairs, US Department of

State to the Legislation and National Security Subcommittee of the Committee on Government Operations, House of Representatives, "UN Peacekeeping: the Effectiveness of the Legal Framework", March 3, 1994.

Bush and Gulf War see Kull. New World Order a big idea: President George Bush, State of the Union Speech, January 29, 1991. US Information Service, the Security Council and the invasion of Kuwait: Lawrence S. Finkelstein, "Kuwait and the UN Security Council, Collective Security Revived?", Department of Political Science, Northern Illinois University, October 10, 1990.

The background to the invasion and the story of Farzad Bazoft, Hussein's intentions, and early and modern history of Iraq: Adel Darwish and Gregory Alexander, *Unholy Babylon*, Victor Gollancz, London, 1991. Lawrence Freedman and Efraim Karsh, *The Gulf Conflict*, Faber and Faber London, 1993. Paul Taylor and A.J.R. Groom, *The UN and the Gulf War, 1990-1991: Back to the Future*, Royal Institute of International Affairs, Discussion Paper 38, 1992.

Powell's overhaul of plans for the Middle East: "A Buffalo Soldier on the Brink", *Guardian*, 11 February, 1991. Gorbachev's objection to the world force: Michael R. Beschloss and Strobe Talbott, *At the Highest Levels*, Little, Brown, New York, 1993.

Public relations company in Security Council: Leonard Doyle, "Saddam Faces UN Deadline to Quit", *Independent*, November 26, 1990. Baker's efforts: Bob Woodward, *The Commanders*, Simon and Schuster, New York, 1991. Bush's warning is in Martin Walker, "Bush Tells Troops of Nuclear War Threat", *Guardian*, November 23, 1990. No role for us: Interview with Giandomenico Picco, New York, April, 1993.

Pérez desperate to leave: John Simpson, "The Old Order Changeth", *The Spectator*, October, 12 1991. Conversation with Saddam Hussein: "When UN Resolutions met Iraqi Resolve", *Guardian*, 12 February, 1991.

Transcript of BBC Interview with Christopher Gunness, 23 January, 1991. UN Doc. UN Information Centre, London, News Summary, 25 April, 1991. Iraq bombed to the stone-age: Under Secretary General for Administration and Management. "Report to the Secretary General of Humanitarian Needs in Kuwait and Iraq in the Immediate Post-Crisis Environment". March 20, 1991, unpublished. Baker comment to Aziz: Eric Rouleau, "America's Unyielding Policy Toward Iraq", *Foreign Affairs*, January 1995.

On Kurds: Groom and Taylor. Martin Walker, "Bush Steering UN to Intervention Role", *Guardian*, April 18, 1991. The lack of money pledged: Frances Williams, "UN Aid Plan for Refugees in Disarray" and "We are Waiting for the UN" is in Phill Reeves, Hugh Pope, Christopher Bellamy and Frances Williams, "Help Failing to Reach Kurds", *Independent*, April 12, 1991. On Lynda Chalker: Leonard Doyle, "UN Chief Criticises Modest Aid for Kurds", *Independent*, 27 April, 1991.

On a stronger Secretary General: Hella Pick, "Tangle in the Arms Trade", *Guardian*, May 7, 1991. Also Simpson.

Former Yugoslavia: Misha Glenny, *The Fall of Yugoslavia*, Penguin, Harmondsworth, 1992. Also Sabrina Petra Ramet, "War in the Balkans", *Foreign Affairs*, Fall 1992.

On hostages: Interview Giandomenico Picco, New York, April, 1993. Elaine Sciolino, "Tea in Teheran: How Hostage Deal was Born", *New York Times*, December 6, 1991. UN Doc, Chronology of Secretary General's Role in Helping to Resolve the Hostage Dilemma Since Early August, 1991, unpublished. Con Coughlin, *Hostage*, Little, Brown, New York, 1992.

Chapter Thirteen, pp. 315 – 355

THE MOGADISHU LINE

Details on the Boutros-Ghali campaign: Interviews with diplomats and UN officials in New York, July, 1994. Medical check-up is in *Secretariat News*, September 1991.

Douglas Hurd's comments on the Security Council: Douglas Hurd, "Little Peace for the Peacekeeper", *Guardian*, January, 13, 1992. Boutros-Ghali new era: *An Agenda for Peace*, Boutros Boutros-Ghali, UN, New York, 1992. Boutros Boutros-Ghali, *Report on the Work of the Organisation from the Forty-Sixth to the Forty-Seventh Session of the General Assembly, September 1992*. Interview with Boutros Boutros-Ghali, New York, July 1994. Security Council summit: Leonard Doyle and Sarah Helm, "Major Wins Support for Showpiece Security Council Summit", *Independent*, Janaury 8, 1992.

Boutros-Ghali's row with the council: Leonard Doyle, "Boutros-Ghali clashes with Security Council on Bosnia Policy", *Independent*, July 27, 1992. Harvey Morris, "Give me the Battalions for Peace", *Independent*, August 3, 1992. Leonard Doyle, "The Big Noise at the UN", *Independent*, August 9, 1992. Julie Flint, "UN crisis over West's Tyranny", *Observer*, August 2, 1992. Leonard Doyle, "The Heavyhand of Boutros-Ghali", *Independent*, July 29, 1992. Patrick E. Tyler, "UN Chief's Dispute with Council Boils Over", *New York Times*, August 3, 1992.

On Somalia and UN criminal negligence. Alex de Waal, "Fiddling while Somalia Starves", *Independent*, August 14, 1992. Telephone interview with Alex de Waal, May, 1995. Rakiya Omaar, "What Somalia Needs Now", *Guardian*, August 14, 1992. Julie Flint, "Aid Groups Argue as Somalis Die", *Observer*, August 30, 1992. A detailed description of the UN's mission to Somalia is in Geoff Simons, *The United Nations*, Macmillan, London, 1994. Also Human Rights Watch, *World Report*, Human Rights Watch, United States, 1994.

Doing God's work: George Bush, Humanitarian Mission to Somalia. Address to the Nation, Washington DC, December 4, 1992, US Department of State Dispatch. The *Los Angeles Times* headline: "Somalia, Bush Sending Troops to Save Millions from Starvation", December 6, 1992. Bush and wonderful mission: John Lancaster, "Amid Ceremony, A Lonely Death", *Washington Post*, January 12, 1993. Smith Hempstone: Michael R. Gordon, "Envoy Asserts Intervention in Somalia is Risky and Not in Interest of US", *New York Times*, December 6, 1992.

Boutros-Ghali and disarmament: John R. Bolton, "Wrong Turn in Somalia", *Foreign Affairs*, January, 1994. Interview New York with Elizabeth Lindenmayer, Department of Peacekeeping Operations, June 1994. Interview with Admiral Jonathan Howe, Alexandria, July 1994. Michael Littlejohns, "Pakistani force in Somalia backed by Security Council", *Financial Times*, June 15, 1993. Richard Dowden, "US and UN at Odds Over Somalia", *Independent*, December 15, 1992. Testing the UN is in: Daniel Williams and John Lancaster, "Somali Violence May Delay US Withdrawal", *Washington Post*, February 26, 1993. US leave: Keith B. Richburg, "UN, US Still Differ on Transfer in Somalia", *Washington Post*, February 4, 1993. Mark Huband, "Somali Relief Agencies Denouce UN", *Guardian*, March 1, 1993. Howe takes over: Mark Fineman, "Somalia Debated as US Hands Mission to UN", *Los Angeles Times*, 5 May, 1993.

The Pakistani murders: Report of the Commission of Inquiry Established Persuant to Security Council Resolution 885 (1993) to investigate armed attacks on UNOSOM II Personnnel which led to casualties among them, Commission members: Hon. Matthew M. S. W. Ngulube, Chairman. Lt Gen Gustav Hagglund, Lt General (ret.) Emmanuel A. Erskine, New York, 24 February 1994, unpublished. Interviews: Lindenmayer, Howe, June, 1994.

Most valuable: Médecins Sans Frontières, *Life, Death and Aid*, Routledge, London, 1993 which addresses the problems inherent in Somalia. Also: "A Report on the Second Annual Peacekeeping Mission, November 2-16, 1993",United Nations Association of the United States of America, March 1994. Mats Berdal, "Fateful Encounter: The United States and UN Peacekeeping", *Survival*, Spring, 1994. Walter S. Clarke, "Testing the World's Resolve in Somalia", *Parameters*, US Army War College Quarterly, Winter 1993-94. Trevor Rowe, "Somalia: Hard lessons for the UN – and the US", *The Interdependent*, UN Association of the USA, Vol 20, Number 1, Spring 1994.

Somalia UN: *UN Chronical*, September 1992, Report of the Secretary General, S/23693, March 11, 1992. Security Council S/23829, April 21, 1992. Report of the Secretary General, S/24480, August 24, 1992. Report of the Secretary General, S/24992, December 19, 1992. Report of the Secretary General, S/26022, July 1, 1993. Report of the Secretary General,

S/1994/12, January 6, 1994.

Clinton quotation after line is crossed: Martin Walker, "Officials Hear Emergence of Clinton Doctrine to Back Beleaguered Peacekeeping Operations with Military Force", *Guardian*, June 14, 1993. Everyone better off disarmed is in Michael Littlejohns: "Pakistani Force in Somali Backed by Security Council", *Financial Times*, June 15, 1993. Italy: Mark Tran, "US Head Diplomatic Effort to Resolve Split with Italy", *Guardian*, July 16, 1993. The mission a mess: interviews, New York. Mark Huband, "Infighting Hampers UN in Somalia", *Guardian*, July 23, 1993.

Clinton speech to the General Assembly: Address by the President of the United States of America, William J. Clinton, to the 48th Session of the UN General Assembly, US Mission to the UN, press release USUN 140-(93). Albright conclusions are in Hella Pick, "Insecurity Council Needs a Rescuer", *Guardian*, June 16, 1993. Clinton and not leaving Somalia: R. W. Apple, Jr, "An Old Cold War Refrain", *New York Times*, 8 October, 1993.

Special Operations: Kirk Spitzer, Gannett News Service, "Special Forces Fate Rides on Somalia Units's Backs", *USA Today*, 27 September, 1993. A detailed account of the Delta-Rangers mission on October 3 is in Rick Atkinson, a two-part series in the *Washington Post*, 30-31 January, 1994. Interviews with Howe, Lindenmayer. Also interviews in Somalia conducted by Jenny Crowther, June 1994. Interview Robert W. Gaskin, Business Executives for National Security, Washington, June, 1994. Walter Reed Hospital: Patrick Sloyan, "Clinton's Quick and Dirty Route to a Fiasco in Somalia", *Guardian*, March 17, 1994.

On Mogadishu line in Bosnia: Robert Fox, "Peacekeepers Draw Line at Fighting Warlords", *Sunday Telegraph*, March 26, 1994. The detail on cutting funds for peacekeeping comes from Steve Dimoff, "Congress Budget Cutting Fervor Threatens US Standing at UN", *The Interdependent*, UN Association of the USA, Autumn, 1993. Dole: Speech, Topeka, Kansas, April 10, 1995, US Information Service.

Cambodia, Testimony to Subcommittee on Asia and Pacific Affairs of the Committee on Foreign Affairs, House of Representatives. Developments in Cambodia, October 27, 1993. Anthony Parsons, *From Cold War to Hot Peace*, Michael Joseph, London, 1995. Elizabeth Becker, "A UN Success Story", *New York Times*, April 28, 1995. Also *United Nations Interventions in Conflict Situations, A submission from Community Aid Abroad, Australia and Oxfam, United Kingdom and Ireland to Ambassador Richard Butler, Chair of the UN Preparatory Committee for the Fiftieth Anniversary*. In possession of the author.

Former Yugoslavia, Boutros-Ghali reluctant, creation of UNPROFOR and extension to Bosnia-Hercegovina: Secretary General's Reports to the Security Council: S/23900, May 12, 1992; S/2400, May 26, 1992; S/24075, June 6, 1992; S/24100, June 15, 1992; S/24263, July 10, 1992; S/24333, 21 July, 1992. Telephone interview with Shashi Tharoor, June, 1995. *Report on the Work of the Organisation from the Forty-Seventh to the Forty-Eighth Session of the General Assembly*, September 1993. Thornberry quote is in: Hugh Pain, "Violations of no-fly zone rife, says UN", *Guardian*, 24 November, 1992.

People try to leave Sarajevo: John F. Burns, "Serbs' Campaign for Ethnic Purity Divides up a Busload of Orphans", *New York Times*, August 3, 1992. Waiting in the rain: Maggie O'Kane, front page news story on the death of newspaper photographer Jordi Puyol, *Guardian*, May 21, 1995.

What Izetbegović was told: Leonard Dolye and Tony Barber, "Islamic Plea to UN over Bosnia's Muslims", *Independent*, May 16, 1992. Rifkind: Anthony Bevins, "Military Aid for Bosnia Ruled Out as Too Risky", *Independent*, November 23, 1992. Razek and failure is in: Ian Traynor, "UN a Failure in Former Yugoslavia", *Guardian*, December 7, 1992. The best analysis of Western inaction is in: Lawrence Freedman, "Why the West Failed", *Foreign Policy*, Winter, 1994. The theory that 1990 was the window of opportunity is in: Michael Kelly, "Surrender and Blame", *New Yorker*, 19 December, 1994. Paddy Ashdown, "Strangulation of a city", *Guardian*. December 17, 1992.

Genocide: Leo Kuper, *Prevention of Genocide*, Yale Universtiy Press, New Haven, 1985. Human rights and Mazowiecki: Felice D. Gaer, "UN Operations in Former Yugoslavia", *Balkan War Report*, September 1994. Also telephone Interview with First Secretary Felicity Wong, New Zealand Mission to the UN, New York, June, 1995. EC Investigative Mission into the Treatment of Muslim Women in the former Yugoslavia, "Report on Preliminary Visit", 18-24 December, 1993. Human Rights and UN Field Operations, *The Lost Agenda*, Human Rights Watch USA, 1993. Christopher Greenwood, "The International Tribunal for former Yugoslavia", *International Affairs*, Vol. 69, October, 1993. Stefanie Grant, "Playing in the Hague", UN Operations in Former Yugoslavia, *Balkan War Report*, September 1994. Albright: Julia Preston, "UN Creates Balkan War Crimes Panel", *Washington Post*, February 23, 1993. "A Tribunal for Beginners", *Balkan War Report*, 1995. Hazel Fox, "An International Tribunal for War crimes: Will the UN Succeed Where Nuremberg failed?", *The World Today*, Vol. 49, October 1993. Evidence of defector: John F. Burns, "Slaughter in the Name of Serbia", *Guardian*, December 3, 1992.

Karadžić and population transfers: Misha Glenny, *The Fall of Yugoslavia*, Penguin, Hamondsworth, 1992. Ed Vulliamy, *Seasons in Hell*, Simon and Schuster, London, 1994. Milošević: John McKay, "Working for a Beta day", *Balkan War Report*, May, 1995. The camps are in Vulliamy. The journalists who first went to Omarska and Trnopolje were from the *Guardian* and two ITN television crews, reporters Penny Marshall and Ian Williams. See also Paddy Ashdown, "When Will you act?" *Guardian*, 13 August, 1992.

The best account of Srebrenica and Morrillon is in Vulliamy. One of only two to witness to the stampede for trucks was Tony Birtley of *ABC News*. Vulliamy uses the full text of Birtley's report in his book. Also telephone interviews with General Philippe Morillon, June, 1995. Aslo *Balkan War Report*, March 1993. Security Council report: S/25700, April 30, 1993. State Department in revolt: Michael R. Gordon, "Twelve in State Department ask Military Move against Serbs", *New York Times*, April 23, 1993. Srebrenica, wake up call: Daniel Williams, "White House Faces Test of its Global Leadership", *Washington Post*, May 2, 1993.

Peacekeeping and safe zones: Telephone interviews with Major-General John Arch MacInnis. See also John A. MacInnis, "Peacekeeping and Postmodern Conflict: A Soldier's View", *Mediterranean Quarterly*, Spring, 1995. Telephone Interviews with Lt-General Lars-Eric Wahlgren. Boutros-Ghali, no more money: Paul Lewis, "Despite Doubts UN to support Balkan Strategy", *New York Times*, May 24, 1993. Boutros-Ghali views: S/1995/4444. May 30, 1995. See also Boutros Boutros-Ghali, Annual Report on the Work of the Organisation, 1994.

Blue helmets hostages and Pentagon view: Testimony before the Committee on Armed Services, US Senate, Situation in Bosnia, December 1, 1994. Shortages in troop deployments comes from Humanitarian Intervention. *Effectiveness of UN operations in Bosnia*, Briefing Report to the Hon. Robert S. Dole, US General Accounting Office, April 1994. The numbers of UN troops in Bosnia and the need for more is in: *Reform of the UN Peacekeeping Operations: A Mandate for Change*, a staff report to the Committee on Foreign Relations, US Senate, August 1993. Also Michael Ross and Art Pine, "Senators See Need to Beef up UN Forces if Air Strikes Ordered", *Los Angeles Times*, May 7, 1993.

Chris Gunness and troops needing direction: Mark Heinrich, "Troops Ask UN to Show the Way", *Guardian*, June 30, 1995. Srebrenica and Dutch: UN Briefing Note, Srebrencia, unpublished.

The quote from Zlatco Dizdarević is in: Zlatco Dizdarević, "The United Nations and Us", *Balkan War Report*, September 1994.

Peacekeepers in Europe: Shashi Tharoor, "United Nations Peacekeeping in Europe", *Survival*, Vol 37, Summer, 1995.

Boutros-Ghali meets ambassadors: Telephone interviews with Shashi Tharoor, July 1995 and ambassadors, New York.

For UN's unrealistic resolutions see Rosalyn Higgins. "The New United Nations and Former Yugoslavia", edited text of the eighteenth Martin Wright Memorial Lecture, Sussex University, March 1, 1993. Disasters more complex: *1995 World Disaster Report*, International Federation of Red Cross and Red Crescent Societies. Hannay quote: Barbara Crossette, "UN Falters in Post-Cold War Peacekeeping but Sees Role as Essential", *New York Times*, December 5, 1994. Richard Butler: Christopher S. Wren, "Mismanagement and Waste erode UN's Best Intentions", *New York Times*, June 23, 1995. Dutch are shamed: Patrick Bishop, "What's Best for Them", *Daily Telegraph*, July 19, 1995. Oxfam, *Poverty Report*, Oxfam, London, 1995.

BIBLIOGRAPHY

Abel, Elie, *The Missiles of October*, Mayflower-Dell, London,1966.

Allsebrook, Mary, *Prototypes of Peacemaking*, The First Forty Years of the UN, Longman , London, 1986.

Ambrose, Stephen E., *Eisenhower Soldier and President* Simon and Schuster, New York, 1990.

Bailey, Sydney D., *The Procedure of the UN Security Council*, Second Edition, Clarendon Press, Oxford, 1988.

Barros, James, *Trygve Lie and the Cold War, The UN Secretary General Pursues Peace, 1946-1953*, Northern Illinois University Press, 1989.

Bassett, Richard, *Waldheim and Austria*, Viking, London, 1988.

Behrstock, Julian, *The Eighth Case: Troubled Times at the United Nations*, University Press of America, New York, 1987.

Beigbeder, Yves, *Threats to the International Civil Service*, Frances Pinter Publishers, London, 1988.

Beigbeder, Yves, *Management Problems in UN Organizations*, Frances Pinter Publishers, London, 1987.

Belfrage, Cedric, *The American Inquisition, 1945-1960*, Thunder's Mouth Press, New York, 1989.

Bennet, A. LeRoy, *International Organizations*, Prentice Hall, New Jersey, 1984.

Boyd, Andrew, *United Nations, Piety Myth and Truth*, Penguin, London, 1962.

Boyd, Andrew, *Fifteen Men on a Powder Keg: A History of the UN Security Council*, Methuen, London, 1971.

Buckley, William F. Jr, *United Nations Journal*, Michael Joseph, London, 1975.

Bulloch, John and Morris, Harvey, *The Gulf War*, Methuen, London 1989.

Carroll, Faye, *South West Africa and the UN*, Greenwood Press, Connecticut, 1967.

Caute, David, *The Great Fear*, Simon and Schuster, New York, 1978.

Churchill, Randolph S. (Ed), *The Sinews of Peace: Post-War speeches by Winston S. Churchill*, Cassell, London, 1948.

Claude, Inis J, *Swords into Plowshares*, Random House, New York, 1959.

Clements, Kevin and Ward, Robin, *Building An International Community*, Allen and Unwin, Canberra, Austrialia, 1994.

Coughlin, Con, *Hostage*, Litle, Brown, New York, 1992.

Dallin, Alexander, *The Soviet Union and the United Nations*, Frederick Praeger, New York, 1962.

Divine, Robert A, *Second Chance*, Atheneum, New York, 1967.

Donner, Frank, *The Age of Surveillance*, Alfred A. Knopf, 1980.

Durch, William (Ed), *The Evolution of Peacekeeping*: *Case Studies and Comparative Analysis*. Macmillan, London, 1994.

Eddy, Paul, Linklater, Magnus, Gillman, Peter and the *Sunday Times* Inisight Team, *The Falklands War*, André Deutsch, London, 1982.

Edwards, Jerome E., *Pat McCarran: Political Boss of Nevada*, University of Nevada Press, Nevada, 1982.

Eisenhower, Dwight D., *Waging Peace, The White House Years*, 1956-1961, Heinemann, London, 1966.

Fasulo, Linda M., *Representing America, Experiences of US Diplomats at the UN*, Facts on File Publications, New York, 1984.

Feis, Herbert, *Between War and Peace*, Princeton University Press, 1960.

Feller, A. H., *United Nations and World Community*, Little, Brown, New York, 1952.

Finger, Seymour Maxwell and Saltzman, Arnold A., *Bending with the Winds, Kurt Waldheim and the UN*, Praeger, New York, 1990.

Fried, Richard M., *Nightmare in Red*, Oxford University Press, New York, 1990.

Fleming, D. F., *The Cold War and Its Origins*, Allen and Unwin, London, 1961.

Foote, Wilder (Ed), *The Servant of Peace: A Selection of the Speeches and Statements of Dag Hammarskjöld*, The Bodley Head, London, 1962.

Franck, Thomas M., *Nation Against Nation*, Oxford University Press, New York, 1985.

Fromuth, Peter (Ed), *A Successor Vision, The UN of Tomorrow*, UN Association of the US, University Press of America, New York, 1988.

Gaddis, John Lewis, *The United States and the Origins of the Cold War*, Columbia University Press, New York, 1972.

Gilbert, Martin, *Auschwitz and the Allies*, Michael Joseph, London, 1981.

Gladwyn, Lord, *The Memoirs of Lord Gladwyn*, Weidenfeld and Nicolson, London, 1972.

Glenny, Misha, *The Fall of Yugoslavia*, Penguin, Harmondsworth, 1992.

Goldblatt, I., *History of South-West Africa*, Jatu and Co., Cape Town, 1971.

Gromyko, Andrei, *Memories, From Stalin to Gorbachev*, Hutchinson, London, 1989.

Hammarskjöld, Dag, *Markings*, Faber and Faber, London, 1964.

Harrelson, Max, *Fires All Around the Horizon*, Praeger, New York, 1989.

Harper, Alan D., *The Politics of Loyalty, The White House and the Communist Issue, 1946-1952*, Greenwood Press, Connecticut, 1969.

Hazzard, Shirley, *Countenance of Truth. The United Nations and the Waldheim Case*, Viking, 1990.

Hellman Ronald G. and Rosenbaum, H. Jon (Ed), *Latin America: The Search for a New International Role*, Sage Publications, London, 1975.

Hersh, Seymour M., *The Target is Destroyed*, Random House, 1986.

Herzstein, Robert Edwin, *Waldheim, The Missing Years*, Grafton Books, London, 1988.

Hiss, Alger, *In the Court of Public Opinion*, John Calder, London, 1957.

Hiss, Alger, *Recollections of a Life*, Arcade Publishing, New York, 1988.

Human Rights Watch, *The Lost Agenda*, Human Rights Watch, New York, 1993.

Johnson, R. W., *The Verdict on KAL 007*, Chatto and Windus, London 1986.

Kelen, Emery, *Peace in their Time*, Alfred A. Knopf, New York, 1963.

Kelen, Emery, *Hammarskjöld*, G.Putnam and Sons, New York, 1966.

Knightley, Phillip, *The Second Oldest Profession*, André Deutsch, London, 1986.

Kyle, Keith, *Suez*, Weidenfeld and Nicholson, London, 1991.

Kuper, Leo, *The Prevention of Genocide*, Yale University Press, New Haven, 1985.

Laxalt, Robert, *Nevada, A Bicentennial History*, University of Nevada Press, Nevada, 1977.

Legum, Colin, *Congo Disaster*, Penguin, London, 1961.

Leuchtenburg, William E., *Franklin D. Roosevelt and the New Deal*, Harper and Row, New York. 1963.

Lie, Trygve, *In the Cause of Peace*, Macmillan, New York, 1954.

Light, Margot, *The Soviet Theory of International Relations*, Wheatsheaf Books, London, 1988

Luard, Evan, *A History of the United Nations. Vol 1: The Years of Western Domination, 1945-1955*, Macmillan, London, 1982.

Luard, Evan, *A History of the United Nations, Vol 2: The Age of Decolonisation, 1955-1965*, Macmillan, London, 1989.

Luard, Evan, *The United Nations: How it Works and What it Does*, Macmillan, London, 1979.

Macmillan, Harold, *Pointing The Way, 1959-1961*, Macmillan, London, 1972.

Meron, Theodor, *The UN Secretariat*, Lexington Books, Lexington, Massachusetts, 1977.

Messenger, Charles, *World War Two, Chronological Atlas*, Bloomsbury, London, 1989.

Moynihan, Daniel Patrick, *A Dangerous Place*, Little, Brown, New York, 1975.

Munoz, Heraldo and Tulchin, Joseph S., *Latin American Nations in World Politics*, Westview Press, Boulder, 1984.

Murphy, Robert, *Diplomat Among Warriors*, Praeger, New York, 1968.

Narasimhan, C V., *The United Nations: An Inside View*, UNITAR, New York, 1988.

Nassif, Ramses, *U Thant in New York, 1961-1971*, C. Hurst and Co., London, 1988.

Nicholas, H. G, *The United Nations as a Political Institution*, Oxford University Press, Oxford, 1975

Palumbo, Michael, *The Waldheim Files*, Faber and Faber, London, 1988.

Parsons, Anthony, *From Cold War to Hot Peace*, Michael Joseph, London, 1995.

Pastor de la Torre, Celso, *Como un Peruano Fue Elegido Secretario Genral de las Naciones Unidas*, Lima, Peru, 1987.

Pike, Frederick B, *The Modern History of Peru*, Weidenfeld and Nicolson, London, 1967.

Pitt, David and Weiss, Thomas G. (Ed), *The Nature of United Nations Bureaucracies*, Croom Helm, Kent, 1986.

Preston, William, Edward, S. Herman and Herbert I. Schiller, *Hope and Folly: The United States and UNESCO, 1945-1985*, University of Minnesota Press, Minneapolis, 1989.

Rhodes-James, Robert, *Anthony Eden*, Weidenfeld and Nicolson, London, 1986.

431

Rieff, David, *Slaughterhouse, Bosnia and the Failure of the West*, Vintage, London, 1995.

Rikhye, Indar Jit, *Military Adviser to the Secretary General, UN Peacekeeping and the Congo Crisis*, Hurst and Company, London, 1993.

Rivlin, Benjamin, *Ralph Bunche: The Man and his Times*, Holmes and Meier, New York, 1990.

Roberts, Adam and Kingsbury, Benedict (Ed), *United Nations, Divided World*, Clarendon Press, Oxford, 1988.

Rosenzweig, Luc and Cohen Bernard, *Le Mystère Waldheim*, Editions Gallimard, Paris, 1986.

Rovine, Arthur W., *The First Fifty Years: The Secretary General in World Politics 1920-1970*, A. W. Sijthoff, Leyden, 1970.

Russel, Ruth B., *A History of the United Nations Charter*, The Brookings Institution, Washington, D.C., 1958.

Schlesinger, Arthur M. Jr, *A Thousand Days: John F. Kennedy in the White House*, André Deutsch, London, 1965.

Schoenberg, Harris O., *A Mandate for Terror*, Shapolsky Publishers Inc., New York, 1989.

Schwebel, Stephen M., *The Secretary General of the United Nations, His Political Powers and Practice*, Greenwood Press, New York, 1952.

Seidman, Hillel, *United Nations, Perfidy and Perversion*, M.P. Press Inc., New York, 1982.

Shevchenko, Arkady N., *Breaking with Moscow*, Alfred A. Knopf, New York, 1985.

Simons, Geoff, *The United Nations: A Chronology of Conflict*, Macmillan, London, 1994.

Soggot, David, *Namibia, The Violent Heritage*, Rex Collings, London, 1986.

Sparks Donald L. and Green, December, *Namibia: The Nation After Independence*. West View Press, Boulder, Colorado, 1992.

Stettinius, Edward R., *The Diaries of Edward R. Stettinius, Jr. 1943-1946*, New Viewpoints, New York, 1975.

Stiff, Peter, *Nine Days of War*, Lemur Books, Alberton, South Africa, 1989.

Stone, I. F., *The Truman Era, 1945-1952*, Little, Brown, New York, 1972.

Thant, U., *View from the UN*, David and Charles, London, 1978.

Thomas, Hugh, *Armed Truce*, Hamish Hamilton, London, 1986.

Tunkin, Grigory, *Politics, Law and Force in the Interstate System*, Academy of International Law, Martinus Nijhoff, 1992.

Ungar, Sanford J., *FBI. An Uncensored look behind the Walls*, Little, Brown, New York, 1975.

UN Institute for Namibia, *Namibia: A Direct UN Responsibility,* Lusaka, 1987.

United Nations, *The Blue Helmets*, The Department of Public Information, United Nations, 1985.

Urquhart, Brian, *Hammarksjöld*, Harper and Row, New York, 1972.

Urquhart, Brian, *Ralph Bunche: An American Life*, W. W. Norton, New York. 1993.

Urquhart, Brian, *A Life in Peace and War*, Weidenfeld and Nicolson, London, 1987.

Vulliamy, Ed, *Seasons in Hell*, Simon and Schuster, London, 1994.

Waldheim, Kurt, *In the Eye of the Storm*, Weidenfeld and Nicholson, London, 1986.

Weinstein, Allen, *Perjury: The Hiss-Chambers Case*, Alfred Knopf, New York, 1978.

Werlich. David P., *Peru: A Short History*, Southern Illinois University Press, Chicago, 1978

Woodward, Bob, *The Commanders*, Simon and Schuster, New York, 1991.

Van Den Haag, Ernest and John P. Conrad, *The UN: In or Out*, Plenum Press, New York, 1987.

Von Hoffman, Nicholas, *Citizen Cohn*, Doubleday, New York, 1988.

ACKNOWLEDGMENTS

There are conflicts in which the United Nations is involved which are not covered in this book: I think particularly of Angola, Sudan, Liberia, Mozambique. Neither was it within the scope of the book to cover the peacekeeping credentials given to Russia in Tajikstan. I am aware that the book is written from a First World view.

Many studies on the UN are produced in academia, and governments conduct their own enquiries, but from a journalist's point of view the UN is one of the world's most under-reported organisations. So much is taken at face value and so little is known. A fog of misinformation envelopes the Secretariat, a situation which ideally suits its member governments. It is not always possible to keep some matters secret for ever and the evidence gathered here will go some way to explain what happened to the world's last, best hope.

The world of international diplomacy is a closed shop and curious outsiders are often dismissed. The covert behaviour practised in this twilight zone helps to ensure that information is reserved for those with an inside track. There is an ever-present inclination towards cover-up. Some were persuaded that an accessible history of the UN needed to be written and there were some notable indiscretions. I thank those involved. Many hundreds of people gave up their time to help me and are too numerous to name.

Many stories in this book are owed to the declassifiers, both in the Public Record Office in Kew and at the National Archives of the US in Washington DC. I thank the archivists for their patience and for skill – and for their photocopiers. I thank particularly John Taylor at the National Archives. Also in Washington I would like to thank Margaret E. Galey, Staff Consultant, Committee on Foreign Affairs, US House of Representatives. I also thank Marjorie Ann Brown of the Library of Congress's Congressional Research Service in the US Congress, Washington. In Washington I thank Steve Dimoff, Editor of the *Washington Weekly Report*, United Nations Association of the United States.

In the UN Secretariat in New York my thanks go to Fred Eckhard and Joe Sills in the Department of Public Information. In the photo-library I would like to thank Joyce Rosenblaum. At the Dag Hammarskjöld library I would like to thank Maureen Ratynski. In the UN archives I am particularly grateful to Marilla Guptil. In the Department of Peacekeeping Operations I thank Kofi Annan, Elizabeth Lindenmayer, and Maurice Baril and I hope they read the book. At the United Nations Association of America I owe particular thanks to Edward C. Luck, President Emeritus, Senior Policy Advisor, UN Association of the USA. I am also grateful to Leonard Doyle and to Chris Gunness.

In Moscow I would like to thank Felix and Nellie Alexeyev and Natasha Souproun. At the University of Liverpool I thank Dr Rory Miller of the Department of Economic and Social History, and Dr Lewis Taylor, Institute of Latin American Studies. For allowing me access to the valuable Peruvian collection in the library, Professor John Fisher, Director of the Institute.

Research was made easier with access to the library of the Royal Institute of International Affairs and I thank Susan Franks, every author's ideal librarian, and all the staff for their help. I am most grateful also to Eileen Murtagh, the Librarian at the Commonwealth Secretariat. At the Commonwealth Secretariat I thank Terence R. Dormer, Chief Project Officer, most helpful on Namibia.

I owe a huge debt to the UN pioneers from the early days. Julia Bazer who edited the first of the Secretary General's annual reports, kept me informed weekly of the latest American attitude towards the UN and she edited the chapters detailing the purges. I thank Julian Behrstock in Paris who read some chapters and made valuable comments. I thank Jack and Shirley Harris in Costa Rica and Lukin Robinson in Canada and Marjorie Zap. With much regret I missed meeting Ben Alper although I spoke with him on the telephone many times. I missed others: David Weintraub, Alfred Van Tassel, Ruth Crawford, Mary Jane Keeney and David Zablodowsky. Some of them could not be traced. The memories of two of the lawyers, Arthur Kinnoy and Marshall Perlin, were invaluable.

I am grateful to James S. Sutterlin and Giandomenico Picco but regret that Javier Pérez de Cuéllar declined to respond to my requests for an interview. I hope he changes his mind.

There were two most valuable publications: Balkan War Report and Africa Confidential. Lin Murray was a formidable reseacher and her moral support was invaluable. Julia Grimes's research was expert. A steadfast Carol Kremer helped more than she knows and was so generous with her time. Thanks to Michael Lee and to Neil Waterman.

Research in Peru would been impossible without dear friend Toni Bard. I thank Brian Low and his wife Anita for their hospitality in Lima. I thank Jenny Crowther for her excellent reporting in both Kigali and Mogadishu. I thank Major General Romeo Dallaire. Anne-Marie Huby at Médecins sans Frontières was patient to a fault with unreasonable requests and so were the doctors with whom I spoke. I thank Gerald Papy, journalist from *La Libre Belgique*.

I thank friends James Bamford, William Wesbrooks and Dallett Norris, Tony and Margaret Grimes, Isabel Hilton, Pauli and Iain Joyce, Patrick Masters, Daphne Norman, Anita Rowe, Sue Snell and Peter and Leni Gillman. S. J. Taylor understands all too well the heavy personal toll and was a great strength. I thank Ann Mansbridge for sound advice. Cynthia Jabs and Jane Rackham gave invaluable support from start to finish. I am grateful to Alice Beckwith who enabled me to continue when it would not otherwise have been possible.

My agent Michael Shaw rescued this book when everything conspired against it and Mark Le Fanu, General Secretary of The Society of Authors, also helped to ensure it would be published. I thank Peter Day of Allison and Busby.

Valerie Green made it possible to write this book and be a mother too. The debt I owe my parents, Mavius and Jim Melvern, is enormous, as was their unwavering love and support. Michael Pye was wise friend and counsellor and both Phill Green and I will always be grateful to him. The original idea came from Phill Green. Without the benefit of his unfailing support and devotion I would not have attempted to tell the UN story. Nor would I have finished it. To Phill Green I dedicate this book.

INDEX